Dreiser-Mencken
LETTERS

Edited by Thomas P. Riggio

University of Pennsylvania Press · Philadelphia

upp

Dreiser-Mencken

LETTERS

The Correspondence of
Theodore Dreiser & H. L. Mencken
1907–1945

VOLUME TWO

Library of Congress Cataloging-in-Publication Data
Dreiser, Theodore, 1871–1945
  Dreiser-Mencken letters.
  Includes index.
  1. Dreiser, Theodore, 1871–1945—Correspondence.
2. Mencken, H. L. (Henry Louis), 1880–1956—
Correspondence.   3. Authors, American—20th century—
Correspondence.   I. Mencken, H. L. (Henry Louis),
1880–1956.   II. Riggio, Thomas P.   III. Title.
PS3507.R55Z485   1986   810'.9'0052   [B]   85-22506
ISBN 0-8122-8008-3 (set : alk. paper)

Printed in the United States of America

Designed by Adrianne Onderdonk Dudden

For Milla

Contents

VOLUME TWO

Illustrations

4

*And Now I Sometimes Wonder
What More
(1919–1923)*

"My work hereafter, if I keep on, will be a good deal more political than literary."
—HLM to TD, 1 October 1920

"And now I sometimes wonder what more. The fireside & a limping old age. Hell."
—TD to HLM, 14 November 1920

After the war years, Dreiser and Mencken surfaced with little money in their pockets but with a sense of having won important battles. Mencken publicized the legacy of the Great War in the terms he helped to create, as a turning point in the history of American culture: "The whole history of the war period is a history of the subsidence of the van Dykes and the rise of the Cabells, Dreisers, Masterses, Andersons, and Sinclair Lewises—in brief, of the men who continued to question the national culture, despite the colossal effort to endow it with a mystical sort of perfection."[1] He spoke for himself, too, when he addressed Dreiser at the start of the twenties: "At fifty years you are not only permanently secure. You have become a sort of national legend. The younger generation is unanimously on your side." To that generation, the two together offered a dramatic instance of literary practice. They had conducted a frontal assault on the bastions of "puritan" morality and routed the stiffcollars that dominated the marketplace. They helped establish a model for critical discourse that was more militant and more tied to social realities than any before it. For writers starting out after the war, they became the central living figures in the sparse literary pantheon of America. In his columns and essays, Mencken played up their earlier struggles, and, as long as he limited himself to Dreiser's pre- *"Genius"* phase, he was willing to advertise him as "by long odds the greatest novelist that America has yet produced."[2]

The public recognition did little to lessen the tensions of the preceding years. In private, they squabbled about the nature of Dreiser's current writing. Becoming defensive, Dreiser concluded that the Baltimorean "lacks for one thing a sense of beauty." [3] Mencken had made famous the novelist's so-called decade of silence after *Sister Carrie* but could not understand the even longer hiatus between *The "Genius"* and *An American Tragedy*. When he chided Dreiser for not completing the novel he had promised in 1915, he was given a quick history lesson: "if I had counted on my novels during this time I would have starved. Imagine *The Bulwark* put out in war times! God Almighty!"

The war and the related trials of *The "Genius"* had, in fact, turned Dreiser in on himself as a writer. For one thing, he felt that his political stance had lost him the freedom to write a novel that reflected contemporary issues—unlike other novelists of his generation, such as Willa Cather and Edith Wharton, whose wartime sympathies did not offend American readers. He continued in these first years of the twenties to work on memoirs and to support himself meagerly on publishers' advances and his writing for magazines. There were more rejection slips than publications, however, and he found that he could sometimes make more selling his old manuscripts to collectors than selling his current writing.

Dreiser grew restless, taking more time away from his writing desk and seeking relief in constant motion. In early 1919 he vacationed in the South and then traveled to Indiana to visit the scenes and acquaintances of his youth. That fall, he left New York and settled in Los Angeles with Helen Richardson, an actress and distant cousin who would eventually become his second wife. Mencken was startled to learn that he had slipped quietly out of Manhattan, and for the next few years he remained puzzled by the resettlement, since Dreiser, partly because of Mencken's loyalty to Estelle Bloom Kubitz, kept his new liaison hidden from him. They did not meet again until 1923, and so the friendship, maintained solely by correspondence, became less immediate and more ritualized.

The changes are striking. First of all, the usual preoccupation with books in progress gave way to the need to reassess their relationship. In the letters of these years, one can hear a note of culmination and even nostalgia. The old critical exchanges are still there, but a fair amount of energy is spent in recapitulating the past. They begin, noticeably, to reflect on the passage of time. Looking back on Mencken's long campaign in his behalf, Dreiser quotes Samuel Johnson on the author of merit who, without a sympathetic critic, "may pass without notice, huddled in the variety of things and thrown into the general miscellany of life." And they indulge in recollections of late-night convocations, which they remember for the good talk, food, and beer. "Will the latter ever be again, I wonder," writes Dreiser, while Mencken's repeated calls for his return to New York suggest he shared the sentiment.

Rarely, however, did the retrospection of this period turn maudlin.

More often, they found ways of converting personal stress into hearty humor. They joked about retiring together, about writing risqué reminiscences of each other, or retreating to a monastery to spend their last years in joint contemplation. The numerous jokes (often of the locker-room variety) about sexual prowess, impotence, illness, and death are a new feature of the correspondence. They begin, for instance, to exchange "famous last words," imagining what they might say on their deathbeds. And Mencken, refashioning an old theme to suit the new day, repeatedly warns Dreiser against "excessive veneries at your age."

Humor, we assume, is a clue to more serious concerns. As their past engagements began to fade, both men found it hard to adjust to the changing order of things. Dreiser's difficulty in finding a shape for his longer fiction paralleled Mencken's increasing uneasiness with literary criticism. Mencken wanted to give up *Smart Set*, which he did in 1923, and find a more suitable platform for the political and social commentary he wanted to write. The critic seemed, at the outset, shaken by the problem of disengaging himself from the complexities of the preceding decade. He felt abandoned, he told Dreiser, by the old warriors who fought against puritanism and nativist politics. "Huneker's autobiography . . . leaves me very depressed. One by one, they drop from the tree." Dreiser's defection—to the "radicals," to Hollywood, away from old-fashioned realism—was the hardest to take.

Mencken's moods of depression came more frequently now. He complained often to Dreiser of being in a "bad state mentally. I begin to believe that I'll never do the books I want to do"—to which Dreiser sent assurance that he had many good years ahead. This was not simply privileged information reserved for an old friend. Mencken's correspondence in this period is spotted with similar revelations to others. "I am in such a low state of health and mind that I feel like jumping into the Chesapeake Bay," he wrote to Amélie Rives, and added that Johns Hopkins physicians had prescribed a regimen of "hard physical labor daily from lunch to dinner" as an antidote.[4] To James Branch Cabell he suggested one source of anxiety: "My own father died at 44—and I am now nearly 42!"[5] Years later, Mencken confided to Dreiser that "since the age of forty I have been full of a sense of human sorrow." Now in his early forties, he began to show signs of hypochondria, and he would joke frequently about symptoms of "menopause."

There are other signs of strain. Most noticeable are Mencken's repeated suggestions that he and Dreiser "get away from visible America." He spoke of the problems facing them at home and considered Germany as a possible haven for serious writing. "The future of both of us, I think, lies on the other side of the water." While he encouraged Dreiser to concentrate on writing novels, to others he was more candid: the novelist, he wrote Ernest Boyd, "was a great fool to give up his old job and try to live on books. It can't be done in America."[6]

Mencken's impulse to expatriate—from the war years to the late sorry entries of his still-unpublished diary—is well documented in his exchange with Dreiser. The letters suggest a source of Mencken's ability to speak to a postwar generation that found other reasons for flight. The impulse, in his own case, ran so deep that a few years in Paris—or, for him, Munich—would not have healed the emotional wounds. Mencken, of course, stayed home, announced that the show was funnier in America, and wrote essays that debunked that impulse and often dazzlingly transformed it into the barbed criticism that fitted the mood of the time. The transformation was only partial, however, and the feelings he shared openly with Dreiser impressed themselves upon the surface of his writing. So much so that Edmund Wilson could observe, in 1929, that among the "fantasies" that allow writers "to take refuge from the perplexities and oppressions about them," Mencken's stands out: "it is," Wilson concluded, "a sort of German university town, where people drink a great deal of beer and devour a great many books, and where they respect the local nobility—if only the Germany of the Empire had not been destroyed by the war!"[7]

Fantasies, however useful as an index to psychic motivations, are less reliable guides to understanding than the record of cumulative achievements. In hindsight, the projections and worries expressed in the letters of this period appear premature—more a matter of midlife jitters than a diminution of real powers. The twenties proved to be a splendid decade for both men. By 1925, Dreiser would make his last and greatest breakthrough as a novelist and, for the first time, realize a nice profit from his fiction. Mencken returned to the *Sunpapers* and in 1920 began the "Monday Articles" column, which ran successfully for eighteen years. In 1924 he co-founded one of the landmarks of modern popular journalism, and his influence, as editor of the *American Mercury*, was greater than ever. In these and other outlets, he channeled whatever fantasies he had into his work. Among other things—and surely with the earlier racial slurs against Dreiser and himself in mind—he helped establish a view of American writing as multiethnic. As Van Wyck Brooks wrote, "More than anyone else perhaps, Mencken broke the way for writers who were descended from 'foreign' stocks and who were not yet sure of their place in the sun."[8]

Mencken, especially, felt intense relief in his new freedom to speak out unchecked and, as it happened, with a new stridency. While this did not win him favor among the more traditional or scholarly critics, he understood that, as he admitted to Carl Van Doren, "the war greatly improved trade for me." [9] Certainly the polemics of the preceding years provided him with an audience prepared and eager for his postwar elaboration of old themes, which he carried on with gusto and often with recklessness. Dreiser's work also showed, though in more subterranean ways, the influence of their earlier concerns. The twenties might be called Dreiser's and Mencken's "American decade," the years in which novelist and critic struggled to synthesize and define the essence of the national experience as they had absorbed it. Their common enterprise, particular in its conceptual thrust, helps explain the basis and the staying power of their long-term ties; their various conclusions suggest something about the precariousness of those ties.

"I incline to the Right, and am a Tory in politics," Mencken announced in 1920. [10] There was a degree of mischievous posturing in this, but, as the often-heated debates with Dreiser show, it was a position that allowed him to be iconoclastic without sacrificing his elitism, a libertarian with a finely tuned sense of class conciousness. In his writing, from the groundbreaking *American Language* to the widely influential *Prejudices* series, Mencken surveyed American habits, ideals, and expression with a brand of aggressive satire that created a landscape populated by near-mythical figures—the booboisie, the Anglo-Saxons, the professors—that impressed themselves on the popular imagination as vividly as Lewis's Babbitt or Fitzgerald's flapper. If historical accuracy (and a certain human dimension) was lost in the creation, there was yet an energetic display of critical intelligence, a model for exposing social pretense and hypocrisy, and, of course, the fun of it all. Dreiser, in the meantime, was moving toward a panoramic exposition of American life understood in terms of crime and punishment, a somber view of societal stratification that he conceived in the form of social tragedy, not satire. It would be too simple to say that where Mencken saw the boob, Dreiser saw the victim; but, as their private discourse became more polarized, there was a strong tendency in this direction. While Dreiser's fiction was not conceived politically, his sympathies, if translated into political terms (as he himself would do in the thirties), were clearly becoming less congenial to Mencken.

They did, however, agree enough to keep the friendship intact. Although Dreiser argued with Mencken's belief that puritans no longer were a threat in literary matters, he relished the critic's treatment of newer targets: Prohibition, politicians like Harding and Coolidge, the "Klu Klux Kritics," Billy Sunday. With a continent separating them, they relaxed enough to resume a number of old rituals. Mencken helped edit the novelist's autobiography, *A Book about Myself*, and—in a friendly gesture to Dreiser—met with John Sumner to work out a compromise to get *The "Genius"* republished. They negotiated for translations of their work into German and traded opinions in their endless dealings with a new brand of publisher, like the shrewd, businesslike Alfred Knopf and the volatile Horace Liveright. Only half in jest, they worked out schemes to manage Dreiser into the Nobel Prize—and split the money.

Throughout these years, their strained intimacy complicated attempts to evaluate each other objectively. Returning to New York in 1923, Dreiser was interviewed by a reporter who asked what he thought of Mencken: "I think he is a great force. For what God only knows. A force to cause people to revalue what values they happen to be conscious of." [11] Mencken, who had to print his ideas about the novelist, had a more difficult time of it now. Though he admired *Twelve Men* (1919), which he saw as a return to Dreiser's major key, his *Smart Set* review of *Hey Rub-a-Dub-Dub* was as scathing as his treatment of *The "Genius"* (see Appendix 2, pp. 793–95). He lampooned Dreiser's attempts at philosophical reflection, noting that "Dreiser is no more fitted to do a book of speculation than Joseph Conrad, say, is fitted to do a college yell." The review resulted in a few months of icy silence, broken only by Mencken's trip to San Francisco, in June 1920, to cover the Democratic national convention. Even then, both men made up lame excuses not to meet. When the novelist published *The Color of a Great City* (1923), Mencken simply did not review it in the *American Mercury*. While he briefly and favorably noted *A Book about Myself*, in private he told Fielding H. Garrison that the book repeats past performances: "One chapter is gorgeous; the next is feeble bosh about some goatish love affair—once with a Bohemian charwoman. Imagine a man remembering all the loose gals of his youth!" [12]

Yet while the silences and the astringent commentary continued, there was also the high praise that Mencken reserved for Dreiser alone among American novelists. Though Mencken was attracting to himself younger literary satellites—like Sinclair Lewis and Joseph Hergesheimer—he did not experience with them the excitement of his early years with Dreiser. As a result, he walked a tightrope in his analysis of Dreiser, and the strain of maintaining a critical balance is apparent in this appraisal sent to Burton Rascoe:

Dreiser is a great artist, but a very ignorant and credulous man. He believes, for example, in the Ouija board. My skepticism, and, above all, my contempt for the peasant, eventually offended him. We are still, of course, very friendly, but his heavy sentimentality and his naive yearning to be a martyr make it impossible for me to take him seriously—that is, as man. As artist, I believe that he has gone backward—but he is still a great man. [13]

The skewed logic of this is uncharacteristic, but it highlights the peculiar mixture of admiration and repulsion both men contended with over the years.

In the same letter to Rascoe, Mencken added a telling line: "I know [personally] no other first-rate artist." It would be difficult to overstate the importance of this, not only for the longevity of the turbulent friendship, but also for its effect on Mencken's writing in the twenties. Throughout this period, the example of Dreiser and the related themes of the war years remained close to Mencken's growing repertoire of prejudices. He began the decade with a series of contentious essays—among them the brilliant "The National Letters" and "On Being American"—that defined anew the predicament of the artist and intellectual in America. The emphasis fell on the isolation of the artist, and his great contemporary model remained Dreiser, whom he placed, in this respect, in the line of Poe and Whitman. For Mencken, these writers mirrored his own sense of isolation, which expressed itself in his laments over the absence of a native aristocracy of the mind, in his attacks on academic critics, and in the creation of the philistine "boob," which he promoted as an American original. In all this Dreiser remained a fixed point of reference, the prime example of the writer both scarred by and triumphant over these forces. While Mencken so defined the action, Dreiser was acutely aware of the supporting role played by the critic in this drama. So, despite bruised egos and blatant infidelities, a mutual sense of debt and of genuine esteem was enough to keep them trying to renew the friendship.

Notes

1. Mencken, "The South Begins to Mutter," *Smart Set* (August 1921), 143–44.
2. Mencken, "An American Troubadour," Baltimore *Evening Sun*, 27 December 1920.
3. Dreiser to Edward H. Smith, 31 January 1921, in Elias, *Letters*, 1:344.
4. Mencken to Rives, 23 January 1922, in Forgue, *Letters*, 232.
5. Mencken to Cabell, 11 May 1922, in Bode, *Letters*, 153.
6. Mencken to Boyd, 9 August 1919, in Forgue, *Letters*, 152.
7. Edmund Wilson, "T. S. Eliot and the Church of England," *The New Republic*, 24 April 1929; repr. in *The Shores of Light* (New York: Farrar, Straus and Giroux, 1952), 439.
8. Van Wyck Brooks, *The Confident Years: 1885–1915* (New York: E. P. Dutton, 1955), 466.
9. Mencken to Van Doren, 20 February 1923, in Forgue, *Letters*, 243.
10. Mencken, "Meditation in E Minor," *The New Republic*, 8 September 1920, 39.
11. Quoted in Dorothy Dudley, *Forgotten Frontiers: Dreiser and the Land of the Free* (New York: Harrison Smith and Robert Haas, 1932), 443.
12. Mencken to Garrison, 2 October 1920, in Forgue, *Letters*, 202.
13. Mencken to Rascoe, undated [summer 1920], in *H. L. Mencken: The American Scene*, ed. Huntington Cairns (New York: Alfred A. Knopf, 1965), 472.

The Correspondence
(1919–1923)

[NYP]

165 West 10th Street
New York City

Jan 3rd 1919

My Dear Mencken:

If your in town next Wednesday evening & can—drop round. Just to stir up the animals. I am inviting some twenty odd people here to discuss that Society I once talked to you about.[1] No propoganda on my part. Its in the hope that some others may be moved to do it. All those named on the enclosed list will be here.[2] I have also invited Nathan & Hopkins.[3]

Dreiser

"A good time will be had by all."
Nine O'clock is the hour.[4]

1. Dreiser's idea was to establish an organization that would support (with both money and advice) struggling writers and artists.
2. The list has not survived.
3. Arthur Hopkins, a theatrical producer.
4. This was placed in the top left-hand corner of the letter.

[UPL]

H. L. Mencken
1524 Hollins St.
Baltimore.

January 3rd. [1919]

Dear Dreiser:-

Unluckily, I can't get to New York Wednesday. I am, in fact, just getting over a bout with what must have been the flu, or maybe beer-drinker's
liver. I am full of aches.

You have picked a good crowd, but with one or two suspicious characters. Be careful of Street. He was once hot for such an organization, and
then joined the Vigilantes and became a spy-hunter. Reedy is another professional patriot. The point is that the professional patriot, at bottom, is
bound to be a Puritan—the leopard cannot change his spots. You will hear
tall talk from such fellows, but when it comes to tackling the Presbyterians
head-on you will find them not present. I speak by experience.

My honest belief is that, while it would be a lot of fun to harass the
Comstocks legally (and hence highly pleasing to me), it would be hard
to accomplish anything. I am seriously considering printing a book in Germany or Switzerland, to get genuine elbow-room.

I have a note from the late Lieut. Hersey, very easy and impudent. I
have not yet replied. He informs me that he is once more on intimate
terms with you.[1]

Yours in Xt.,
M

1. Harold Hersey quarreled with Dreiser, who thought he was trying to profit from
his friendship, after Hersey announced his intent to publish an account of his part in
the suppression of *The "Genius."*

[NYP]

165 West 10th Street
New York City

Jan 6—1919

Dear Mencken:

The fact is there are two or more schemes on foot here. Auerbach[1] has
$500000 of August Belmont's money or can get it—to be invested in an all
arts encouraging club (Pish—Tush—Slush!) to be built in N.Y. Liveright
has a guy with $100,000 with which he wants to do something Noble. I

think more trashy clubs ought to be headed off. There is the possibility (?) of an all arts league for criticism and endorsement with money for honorariums or awards ala Noble.[2] There is I say—the possibility. The town is full of schemes. If a few people would set their faces against mush and silly trade unions like the Authors League mush would be avoided. (And therein lies deeply concealed a glistening bit of wit, H. L.) That's why I wanted you here to help frost bite these people for they are going to move anyhow soon and they might as well have a little cool poison poured in their veins

Dreiser

Hersey is around here looking like a dragonfly. He is dying to be restored to your good graces   Why not be civil to him—After all it's a short, sad life

1. Joseph Auerbach was the attorney of the financier Major August Belmont (1853–1926).
2. Dreiser means Nobel.

[UPL]

H. L. Mencken
1524 Hollins St.
Baltimore.

January 7th [1919]

Dear Dreiser:-

  I have myself heard of various schemes and schemers. The majority, of course, are proposed by gentlemen looking for advertisement. My inclination is to stand off and let them try their wings, but without getting involved. The simple truth is that I detest all movements and all uplifters, and can't throttle my dislike of them even when they are more or less sane and honest. I am against Puritanism to the last gasp, but when anti-Puritanism comes to a program and a theory I find myself against it almost as strongly. This is a temperamental lack that I can't help. I'd spoil even a good enterprise if I had anything to do with it.

  As I see it, your own best course is plain. Get every advantage out of the thing that you can find in it, but don't commit yourself—don't let them use you as a stalking horse—above all, don't let them parade you as a martyr. Be aloof and they will think a great deal more of you. After all, you are about the only man in America whose sufferings at the hands of the Puritans are worth discussing. The rest are lice—their complete obliteration would be no loss. I shall probably go into this in my next book. For the first time I shall spit on my hands and tell the whole truth.

Why waste time upon such a silly fellow as Hersey? He is the worst sort of lion-hunter, and is bound to compromise and embarass one soon or late. I surely owe absolutely nothing to him or to any one like him, and so I am disinclined to be polite. The older I get the more I am convinced that, if I am ever to do anything worth a damn, it must be done entirely alone. Moreover, I am more comfortable that way.

I am still somewhat wobbly, but am once more able to work. I have a pile of editorial work accumulated.

Yours in Xt.,

M

P.S.—I hope you have paid your tribute to Roosevelt.[1] True enough, the man was a liar, a braggart, a bully and a fraud, but let us not speak evil of the dead. I hear that the Trinity is to be enlarged to let in Woodrow.

1. Theodore Roosevelt had died the day before.

[UPL]

SMART SET
A Magazine of Cleverness
25 West 45th Street
New York

January 28th [1919]

Dear Dreiser:-

1. George Gordon is a young man named Charles G. Baldwin. He runs a stock farm at Laurel, Md. His one book, on Shakespeare, is rather hollow, but I am inclined to think that he will do fairly good work hereafter. The trouble with the American Writers Series is that it has been started off with an execrable book on the poets by Howard W. Cook, of the Moffat-Yard staff. This book is almost fabulously idiotic; it crabs the whole series. I don't see why you should waste time rewriting for Baldwin what is already printed in your Hoosier Holiday and in my Prefaces book. He says that he "wants" to read Sister Carrie. Surely, if he hasn't read Sister Carrie he is badly equipped to write about you—or about any other living American novelist.

3.[1] I know nothing about La Mayorga and her book of one-acters.[2] On general principles, I am opposed to submitting to these innumerable anthology grafters. You will note that Jones, apparently tired of them, has started to tax them. Your appearance in the book will do you little good. A few good dramatists, such as Eugene O'Neill are to be in it—but don't forget the Kreymborgs and other such villagers.[3] I have a feeling that a good deal of reserve is the best thing for you; they always value a man more when he is sniffish.

4. I have laid in 300 bottles of wine, so do not despair.[4]

5. Have you read My Antonia, by Willa Cather? Give it your eye.

In Xt.,

M

1. Mencken miscounted here and skipped from 1 to 3.
2. Margaret Gardner Mayorga published an anthology of Little Theatre plays, *Representative One-act Plays by American Authors* (1919). Dreiser did not appear in the book.
3. Mencken is referring to the poet and critic Alfred Kreymborg, whom he associates with the Greenwich Village group he disliked so much.
4. Nebraska had recently become the thirty-sixth state to ratify the Eighteenth Amendment, making Prohibition effective in January 1920.

[UPL]

H. L. Mencken
1524 Hollins St.
Baltimore

January 30th [1919]

Dear Dreiser:-

1. The autograph question is almost insoluble. According to an article by Guido Bruno in Pearson's there are grafters who make a business of getting them to sell. On the other hand, it seems ungracious to refuse a man who may be a very sincere and useful reader. Today I had a letter announcing the shipment of all my books, whatever that may mean. It will take 15 or 20 minutes to unpack them, inscribe them and repack them. And it will take almost as long if I merely tie up the package unopened, readdress it to the sender and take it to the parcels post office. Probably the best solution would be to demand a contribution to some charity. But I don't know any charity worth contributing to.

2. You are far too generous to "The Great Hunger."[1] It is a typical piece of Norwegian sentimentality, and I am removing its hide in the March Smart Set. This Cook tends to become an impudent fellow.[2] His book on poetry, lately published, is fearful crap. How Galsworthy came to

fall for The Great Hunger I can't imagine. Probably it was done by his own publisher.

3. If you actually know law, you are probably familiar with Section 3,717 of the Revised Statutes. It provides a penalty of 3 years for charging a man falsely, by mail, with any violation of the Postal Laws.

4. Incidently, I got proof yesterday that letters are still being opened in the postoffice. On January 22 I wrote a note to a man in Washington. It reached him January 27th, obviously opened, with two extra one-cent stamps, and showing the stamp of the War Department postoffice   The thing was really too obvious. The letter was plainly diverted to the War Department, there opened, then sealed, and then openly remailed in Washington, with two cents local postage added. In brief, they do not even take the trouble to conceal it.

5. What of "The Bulwark"? I think the Spring would be a good time to print it.

Yours in Xt.,
M

1. *The Great Hunger* (1919), by Johan Bojer.
2. Howard Willard Cook, of the editorial department of Moffat, Yard & Co., sent Dreiser an advance copy, along with a favorable review by John Galsworthy. Dreiser responded warmly to the novel but criticized it for being too much of a religious tract (see Dreiser to Cook, 29 January 1919, in Elias, *Letters*, 1:257–58).

[UPL]

H. L. Mencken
1524 Hollins St.
Baltimore.

February 1st. [1919]

Dear Dreiser:-

1. I have an impression that the Nouvelle Revue Francaise is a respectable magazine, somewhat on the order of the New English Review.[1] But I am uncertain, and am asking Nathan to let you know. On general principles, I think you should embrace every opportunity to get into French. In this case, you don't risk much. "The Financier", as a piece of property, is worth far less than any other of your novels. If I were in your place, I'd let Gallinard have it, and then use its appearance as a means of planting "Sister Carrie", "Jennie Gerhardt" and "The Titan". To be translated at all is a great benefit.

2. "The Orf'cer Boy" is being set as a one-act opera by the Anglo-American composer, Emil Hugendubel. Beware of the Copyright Act! [2]

3. To prove my absolute disinterestedness, I offer you one of those sanitary indoor closets entirely free of charge, if only you will agree to use it. It pains me to think of you going out into the yard in cold weather.

4. A man named Keating—George T.—has been writing to me. I had to be polite to him because our backer, Crowe, is under obligations to him. He hints that he had some sort of transaction or contact with you, apparently in the matter of "The 'Genius'". He seems to be wealthy. His aim seems to be to get your autograph. I have advised him that you and I are not on speaking terms, and that I can't help him.

5. Why in hell don't you move out of New York, settle down in some small town, and finish "The Bulwark?" In brief, get away from visible America. My own scheme is to move to Munich as soon as I can shake off my obligations. I have five or six books to write, wholly unlike anything I have yet done. Trying to write them while in active contact with American life would be like trying to read in a nail-factory.

In nomine Domine
M.

1. The French magazine wanted to publish sections of *The Financier* in translation.

2. Mencken is responding jokingly to a request by Dreiser in a letter of 31 January 1919: "I am thinking of trying to sell 'The Orf'cer Boy' for you to one of our best magazines—the Pictorial Review maybe. Have you any objection." [NYP] (See Appendix 2, pp. 804–5, for text of "The Orf'cer Boy.")

[NYP]

165 West 10th Street
New York City

Feb 3rd 1919

My Dear H. L. M:

Your remarks anent "The Bulwark" are the reason for this letter. I have the feeling that you are under the impression that I am idling in the extended arms of a harem—dreaming sweet dreams and killing time. It is your Dreiser complex I fear. As a matter of fact the last three or four years have been the most strenuous of my life. As a kid I idled a lot doing only the most necessary things. For one thing I have been working on a "History of Myself" Vols 1 & 2 of which are now done. I need only do two more to complete it. I have gathered and arranged in my mind the data for four or five novels of great import to me   I wrote <u>Free</u>, "The Hoosier Holiday", "Plays of the Natural and the Supernatural", <u>The Hand of the Potter</u>. This spring, after much deliberation I am publishing "<u>Twelve Men</u>", a book of characters—almost novels in themselves and the only way I have of disposing of a lot of material which would annoy me because I could not take the time to novelize it all. To me it is one of my best things and seven of the features were done within the last 10 months. At the same time I have done seven short stories, all above the <u>Free</u> average—or nearly all, and have plans for many more, a selection from which will make an excellent book. I have a new drama half done. I had thought first, this spring, of issuing a book of essays, some thirty one of which are lying here complete. It looks now as though I may have to throw them over beyond the fall as <u>The Hand of the Potter</u> may be released for publication and issued then.[1] These things had to be done to relieve a psychic urge in me. It is useless to say they should not. A man must express himself in the field of his greatest craving. In addition there are here over 200 "poems" (the word is questionable)—the product of this same period. There are also a volume of short <u>color</u> sketches, the product of an earlier period which Booth has long wanted to illustrate and publish as a portfolio.[2] All these, barring the plays, fill perhaps a psychic interlude. The stories, which I am very pleased to find that I can do provide a median for a type of mood—that with me has no other avenue of expression. The plays the same. I like tragedy and am looking for a great picture to be done briefly

As for ways & means—if I had counted on my novels during this time I would have starved   Imagine the Bulwark put out in war times(!). God Almighty! And as for The "Genius"—I had it all arranged some time ago for Boni to pay Jones $2500 & make me a 5 years contract—and then he jumped the price to $5,000 after refusing to answer even a telephone call for weeks! See enclosed letters.[3] Even now he refuses to change though he wont publish it himself unless guaranteed immunity from loss & prosecution! My stories & <u>The Hand of the Potter</u> have tided me over nicely. If it hadn't been for short stories I'd be out in the snow sure enough. They have kept me going in other things. They will probably permit the completion of The Bulwark and other novels   Personally, at this age, I have concluded that literature is a beggars game—but if you are born a thief—a thief you are & jails must be made the best of

Th D

1. *The Hand of the Potter* was published on 20 September 1919.
2. This eventually became *The Color of a Great City* (1923), but the illustrations were done by C. B. Falls, not Franklin Booth.
3. The letters have disappeared.

[UPL]

H. L. Mencken
1524 Hollins St.
Baltimore.

February 4th [1919]

Dear Dreiser:-

1. I get the notion that I gave you the notion that I have the notion that you have been loafing. Nothing could be more inaccurate. I know very well that you have been sweating blood. But it so happens that "The Bulwark" sticks in my mind, and so I am eager to see it on paper. The "Twelve Men" book, if I understand the plan of it, is an excellent idea. What is more, it lies exactly under your hand—you can do it very effectively. All the other schemes are interesting too, save the publication of "The Hand of the Potter". As you know, I believe it will do you damage and make your position very difficult. Following a clean victory over the Comstocks in "The 'Genius'" matter, it would have been safe enough. But after failing to stop them, it will only give them (and all their friends on the newspapers) the precise chance they look for. In brief, publication of it will be a docile baring of the neck—highly delightful to the moral mind. They will not stop at mere accusations of polluting the innocent. They will seize on the perversion, roll it on the tongue, and quickly get you into training as the American Oscar Wilde. And against that there is no defense. I am opposed to hopeless fights. They not only injure a man; they make him ridiculous.

2. Don't get the notion that I give my imprimatur to Baldwin. He simply came to me as many other people come, and I listened to him for a couple of hours. So far he has done absolutely nothing worth reading. His proposal to write about you without having read your novels is so lovely that I shall discourse on it later on. Tell him to go buy your books. And hold all his letters. If any unpleasantness follows I may be able to use them effectively.

3. The Jones business is not surprising. Jones is simply a merchant trying to drive a good bargain. His fundamental motive, of course, is to recover advance royalties. Your remedy is to sue him for damages for his failure to carry out his contract. He doesn't own the book; he merely has your license to print it. If he fails to do so, the rights revert to you. Liveright ought to be willing to finance such a suit. In case you win, he will get the book without paying Jones anything. As for the advance royalties, Jones' only remedy is to sue you for their recovery. But the thing could be better arranged by friendly mediation. My impression is that Jones would come to terms if properly approached. More difficult is the question of the

future of the book. If it is raided again, you will have the whole song and dance over again. Why be so eager to reprint it? My notion is that it does you far more good suppressed than it ever could have done you printed. The possible royalties in it are small. It gives an author a romantic glamour to have a suppressed book on his list. Remember this primary principle of the literary art: A man is always admired most, not by those who have read him, but by those who have merely heard about him.

4. I have started a book to be called "The National Letters". It will be the most violent philippic since the speech of the late Dr. J. C. Josephson on the scribes and the pharisees.

Yours in Xt.,
M

[UPL]

H. L. Mencken
1524 Hollins St.
Baltimore.

February 11th [1919]

Dear Dreiser:-

I shall read "The Hand of the Potter" with the highest attention. Maybe it will strike me quite differently than it did in ms. My objection then, of course, was not so much to the play intrinsically as to the folly of giving the Comstocks so noble an opportunity with the Genius case under weigh. That objection now fades. Far worse attacks on free speech than any Comstock ever dreamed of are now commonplace, and the end is not yet.

If you crave intellectual entertainment, send $1.50 to the Superintendent of Documents, Government Printing Office, for a month's subscription to the Congressional Record. Borah, France of Maryland and a few others are carrying on a fight for free speech that gets no notice in the newspapers. They will be beaten. See especially the Record for February 8th. The single copy may be had for 10 cents.

I have at last got the first four pages of my next book[1] on paper—it took months to get so far. The volume will be a slaughter-house. Absolutely no guilty man will escape. Let me have a private list of your special enemies. I shall even denounce myself.

Yours in Xt.,
M

1. *Prejudices: First Series* (1919).

[UPL]

H. L. Mencken
1524 Hollins St.
Baltimore.

February 19th [1919]

Dear Dreiser:-

In the Mercure de France for January 16th, page 249, you will find yourself highly lathered in a French article by Vincent O'Sullivan. On the same page I am introduced as the noblest American critic since Poe. All this should be awful news for patriots. The New York Times will be in a sweat.

After many disappointments, the Second Coming of Christ is here. Josephus Daniels is Mark, House is Luke, Burleson is Matthew and Jim Ham Lewis is John.[1] I nominate you for Judas and myself for Pontius Pilate.

Yours in Xt.,
M

1. Josephus Daniels, journalist, secretary of the navy in Woodrow Wilson's administration; Edward M. House, politician from Texas and diplomat in Wilson's administration; Albert Sidney Burleson, postmaster general in 1919; James Hamilton Lewis, Democratic senator from Illinois and a strong supporter of Wilson.

[UPL]

H. L. Mencken
1524 Hollins St.
Baltimore.

March 26th [1919]

Dear Dreiser:-

1. Now is the time for you to begin unloading your cellar full of "Geniuses". Note the price in McGee's catalogue.[1]

2. I hear that you and Jones are starting a magazine.[2] Is this mere pishposh, or is there some fact in it?

The Wiessner Brewery here sold its last keg of beer yesterday. Adolph Bornschein, the assistant brewmaster, blew out his brains as the wagon left the yard.

Yours in Xt.,
M

1. Mencken enclosed a page from the J. B. McGee book firm, advertising a first edition of The "Genius" for $12.50.
2. J. Jefferson Jones, American representative of the John Lane Co.

[NYP]

165 West 10th Street
New York

March 28—1919

Dear Mencken:

I am using Yewdale and Liveright[1] to test an idea of mine which springs partly from "The Best Short Stories of 1919" school of art and a suggestion made by Cahan.[2] I have persuaded Liveright to bring out four magazines or issues in <u>book form</u> for one year the contents to be oked by me. The collecting and editing will be done by Yewdale under my supervision. However there being no satisfactory material—assuming such a state to exist—there will be no books. At present I am on the trail of a few things. Each issue is to be limited to ten features—and features only. The contributors are to be paid a royalty—pro rata—on the sale of the book. It will be placed—as a book—in all hotels, book stores, stations etc and old issues will be reprinted as long as the demand keeps up. I fancy you & Nathan may know of things too strong for any present day magazine but genuinely fine. If you do and want to help—notify me or better yet Merton S. Yewdale, care Boni & Liveright   I only want big things   We haven't settled on a name although a few have been thought of. As for you—one of your most terrorizing & defiant flights would suit me exactly—or a satire like The Concert? (Was it?)[3]

Dreiser

A group of poems by a man like Neihardt, George Sterling[4] or some other punch would fall in with my idea of one feature

1. Merton S. Yewdale, editor at the John Lane Co.; Horace Liveright, publisher.
2. Abraham Cahan (1860–1951), novelist and editor of the *Jewish Daily Forward*.
3. Dreiser means "The Artist" (see Mencken to Dreiser, 15 September 1909, n.1).
4. John G. Neihardt, novelist, poet, educator; George Sterling (1869–1926), poet, dramatist, critic.

[UPL]

H. L. Mencken
1524 Hollins St.
Baltimore.

March 29th [1919]

Dear Dreiser:-

The German mind is standardized. I thought of that book magazine idea two years ago. You pumped it out of me via Spafford or the Ouija board.[1] I think it is excellent, provided decent stuff can be found. My one doubt springs out of the fearful difficulties I have encountered with the Smart Set. The obvious title is The American Quarterly. I offer you the Declaration of Independence translated into the American language, with an introduction showing that the average American cannot understand the original.[2] My share of the royalty to be payable to the German Red Cross.

I sent you "The American Language" today. It is a gaudy piece of buncombe, rather neatly done.

Yours in Xt.,

M

1. Jessie Spafford was a fortune teller living in New York to whom Dreiser, Mencken, and their friends went for amusement. She appears as "Giff" in *A Gallery of Women*, where Dreiser seems open to the possibility that she is clairvoyant. Mencken was clearly more skeptical of her powers.

2. Mencken appended the Declaration of Independence, transcribed into modern American English, to the first edition of *The American Language*, but he later removed it as a cautionary measure against attack by the "patriots."

[NYP]

165 West 10th Street
New York City

April 1—1919

M:

Yes, I wormed it out of Spaff. She finally admitted that you were thinking of it and had been for exactly two years   Have respect for fortune tellers. They are an asset.

Betimes, send on that Declaration of Independence. It sounds promising. I believe striking material for a few issues can be gathered. Are we at liberty to use "American Quarterly"   I would be glad to put over a few issues just as samples—or a mode.[1]

D

1. Horace Liveright agreed to publish "The American Quarterly," a book-magazine that would promote realistic fiction. However, no one, including Dreiser, was willing to take on the burden of editing it.

[UPL]

H. L. Mencken
1524 Hollins St.
Baltimore.

Thursday. [3 April 1919]

Dear Dreiser:-

I have just read the sheets of "Twelve Men" and hasten to present arms. If you have ever done anything better than the portraits of your brother and of Muldoon, then it is hidden in your private archives and I have not seen it. The book, as a whole, is a capital piece of work. An we were nearer, I should haul you out and flood you with beer.

Yours in Sso. Corde Jesu,
M

[NYP]

165 West 10th Street
New York City

April 4—1919

Dear Mencken:

Thanks for this imposing tome.[1] It looks like volume six of the "Crowned Masterpieces of American fiction." Your works now range in size from a peice of toilet paper to Walker's Rhyming Dictionary. Well, such are the fruits as well as the rewards of industry. Why dont you compose an American Encyclopedia Britannica   I shall look into this of yours some restful Sunday morning

By the way would you bar European and especially English stuff from The American Quarterly   Liveright thinks not but I think yes

D

1. *The American Language.*

[UPL]

H. L. Mencken
1524 Hollins St.
Baltimore.

April 5th [1919]

Dear Dreiser:-

1. The American Quarterly, of course, ought to be American, but suppose an Englishman or a German came along with a first-rate article on

some phase of American Kultur? I think I'd leave the matter open. Don't burden yourself with rules.

2. Keep the reins firmly in your hands. Yewdale can't edit the thing under your supervision. Either you are editor or you are not editor. The important thing is to see the mss. as they come in. That is the way you will unearth new ones.

3. Twelve Men tickles me much, particularly the chapters on your brother and Muldoon. Who was Peter? Send me a private list of the men. I remember the Jew speculator, but can't remember his name. Lyon is very well done.

4. Obviously, Twelve Women ought to follow.

In Xt.,
M.

[NYP]

165 West 10th Street
New York City

April 8—1919

Dear Mencken:

Of course I intend personally to examine all the stuff that goes in the magazine & ok it. Also all that I solicit. Things unsolicited will be examined by Yewdale and others. Hes a good book maker and editor and is willing to do the work for little or nothing—just to be doing it. How would it do to revise The Seven Arts¹ as a title. Also why not a council or board of directors   I would gladly whack up the responsibility so long as a really good thing appeared. The men in Twelve Men are:

1. Peter (P. B. McCord)
2. The Doer of the Word (Charley Potter—I think)
3. Paul
4. The Country Doctor (Dr. Woolley—of Warsaw)²
5. Culhane (Muldoon)³
6. A True Patriarch (? Whitside I think)⁴
7. DeMaupassant Jr. (Lyon)⁵
8. The Village Feudists (Dont Remember)
9. Vanity, Vanity (J. G. Robin)⁶
10. Rourke (Burke—a foreman)
11. A Mayor & His People (Cant Recall)
12. W. L. S. (W. Louis Sonntag, Jr.)⁷

Please dont mention McCords name—one of his brothers is in the army—well placed & may resent it   He is a West Pointer. J. G. Robin is still around—a failure. It would be a kindness not to lug him into the light. Again Mrs. Lyon may kick & Muldoon—but.

For years I have planned a volume to be entitled "A Gallery of Women".

God what a work! if I could do it truly—The ghosts of Puritans would rise and gibber in the streets.

Dreiser

1. In 1917 *Seven Arts* magazine came under pressure for its allegedly pro-German stance, mainly as a result of Randolph Bourne's antiwar articles, and the journal did not survive the attack.
2. Dreiser spent a number of his childhood years in Warsaw, Indiana, and Wooley was the family doctor there.
3. William Muldoon ran a health spa in Westchester, New York. Dreiser went there in 1903 to recover from a nervous breakdown.
4. Not Whitside but the father of Sara White, Dreiser's estranged wife at this time.
5. Harris Merton Lyon.
6. Joseph G. Robin, a failed financier who turned to writing under the pseudonym Odin Gregory.
7. The illustrator W. Louis Sonntag (1822–1900).

[NYP]

April 9—1919

Do you know Jacques Loeb?[1] If so would you give me a letter of introduction to him. Or possibly you know Simon Flexner.[2] He would do nearly as well.

Th.D

1. Jacques Loeb (1859–1934), biologist. Loeb's theory of animal tropism was an early influence on Dreiser's thought.
2. Simon Flexner (1863–1943), a famous pathologist.

[UPL]

H. L. Mencken
1524 Hollins St.
Baltimore.

April 16th [1919]

Dear Dreiser:-

The Cook business is irritating, but not astonishing.[1] The fellow has been cadging free stuff for some time, and deserves to be exposed. I shall do it anon. I assume that you are absolutely sure of the text of your letter.

Did he also try you on Fuessle? The Fuessle novel,[2] for two or three chapters, was a very fair imitation of you. After that it degenerated into bull-shit. I pay my devotions to it in the June Smart Set. Fuessle is an eighth-rater.

The Constitutionfest proves anew that Americans are absolutely devoid of humor. Why not send in a prose threnody? You will be just in time for the funeral.

Yours in Xt.,

M

1. David Karsner, then on the staff of the New York *Call*, wrote Howard W. Cook, an editor at Moffat, Yard & Co., saying that Cook should have printed Dreiser's full statement about Johan Bojer's *The Great Hunger*, not just four lines of endorsement (see Mencken to Dreiser, 30 January 1919, n.2). On 10 April 1919, Cook wrote Dreiser a letter of apology, saying that he did not "mean to play up a book on false pretenses." [UPL]

2. *The Flail* (1919), by Newton A. Fuessle.

[NYP]

April 25—1919

Dear HLM:

What about that mss you were going to offer. I have under consideration an essay by the late Randolph Bourne, a story by Wood C. (Eugene) & a poem by Masters

D

[UPL]

H. L. Mencken
1524 Hollins St.
Baltimore.

April 26th [1919]

Dear Dreiser:-

Thanks for "Twelve Men". Liveright has made a very good looking book, barring the bad drawing by Brodzky on the slip-cover. There is one whooping typographical error: novitiate for novice on page 76. But what would you? My American Language, after five careful readings, has twenty.

A Catholic bastile for bad boys burned down here yesterday. Two firemen were killed, but not a single holy monk had his hide singed. Everything burned—save the chapel! A cross on top of the central tower is still there! Put that in your pipe and smoke it.

Some time or other let us have a session alone. There are various matters worth going into, some literary and some political. We get nowhere with others present—even very charming others. Perhaps we might hold an executive session, and then to the victuals and the gals. Or perchance we might get drunk.

I offer even money that Woodrow's impeachment is moved at the next meeting of the Narrenhaus.[1]

M

1. Madhouse.

[UPL]

H. L. Mencken
1524 Hollins St.
Baltimore.

April 28th [1919]

Dear Dreiser:-

I had no notion that you were proceeding with the new magazine so fast. I am having a copy made of my translation of the Declaration of Independence into American. The chances are that it is too loud, but it may give you a tickle.

The Baltimore Sun is to review "Twelve Men" in terms of encomium.

Yours,
M

[NYP]

April 29—1919

Yes, anything you say. A stag beer fest is ideal   I like nothing better & can blab till dawn. Give me day or two notice. That language book of yours really interests me. What a mine Ring Lardner has proved.

D

There are various things I want to talk about

H. L. Mencken
1524 Hollins St.
Baltimore.

May 2nd. [1919]

Dear Dreiser:-

1. Next to the Times' notice of "Twelve Men" is a review praising the latest book by Robert W. Chambers.[1] I shall call attention to it.

2. Rascoe, of the Chicago Tribune, writes that "Twelve Men" has fetched him, and that he is going to do a gaudy review.[2]

3. I am hauled to New York unexpectedly Sunday. Will you be in town, say Wednesday? I don't know what business is afoot, but I'll call you up. The office is working me hard and driving me nutty. I should be a kept man. Business gets me into a hell of a state.

M.

1. The New York *Times Review of Books* of 27 April carried a notice of *Twelve Men* in which the reviewer wrote of being "profoundly bored" by the book; repr. in Salzman, 324–25.

2. Burton Rascoe, "Dreiser Gives Us His Best Effort in 'Twelve Men,'" Chicago *Daily Tribune*, 3 May 1919, 12; repr. in Salzman, 329–31.

165 West 10th Street
New York City

May 4th 1919

Dear M:

Yes—chains & slavery being my lot in life I will still be here Wednesday unless I am in hell. Dives, Tantalus & myself will open a book booth when I get there. The enclosed is something fresh from Chicago.[1]

D

1. This has not survived with the letter.

SMART SET
A Magazine of Cleverness
25 West 45th Street
New York

May 6, 1919

Dear Dreiser:

Such an infernal mess of work has fallen upon me that I doubt that I'll be able to get down tomorrow as I had hoped. I have a pile of manuscripts at least six feet high in front of me. How long will you be in New York? That is, this Spring. I assume that you will be here when I return in about two weeks. Why not let us arrange by mail for a session? There are half a dozen things that ought to be gone over.

Sincerely yours in Xt,
M.

SMART SET
A Magazine of Cleverness
25 West 45th Street
New York

May 7, 1919

Dear Dreiser:

As I expected, I am forced to go home at noon today. I will probably be back next week.

It would be impossible at the moment, of course, to print my translation of the Declaration. The Espionage Act[1] specifically forbids making fun of any of the basic ideas of the Republic. But once the Act expires by limitation I'll be delighted to do the thing. My present plan is to add a translation of the Constitution, including the amendments, and one of Lincoln's Gettysburg speech, and to preface them with a note arguing that all of these things are now incomprehensible to the average American. I shall support this argument by citing passages plainly beyond his understanding.

The "C.B." of the Baltimore Evening Sun is apparently Constance Black. Mrs. Black is an English woman and the wife of one of the owners of the paper. I know her very well. She is a great admirer of yours and constantly asks me to invite her to the party the next time you are in Baltimore. She is especially enthusiatic over "Twelve Men".

Yours in Xt,

M.

1. Passed by Congress in June 1917.

H. L. Mencken
1524 Hollins St.
Baltimore.

May 8th [1919]

Dear Dreiser:-

My advice is to avoid this, at all hazards. If Viereck[1] were out of it, I'd say sign it, but with him in it it is bound to be a mess. If he is genuinely interested in the thing, and not merely looking for advertising, he should withdraw himself and give it a chance. The question whether or not he deserves his bad reputation is beside the point. The point is that he has it. My personal impression is that he is a vain, hollow and intensely disagreeable fellow. He did more harm to the German case in America than half of the English press-agents. I am against him because I don't trust him: he will crab things and thus spoil the whole enterprise. The Rothschilds used to have a rule against employing unlucky men. It is equally disagreeable to deal with disreputable and imprudent men.

In your place, I'd write to Viereck telling him frankly that he ought to get out of it.

Yours in Xt.,

M

1. George Sylvester Viereck (1884–1962), journalist, author, poet. Viereck's pro-German sympathies during World War I caused him legal troubles that Dreiser and Mencken feared for themselves. Mencken is here suggesting that Dreiser not sign a petition in support of the French socialist Henri Barbusse.

[UPL]

H. L. Mencken
1524 Hollins St.
Baltimore.

May 14th [1919]

Dear Dreiser:-

I surely hope your beauty is not spoiled by the accident. There is a good lawyer in Essex street, by name Irving Noblestone. Mention my name. He takes only 50% and expenses. Let me hear what the x-ray shows.[1] Don't let them flash it on your seeds. Ten seconds exposure will shrivel them.

Rascoe sends in the enclosed. How in hell he ever got the notion that I laid violent hands on "Sister Carrie", God alone knows. The origin of such fables is a great mystery.

My prayers follow you.

Yours in Xt.,
H. L. M.

1. Dreiser was hit by a car as he crossed Columbus Circle and suffered, among other injuries, two broken ribs. He did not press charges against the driver.

[UPL]

H. L. Mencken
1524 Hollins St.
Baltimore.

May 22nd [1919]

Dear Dreiser:-

The enclosed is from the Chicago Tribune.[1]

I have an idea for an article burlesquing the professional shit-heels who now propose to rewrite American history in the English interest. My plan is to review several mythical works of that sort, and incidently prove that the Germans caused the War of 1812, and were responsible for the Fort Pillow massacre, the Crime of '73 and the Johnstown Flood. It should make a juicy piece of buffonery.

Have your agents inform me of your condition. Be sure to keep the x-rays off your gonads.

In Xt.,
M

1. The clipping from the *Tribune* of 18 May 1919 was of Dreiser's story "Love," which was republished as "Chains" in *Chains* (1927).

[NYP]

Mrs. D. M. Parrys Residence
Indianapolis, Ind.

June 26—1919

Dear H. L. M:

Who is L. C. Hartmann (?) of Baltimore? And kindly refrain from commenting on this letter. Will be back early next week so you can address me there.[1]

Dreiser

1. Dreiser paid a visit to Indiana, particularly to see his grade-school teacher, May Calvert Baker. He traveled to Indianapolis to meet a friend from his Chicago newspaper days, the editor John Maxwell.

[UPL]

H. L. Mencken
1524 Hollins St.
Baltimore.

June 29th [1919]

Dear Dreiser:-

L. C. Hartmann is a damned fool—one of the town nuts. He writes endless letters in a big, round, bank clerk's hand. Don't answer them.

Your stationary leads me to suspect that you have abandoned literature and are being kept. Well, that is also an art like another.

How are your ribs? I hope all the pain is gone.

Yours,
Mencken

[UPL]

H. L. Mencken
1524 Hollins St.
Baltimore.

July 11th [1919]

Dear Dreiser:-

This Frenchman is prof. of French at Smith College and the author of several very fair books in that dialect.[1] I have advised him to read all of your books before writing about you. But soon or late he will be good for a thumping article. Return his letter.

Woodrow's bosh will fetch the boobs again. His speeches are really quite astounding. He makes denial of the plainest facts—and gets away with it.

The leading bookseller here told me yesterday that he often got inquiries for The Bulwark.

Yours,

M

1. Professor R. Michaud wrote Mencken, saying that he had been impressed by *The "Genius"* and wanted to write "A French View of Dreiser" for *Smart Set*. [UPL]

[UPL]

H. L. Mencken
1524 Hollins St.
Baltimore

August 12th [1919]

Dear Dreiser:-

I have a letter from Vincent O'Sullivan,[1] who is in Paris, saying that Payot, the French publisher, tells him he is to do "Sister Carrie" and my preface book in French. Do you know anything of this? The French rights to the preface book have been in the hands of Curtis Brown, of London, and about two months ago he reported to Knopf that the Frenchwoman who proposed to translate it had fallen down. Evidently, there have been further negotiations. If you have any news of the matter let me hear it.

I went to hospital this morning expecting to have a papilloma removed from my rectum and to be laid up two weeks. On the table it turned out that there was an error in diagnosis, and so I got off with nothing more than a very sore arse. The dilation must have been to a diameter of at least 18 inches: I could have given birth to a child of 2 years. Imagine a surgeon honest enough, in the presence of nurses and other surgeons, to admit his error and send me off without operation! His name is Bloodgood. Inscribe his name on the roll. He says local manipulation will fix me up.

Yours in Xt.,

Mencken

1. Vincent O'Sullivan, journalist, critic, author.

[NYP]

Aug 13—1919

Dear Mencken:

I know nothing of this French thing. Curtis Brown once offered me 15 pounds for the Holland rights of Sister Carrie & I agreed but never heard anything more so I still have the rights I assume. The Tanchnitz edition people either stole or secured from some English publisher without my consent the right to publish Carrie as the Castaway.[1] At any rate it was so published and I never got a cent. I would like to see Carrie translated into French, Jennie Gerhardt into German and the Financier & Titan into Russian. But—

By the way I noticed on the check for Sanctuary a statement to the effect that I waived all rights. Since I was practically giving the thing away I assume there is nothing to this.

I extend my profound respect to the surgeon who had the decency to do as yours did. After all we all do a few decent things in our lives—or—may I not cautiously add—I hope so

Dreiser

1. There is no record of such an edition.

[UPL]

H. L. Mencken
1524 Hollins St.
Baltimore.

August 14th, 1919.

Dear Dreiser:-

Pay no attention to that notice on the check. It is there by legal advice, as a protection against copyright difficulties. Let this be sufficient acknowledgement that you retain all rights to "Sanctuary", in all countries, saving only the first American and English serial rights. If you ever want a formal transfer, simply ask for it.

Once communications are open, I think I may be able to arrange a German translation of "Jennie Gerhardt". I believe that you will see many translations of your books within the next five years.

Preserve the name of that surgeon: Bloodgood. He is a son-in-law to old Henry Holt, the publisher. I have known him ten years. My tail is still sore, but that is largely due to the stretching it got when he inserted his telescope. This suggests a good means of suicide. Get one of those telescopes, drive it up the bum, and blow in prussic acid in gaseous form. But maybe the scheme is impracticable. It would probably require a valet to help.

Yours,

M.

[NYP]

Aug 19—1919

Do you know anyone who would make a good London (incidently foreign) agent for Liveright—someone who would especially and particularly look after his interests. He had this fellow Edward J. OBrien, only he seems to have disappeared. A good suggestion will be welcomed—Some resident in London would be best

Th D

The right man might do you a few good turns.

[UPL]

H. L. Mencken
1524 Hollins St.
Baltimore.

August 22nd [1919]

Dear Dreiser:-

This morning comes a letter from Boyd[1] saying that he has sent in his resignation from the consular service and will go back to England September 1st. His permanent address is 11 Upper Fitzwilliam street, Dublin. If Liveright can get hold of him it will be a good job for Liveright.

Yours,

M

Boyd says Georg Brandes[2] told him that Gyldendal (Ibsen's publisher) is considering Danish translations of "Sister Carrie" and "Jennie Gerhardt"[3]

1. Ernest Boyd.
2. Georg Brandes, a famous Scandinavian critic.
3. The postscript is handwritten.

[UPL]

SMART SET
A Magazine of Cleverness
25 West 45th Street
New York

August 28, 1919

Dear Dreiser:

I encountered Liveright accidentally last night and had a long talk with him. He was somewhat in liquor but still able to converse. He tells me that he rather inclines to a plan I once mentioned to you, to wit, to transfer your book of essays[1] to Knopf and to bring it out as one of the Free Lance books which I am editing for him. Knopf himself, of course, would agree with great pleasure. Please give your thought to this matter. As your book stands it is apparently a great deal too long for the series. The books I am printing will not run over about 60,000 words each, but if you incline to go in that may be very easily surmounted by using half of the stuff and keeping the rest for another book. My own view is that 125,000 words is too long in any case. The reader will pay just as much for half the stuff and then come back and pay the same sum again for the other half.

I am writing to Boyd. As I understand it, his plan is to move to London. He there expects to represent American publishers and authors. It is unnecessary to call his attention to your books. They occupy the first place on his list and, as you probably know, he has made various efforts to inspire a French translation of "Sister Carrie".

I inclose both your table of contents and the Liveright letter.

Yours,
M

1. *Hey Rub-a-Dub-Dub* (1920).

[UPL]

H. L. Mencken
1524 Hollins St.
Baltimore.

September 3rd [1919]

Dear Dreiser:-

We have used so very much stuff regarding the American of late that I hesitate to take on any more.[1] My last four or five articles have dealt chiefly with his failings, Nathan has flogged him in "The American Credo", and there have been other things. Have you anything else in hand?

I wrote to you last week about a proposal to take over your philosophical work from Liveright. Give this your thought. The advantages from my side, of course, are plain enough, but whether it would be to your advantage remains to be determined. Both Liveright and Knopf are willing.

Have you got any of your gallery of women sketches finished?

Hay-fever has me by the ear and I feel very badly.

We are notified of an advance of 35% in printing costs October 1st. This is the third. One more, and we'll be ready for the dump.

Yours,
M

1. On 30 August 1919, Dreiser had sent Mencken an unidentified essay that he wanted to sell for "a modest price." [NYP]

[NYP]

165 West 10th Street
New York City

Sept 4—1919

Dear Mencken:

None of the papers you mention are ready,—for publication at any rate. As for the essays—as I once suggested to Liveright—I would prefer that Knopf (this for the novelty of it merely) should bring out the volume first and then hand it over to Liverights catalogue later. B & L[1] are almost worthless as advertisers & distributors for me at least. They did nothing with Twelve Men—a book which I am positive can still be sold widely by advertising. My terms to Liveright, and these will hold for Knopf, are 20%—a five year contract, and no rights other than those of publishing in book form. I would be pleased if B & L could still be persuaded to thus arrange but after throwing cold water on the project for some time they have now become enthusiastic—at least Fleischman[2] has—I doubt if they will consent. I should like to see Knopf take it over for a period just to see what if anything he would do with it. If you can persuade B & L to this first arrangement I would prefer it.

Dreiser

Now that the book[3] is drawing near to issue I have no difficulty in finding periodical publishers—when it is too late.

1. Boni & Liveright.
2. Leon Fleischman, vice-president and treasurer of the Liveright firm.
3. *Hey Rub-a-Dub-Dub* (1920).

[UPL]

H. L. Mencken
1524 Hollins St.
Baltimore.

September 7th [1919]

Dear Dreiser:-

For the Free Lance series the book you outline is impossible for two reasons. On the one hand, it apparently runs well over 100,000 words, and the books in the series are to be but 50,000 words, or even less. On the other hand, it would be out of the question for Knopf to pay 20% on a book selling for $1.50. But I rather think that he might do it as an independent book. At all events, it is worth looking into. Just what Liveright's attitude toward it is I couldn't quite make out when I met him. He was in a state of liquor and agreed with anything said by anyone else. Fleishmann somehow made a good impression on me. He seemed a very sensible fellow. The simplest scheme would be for you to talk the thing over with Knopf—of course with Liveright's knowledge. I'll arrange it at any time you say. As for Liveright, I think I could induce him to consent—that is, in case he showed any morning-after reluctance. I agree with you that Knopf would probably do better with such a book.

Liveright, by the way, told me of a general rumor that I am a partner of Knopf. This is absolutely untrue. Such a thing has never been discussed, or even mentioned. My sole connection with him is as an author. Naturally, on account of my Smart Set job, I see and hear of a good many MS., and I tell him of the more promising ones. But that is a mere matter of friendly interest and I get nothing for it. In the Free Lance series I get a small royalty as editor. In the case of Nietzsche's "Antichrist"[1] it will be 5%. But in the case of the Howe book it will be but 1%. It varies with the book. In case a book of yours went into the series I'd of course waive all royalties.

Yours,
Mencken

1. In 1920, Knopf published Mencken's translation of *The Antichrist*.

[NYP]

165 West 10th Street
New York City

Sept 10—1919

Dear Mencken:

My feeling about Knopf & Hey Rub-a-Dub-Dub is as follows. If the length of the book is to exclude it from the series and the series is the thing I would prefer to let Liveright proceed & then permit a smaller book to be selected from it. In that case I think it might be advisable to use a different title. "The King is Naked" still appeals to me as strongest & best.

Dreiser

[UPL]

H. L. Mencken
1524 Hollins St.
Baltimore.

September 11th. [1919]

Dear Dreiser:-

The conditions governing the series make it impossible to do a book of more than 60,000 words. As for me, I am against a 125,000 word book on general grounds, but there you probably disagree. Let Liveright do the Rub-a-Dub-Dub, and we'll talk of a book for the series when we meet. I have an idea for one that will be very easy to write and that won't interfere with Rub-a-Dub at all. The King is Naked is an excellent title.

I am full of hay-fever, asthma, etc., and feel like hell.

Yours,
Mencken

[NYP]

165 West 10th Street
New York City

Sept. 12—1919

Do me a favor. Make me a present of 10 copies of your issue containing *Sanctuary*.[1]

Yours
Ignatius Donnelly.

1. Dreiser's story "Sanctuary" appeared in the October issue of *Smart Set*.

[UPL]

H. L. Mencken
1524 Hollins St.
Baltimore.

September 25th [1919]

Dear Dreiser:-

That old bitch is forever at the bat.[1] I am waiting patiently for her to write a book. The Lord God Jehovah, soon or late, always delivers them into my hands.

At 100,000 words, your book is still much too long for the Knopf series. But Liveright should be able to do some business with it.

My own book seems to be held up by the printing difficulties. I'll send you a copy as soon as it comes in. If the printers keep on, we'll be down and out. It is already almost impossible to print a magazine of small circulation without loss.

I am over hay-fever. It was very mild. I ascribe this favorable issue to your prayers. Aux pieds du Sacré-Coeur j'ai prie pour vous!

Yours,
Mencken

1. Probably a reference to a reviewer.

[NYP]

c/o General Delivery
Los Angeles, Cal.

Nov. 3rd 1919

Dear Mencken:

Did you grant Andre Tridon permission to use your name in connection with this psychoanalytic study league?[1] I note in a letter addressed to me that he has used mine and after I specifically disclaimed any interest in the idea. The enclosed from A. A. Brill[2] sent to me, why I dont know— unless Tridon has been using my name to him makes Tridons game look a little thin. What do you suggest?

Coming west I saw a desert in Arizona which makes me long to retire to the wilds. Sand & cacti & the most wonderful bare & inhospitable mountains I ever saw. I welcomed the whole damn thing as an ideal home for a withering sage. Come west sometime & look it over

Dreiser

Please send me any word of Gloom.[3] Marion writes she is sick. I will pay operating expenses

1. On 21 September 1919, André Tridon wrote Dreiser that he was starting an "Association for Psychoanalytic Study" and wanted him to join. [UPL] Later Tridon asked Dreiser to become a member of the executive committee and to speak to the group about *The Hand of the Potter*. He added that Mencken had joined the organization.

2. A. A. Brill (1874–1948), psychiatrist, author, and early translator of Freud.

3. Estelle Bloom Kubitz.

[UPL]

H. L. Mencken
1524 Hollins St.
Baltimore.

November 8th [1919]

Dear Dreiser:-

I saw Gloom in New York last week. She was in pretty good shape, and went out for the first time while I was in town. She had had a chronic appendicitis, keeping her in bed for two weeks. I don't think there is any danger, but the appendix ought to come out—that is, if the diagnosis was correct.

The Tridon matter seems to me to be too trivial to bother about. Tridon wrote to me, announcing that he had written a book. I replied politely, suggesting that he do a book psychoanalyzing the Puritan mind. Next came his circular with my name. I protested—but only very feebly. It seems to me useless to combat such impudences. My name is often used by political agitators of one sort or another. I don't give a damn what any American thinks of me, and hence do not get into sweats about such things. Tridon, I hear, is half starving.

The desert doesn't lure me. But I have my eye on a place in Howard county, Maryland, planted to apples and grapes, with a row of hop-vines to boot. Meanwhile, I am taking lessons from a brewmaster and a wine-squeezer. Gott mit uns!

What in hell are you doing in Los, among all the New Thoughters, swamis and other such vermin. I hear that all the old maids west of the Mississippi flock to the town in the hope of being debauched. I surely hope you don't risk your old fowling-piece on any such game.

You will, with your accustomed sagacity, mistake the enclosed card for a practical joke.[1] Well, go on thinking so. Miss W. is a very pretty girl, has read your books, and views you with respect. If, throttling your low suspicions, you do yourself the favor of calling on her and her mother, give them both my best regards. Tell Mrs. W. that I am still agin Prohibition.

Helen Richardson (University of Pennsylvania Library)

She is a clever woman, and actually took to the stump against it when the matter was up in California.

Yours in Xt.

M

Why General Delivery?[2] Are you staying at the railroad yards?[3]

1. The card has disappeared, but it is obviously from "Miss W," who is Ruth Wightman, a friend of Mencken and the Bloom sisters.
2. Dreiser had gone to Los Angeles with Helen Richardson, who would eventually become his second wife. Having recently broken his relation with Estelle Bloom Kubitz, he wanted as much privacy as he could manage.
3. The postscript is handwritten.

[UPL]

H. L. Mencken
1524 Hollins St.
Baltimore.

November 19th [1919]

Dear Dreiser:-

I saw Gloom in New York last week and she looked pretty well, though somewhat peaked, but now Marion writes that she is laid up again. All the symptoms relate themselves to her chronic appendicitis. Marion wants to take her to Galen Hall for a "rest"—an expensive and idiotic idea. What she needs is an operation. I am writing to her by this mail, telling her so.

If Jake[1] can't arrange the thing satisfactorily in New York I can have it done here, and at a minimum of expense. Bloodgood will charge any fee I tell him, and the hospital bill, etc., needn't be large. It is absolute insanity to treat such a condition medically. It simply can't be done. She may get some temporary relief, but she'll be laid up again soon or late. And if the thing ever becomes suddenly acute there will be hell to pay.

I forgot to send you the card last week. I enclose it herewith. No monkey-business, darling. The ladies are friends of mine.

Yours in Xt.,

M

Hugh Walpole now publicly announces that I am the white hope of American criticism. He picked out a good pro-English propagandist.

1. Jake, whose last name is unknown, was a medical doctor who appears as Walter La Grange in Dreiser's story "Regina" in *A Gallery of Women*.

P.O. Box 181
Los Ange

Nov 23rd 1919

Dear Menck:

I wired you as to Gloom so there's no more to say as to that. Be as economical as possible as I'm up again a legal battle between Jones & Liveright over The Bulwark & may be able to draw nothing for some time. Jones—the swine—claims a contract when none exists—and bases it on money owing him and a "next full length novel" clause in The "Genius" contract![1] At the same time he has 500 copies of The "Genius" which I can sell out here for $10⁰⁰ each which would yield him $5000 and pay up my indebtedness three times over & he wont release & wont do a damn thing. Liveright is willing to stand the suit but not an uncertain side expense

Notice: I will not accept cards of introduction from you to females. Even though I met them they would be under suspicion to their dying hour. No bunk traps are to be sprung that-a-way. Under separate cover I am mailing you some of the writings of W. H. Wright.[2] He is here singing the praises of lousy cafes that are so poor they are a joke—at so much a line—to catch the scrubby tourist. If you could see these cafes you'd know what swill there is. Send the clippings on to Gloom.

Love—but advice or introductions go here.

D

1. Horace Liveright was negotiating with J. Jefferson Jones of the John Lane Company, in an attempt to take over Dreiser's books under the Lane imprint. Jones responded that Dreiser owed $2,143.06 to John Lane and that Dreiser's contract required that Lane get his next novel. Dreiser, of course, claimed the contract was void since Lane had withdrawn *The "Genius."* Liveright eventually gave Dreiser a $4,000 advance on *The Bulwark*, but he never saw the book completed.

2. Willard Huntington Wright returned to California after leaving the New York *Evening Mail* during the war years.

H. L. Mencken
1524 Hollins St.
Baltimore.

November 29th [1919]

Dear Dreiser:-

I enclose a translation.[1] My model is H. E. Krehbiel's translations of the Heine songs. The fellow's writing is not bad, but now and then he runs letters together in such a way that I can't make out just what he is saying. German script is hard to read,—particularly when a German uses the Latin letters. The Gothic is much easier, because it is clearer.

Obviously, he is a familiar German type—the over-educated numskull. The German universities suck them in, and then spew them out half crazed— melancholy, useless men. I have known many. Let us thank God that you and I never had no education.

I have ordered a cartload of books from Munich and they are beginning to come in. There is much very interesting stuff, about the war and in pure literature. There is no good book in German on latter-day American literature. I think I shall tackle it—doing it, of course, in English.

Yours in Xt.,

M

What is your address? General Delivery is a pickpocket's address.

1. Dreiser had sent Mencken a letter written in German by Richard H. A. Schofer, asking him to translate it since "my knowledge of German has all gone flooey." [NYP] Schofer's letter praises Dreiser as the one contemporary American writer worth reading.

[UPL]

H. L. Mencken
1524 Hollins St.
Baltimore.

November 30th [1919]

Dear Dreiser:-

Your suspicions, as usual, are grossly inaccurate. Miss W. is connected with the movies, is a very intelligent girl, and writes to me that she has a notion that she may be able to sell the movie rights to Jennie. So put on your Sunday clothes and go to see her and her mother. Kiss their hands for me.

The Jones imbroglio seems almost insoluble. Why don't you propose arbitration to him? The whole business rests on the vicious system of paying advance royalties. I believe it is bad for the publisher and worse for the author. It inevitably makes a slave of the latter, or, at all events, jockeys him into such a position that he can't fight the publisher on equal terms. Let me know what happens.

Yours,

M

[NYP]

P.O. Box 181
Los Angeles

Dec 14—1919

What a dog you are to return such a daub of a translation. You ought to be ashamed of yourself. And as for Ruth Wightman—now I get a letter from Gloom urging me to corrupt her. Gad—is there no rest for the wicked! As for my address P.O. Box 181 is all you get. You are as dictatorial and commandeering as a German uncle. Well, I'll see Ruth Wightman

Dreiser

[UPL]

H. L. Mencken
1524 Hollins St.
Baltimore.

December 20th [1919]

Dear Dreiser:-

I know nothing of Dr. Heinecke. Some time ago I had a letter from Mrs. Kuno Meyer, the American widow of the great Gaelic scholar. She is in Berne, negotiating translations from English into German and vice versa. I wrote to Liveright about her. Since then I have received a warning from Berlin that she knows very little German, and is a Kansas patriot. Maybe she and Heinecke are in business together.

I still insist that a postoffice box is the address of a pickpocket. If you go to see Ruth Wightman, you will find a very nice girl. Give my best regards to her mother.

This will be a very wet Christmas. I am booked for three under-the-table parties, all stag.

Yours in Xt.,
M

What in hell are you doing in the Methodist paradise? Why be so mysterious? If you are acting in the movies, don't hesitate to admit it.

H. L. Mencken
1524 Hollins St.
Baltimore.

January 2nd [1920]

Dear Dreiser:-

Meredith Janvier, of 14 west Hamilton street, Baltimore, who deals in first editions and mss., tells me that he has a customer who yearns to own one of your mss. He would be content with a very short one—say a short story. If Janvier writes to you, you may trust him fully. I have known him for years.

By this mail I am sending you a copy of "Heliogabalus", a play inspired by "The Hand of the Potter".[1] Hurtig and Seaman will produce it anon. The French rights have been sold to Sarah Bernhardt, who will play Heliogabalus herself. We have received $20 advance royalties.

Your Christmas telegram[2] deceived my family, which mistook the signatures for misspellings of William Dean Howells, Orison Swett Marden, Harold Bell Wright, Irvin Cobb, etc. Result: I am viewed with great respect.

The young Wightman writes that she thinks you are a handsome dog, but that your manners are those of a railroad boarding-house.

Yours in Xt.,
Mencken

1. *Heliogabalus, a Buffoonery in Three Acts* (1920), by Mencken and George Jean Nathan.
2. On Christmas day 1919, Dreiser had sent Mencken a telegram, which he signed using names such as Roscoe Skunkwiller and Bettina Fishbone. Those signing were supposed to be authors, and the message was one of thanks to Mencken for, among other things, "broadening and brightening our outlook and emphasizing that optimism and spirit of Christmas helpfulness so necessary to great writers" (see Elias, *Letters*, 1:265, n.1).

[UPL]

SMART SET
A Magazine of Cleverness
George Jean Nathan ⎫
and   ⎬ Editors
H. L. Mencken ⎭
25 West 45th Street
New York

January 6, 1920

PAS AUF!

Revenge is sweet. Beware of the ides of January. Take warning that the first counter-attack in answer to your insulting telegram will be made anon. Beware! No guilty man ever escapes.

PAS AUF!
A Friend

[UPL]

Law Offices
Garfunkel, Fishbein, Spritzwasser & Garfunkel
21 West 42nd Street
New York

7 January 1920

Mr H L Mencken
   1524 Hollins Street
   Baltimore, Md
Dear Sir

We are advised by a mutual friend who asks that his name be withheld that you would be interested in the Pamphlet "How to Circumvent the Mann Law" prepared by our Mr. Spritzwasser. The price of the booklet is Five Dollars, less 20% in quantities of one dozen. We can recommend it most highly to those whose have affectionate natures and whose occupation requires them to do travelling of an interstate nature. Appreciating your order as well as the names of any of your friends who might be in need of just such counsel as this, we are,

Very truly yours
J Choate Kaplan[1]

1. J. Choate Kaplan was a member of the law firm of Garfunkel, Fishbein, Spritz-wasser & Garfunkel, according to the stationery Mencken used to send this letter. This is the promised response to Dreiser's telegram.

[NYP]

P.O. Box 181
Los Angeles
Calif.

Jan 23—1920

Dear Mencken:

I see by a copy of the Mirror to hand today that either Masters [1] or Karl Kitchen has sent Reedy that copy of the telegram to you. [2] I didn't intend that, since Reedy & I are on the outs now, but I hope you dont mind the joking anyhow. A letter from Mr. Janvier wants a short mss of mine. I have been offered $1000 for the original of Jennie Gerhardt & turned it down. I have been paid $100 for autographing a set of my books. How much ought I to ask for the original of "Sanctuary" say—or <u>Laughing Gas</u>.

The place is full of healers, chiropractors, chiropodists, Christian Scientists, New Thoughters, Methodists, Baptists, Ana-Baptists and movie actors   My landlord brackets "Praise the Lord" with "Good morning"— & then swindles me on the gas bill. This climate is 90 per cent over advertised. Theres not one decent restaurant & the drinking water has alkali in it. I have lost 10 pounds in weight

Phryne Euphrosina Weiskittle, the well known local poetess of love & new thought preacher asks me to add her name to the telegram to you—if not too late   Also Arthur Pennieswad Buchstobeel, the well know local Democratic portrait painter. Once more Eamoun Padriac Toonty, the local Glana Gael novelist says he reveres you above all critics. Really, you are coming on aren't you

Thermystes VII

1. Edgar Lee Masters.
2. As "Grateful Authors," Dreiser's telegram to Mencken appeared in *Reedy's Mirror* 29(8 January 1920), 27.

[UPL-H]

H. L. Mencken
1524 Hollins St.
Baltimore.

Jan 27th [1920]

Dear Dreiser:

I suspect that you sent that telegram to Reedy yourself. It has been reprinted in the East. Reedy doesn't like me: I consider him an ass, and never mention him. The joke is that the average boob will read the text without reading the signatures, and so go away with the notion that it was sent by Irvin Cobb, Henry van Dyke and Kathleen Norris. But pas auf! My revenge is under way. The few days in jail won't hurt you. Don't resist the officer!

The suppression of "Jurgen" by the Comstocks is a lovely spectacle.[1] Guy Holt[2] says he will fight. But the game is rather hopeless. The London <u>Atheneum</u> lately printed an article inviting me to move to England. I think I shall accept.

Yours in Xt.

M

1. *Jurgen* (1919), by the Virginia novelist James Branch Cabell, was attacked on the ground of immorality, but this led only to increased sales of the book.
2. Guy Holt was an editor at McBride & Co., the publisher of *Jurgen*.

[UPL]

H. L. Mencken
1524 Hollins St.
Baltimore.

February 2nd [1920]

Dear Dreiser:-

I think $75 or $100 would be a fair price for a short story ms. I am asking Liveright to send me some copies of the "Free" and "Twelve Men" pamphlets, and shall send them abroad. The future of both of us, I think, lies on the other side of the water. Next year I hope to do a book for publication in German only—on American literature and civilization. It will be sweet stuff.

Yours,

M

Nathan and I often talk of the possibility of getting you into the magazine, but put it off for a simple reason. That is, we have gathered the idea that you think we drove hard bargains with you in the past, and so made an excessive profit on you. This is not true. You apparently share the general notion that we are full of money—another delusion. We have had a very tough struggle with The Smart Set from the start, and have kept it going without a cent of outside help. It has had to pay for itself. Well, the net result of all that effort is that, after 5 1/2 years, it yet owes each of us 11 months of the smallest salaries drawn by any magazine editors in New York, and has not paid us a single cent in dividends. We have gone on with it for various reasons. First, we enjoy monkeying with it. Secondly, we like to dig up new authors and give them their chance. Thirdly, there is the sporting interest: it is pleasant to overcome difficulties. Fourthly, running the magazine gives us a certain prestige, and helps our books. Both of us have made a living by other devices, often onerous. I held a newspaper job until the middle of 1917, and have lately resumed it. Nathan has done a great deal of hard hack work. We started the Parisienne to get money, sold out to get rid of too much work—and are now starting another magazine. The common view in New York seems to be that we got $100,000 for the Parisienne. I only wish we had. And what we got is nearly all gone. If it hadn't been for the fact that each of us has a small independent income, we'd have been down and out a dozen times.

All this for your private eye. I don't offer it as a reason why you should do any work for us. I go into it simply to purge your mind of any notion that you may harbor that we are Shylocks. We are sinful, but that is not one of our crimes. In my autobiography, announced by Knopf for the fall of 1950, I shall tell the whole story in detail, giving actual figures.

[UPL]

H. L. Mencken
1524 Hollins St.
Baltimore.

February 3rd [1920]

Dear Dreiser:-

I have been in communication with Herman Scheffauer, who is now in Berlin, about German translations. He is very friendly to both of us, and has gone to the length of approaching the Kurt Wolff Verlag, a very good publishing house, in Leipzig. He says that he has been met with great friendliness: Wolf wants to introduce a few salient Americans of German blood to German audiences. I incline to go with Scheffauer as far as he chooses. He is a sound man and has had a good deal of experience. His suggestion is that you choose a couple of your books as most probably suitable for translation, send them to him in Berlin, and let him go on with the negotiations. What do you think of it? My own suggestions are Jennie Gerhardt and Twelve Men. I think the Germans would understand both. Or maybe substitute The Titan for Twelve Men. If you are interested, Scheffauer's full name and address follow:

Herrn Herman G. Scheffauer,
Cunostrasse 48, III
Berlin-Grunewald,
Germany.

I am more and more convinced that we had better reach out for European audiences. The United States will go from bad to worse. Beginning with On Democracy all my books will be published in England simultaneously, and I shall make every effort to get them into German and French. It will be safe, I think, to allow Scheffauer to arrange terms. On account of the state of exchange, we'll get next to nothing from the first book or two, but after that we should get a fair royalty.

Yours,

M

On second thought, The Titan is much better for the purpose than Twelve Men.[1]

M

1. The postscript is handwritten.

[NYP]

P.O. Box 181
Los Angeles
Calf.

Feb 9—1920

Dear Mencken:
I'll be glad to have copies of <u>Jennie Gerhardt</u> and The <u>Titan</u> sent to Scheffauer but since you know him I wish you would discuss trans. & deals with him for me. By the way how does one renew a copyright now. I want to renew my Sister Carrie contract in my own name. Thanks for thinking of me in connection with Scheffauer.

Dreiser

In one of your letters you write the <u>Ides</u> of January. I fancy you mean the Idees of January.

[UPL]

H. L. Mencken
1524 Hollins St.
Baltimore.

February 11th [1920]

Dear Dreiser:-
Thanks very much for <u>Hey-Rub-a-Dub Dub</u>. The title will cause a lifting of eyebrows at Harvard and Yale. You are, I dessay, a low fellow, and

use the flat a in your speech. My one complaint is that you give the boobs too much for their money. You could have made two books of your material, and so jockeyed the thing that one would sell the other. Lieberecht has done a very good job of printing.

Guy Holt, of McBride & Co., is coming here tonight to palaver about the Cabell case. What can be done about it, God knows. I wrote and had the Baltimore Sun print the enclosed editorial, but regarding further proceedings I am stumped.[1] Holt is full of vain hopes that he will be able to put critics on the stand. Comstock, who drew the law, made it impossible. My advice to Holt is to put Cabell on the stand, and have him dispute every indecent meaning alleged by the Comstocks—in other words, have him swear that the meaning in each case is something harmless, and that all obscenity is imagined by the Comstocks.

In 1919 my books earned more than $1,200. This fills me with amazement. The most I ever got in any single year before that was $200. The first series of Prejudices has sold 1,700 copies and is being reprinted. After all, I must be a meritorious fellow.

Madeleine is now selling for $10.[2] Three cheers for Jesus!

I have got some of those pamphlets from Boni, and shall put them where they will do some good.

Yours,

M

1. Mencken enclosed "Jurgen and the Moralists" (31 January 1920), which argues for the novel on the basis of its "beautiful style" and its good reception abroad.
2. *Madeleine*, by J. Kavanaugh.

[UPL]

H. L. Mencken
1524 Hollins St.
Baltimore.

February 14th [1920]

Dear Dreiser:-

If Scheffauer's efforts develop anything I'll be glad to discuss the business with him. He is, of course, disinterested. What he wants to do is to set up an interchange of books. He will introduce you as a former Bavarian brew-worker, still scarcely able to speak English. Look for a notice that you have been elected an honorary member of the Hessen-Nassauer Liedertafel.

By the way, I have a letter from Mrs. Kuno Meyer saying that Rudolph

Kommer, who says he is a friend of yours, has given the rights to your books to one Dr. Heinecke. I suppose Kommer is a fraud. I have been suspicious of the whole Meyer-Heinecke outfit. Old Kuno was a fine fellow, but his widow is a Kansas Presbyterian. It might be well for you to drop a line to Mrs. Meyer, warning her to beware of Kommer. Her address is Länggass strasse 26, Bern, Switzerland.

The copyright to "Sister Carrie" has not run out, and so you can't renew it. Harper apparently took over the Doubleday copyright, dated 1900, but Liveright prints a new copyright notice in his own name, dated 1917. Was the copyright ever actually transferred from Doubleday to Liveright, via Harper? If not, then Doubleday still owns it. Find out who actually owns it now, and have him transfer it to you. You apparently have no legal right to it, unless you bought it back from Doubleday when you took over the plates. But it is not a matter of much importance. No matter who owns the copyright, they have to pay you royalties by the original contract. Doubleday could not sell more than he owned, and he merely owned the copyright subject to royalties. In case there is any dispute, you had better get a lawyer. Stern, of the Authors League, is probably the best for such business.

—Holt, of McBride & Co., dropped off to see me the other night. He turns out to be a very young fellow. He says that his boss, McBride, who has just got back from Europe, is a moralist. I foresee another Jones manoeuvre,[1] with Cabell the victim.

Yours in Xt.,

M

1. J. Jefferson Jones who, as the American representative of the John Lane Co., did not give Dreiser strong support during the suppression of *The "Genius."*

[NYP]

P.O. Box 181
Los Angeles.

Feb. 20—1920

Dear Mencken:

All I know of Kommer is that he came to this country in 1917—just before we broke with Germany, was gathering up books to submit to Berlin & Vienna publishers. He wanted a copy of Sister Carrie and one of The Hand of the Potter to read. Finally he asked if he might submit them in Berlin & Vienna with a view to translation & publication. To this I agreed, terms to be submitted to me direct. I sent you a letter in which he said that he was retiring from the agency field & had turned the books over to one Dr. Heinecke for submission to publishers. I have had no word from Heinecke & so presume he has done nothing at all. If you know Mrs. Meyer why not communicate these facts & ask her what's what.

You are wrong as to Sister Carrie   The mss was not completed until May—1900 & not ready to be copyrighted before Sept 1900. It was not issued until October 1900. So I have several months as I see it in which to arrange for a renewal. It was not published in England until 1901

I am sir, gravely & respectfully
Lenine Trotsky Goldman

Thanks to you (?) I have sold the original of <u>Free</u> for $100⁰⁰ but I'm through at that price. I haven't so many & I'll hold them I think for a better market later on—or my heirs & assigns can sell them.

I have received & signed a James Branch Cabell protest. Far more important & decent would be a defense fund to which I will gladly contribute. What the hells use are kind words. And what good is the lousy Authors League with its shabby jealousies   Money talks & a good lawyer hired for the job would nag the soul out of these book improvers—their directors & supporters. The "Genius" case so far has cost me personally over $2000. Ask Gloom. And I cant afford it

[UPL]

H. L. Mencken
1524 Hollins St.
Baltimore.

February 28th [1920]

Dear Dreiser:-

Your story agrees substantially with Mrs. Meyer's. She says that Rudolph Kommer turned over the books—"gave the rights"—to Dr. William Heinecke, who runs the so-called International Literary Bureau. Scheffauer, of course, is a vastly better man to handle them. I had a letter from him yesterday saying that the German publisher he had interested was constantly asking him for the books. I doubt that Kommer's farming-out of the rights is valid. Surely you don't want Heinecke to be horning in and spilling the beans, in case Scheffauer arranges for a translation. To avoid that I suggest that you write a letter to Scheffauer direct, authorizing him to carry on negotiations and putting the matter of compensation into his hands. If I were between the two of you the complication would simply make for difficulties and misunderstandings. Direct negotiations are better. Scheffauer's address is

Herman George Scheffauer,
Cunostrasse 48/III,
Berlin-Grunewald, Germany.

McBride is, and should be, able to pay for defending the Cabell case. It would be rather embarassing to offer him money. If Cabell were the defendant it would be a different story. Needless to say, I'll be glad to contribute to any necessary fund. Like you, I doubt the value of protests. In case Sumner is defeated I shall press Cabell with all arms to institute suit. Then it will be a good time to raise a war fund.

Yours,
Mencken

I think $100 was a fair price for a short ms., though I had nothing to do with fixing it. I have been told that Joseph Conrad sells his <u>book</u> mss. to that Irish lawyer (whose name I forget) for $1,000 each. A man must be dead to get much more.

[NYP]

P.O. Box 181
Los Angeles
Calif

Mch. 2nd 1920.

Dear Mencken:

Enclosed is a letter from Dr. Heinecke which sounds rather promising. I am wondering as to probable worth in connection with a country like France. Do you know anything concerning his agent here—Frederick H. Marteus. I have heard of him, but in just what connection I cannot say

A most cynical & amusing article could be done on this burg—"The Queen City of the Angels" (which is its original Spanish name) if I thought any magazine would be interested.

D

Saw Wright[1] the other day. He is off the Frisco paper & connected with Ferdinand Pinney (Affinity) Earle,[2] who has a new moving picture Co. here. He looks fine—has a car & cutie.

1. Willard Huntington Wright.
2. Ferdinand Pinney Earle, motion picture director.

[UPL]

H. L. Mencken
1524 Hollins St.
Baltimore.

March 3rd [1920]

Dear Dreiser:-

I agree with you. But the Protest was not my invention. I have told Clark that I'll be glad to put up whatever anyone else puts up. So far, no word from him.

I shall put Hey Rub-a-Dub-Dub to the torture in the May Smart Set, out in a month.[1]

The Baltimore Sun wants me to go to San Francisco to cover the national convention. I incline to do it, if business allows. How long does it take to get to Los Angeles from San? Or are you going to the convention too?

In Xt.,
M

1. "More Notes from a Diary," *Smart Set* 62 (May 1920), 138–40. Mencken did come down hard on the book, stressing Dreiser's lack of talent for abstract speculation: "He lacks the mental agility, the insinuating suavity, the necessary capacity for romanticizing a syllogism" (see Appendix 2, pp. 793–95).

[NYP]

P.O. Box 181
Los Angeles.

Mch. 11—1920.

Dear Mencken:

Yes, I am thinking of moving up to Frisco after April. Its too cold there yet. The only reason I stay here is to keep from freezing elsewhere and its not warm here. People who come here between November & April—or May expecting to find warm clear days are misled   We have had twenty dark gray or rainy days (all dull) out of 22 straight & the same are continuing now. If I'm in Frisco by June I'd be delighted to see you again. Dont waste any time on L.A. It isnt worth it. I'm stuck in the outskirts writing   The best hotels are at Santa Barbara & San Diego

D

What is the name of the critic who reviews for the Washington Star

[UPL]

H. L. Mencken
1524 Hollins St.
Baltimore.

March 15th [1920]

Dear Dreiser:-

I don't know the name of the Washington Star critic. The chances are that the stuff is written by Philander Johnson.[1]

Beware of San Francisco in convention time—or get your quarters in advance. The hotels will charge about $20 a day. More about this anon. I think I'll get there about June 26th.

Yours,

M

1. Philander Chase Johnson (1866–1939), drama critic, humorist, journalist. Johnson wrote daily verses for the Washington *Star* and created the popular character of Senator Sorghum.

[NYP]

P.O. Box 181
Los Angeles

June 21—1920

Dear Mencken:

I am as much interested in the Democratic Convention as such as I am in eight Jews playing pinochle. However your very good self & San Francisco are two different and very much better things. That I will get up there is at this writing a little uncertain. If I can arrange it I will and will let you know. I think you ought to see this burg & perhaps San Diego before returning. If you come this way I will use whatever time you have to spare in showing you the bits that have interested me.

Dreiser

[UPL]

HOTEL ST. FRANCIS
Union Square
San Francisco

Friday [25 June 1920]

Dear Dreiser:-

God knows if I get to Los Angeles. My inclination is that way, but all the master-minds tell me that the trip home by that route at this season is infernally hot. Moreover, there is a special car for literati routed via Canada. I'll know more in a day or two. If you come up, wire me as above—room 1015. I doubt that you can get a room anywhere.

George Sterling was here when I got in. I am to meet him at 10 o'clock tonight to test the wines of the country. On the train I had plenty to drink—some of my own stock, and some provided by gentlemen from Kentucky.

The convention promises to be tame—that is, for a Democratic show. God have mercy on us all.

Yours,
M

[NYP]

P.O. Box 181
Los Angeles.

July 3rd 1920

Dear Mencken:

I suppose you'll being going northward—no doubt the better way. Sorry you couldn't see this burg. Its interesting—ideal summer weather here. My regards to Sterling—and George Douglas[1]—if you see them. Would that I knew of a cellar of wine here.

Dreiser

1. George Douglas, Australian-born journalist and critic, was literary editor of the *San Francisco Bulletin* in 1920.

[UPL]

HOTEL ST. FRANCIS
Union Square
San Francisco

Sunday [4 July 1920]

Dear Dreiser:-

It now looks certain that I'll be unable to come to Los Angeles. These scoundrels are so long winded that I must now start home immediately they shut down. I thought they would finish Saturday morning. Damn the luck!

George Sterling has treated me like a visiting profiteer. The other night, in my presence, a girl crazed by love stabbed him, but he is still able to walk. Yesterday his surgeons ordered him on the water wagon. His wounds had begun to run light wines and beers.

Yours,
M

[NYP]

P.O. Box 181
Los Angeles

July 21—1920

Dear Mencken:

I wish I might interest you as a critic—and as a critic only—in John Maxwells Cecilian theory of Shakespeare.[1] John is an old friend of mine—in fact he gave me my start in the newspaper world. He is today connected with the Indianapolis Star. As I informed you last year—in the hope of interesting you he has in the judgement of many compentent men solved the question of who Shakespeare was. I have read the work from the first to last & have been fascinated. It is a great peice of scholarship—as good as any done anywhere at any time. Maxwell spent seven years & $10,000 of his own money sifting the data   He deserves recognition before the data is swiped by garbling Shakespearean theives. I have interested Liveright but before doing anything he has turned the mss over to one Dr. Rosenbach of Phila. who is a pundit as I hear and a friend to the Furness group of Shakespeareans.[2] Rosenbach has held the mss 8 months. What he is doing with it—who is reading it—or making notes from it God only knows. The mss ought to be read by an honest critic of standing so that the feat accomplished—the propounding of the Cecilian theory may be credited to Maxwell. If I could interest you I would like you to ask Liveright for the loan of the mss with a vow to such examination. It is a great work. You will honor yourself by interesting yourself in it. Maxwells address is

John Maxwell,
Hotel Seminole
Indianapolis, Ind.

Dreiser

1. John Milo Maxwell (1866–1929), editor, author. In 1892 Dreiser met Maxwell, who was copy editor for the *Chicago Daily Globe*. The young Dreiser was impressed by the veteran editor who helped smooth the way for him on the big city newspaper (see *Newspaper Days*, chaps. 7–14). In 1920, Maxwell was at work on a long study, "The Man behind the Mask," which tried to prove that Shakespeare's plays had been written by Robert Cecil, first earl of Salisbury. Dreiser encouraged him in this folly and tried for years to find him a publisher.

2. Dreiser is referring to Dr. A. S. W. Rosenbach and to an editor of the *New Variorum* Shakespeare, Horace Howard Furness, Jr.

[UPL]

[after 21 July 1920]

I never could pump up any interest in this Cecil-Bacon business. Who gives a damn who wrote the Shakespeare plays? The evidence is massive that Shakespeare lived, and that all his friends thought he wrote them. Personally, I believe that they were all written by Beethoven.

M.

[NYP]

P.O. Box 181
Los Angeles

Aug 4—1920

Dear Mencken:

Thanks for the Maxwell letter.[1] I'll get the mss to you in some way. I suppose you read of Reedys death. You didn't like him but he was a great book man a little vain, an ass in war, but still a fellow. I'm sorry he's gone.

The reason I stay here is—because this summer climate is without exception the finest I have ever known   Sky, mountains, the sea, light, temperature and a sensuous wind combine to make it perfect. 88 to 90 at noon. Cool winds & a blanket at night—and every night. No flies, no mosquitos, no gnats, ants cockroaches or bugs of any kind   Name me a better summer world with—of course—the exception of Baltimore

Th.D.

1. This letter is missing.

[UPL]

H. L. Mencken
1524 Hollins St.
Baltimore.

August 7th [1920]

Dear Dreiser:-

1. Observe within, the mooing of an old cow. Refresh my memory. Didn't Austin[1] assure you of her indignation against the Comstocks, and then refuse to sign the Protest? Let me know about this.

2. I have heard nothing so far about the Shakespeare book. The subject is one in which my ignorance shines.

3. Yesterday, coming down from New York on the train, I read a first novel by a Detroit lawyer that would delight you. The fellow shows a very high talent. If this is actually his first work, then he will be heard from.

4. I have got over the San Francisco shambles. Now for hay fever. Sterling writes that he and a few others emptied a 50 gallon barrel of wine at the Grove. Life out there is very wild.

5. What in hell has become of the Bulwark?

6. I am making ready to tackle On Democracy. It will be awful stuff, I do believe.

7. The other day a dog peed on me. A bad sign.[2]

Yours,
Mencken

1. Mary Austin (1868–1934), poet, critic, novelist.
2. There is a standing joke between Dreiser and Mencken about the dogs that urinated on Poe's grave in Baltimore. Moreover, Mencken made a habit of taking friends to the spot, after an evening of music and beer, to perform the same rite.

[UPL]

H. L. Mencken
1524 Hollins St.
Baltimore.

August 11th [1920]

Dear Dreiser:-

You are getting too damned refined. What could be more comforting than a few tame roaches? Some time ago I put a turtle into my back-yard and he began to eat the cellar-bugs, shit-bugs, etc. I killed the turtle at once. When you are in the death-house, waiting to go to the chair, you will thank God for a few bed-bugs.

Boyd is in New York. He got himself a job writing editorials for the

Evening Post—very good luck for him. He was down here week before last for an evening at the pots; I see him every time I go to New York. He begs to be remembered. He reports that life is impossible in Ireland.

Hay fever is due to floor me next week. I feel like a poor working girl waiting to be accouched.

Yours in Xt.,
M

P.O. Box 181
Los Angeles

Aug 13—1920

Dear H. L. M.

Yes, Mary Austin is the same who once argued against literary oppression and then refused to sign. As I understand it she combined with Augustus Thomas, Hamlin Garland, the author of Pigs is Pigs[1] and some others to prevent the Authors League from taking a stand in my behalf. An honest appreciation of my defects as a writer was probably at the bottom of it all. But she doesn't seem to know that you hail from Baltimore & refuse to be pried loose   Years ago—about 1904—or 5—she wrote one good book as I recall it—a picture of Arizona The Land of Little Rain   Since then nothing of import to me. Her style is now loggy & pretentious and she is sour & crusty—a kind of logger in petticoats. If Frank had praised her— not a word I fancy.

A spirit message informs me that the dog who so offended you now houses the migrated soul of Edgar Allen Poe, who thus retaliates.

In July I read your summary of the American literary scene.[2] I can't tell you how wise and compact and sound I thought it—a fascinating peice of writing

Dreiser

I have finished a book which teeters between two titles—Newspaper Days and A Novel About Myself   I also have about completed a second book of 15 short stories. The Bulwark lags but should be along by Christmas or if not that—then a novel of equal force.

1. Ellis Parker Butler, who eventually did sign the protest.
2. "Observations upon the National Letters," *Smart Set* 62(July 1920), 138–44.

[UPL]

H. L. Mencken
1524 Hollins St.
Baltimore.

August 20th [1920]

Dear Dreiser:-

I shall come to the case of the old cow in due course. She is a dirty old slut.

That article on the American literary scene was a small part of a very long essay in Prejudices II—about 23,000 words.[1] I'll send you the book when it comes out, in October. I made the index of the book the other day and found that, next to Jesus, Ludendorff and Liveright, you were mentioned in the text more than any other man. In one place I say flatly that you are a promising fellow, and will make a splash when you get your growth.

The Newspaper Days stuff interests me a great deal. You told me of it years ago. Is it ready?

I still cling to the notion that a lot of money could be made by reissuing The "Genius" with all of the passages complained of cut out of the plates, leaving white blanks, and with a special preface by the author. It would be easy to talk Jones into it. You could sell 5,000 in two months. The publicity would be enormous.

Boyd is in New York and I see him regularly. Send him a line of welcome. He is working for the Evening Post, and can be reached there. I have given him some beer. But not enough. The aim is to tease him and so keep him wild.

Yours,
Mencken

1. "The National Letters," in *Prejudices: Second Series* (1920).

[NYP]

P.O. Box 181
Los Angeles
Calif.

Aug 27—1920

Dear Mencken:

While I would like to see the scheme proposed by you—anent The "Genius" tried, it is useless to appeal to Jones. At this moment a suit is being waged in one of the Federal Circuit Courts of New York, by me, to compel Jones to return the book to me without cost—and with damages. I may lose—and again I may not. Jones asks $5000—for the copies—(500) paper for 5000[1]—and the plates. The plates by the way are in my possession in New York now.

Again it is useless to appeal to Liveright. He has no money—or at least he will not expend it in my behalf. Quietly and under cover I am negotiating a return to Harper & Brothers. All my books published by Liveright are published on a 5 year lease, so I need only assign the leases to Harpers or any other firm. I have the feeling that Liveright cannot sell books for me. Harpers & the Century have always done well with mine. A Traveler at Forty has sold 10,000[2] and a new 5,000 edition at $3^{50} in cheaper paper has been issued. The original 1st sold for $1.80

I wish you could induce Knopf—or some other publisher to undertake your idea—and you censor the book. It is strong demand. I must have autographed so far 200 which have been picked up by admirers at $7, $10 and $15^{00}. I paid $10 for one last spring & there is one here held at $25^{00}! I would allow you a percentage on the sales for the work

Gloom[3] has the final version of A Novel About Myself and can let you see a copy later if you wish. I am not submitting it for publication now as I expect to sell certain portions of it to magazines for serial use. Please dont mention it by any title as yet. I want to sell it serially.

Under separate cover I sent you an English proposal (Constable & Co—Limited) to gather all my books under one roof in England. My letter to them[4] may seem a little flippant although I do not mean it to be. I am so tired of lofty English pretentions in connection with books—especially American ones that I could not help stating how I feel. If I cannot make any money in books published in England I see no use in publishing them there.

Th.D

I will write Boyd as you say—but cannot find his first name at present

1. Robert. H. Elias suggests that Dreiser means that "there were 500 bound copies and 5000 sets of unbound sheets" (see Elias, *Letters*, 1:275, n.1).

2. The record shows that the book had sold a little less than half this amount by this time.

3. Estelle Bloom Kubitz.

4. See Dreiser to Constable and Company, Ltd., 26 August 1920, in Elias, *Letters*, 1:271–74.

[UPL]

H. L. Mencken
1524 Hollins St.
Baltimore.

September 2nd [1920]

Dear Dreiser:-

I'll drop in to see Jones the next time I am in New York, and find out what is in his mind. I had not heard of the suit in the Federal courts, though I knew that you were planning it. It offers a good way out. What boggles the whole situation is Jones' and Liveright's claims for royalties advanced. Both are poor sportsmen, especially Liveright. I was always in doubt about your alliance with him. He now has a great deal of money, obtaining from some new Jew backer. Confidentially, he is forever approaching Nathan and me, and lately he offered us a blank contract, including even 50% royalty. But we are too comfortable with Knopf. He gets out good-looking books—not abortions, like Jones and Liveright—, he pays royalties promptly, and he is a good drummer. Three years ago Jones printed my burlesques book. It got out of print and he let it die. Knopf bought the plates, and actually sold 50% more on a reprint than Jones had sold of the original edition. Lately Knopf has reprinted my Prefaces for the second time, though it is three years old, and such a book seldom lives two years. He is also in the third edition of Prejudices I, though it is an annual, and Prejudices II will be out in a month. But he couldn't afford to buy off Jones and Liveright. I have talked to him about it often. He sells books, but he lacks the capital for such enterprises. I have a feeling that both Harpers and the Century are sick. Of the two, I prefer the Century, on account of Tom Smith. But he may leave at any time.

I think your letter to Constable is rather sniffish, but on the whole you are right. It is, however, rather useless to ask a publisher to guarantee sales; he simply can't do it; he sells as many as he can. As you know, I am strongly against the advance royalty plan. It makes for rows inevitably. I know of no case in which it has failed. Constable is a reputable publisher, and if he had all of your books he should be able to do a lot with them. He is quite right to hesitate to go ahead without the novels. In the long run, they will outsell everything else. You got very small royalties from England on account of the sale-of-sheets system. It cuts royalties to pieces, and takes away all incentive to sell books. Fisher Unwin bought 500 sheets of my Nietzsche in 1908 and still has some of them. Meanwhile, the book has gone through four editions in the U.S.

Scheffauer writes that he has interested a German publisher in several of your novels. On account of the Heinecke arrangement I have advised him to write to you direct. German royalties, on account of the exchange situation, amount to little today. Indirectly, the results are excellent. For this reason, I am giving some of my own stuff to any German translator who will translate it and get it published. Already I have been in Jugend, Der Tagebuch, Die Glocke and other magazines. Don't say these indirect results are worthless. Until I got a few good notices in France and England, I was sneered at at home. Now they treat me so politely, in the main, that I am embarassed. But this politeness sells books. My sales are now at least three times what they were a year and a half ago. The whole change began with a few favorable notices abroad. You yourself owe more to English notices than to American notices. Sister Carrie was made in England, and it was in England that the Genius suppression was converted into a celebrated case. Without English support, Cabell is dying of lack of interest.

E. A. Boyd is the name. In care of the Evening Post, edit. dept.

I am down with hay-fever.

Mencken

I note that you still cling to your pickpocket's address. It is generally believed here in the East that you are being kept in Los Angeles by a fat woman, the widow of a Bismarck herring importer. The other day I was told that she had bought you a gold watch, fully jewelled, and a Ford painted blue. Congratulations.

If you want to, tell Gloom to send me Newspaper Days. (<u>Collect</u>) Every time I see her it costs me a bottle of absinthe cocktails.[1]

1. The postscript is handwritten.

[NYP]

P.O. Box 181
Los Angeles

Sept 5—1920

Dear Mencken:

In The Dial for August appeared a most inspired sketch of me by an artist by the name of Stuart Davis.[1] I wouldn't mention it save that the thing has force & originality & you might like a copy to paste in one of the books. It certainly is an interpretation, in one way.

Dreiser

1. The Stuart Davis drawing of Dreiser shows him as a dark figure with cane in hand, walking in an urban setting, and apparently talking with an ominous-looking

man on the street. This is one in a series by Davis, the others being of Dostoevsky, John Synge, and N. Ostrovsky.

[UPL]

H. L. Mencken
1524 Hollins St.
Baltimore.

September 11th [1920]

Dear Dreiser:-

I'll take a look at the Dial woodcut at once. By the way, Gloom gave me that Bordfelt oil to keep in safety while her place was closed during the summer, and I have decided to steal it. When I die it goes to the National Museum.

I am hay-feverish and full of sadness. The other day in New York (a chronic sucker) I took 400 cc. of a new horse-serum antitoxin in the arm. For 24 hours I was free of the damned pestilence, but then it became worse than ever. However, it will be over in a week. If you can get hold of the New Republic of Sept. 8th, take a look at my article.[1] I shall follow it up.

Yours in Xt.,
M

Scheffauer writes that Kurt Wolff, a leading German publisher, wants to do The Financier. I have told him to write to you direct.

1. "Meditation in E minor," in which Mencken outlines, with great gusto, his "Tory" political views and class loyalties.

[NYP]

P.O. Box 181
Los Angeles
Calif.

Sept 7—1920

Dear Mencken:

I see by this pamphlet concerning you (Fanfare)[1] that you are 40 this 12th day of Sept. Many better returns than have ever yet been. That matter by Rascoe is excellent. I had no idea that he was so rotund. Someday, if I ever find time to do Literary Experiences you will find another angle of yourself suggested—no more—because I have never known you really

Th.D

1. *H. L. Mencken: Fanfare* was issued by Knopf in 1920 and includes an article by Burton Rascoe that was first published as a review of *A Book of Prefaces* in Rascoe's column in the *Chicago Sunday Tribune* (11 November 1917).

[UPL]

H. L. Mencken
1524 Hollins St.
Baltimore.

September 13th [1920]

Dear Dreiser:-

If you ever put me into that book, all I ask is that you speak of me as one who loved God and tried to keep His Commandments. Please don't mention my beauty: it has been my curse.

Rascoe is a young fellow of much promise. He has a sound education and writes very well. Unluckily, he has a wife and children, and so it is hard for him to avoid newspaper slavery. The Tribune fired him a few months ago, and he is now rusticating in Oklahoma. But I think he'll be back in the mines before very long.

You say you have never known me really. No doubt you recall the story of the Irishman who dropped his sandwich in the gutter. "Mike," he said to his friend, "have you ever tasted horse-piss". "No," said the friend. "Well, said the sandwich-dropper, "you ain't missed much".

Huneker's autobiography[1] is chiefly crap, but with some excellent spots.

Hay-fever has me by the ear.

Yours,
M

1. *Steeplejack* (1920).

[UPL]

H. L. Mencken
1524 Hollins St.
Baltimore.

September 17th [1920]

Dear Dreiser:-

I have just viewed the Stuart Davis portrait. It reduces your height by four feet and makes you look like a talented East Side free-verse poet. Who is the other fellow?[1] The nose is obviously Huneker's.

Huneker's autobiography, by the way, is crap. The old boy tries his damndest to appear respectable, and even assures everybody that he is a 100% American. The book leaves me very depressed. One by one they drop from the tree!

I am in great physical discomfort. I took some horse-serum antitoxin for hay-fever. The hay-fever blew up within a week, but I have severe anaphylaxis from the serum, with urticaria (huge hives) all over my arms and legs. One even showed today on my gospel-pipe, forcing me to cancel a literary engagement. Such are the evil humors of God. I feel as sick as Woodrow[2] the day after the heart of the world was broken in Maine.

Get hold of the New Republic for Sept. 8 and read my article. It is the first of a series.

Yours in Xt.,
HLM.

1. See Dreiser to Mencken, 5 September 1920, n.1.
2. Mencken is referring to the severe stroke that Woodrow Wilson had in 1919.

[NYP-T]

P.O. Box 181
Los Angeles

Sept. 20, 1920.[1]

Dear Mencken:

In your letter of September second you make several statements which indicate that you do not understand this "Genius" situation. After saying that you are going to see Jones (presumably about releasing The "Genius") you add "what boggles the whole situation is Jones' and Liveright's claim for royalties advanced." If you are referring to the "Genius" Liveright has no claim in connection with it in any way. He has not advanced me any money in connection with that and has persistently refused to take any interest in it so I cannot see how these alleged respective claims come in.

If you are referring to Jones' alleged advance royalties on The Bulwark you are referring to something about which you know little. In my suit in the Federal Court I am proving—by letters and semi-annual statements that instead of Jones advancing me any money directly against The Bulwark he advanced it under an agreement as to a general drawing account against all my books. He has no contract covering The Bulwark and at the time he asked me to sign one I refused. The several blank contracts offered me by him are here in my desk now. He claims that I owe him $2,000 and interest on The Bulwark. Yet regularly he charges off all returns on all my books now with him to my indebtedness. At the same time, although The "Genius" has never been stopped in any state but New York—and although the P. O. Department assured him that it would refuse to prosecute—and although he has a letter from the Federal District Attorney for New York absolving the book, he holds up all the books in his possession, refuses to restock my books anywhere and generally conducts himself as a tenth rate Christian Moralist would anywhere.

At the time of The "Genius" fight—although he had a cable from Wells and others and the signatures of 500 writers, and the letter from the United States District Attorney and the word of the U.S.P.O. he refused to make a single statement or pay for a single ad in any paper showing the other side of the charge. J. Jefferson J. can kiss my ass. I don't want him to republish The "Genius" and I want him to let go of my property. He has cost me a lot of money and if I win this Federal case I'll make him come across with the books and some cash.

Now as to the advance royalty idea in general—several times this winter you have written about the crime of advanced royalties and seem to be conducting some small ethical war of your own, tending to improve the morals of publishers and authors. So be. The idea does not interest me. I am and have been conducting an individual struggle to live and write and I will continue so to do as my best wits help me and not otherwise. In my labors so far I have had much advice but no practical cash aid other than I could extract by some well laid device of my own. It is true that Harpers, Century, Lane and Liveright have advanced me at different times sums on which The Financier, The Titan, The "Genius", A Hoosier Holiday and some others were written. I paid Century and Harpers in full and they now send me checks. To Lane I owe $2,000, which long ago, if he had not laid down on my books, he could have taken in via sales. Because of non-distribution by him—A Hoosier Holiday sells here for $7.50 and $10.00.

The Titan for $7.50. Plays of the Natural for $3 and $4—The "Genius" for $15.00 and up. It is just as true in Frisco, Seattle, Denver, St. Louis, Indianapolis and elsewhere. I know because I have investigated. I offered him $5 cash for 100 copies of The "Genius" and he refused to sell one. There was $500 on this alleged indebtedness from a responsible agent here. I paid $10.00 for a copy myself last May because I had to have it.

Another phase of the thing. When I went to Jones he was delighted to get me and agreed forthwith to a general drawing account. During my stay he assured me that my identification with his firm was of <u>cash</u> advertising value to him. He assured me that he owed not only your name and Nathan's but a number of others—Sherwood Anderson for one and Wright for another—to my presence on his list. In proof of the fact that I was of service to him I can cite that I gave him the refusal of "The Spoon River Anthology"—which his reader rejected and of which MacMillan sold 60,000 in one year—also Carl Sandburg's <u>Chicago</u> <u>Poems</u> which Sandburg sent to me—and which he also rejected, saying that it was an imitation of Masters. Also I sent him Anderson's first and second books. He told me that my name had attracted to him better people than otherwise would have come to him and John Lane personally assured me that ever since he had lost Gertrude Atherton he had been looking for an American name on his list to conjure with and that now that he had me he was satisfied that he would do better.

Now coming back to the advance royalty idea—if a writer's name is of some value from an advertising point of view to a publisher why shouldn't he pay him for it?—or make it up to him in some other way by advancing royalties for instance. You seem to realize the point well enough for you cite with considerable gusto that Liveright was willing to pay you and Nathan royalties up to 50 per cent. For what? Because he expected to make it out of your books? Like hell. He was considering the advertising or drawing power of your name. And if its such a crime to take royalties in advance how about higher royalties than a book can possibly earn? And if the poor publisher is so helpless that he can be slicked into advancing cash to designing authors how is it that he comes around with offers of royalties up to 50 per cent, which he cannot possibly earn in order to get a name. I know for a fact that Liveright has paid and does now pay from 2 1/2 to 5 per cent on books brought to him by Lewisohn[2] and some others. If so— and if he can do this and still pay the author and in other cases advance working capital to 78 different breeds of kykes on books to be translated or written, why can't he advance me money on a book especially when I have drawn to him better names than he ever had. If you want to know whether he considers—or did—that my name was of value to him over and above the cash returns on my books, consider the fact that I threatened to leave him flat last August and called him up and told him to go to hell and that he came down to my place and literally—not figuratively—wept—and agreed to do anything within reason if I would stay. And now you assure me that he is beefing about money advanced me—"boggling matters" in regard to me. If so he will get a real opportunity to beef soon. I owe him less than $1,600 against which he has five books—all selling. He has only five year contracts in each case and I can fix him neatly.

Once again to get back to this advance royalty crime. When I was at Harpers Major Leigh and Duneka were both in charge and I talked over this whole advance idea with them.[3] Major Leigh assured me that he considered it one of the best investments a clever publisher could make and cited a dozen instances (Bachellor—"Eben Holden" for instance)[4] where Harpers had scored heavily by aiding certain men to write. When Paul[5] was in the song business it was an axiom with his firm that the slickest thing they could do was to get hold of and stake possible geniuses in the field until such time as they should ring the bell—and to this day Feist, Witmark, Haviland and others carry people on salary—not because of a past success—but because of prospective successes. Grubstaking is not only common in trade but it is good business. If I ever run a successful restaurant or grocery business anywhere—and could prove it—I could go to a bank here and get an advance. They even advertise the fact.

However I am not here to prove what everybody knows—and if it were not true it would make no difference in my case. I am out to write and make a living, and until such time as some Maecenas or well to do relative comes forward to make me comfortable for life I will invent or employ such devices as I can to work and live. If you feel this to be a vast moral crime or something that "boggles" something call the police.

Dreiser

PS. In regard to my present social state here your informant has not the color of the Ford quite correct. It is cream and light blue. The watch, however, is as described.

N. B. This additional thought occurs to me. If Liveright can afford to offer you a 50 per cent royalty and he thinks so highly of me that he is moved to tears, why can't he afford to stand for an advance of $2,000 in my case? Incidentally Gloom writes me that Cox, the old and new book man who supplies libraries, assures her that he can get all the "Geniuses" he wants from a publisher in Australia at $2.50 and that he does, selling to whomsoever wants them. This Australian publisher leases or buys from Lane in London and according to Lane's statements not a copy of the "Genius" has been sold since 1917. But I suppose, as you say, these two publishers "cannot afford" to do better by me.

1. This is misdated; it was written sometime before Mencken's letter of 18 September.
2. Ludwig Lewisohn.
3. F. T. Leigh was vice-president and Frederick A. Duneka secretary of Harper's when the firm became Dreiser's publisher in 1911.
4. Irving Bacheller's novel *Eben Holden* (1900) sold over a million copies.
5. Dreiser's brother, the songwriter Paul Dresser.

[UPL]

H. L. Mencken
1524 Hollins St.
Baltimore.

September 18th [1920]

Dear Dreiser:-

For God's sake, desist! Now, it appears, I am a moralist. It simply ain't so. No one is more delighted than I am when an author horns a publisher, but my contention is simply this: that advance royalties benefit the publisher vastly more than they benefit the author. Your own evidence proves it: all the publishers are in favor of them, and pay them with oleaginous alacrity. But I submit nevertheless that, after an author has accepted them, he is in an unfavorable position to fight a publisher who plays yellow—that the counter claim always weakens his direct claim. But I am surely not carrying on any campaign against them. I refuse to accept them chiefly, I suppose, because I have never needed them—not by the patronage of some Maecenas or some rich relative, but merely by the fortunes of war. I advise every author to refuse too, when he can.

Please don't get the notion that Liveright is bawling about any advance he may have made to you. So far as I am concerned, he has never mentioned the subject. Nor has he ever offered me any royalty, 50% or otherwise, directly; he has simply done some scouting. All this in justice to Liveright, whom I surely do not admire. But you are bound to quarrel with such a fellow soon or late, and when the quarrel comes his advances give him a chance to knock you in the head. As for the Jones proposal, I retire precipitately. It will be useless to tackle him until the case in the Federal courts is decided, and if the verdict is in your favor then you will have the whole situation in your hands.

Where is your case being tried, and when is it called? No one here in the East seems to have heard of it; at all events, I have never heard anyone mention it.

Yours,
Mencken

P.O. Box 181
Los Angeles

Sept 22nd 1920

Dear Mencken:

In regard to the Bror Nordfeldt Portrait of me Please note: neither the canvas nor the frame belong to me. They belong to the artist, who loaned them to me. Nordfelt is a peripatetic Swede who was last (November 1920) in Sante Fe, N.M.[1] He may now be anywhere—India, Argentina or Baltimore. When he shows up—or demands the portrait—and by & with the consent of Gloom—you may keep the picture. If he never shows up it is yours, but he may call at any time. Hes a very interesting fellow & you might like him. As for Kurt Wolf, I'll be glad to deal with him. The Heinecke thing seems to have disappeared

Dreiser

In regard to my last long letter all I can say is that whether intentionally or not,—& sometimes I suspect intention, you have the happy faculty of getting a rise out of me. I hear that Frank Harris has written a volume—Contemporary Portraits—2nd series—in which he disposes of me as a bag of mush.[2] All I can say of Harris is that he is the Eva Tanguay of letters.[3]

1. Dreiser knew the painter Bror Nordfeldt when he lived in Greenwich Village; he obviously has another year in mind.
2. Harris's portrait was not excessively harsh, but it did use personal interviews to portray Dreiser as sexually insecure, and it praised his early writing at the expense of *The "Genius"* and later work.
3. Eva Tanguay (1878–1947) was a vaudeville queen who was considered something of an exhibitionist.

SMART SET
A Magazine of Cleverness
George Jean Nathan ⎫
and ⎬ Editors
H. L. Mencken ⎭

[after 22 September 1920]

Dear Dreiser:

Of course I understand that Nordfelt owns the portrait. It simply seemed to me to be safer in my house than in Gloom's, with her away—and she agreed. Maybe you'll want it yourself some day, when you are rich and build a palace. If so, let me know.

The Harris chapter is <u>not</u> an attack on you. Harris is probably trying to be very nice. He is a curious fish—enormously vain @ touchy. I never see him because I dislike quarreling, and he is very quarrelsome.

Gloom sent me the ms of "Newspaper Days". Of this, more when I get back to Baltimore. There is very fine stuff in it. I incline to think that, as it stands, it is a bit longish. I wish you had done a whole book on your brother. At the S.F. National Convention there was an hour when he lived again. All his songs were sung, and they moved 10,000 people quite as powerfully as they used to in his own day. It was a really impressive scene. Unluckily, I was tight that night, and so could not describe it adequately. No one else, I suppose, thought of him. Such is the curious, obscure power of the man who imagines things.

When are you coming back? I heard the other day that the husband of the lady who is keeping you has got out of jail and is about to go west. A word to the wise!

Truly yours

M[1]

1. Mencken enclosed with this letter a brief review of Frank Harris's *Contemporary Portraits*, by Arthur H. Moss, who compared Harris's weak chapter on Dreiser to "Mencken's masterly article on that ponderous genius" (*The Quill*, October 1920, 12). Mencken laughed over the misspelling of Dreiser ("Dreisler") and beside "masterly" he wrote "Jesus, save me."

[NYP]

P.O. Box 181

Los Angeles

Sept. 23rd 1920

Dear Mencken:

Anent Huneker:

The truth is that you are an idealist in things literary or where character is concerned and expect men to ring centre 100 times out of 100. Many of Hunekers earlier critical estimates and interpretations are excellent— quite generous and fascinating   What matter now, if when he is old he dodders. Wait till you are 60 or 70—and see how you do. My quarrel with his earlier work was that in many cases he was the very last to discover certain people especially Americans like Davies,[1] and, so far as I know, he never said a word about Inness[2] until after 1910. I may be wrong. He waited until all the European reports were in and then generalized upon them—a safe bet   Despite that he was & is a fine writer, interpretive and illuminating. He was certainly very much needed over here. Beside you however—and I say it in all fairness—he is as a pop-gun to a howitzer. You blaze new trails—seek poor sprouts under the weeds—& chop down all the choking ones for miles around. You almost kill the new things with sunlight. In addition you run into the offing and yell until a crowd collects. Excellent and wonderful. May your snickersnee grow heavier and sharper. But dont expect the bell to be rung every trip.

And remember Wright. In 1912 I warned you he was stealing your stuff—and revamping it. He had dropped a little tube into your well & was trying to siphon you out   He even assumed himself the larger figure—and began spouting to me until I threw him out. But to you—the idealist once more—he was a little tin Jesus. And now see.[3]

Well it is your typical stunt & your typical experience. You will probably continue for years to come to bring in tin cans from the street and set them on the mantel. But in view of past flops—you might be careful—& not too hard on your idols once they are out in the street again. I like the Stuart Davis sketch of me very much. It makes me laugh.

Dreiser

1. Arthur B. Davis, painter.
2. George Inness, painter.
3. During the war, Mencken and Willard Huntington Wright ended their friendship. Wright had been working for the New York *Evening Mail*, and when a secretary spied on him he wrote a letter, as bait, that was outrageously unpatriotic. In the process, he implicated one of Mencken's friends. The letter was exposed as a hoax, but not until Mencken's friend was investigated by the Secret Service and given publicity that Mencken resented.

[UPL]

H. L. Mencken
1524 Hollins St.
Baltimore.

October 1st [1920]

Dear Dreiser:-

Of course I don't believe that you would blab a confidential communication.[1] But I saw a row looming up, and I have had a belly full of rows these last years. I am constantly tempted to throw up the literary business, buy a dog-house in Maryland, and live on $100 a month, writing one book a year. But by the time one mess is finished I am in another. I'll probably die in full regalia, wearing even a condom.

What you say of my high services to art is pleasant, but rhetorical. There is nothing much to do here save hatchet idiots. The country is irrevocably rotten. My work hereafter, if I keep on, will be a good deal more political than literary. In Prejudices II I skin Roosevelt's carcass. In Prejudices III I hope to tear out the cold bowels of Woodrow. A pox upon all such swine! May they sweat in hell forever!

The Wright episode was disagreeable, but I have no regrets. I got him every job he ever had in the East, supported him when he was in need, and stood up for him against the crowd. In reply he robbed me of money and lied about me. But consider his state today—full of drugs, hopeless, jobless and living by petty graft.[2]

I read the newspaper book. It is full of excellent stuff. Some of the newspaper chapters are gorgeous. The defect that I see in it is a certain flabbiness in form. Considering the great space given to the beginning of the S.W.[3] episode, it seems to me that the thing is dismissed too briefly at the end. So with the Alice business. This objection, of course, would fade if the book were printed as one volume in a series—that is, if it were clearly understood that another volume would follow. Such a volume should follow. For this reason I think that Newspaper Days is a better title than A Novel About Myself. If you use the latter, what will you call the succeeding and preceeding volumes?

In places you philosophize, I think, at too great length. Again, I dislike the picking up of stuff from Twelve Men (the McCord episode). Yet again, the affair with the Bohemian woman is a bit wheezy—the sort of thing that all of us have at 22. It is true, of course, but it is also true that you shit your pants in 1884—and that is not mentioned. I don't think the Comstocks will bother the book. Changing a few words would stump them completely. Altogether the book is a bit too long. It would be more effective if some of the thinner discourses were cut down. But there is enough good stuff in it to justify it.

You missed a fine chance when you didn't write a whole book about your brother. The idea dawned on me that day at San Francisco. We have biographies of all sorts of eighth-rate politicians, preachers, cheesemongers, etc. Why not a full-length book on a genuine American original, what we Huns call a Kopf?[4] I don't think the Twelve Men chapter has ruined it. What of his early days? How did he write his songs?

I don't object to Huneker growing senile; I object to him recanting so ignominiously. I enclose a tender review of his book.[5] He deserved an attack with good German artillery. Also I enclose a patriotic piece.

The Liveright letter is very amusing.[6] A love affair, by God! He talks and talks.

I met W. L. George[7] last night in New York. He will be in Los Angeles toward Christmas. Do you want to see him?

I returned the MS. to Gloom, and gave her a bottle of vermouth.
God save the Republic!

Yours,
M

1. On 24 September 1920, Dreiser wrote to Mencken saying that he did not use Mencken's private opinions to him in a letter to Liveright.
2. Willard Huntington Wright had become addicted to drugs and later, after a period of hospitalization, he turned to writing the popular Philo Vance detective stories under the pseudonym S. S. Van Dine.
3. Sara White, Dreiser's first wife.
4. A talented man.
5. Mencken sent advance copies of his review of Huneker's *Steeplejack* (*Smart Set* 63 [December 1920], 140–42).
6. This is missing.
7. W. L. George, British novelist.

[NYP]

P.O. Box 181
Los Angeles

Sept. 30—1920.

Dear Mencken:
I have written John Maxwell, of Indianapolis—to send his mss to you—collect—insured. Please pay the bill <u>if</u> it <u>comes</u> & send the bill to me

Dreiser
When done with mss hold until you hear from me

[NYP]

P.O. Box 181
Los Angeles

Oct 4—1920

H. L. M.
Harris has combed my more personal & intimate books for statements & confessions regarding myself—and put them without authority or indication of any kind into my mouth. Before this he attacked me in Pearsons as anti-German![1] in order to curry favor with German readers. Judge for yourself.

Dreiser

1. Frank Harris, "Theodore Dreiser," *Pearson's Magazine* 39 (October 1918), 346–51.

[UPL]

H. L. Mencken
1524 Hollins St.
Baltimore.

October 6th [1920]

Dear Dreiser:-

It shall be done.[1] The MS. is not yet here,[2] but the Gracchus book has come in.[3] Have I got to read a whole book of blank verse? If so, a pox upon you for inflicting it upon me.

Sterling says that you are going to San Francisco. I lost a couple of neckties and a brand-new undershirt there. If you find them hanging over the foot of the bed please return them.

Yours in Xt.,
M

I have not asked anyone to inflict this on you. Please don't let the author or Liveright use my name to persuade you to do it.[4]

If you write W. L. George just indicate to him that I am in Los Angeles. I have a letter direct from N.Y., but he may be gone from there when my answer arrives.[5]

D

1. Dreiser circled this line and wrote in "Thanks."
2. John Maxwell's manuscript.
3. *Caius Gracchus* (1920), a verse tragedy by Odin Gregory, for which Dreiser wrote the introduction. Odin Gregory was the pseudonym of Joseph G. Robin, a businessman-turned-author; he was the model for the central character in "'Vanity, Vanity,' Saith the Preacher" (*Twelve Men*).
4. Dreiser added this at the end of the letter, and returned it to Mencken.
5. Dreiser placed this message at the top right-hand corner of the page.

[NYP]

P.O. Box 181
Los Angeles

Oct 8—1920

Dear M—

Thanks for Huneker and <u>Star Spangled Men</u>.[1] That last is certainly Spangled satire. At times you remind me of an athlete leaping lightly from test to test, a devout Moslem whirling his sacred prayers, a scaly rattler fencing with a gopher. After all the gyrations of these lice for five years what fine comforting commentary. While I laughed I thanked heaven for the blood being drawn. I actually hope you finish Woodrow.[2] Why not a small brochure on that nobleman alone?

In regard to <u>Newspaper Days</u> I agree with all you say. Would that I could induce you to show Gloom—with pencil marks—where & how to cut. The thing is not going to any publisher yet. Also to write me the chapter heads. The reason I put in the McCord & other stuff is this. Aside from a few critics who follow all of one's work most readers take up only one or two books   Nearly every book stands on its own legs—is read discoupled in the mind from every other. Hence the complete data about characters. However this stuff can come out—& the Bohemian woman stuff. This is only a part of a four or five-Vol. <u>History of Myself</u>. Vol. 1 is done—lying typewritten in my trunk at 165.[3] In case of my death go & get it—or send Gloom. Vol III—Literary Experiences is under way. I do a small bit—now & then.[4] Ah, the opportunity that lies there, my good brother—the nobles of the nineties & nineteen tens! I once thought of a book about Paul. But he appears fairly well drawn in Vols. 1 2 & 3—youth, fame & death   In <u>Newspaper Days</u>, supposing you trouble to indicate to Gloom the places—cut the dull philosophy by all means. I want the book to be readable.

Anent W. L. George. No—I don't want to see him. My experiences with literary men make me curse. I like a man anywhere, and if he chances to be one—and really wants to see me, he will get in touch with me direct—and in the right spirit. Otherwise his books suffice. Thank god for private letter boxes, obscure neighborhoods & people who think you are in the real estate or insurance business

Th.D

Your comment on Wright sounds like a religionist who has seen the wicked properly bewrayed. But I cannot pity him because he is a dog—really & truly

1. "Star Spangled Men," *New Republic* 24 (29 September 1920), 118—20. Mencken's satire on military decorations turns into an attack on anti-German civilians and their conduct during the war.

2. Woodrow Wilson.

3. Dreiser's New York address was 165 West 10th Street. The first volume became *Dawn* (1931).

4. Dreiser never published such a volume, and nothing remains of it in manuscript.

[UPL]

H. L. Mencken
1524 Hollins St.
Baltimore.

October 11th [1920]

Dear Dreiser:-

You take the Harris chapter too seriously. After all, the general tone of it is very friendly. He puts you into a book on all fours with men that he regards as great, and elects you to the sodality. I begin to believe that any writing about a man does him good—that even when it is deliberately unfriendly it makes friends for him. Moreover, unfriendly stuff puts a man on his guard. This I know from my own experience: that I have learned more from attacks than from praise. In even the most vicious of them there is a touch or two of plausibility. There is always something embarassing about unqualified praise. A man knows, down in his heart, that he doesn't deserve it. When he sees all his petty bluffs and affectations accepted seriously, the sole result is to make him lose respect for the victim. During the war I was belabored constantly by patriotic gents. Some weeks ten or twelve columns of denunciation would come in. Some of it was so violent that I began to look for libel, hoping to turn an honest dollar by entering some suits and then compromising. But the allegations (save the occasional charge that I was a Jew) were so sound that it would have been ridiculous to complain. The fundamental charge was always that I was a foul agent of German Kultur, seeking to poison the wells of the Republic. Well, this was true, at least in a general sense. The Puritans had a right to defend their country.

Harris is a quarrelsome fellow, with a mind full of suspicions. In Pearson's of this month he prints an attack on me by Middleton Murry. Well, what of it? The attack is apparently honest. Murry has printed two favorable articles about me in the Athenaeum and Harris once printed a long one. If the two of them think that I am wrong in the present case, maybe I am wrong. In any case, I am still alive, and able to work.

So saith the preacher. I doubt that you have any reasonable complaint against Harris and company, or against the world in general. At fifty years you are not only permanently secure; you have become a sort of national legend. The younger generation is almost unanimously on your side. The professors have been beaten, and they know it.

George Sterling writes that he has laid in 4 barrels of grappo and 25 head of gals to entertain you. Beware! He dam near finished me in 24 hours.

Yours,
M

[UPL]

SMART SET
A Magazine of Cleverness
George Jean Nathan
and   } Editors
H. L. Mencken

October 12th [1920]

Dear Dreiser:-

You mistake me, my dear Emil. I don't cite Wright's collapse as a proof of the justice of God; I cite it as a reason why I can't wallop him. He is down and out. You begin to see moral banshees. This is three times within two months that you have accused me of being a Christian. I begin to have Freudian suspicions. You hear the whisper of Jesus in your own ear.

Thanks very much for the Hand of the Potter circular. I hope you send one to Nathan. The history of the play is particularly interesting.

If you can wait a bit I'll be very glad to go through Newspaper Days again and scheme out a few cuts. The best of it is so fine that it seems a pity to let the thing down here and there. I think that Gloom told me she was taking the MS. to Udall.[1] In any case I'll get hold of her. I see no reason why the Bohemian woman episode should be cut out entirely. Maybe, on re-reading the MS., I'll conclude that it ought to stay in as it stands. As for McCord, wouldn't it suffice to refer to Twelve Men? Let the swine buy it.

I suppose George will try to find you. I have not mentioned the matter to him, but if he asks me flatly for a card to you I can't very well refuse. I am surely not one to cultivate these visitors. George, Walpole and Dunsany came to me.[2] Walpole turned out to be a capital fellow, and George seems very decent. Dunsany is an ass. I have met none of the others, save Sassoon.[3] I ran into him on the street one day, with Louis Untermeyer.

Write to Gloom, and tell her to send me the MS., or to leave it at the Smart Set office. I am in Baltimore.

God save the Republic!

Yours,
HLM.

The insurance business? Bah! They suspect you of being a swami.[4]

1. Mencken means Merton S. Yewdale, an editor at the John Lane Co.
2. The British authors Lord Dunsany (see Mencken to Dreiser, 29 November 1915, n.1) and Hugh Walpole.
3. The British poet Siegfried Sassoon.
4. The postscript is handwritten.

[NYP]

<u>P.O. Box 181</u>

Oct. 25—1920

Dear Mencken:

Thanks for your word as to <u>Newspaper Days</u>. I am in no hurry. Will you decorate it with some gaudy chapter heads? I have been up to S.F. and am locoed. I expect to move to & spend my declining years there. In the lankwutch of my late fat brother—"a city, sport—a city." George Sterling hovers over it like a burnished black Holy Ghost—a bird in short   That dear Powell Street is in my blood. Nightly I was led to my room full to the ears. Oh, happy land—oh shapely Succubi. If Hamburg—(such is my name for this place) were only full of Friscans   But what's the use. They have the wind & sea & scenery & gay seeking souls every one. Paris, N.Y. New Orleans and Frisco—and you may put them in any order you like.

Enclosed is an interesting Indiana development.[1] Send it in to Gloom & then back here

D.

You know that secretly you are falling back into the arms of Christ—& making your peace with God. I have it from the Nick Harris detective agency that every Wednesday & Sunday nights you are to be seen slipping into the side door of the Buryher St. M.E. Church—wearing a plug hat and a heavy mat of grey-green whiskers. Oh the perfidy of fearsome, snivelling Christian age!

P.S. Can you suggest any way by which I can find out whether Stern Brothers—(42nd St N.Y.) recently held a sale of Sister Carries at 98 cents. I hear so & would like to know the number put on sale. I own Sister Carrie—plates & rights. The same are leased to B&L for royalty. It was specifically understood that the book was to be sold at 2^{00}. If I can establish this as a fact I will have a heart to heart talk with Liveright. I doubt if he is straight with me.

---

1. A reference to recent letters to Dreiser from the Indiana Society of the Sons of the American Revolution about plans to honor Paul Dresser and to bring his remains back to Terre Haute, Indiana. [UPL]

[UPL]

H. L. Mencken
1524 Hollins St.
Baltimore.

October 30th [1920]

Dear Dreiser:-

I incline to think that the best way to find out about the Stern matter would be to write to the book buyer at Stern Bros direct, telling him that you have heard of the sale and are eager to find out how many copies were sold—that is, as a matter of auctorial paternal feeling. If he bites, then ask him what he charged. He will answer you sooner than he would answer anyone else.

San Francisco evidently made the same smash with you that it did with me. The town is actually almost unbelievable. Let us keep it in reserve for our declining years. What would be more charming than to settle there, put in a couple of clean colored girls to cook for us, and spend our senility discussing the wisdom and majesty of God? You could sleep out (with some gal from Bigins) on the days when I was drunk. Sterling, by that time, will be chained to the wall in some psychopathic ward. He already labors under delusions of sexual grandeur. The girls told me confidentially that a rainy Sunday exhausted him; they said that even I was better. What joy there will be in hell the day he gets there!

Your agents are inaccurate. It is true that I frequent houses of worship, but not to pray. I go there to pick pockets. The magazine business is so damned bad that it is either that, or work. Paper is now so enormously expensive that only the rich can afford to have diarrhoea. I always use the Gideon Bible at the Algonquin.

I have forwarded the Maxwell letter to Gloom. If you go to the unveiling of the monument, invite me to go along.

God help Ireland!

Yours,
Mencken

[NYP]

P.O. Box 181
Los Angeles

Nov. 1—1920

Dear Mencken:

Can you do anything to further the idea put forth in this letter.[1] I would like to see Pauls body taken down there—just because of the sentiment of the thing. He lies in St. Boniface—a cheap, 10th rate Catholic cemetery on the North Side of Chicago. I doubt if there is anything more than a one foot stone—if so much. If the state legislature would do this an interesting memorial might be erected—something different to a lousy tombstone— if only some one would give them idea. Couldn't you say something to guide them. A little publicity & your favor will make all of them out there very keen. I enclose something from the morning Examiner here about you and L.A.²

D

If any mention is made will you see that copies reach the enclosed "list"³

1. Dreiser enclosed the letter he received, on 26 October 1920, from Charles Timothy Jewett, trustee of the Indiana Society of the Sons of the American Revolution. Jewett spoke about creating a "Paul Dresser Drive" in Terre Haute and making Indiana "the final resting place for the ashes of the singer who brought fame and wholesome sentiment to the poetic Wabash." [UPL]
2. This has not survived.
3. Dreiser wrote this at the top of the letter and enclosed a list of Indiana notables who were to receive notice of the memorial plans for his brother.

[UPL]

The Smart Set.
25 W. 45th St.
New York City,
N.Y.

Nov. 9, 1920

Dear Dreiser:

Certainly I'll promote the Paul Dresser memorial. It must be handled discreetly. I hope you invite me to the ceremonies. It's too bad that you never did a complete book on him instead of a sketch. It isn't too late yet, in my judgement. The sketch in Twelve Men wouldn't interfere. He was what the Germans call a "kopf". The Examiner piece is excellent.

M.

[NYP]

P.O. Box 181
Los Angeles

Nov. 14—1920

Dear Mencken:

I don't know whether you are kidding me about wanting an invitation to the P.D. ceremonies and I cant say that there will ever be any ceremonies—but if there are & youd like to come—assuming that I am invited—theres no one in the world I'd rather have by me all the way through for I certainly would need substantial intellectual support of some kind. As Duffy[1] used to say—"one needs to acquire the power of simulating conviction". So if I go you go—if you will & I'll be very much flattered—and Paul would be too, I know.

Some one suggests a Paul Dresser night out there with all his songs sung & it would be interesting—a gala occasion I bet.

Sterling says he is in doubt whether he will let you live in S.F—that your not worthy of its Bohemian resources—that you select impregnable virgins and cling to water as it were your hearts blood. How so? Come through?

Enclosed are two clippings sent on here—which Please return. I note that your list—at last—is the one approved. You weild a big stick & no doubt of it. And looking at these things makes me think that this is as fit a time as any for me to acknowledge your services to yours truly. In his introduction to Erewhon Hackett (Francis) quotes Samuel Johnson as saying—"though it should happen that an author is capable of excelling, yet his merit may pass without notice huddled in the variety of things and thrown into the general miscellany of life". And he adds: "It is even truer as Dr. Johnson adds, that readers "more frequently require to be reminded than informed"—a very clear perception of a fact.

And looking back on myself I know now that except for your valiant and unwearied and even murderous assaults and onslaughts in my behalf I should now be little farther than in 1910. You opened with big guns & little & kept them going. The fact that a few white flags began to appear is due to you & you alone. And now I sometimes wonder what more. The fireside & a limping old age. Hell.

But I will take you up on bachelors hall in S.F.—I will, by God.

D.

Prejudices is here & as usual I fare better than I deserve   The two things that kill me are Roosevelt and Exeunt Omnes. You have that big Rhinoceros measured exactly. Sometime collect twenty or thirty of your best things in one book. Put in Spangled Men, Roosevelt, Exeunt Omnes & that thing I once read in the Smart Set about women—a scream. That will be a book.

1. Richard Duffy, an editor at *Ainslee's Magazine* and a friend of Dreiser since 1898.

[UPL]

H. L. Mencken
1524 Hollins St.
Baltimore.

November 15th [1920]

Dear Dreiser:-

It is in my mind that you once told me the following: That in the days when Mark Twain lived in Fifth avenue he would sometimes come down to a saloon in 4th street or thereabout, and deliver a tirade against his wife. I am certain about the fact, but can't remember whether it was you who told me of it or someone else, though my recollection is that it was you. The other day I met Van Wyck Brooks, author of the very excellent study, "The Ordeal of Mark Twain". Brooks' whole book is based upon the thesis that Mark's wife was a curse to him, despite the apparent amity of their relations. In discussing the matter, I told him of Mark's tirades. He was naturally much interested, since they supported his case. But I was a bit uncertain. What do you know about it?

Gloom reports that "Newspaper Days" is still in the hands of Udale. Why have chapter headings? Have you any reason? My feeling is that they would do no good.

Yours,

M

I had a long talk the other day with Frank Harris. My conclusion is as before: that his intentions were perfectly good. He is getting old—66,— He wrote his own opinion of Mark[1] into his discussion of you—an annoying thing, but one that, in critical writing, it is often extraordinarily difficult to avoid. The old boy seems somehow pathetic. He is crazy to sell out and go to Europe.

M.

---

1. Dreiser had sent Mencken an undated note that reads as follows: "On page 97—of Contemporary Portraits, I am quoted as saying that Twain is negligible. What swill. You know that I admire him intensely. Huckleberry Finn—negligible! The Mysterious Stranger negligible!" [NYP]

[UPL]

H. L. Mencken
1524 Hollins St.
Baltimore.

November 20th [1920]

Dear Dreiser:-

1. I have asked Gloom to get the MS. from Yewdale as soon as he has finished with it, and to leave it at the Smart Set office to be forwarded to me. So far I have not heard from her, but she is always diligent in such matters.

2. Without the MS. by me, it is impossible to suggest chapters for serial publication. But a number of them are in the book, and I'll make a list when I go through the MS. again.

3. Are you set on chapter headings? Somehow, I have a feeling that they would not help the book. It seems to me that it needs relatively little changing. Now and then you got lost in your story, but not often.

4. I am quite serious about going to the Paul Dresser ceremony. The Baltimore Sun would be glad to pay my expenses. The concert of his songs would be superb; they are genuinely fine folk-music, and much better than you think. I shall try to give some help with an article in the Smart Set and one in the Sun. Let us buckle down to the thing, and we'll convert the celebration into a national affair. He deserves it, absolutely. A man who can do what he did that afternoon at San Francisco is extraordinarily rare.

5. Sterling is a low libeller. I drank alcohol each and every day I was in San Francisco, whereas he had to go on the water-wagon and remained there six days running. It is true that I consorted with a virgin and that she is a virgin still, but that is simply because I was very tired and she was very amiable. Sterling announced months in advance that he had a boudoir companion for me—that all I'd have to do would be to go to her place and hang up my hat. But when I arrived she was non est, and so I had to scratch around on my own hook, seeking both sparring partners and a virgin to sooth me with her talk. I had a hell of a good time. George was superb, but history must record that he went on the water wagon. So much in simple justice to my honor. I would not have any reputable man think that I was actually sober in San Francisco. As a matter of fact, I came down with a severe alcoholic gastritis, and was ill in bed all the way home on the train—a ghastly experience. If you ever hear anyone say that I was sober, please call him a liar. I am touchy on such points.

6. You greatly overestimate my services to you. You were squarely on your legs before I came into contact with you or wrote a line about you,

and you would have made the same progress if I had been hanged in 1902, perhaps more.

7. The combat of novelists is very interesting. If I had the list to make I'd leave out Atherton, a great fraud, and put in Hergesheimer, and maybe add a question mark to the name of Tarkington.[1] Hergesheimer's Java Head is far better than any <u>novel</u> that Tarkington has done; his short stories—e.g., Beaucaire and the Penrod pieces—are something different. Atherton belongs to the Amélie Rives group;[2] she lacks brains. Cabell has been made by the Jurgen case. He is tickled sick. Curiously enough, W. L. George does not like him. I see the reason: George is an implacable realist. Walpole, on the other hand, thinks that Jurgen is superb. George has asked me to do an article on him for Vanity Fair. When he reaches Los Angeles, take a look at him. He is not impressive, but he has a head on him.

8. The Writers' Club consists of contributors to Snappy Stories, the Parisienne, etc.

9. My apologies for this too long letter. Get right with God!

Yours,
Mencken

1. The novelists Gertrude Atherton, Joseph Hergesheimer, and Booth Tarkington.
2. Atherton and Amélie Rives belong to the so-called "Erotic School" of writers, a late nineteenth-century group that reacted against conservative views of sex in fiction.

[NYP]

P.O. Box 181
Los Angeles

Dec. 2nd 1920

Dear Mencken:

Here is the Mark Twain stuff in brief.

Introduced to Twain by the late and aged Henry M. Alden—then Editor of Harpers back in—well—roughly 1905—6—or 7 I should say. Introduction very casual. I happened to be in the office. Later—courtesy of Philip Verrill Mighels—now dead I believe (?)—author of "Bruver Jim's Baby" (!) ran into Twain one later afternoon in the back room—or last half of the saloon at N.W. corner Irving Place & 14th St. He was lit up—and alone. Mighels seemed to know him & we were waved to a seat. Generalities for say four or five minutes—then conversation veered to American & he made some humorous remark about this being the land of notions— and that you had to respect 'em. All I can recall is that he talked on banteringly about Americas faith in God, its self conviction of the reality of sin, the truth that the lands notions were separate from its necessities and natural impulses and actions and that like good drinkers it took both "straight". Then he took up the American notion that all marriages were made in heaven—or ought to be if they weren't and that all married people were happy—or ought to be. If they weren't they still ought to be in the thought that they were suffering in a righteous cause—that of God & humanity   It was then that he referred to his wife, slapping a hand on the table and saying "Now take me & my wife"—or something like that. "She is a good enough woman—none better—kind hearted his best interests" etc. The substance of it was that Americans thought him happy—or that he oughta be—in the love and care and protection of one woman, whereas the fact was—I do not venture to quote his exact words—that he was damned unhappy—just like most other men—but that for her sake—or the children—or his standing or something he had to keep up appearances. "A man gets to the place finally where it aint worth while doing anything about it"—In substance that was one of his remarks[1]

I talked to him afterwards—cold sober—at two different public dinners. On those occasions with me he was more reserved but humorous

The reason that I was impressed was that I like a dunce thought him a fine example of American marital bliss etc—very different to my humble self for instance—me being a low dog

Later on Duneka and Major Leigh—down at Harpers told me with great amusement—and as though they had saved a great man from a dreadful error—how he would bring down & submit for Harpers (!) Magazine or a possible book various Rabelasian tales (I saw the ms of three) which "if published would have done for him completely." They told me the plots—really amusing & Rabelasian things which ought to be circulated now. They told me that he was always complaining of the limits of the American mind & so his limitations as a writer & how strictly he was made to walk the chalk when he wanted to write such different kinds of things. I think Wells[2] of Harpers knows all about this.

D

Have recently finished reading "Mooncalf" by Dell[3] & "Poor White" by Anderson. Dells book is infinitely the better—a fine work—Andersons is labored and uncertain—poorly modeled & rocks like a ship in a storm. I cant see it as anything but a fine idea very poorly done

1. In a letter to Robert H. Elias, Bernard DeVoto argued hotly against the facts as Dreiser states them here (see Elias, *Letters*, 1:306, nn. 1 and 2). Dreiser's statements are suspicious, if only because Mrs. Clemens died in 1904.
2. Thomas B. Wells, editor of *Harper's Monthly Magazine*.
3. Floyd Dell.

[UPL]

SMART SET
A Magazine of Cleverness
George Jean Nathan ⎤
and　　　　　 ⎬ Editors
H. L. Mencken ⎦
25 West 45th Street
New York

December 1, 1920

Dear Dreiser:

I believe that Lengel is right about the length of the book and also about some of the writing in it.[1] His reaction is apparently the same as mine. I doubt, however, that he is right about postponing it. I see no reason whatsoever why it should not be published forthwith. Rid of one or two weak spots, it will stand up among the best of your books. He may be right about the postponing of "The Genius". If you had done so for five years, I am inclined to think that you would have changed the book somewhat and that these changes would have prevented the Comstock explosion. Nevertheless, I am thoroughly convinced that the Comstock explosion in the long run was very profitable to you, as a similar attack has been to Cabell. It seems to me that you can, at the present stage of your life, afford to print any book you please. I doubt that many readers liked "Hey Rub-A-Dub-Dub", but it would be absurd to argue that the publication of it had done you any damage. As a matter of fact, it pays now and then to mystify the public. It (the public) always confuses the unintelligible with the superior.

Hergesheimer has been elected a member of the National Institute and I have a letter from him indicating that he will accept. This fact offers me no surprise. He is precisely the sort of man that these cads know how to win. Let him be damned forevermore. I offer one thousand to one that Cabell, if he is ever elected, will refuse in a prompt and obscene manner. As for yourself, I assume without argument that if they ever sent you the summons, you'd shoot the messenger.

Yours,

Mencken

Gloom reports that Yewdale still has the "Newspaper Days" ms.[2]

1. Along with an undated note written after 15 November, Dreiser sent to Mencken a letter he had received from William Lengel, praising and criticizing the manuscript of *A Novel about Myself*. Lengel argues that Dreiser should not publish the book until he writes another successful novel. He had earlier, he mentions, advised Dreiser to hold back on *The "Genius"* for five years. Dreiser's note to Mencken reads: "What do you think of the several points in this letter." [NYP]

2. The postscript is handwritten.

SMART SET
A Magazine of Cleverness
George Jean Nathan ⎫
and   ⎬ Editors
H. L. Mencken ⎭
25 West 45th Street
New York

December 3, 1920

Dear Dreiser:-

Gloom seems to be in very good shape. I saw her within twenty-four hours of the operation and she was in excellent spirits, fully recovered from the anaesthetic nausea and suffering from little discomfort. Lobsenz apparently made a good job. I have sent her a box of cigarettes and a bible. She should be able to write a letter within a day or two.

It was a good thing that the appendix was removed. It turned out to be in a very dangerous state. Fortunately, the doctor got it out before any actual damage was done. The effect of the operation will be to make her put on between sixty and eighty pounds weight. Within six months she will look like a Philadelphia pie-woman.

Yours,
M

P.O. Box 181
Los Angeles

Dec 6—1920

Dear Mencken:

1. Have no fear. The National Institute of whatever it is will never elect me a member.[1] If it should I shall either reject it outright or offer to sell it for a dollar to whoever will buy. A Litt. D. from any source up, down or around would be dropped in the nearest ash can. However if any society or person or university comes accross with a suitable offer of <u>cash</u> it will be accepted. I will take the Nobel Prize or any other cash prize having no strings attached and no one "being looking" at the time

2. As for The "Genius" we shall ever disagree at certain points. Despite Lengel—& as you say—its publication has done me a great good. Its grip on a certain type of mind is phenomenal and the type of mind is not rediculous—only romantic and imaginative. I will not change it though if I could I would reissue it in the form you suggested.

3. As for <u>Hey</u> <u>Rub-A-Dub-Dub</u> will you believe it when I tell you it is outselling <u>Twelve</u> <u>Men</u>   I have to laugh when you speak of parts of it as unintelligible. I am convinced after long observation that you have no least taste for speculation. Years ago when I showed you a rough draft of Equation Inevitable you sent it back with the comment that you did not know what I was talking about. And I assume that you are still convinced that I do not know what I am talking about. Mere mumbling as it were. God—what a funny world. Yet we all have our blind spots. I will agree that I have mine.

Thanks for the Gloom telegram. I am so sorry about her. There is a strange & beautiful mind & a beautiful temperament. If ever I can turn a cash trick I will pension her for life. Her simple little needs & tastes have a color that is all sheer beauty to me

And thanks for your willingness to edit <u>A</u> <u>Novel</u> <u>About</u> <u>Myself</u>. Let the chapter heads go. I am going to ask Lengel to point out specifically if he will—the places or bits that most offend him—I do not believe that the book should not be published now. He gets that swill from Liveright who is insane on the subject of publishing a novel by me   But I am most anxious to have you point out parts that might be sold before hand as magazine papers.

D.

<u>Once</u> <u>More</u>:
Your judgement as to Poor White is very wrong   Dell has written a book 10 times as good—beautiful in its simplicity, sincerity, force & style. So we differ again, I suppose. And now I think he is down on me for saying that he has novelized the 1st one third of his life!

1. In 1935 Dreiser, with Mencken's full support, declined an invitation from the Institute of Arts and Letters.

[UPL]

1524 Hollins St.
Baltimore, Md.

Dec. 5, 1920

Dear Dreiser:
I have just finished "<u>A</u> <u>Novel</u> <u>About</u> <u>Myself</u>". It is full of excellent stuff, quite wonderful in places. Some of the newspaper chapters are gorgeous. The only defect that I see in it, as it stands, unedited, I presume, is a certain flabbiness of form. Here and there, in connection with the narrating of certain incidents, it tends to let down, but not so very much at that. All could be remedied by a few judicious cuts. And even if

these were not made, the force of the work as a whole would not be invalidated. Rid of one or two weak spots it will certainly stand up among the best of your books.

Specifically, the things of which I complain, and which can and no doubt will be remedied in the editing, are as follows:

1. Considering the great space given to the beginning of the S.W. episode, it seems to me that the thing is dismissed too briefly at the end.

2. So with the Alice business.

Since the book is quite frankly a section of your life, and pretends to be nothing more, I can see how these objections would fade, supposing this volume were preceded by one relating your youth and were followed by another relating your subsequent experiences. These volumes should be written.

3. In places you philosophize too much, or, at least, I think so. Yet these preachments can be easily reduced and I do not advocate their elimination by any means.

4. Again, I dislike the picking up of stuff from twelve men. (The McCord incident in particular.) Wouldn't it suffice to refer to Twelve Men. Let the swine buy that book.

5. Yet again, the affair with the Bohemian woman is a bit wheezy,——the sort of thing all of us do at 22. It is all true of course, but so is it that at some time or other you wore a celluloid collar or, that you contemplated small poculations. We all did. Yet these things are not mentioned. But again, this is not to say that I think that the episode should be eliminated. It may be that on rereading the book, I'll conclude that it ought to stay in as it stands. Cutting is probably what it needs. If you can wait a bit I will be very glad to go through the book again and scheme out a few cuts. The best of it is so very fine that it seems a pity to let the thing down here and there.

6. Now as to Lengel's argument that the book ought to be postponed for five years. I cannot see that. I see no reason whatsoever, why it should not be published forthwith. Rid, as I say, of one or two weak spots, it will stand with the best of your books. He may be right when he says that it would have been better if you had postponed publishing The "Genius" for five years. If you had, it is possible that you would have changed it somewhat, and that these changes would have obviated the Comstock explosion. Nevertheless, I am thoroughly convinced that the Comstock explosion was, in the long run, very profitable to you, as a similar attack has been to Cabell. And how could you have had that explosion without publishing the book as it is?—and when you did really.

And anyhow, I am convinced that at the present stage of your life you can afford to print any book you please. I do not believe that Lengel (and some few others, perhaps), realize how you have grown,—that is, how thoroughly you have captured the imagination of the younger genera- tion,—the tremendous color and appeal your personality and your view- point have for them. But as a critic reading manuscripts, I see it every day. You have followers and imitators on every hand. They expect the daring and the different from you. So it is that I say that you can publish what you choose.

I wish you would do a whole book about your brother Paul. It is not too late yet. After all that sketch in Twelve Men merely scratched the ground. There was a fellow, one out of many.

HLM¹

1. Dreiser sent a copy of this letter to Lengel who responded to the penultimate paragraph and wrote back that "Mencken has it all wrong . . . I don't believe any of your books have sold 1/10 of what they should." [UPL]

[UPL]

H. L. Mencken
1524 Hollins St.
Baltimore.

December 11th [1920]

Dear Dreiser:-

Thanks for the letter about Mark.¹ I am telling Brooks the substance of it, but shall not give him a copy, and am asking him never to quote you without specific authority. The conversation exactly bears out the theory he maintains with great effect in his book.

I am handing over the manna to Dr. Deetjen, a local connoisseur who collects historical curiosities. He has the ear of John the Baptist, the hymen of Mary Magdala, and two large logs from the True Cross.

I agree with you about the Dell and Anderson books. Anderson is struggling to express himself, but so far has not succeeded, save in Wines- burg, Ohio. Have you read Sinclair Lewis' Main Street? It is the work of a Saturday Evening Postista, but it has its brilliant moments. All the other new novels I have seen are crap.

The best book of late is The Behavior of Crowds, by one Martin,² published by Harper. Toward the last there is a fine slating of the Ameri- can mind.

Get right with God!

Yours,
Mencken

December 11th
Later
Dear Dreiser:-

Your two letters have just come in.

I incline to think that the French offer is very fair. At all events, it is a good deal to have such a man as Bazalgette sponsor you. You made a grave mistake when you turned down the German offer. If it is renewed, take it. How in hell can those poor devils pay you cash today? You are becoming a usurer.

We are not apart on the Anderson-Dell matter. The Dell book is far better than Anderson's. But I believe that Anderson, at bottom, is a much bigger man. Winesburg was far above anything Dell will ever write. So on The Genius. I have no objection to the realism of it, which seems to me to be quite harmless. But parts of it seem to me to be excessively dull, as I wrote in my review of it and in Prefaces. My objection to Hey-Rub-a-Dub-Dub is not that it is unintelligible, but that some of it seems to me to be unintelligent—that is, far out of accord with my private notion of what is important, and interesting and true.

The fact that it outsells Twelve Men supports my view. Twelve Men is a vastly better piece of work. Hey-Rub-a-Dub-Dub largely appeals, I believe, to the defectively educated. It certainly can't seem as wonderful to a man who has read, say, Nietzsche, Schopenhauer, Spencer, Huxley, Ostwald, Haeckel and Sumner as to one who has not read them. I don't think you argue well. I could have done the book much better myself, whereas I couldn't have done a single chapter of Twelve Men or Sister Carrie.

But all this is unimportant. You are writing your books, and I am writing mine. Do your damndest, and may the good Lord Jesus watch over you. When you offend my pruderies I shall bawl, but I'd consider you an ass if you let it influence you.

Yewdale still has the Newspaper Days MS. I suppose that Gloom will get it back when she gets out of hospital. My office has called up to inquire about her. She had a bad cough for four days, but she is now all right. The cough was not significant. Unable to clear her throat, her pipes got clogged up. Jake did a good job.[3] He is a decent Jew.

Things have come to such a pass in New York that the girl now pays the hotel bill. Thus we approach the ideal. Before I die I'll be kept.

M

1. Mark Twain (see Dreiser to Mencken, 2 December 1920).
2. Everett Dean Martin's book was the first important sociological study of mob psychology.
3. Jake was the doctor who treated Estelle Kubitz.

P.O. Box 181
Los Angeles
Cal.

Dec. 20, 1920.

Dear Mencken:

Thou canst not pick a quarrel with me anent, <u>Hey</u>, <u>Rub</u>. Are you not satisfied. You now have <u>A Traveler at Forty</u>, The "<u>Genius</u>" <u>The Hand of the Potter</u> and <u>Hey</u>, <u>Rub</u> on your blacklist. They are all, alike worthless. Granted. This is the merry yule-log,—I mean tide. Peace! Peace!—and go before I clip thy left ear. Would I had a case of Scotch and a keg of good old Pilsener. This accursed land.

The Author of Twelve Men

I have news that the next Indiana Assembly will certainly vote a round sum for not only a monument for the late genial P.D. (pax) but also a something extra for the drinks on that festive occasion. If only he were here to go along to his own funeral as it were.

SMART SET
A Magazine of Cleverness
George Jean Nathan ⎫
and ⎬Editors
H. L. Mencken ⎭

[after 25 December 1920]

Dear Dreiser:

Bravo. I think the German translation will do you a lot of good.[1]
I spent Christmas in prayer.

Enrico Pishposh

1. Dreiser had been negotiating a German translation of *The Financier*, but nothing came of it.

[NYP-T]

P.O. Box 181
Los Angeles,
Cal.

Jan 2nd., 1920.[1]

Fairest Mencken:

I hereby make you as sound a business proposition as will come to you this blessed year of our dear Lord, 1921. I would like to have the Noble prize,—not that I deserve it but that it appeals to me as a nice bit of change. You are in a position to make a large noise looking to that result. If not that, then you are in a position to influence or at worst suborn certain agencies whose work in that direction would in all likelyhood bring about that comforting result. Start the ball and if I snake the forty thousand— isn't that what the lucky mut is supposed to draw?—you get five thousand, or, between twelve and thirteen percent. This sounds a little Abe Rufe-ish I know, but then forty thousand, in these hard times.

Think this over. Where else can you pick up five thousand for a few kind words, judiciously uttered. Not that I would corrupt an honest man or anything like that, but think of Woodrow. One thousand on the side for George,[2] if he will privily aid and abet the idea.

I was flat on my back over Christmas, otherwise you would have received a most graceful reminder. But, you have a birthday, and, there are other feast days.

Dreiser

Don't forget. This is a sporting proposition and I never welch.

1. Misdated by Dreiser.
2. George Jean Nathan.

[UPL]

H. L. Mencken
1524 Hollins St.
Baltimore.

January 9th [1921]

Dear Dreiser:-

You forget two things, viz:

1. Every candidate must be nominated by some learned body, e.g., the National Institute of Arts and Letters.

2. Every candidate must be of good moral character.

Nevertheless, I have an idea of a possible proceedure, and shall attempt it. It involves working through a Dane.

Are you unaware that the $40,000 is now reduced to $29,000 by the unfavorable exchange? Do you still offer $5,000?

It is Nobel, not Noble.

> Yours for God,
> H. L. M.

[UPL]

Law Offices
Garfunkel, Fishbein, Spritzwasser & Garfunkel
21 West 42nd Street
New York

January 10th, 1921.

LEWIN VS. DREISER, In Equity

Dear Sir:-

We have been instructed by our client, Miss Adelaide Lewin, at present of 172 west 13th street, New York, to enter suit against you in the sum of ten thousand dollars ($10,000) for assault and personal injuries. In view of your public position and the unpleasant scandal that might accompany a public trial of this issue, it occurs to us that you may desire to settle the case privately. If we are correct in this surmise, will you please let us have the name of your New York attorney. We understand that you are at present out of the city.

Miss Lewin complains that her letters to you regarding her hospital bill and the care of her child, since deceased, have gone unanswered. It may be that you did not receive them. She is now engaged to be married. We trust that you join us in a wish to settle this case amicably before that date. She contends that your access to her person was gained by force and fraud.

Awaiting an early reply,

> Very truly yours,
> J. Choate Kaplan [1]

1. This is signed in Mencken's hand.

[UPL]

H. L. Mencken
1524 Hollins St.
Baltimore.

January 10th [1921]

Dear Dreiser:-

I'll get through the MS. at the first chance; it may be a couple of weeks.

Sterling's adulterous career has at last landed him on the red-hot hooks of God's vengeance. Let us take warning. I have a good mind to swear off on adultery next New Years.

You amaze me by your suggestion that I go into the movies. I am poor, but proud. Rather be a dog and bay the moon than such a Roman.

Yours for the New Jerusalem
M

[UPL]

H. L. Mencken
1524 Hollins St.
Baltimore.

January 11th [1921]

Dear Dreiser:-

I have just read Fort's "Book of the Damned", and note your remarks upon it on the slip-cover.[1] Are these remarks authentic or merely imaginary, as in the case of the Norwegian book? If they are authentic, what is the notion that you gather from the book? Is it that Fort seriously maintains that there is an Upper Saragossa Sea somewhere in the air, and that all of the meteors, blood, frogs and other things he lists dropped out of it? This is what I make him out to mean, but it seems quite incredible. The thing leaves me puzzled. His doctrine of continuity is anything but new. In fact, all biologists subscribe to it. He seems to be enormously ignorant of elementary science, particularly biology.

I have lately got in several huge stacks of German books, pamphlets, magazines and newspapers—a lot of very fine stuff. The Ludendorff book is superb,[2] and the stenographic record of his testimony before the Reichstag Investigating Commitee (of Jews, Socialists, democrats and other such swine) is even better. He called names in a firm, loud voice, and thumped the table with his fist.

I have been invited to write for the Yale Review and the New Republic. Your prayers are answered. The Christian Herald is thinking it over.

What are you doing in Los Angeles? The town must be unspeakable—a huge den of Baptists.

Yours in Xt.,
Mencken

1. Charles H. Fort (1874–1932), journalist, author. Fort was an eccentric mystic who waged a private war against modern science. For years Dreiser championed his cause with publishers, trying to get Fort's rather bizarre books into print.

2. *The General Staff and Its Problems: The History of the Relations between the High Command and the German Imperial Government as Revealed by Official Documents* (1920), by Erich Ludendorff (1865–1937).

[NYP-T]

P.O. Box 181
Los Angeles, Cal.

Jan. 15, 1921

Dear Mr. Menckheimer:

Your inquiry of the 9th. inst. received. Notwithstanding the few objections registered at the left, will say, that proposition, while strenuous, will be met, nearly. We feel that four thousand to you, and five hundred to party named X, in case he is included, would be nearer justice and truth, the rate of exchange being as it is. In case exchange becomes normal, original proposition holds.

Respectfully,
T. D. Greasidick

Shylock!
Extortioner!
Buccaneer!
Leech!
Ravager!
Hawk!
Vulture!
Glutton!
Profiteer!
Monopolist!
Gouger!
Miser!
Rackrent!
Jew!
Parasite!
Catchpenny!
Skinflint!
Mercenary!
Jack Cade!
Tyrant!
Harpagon!

Theif!
Pillager!
Blackmailer!
Brigand!
Direptor!
Latrocine!
Burglar!
Nim!
Pilferer!
Crimp!
Looter!
Rifler!
Pickeer!
Swindler!
Bushwhacker!
Freebooter!
Bandit!
Wrecker!
Pick-pocket!
Spoiler!
Dacoit!

Usurer!   Corsair!
Tight-wad!   Jobber!
Money-gut!   Nip-clutch!
Dun!   Throttler!
Wolf!   Cut-purse!
Fortune hunter!   Pick-purse!
Dives!   Claude Duval!
Nest-featherer!   Blackleg!
Mammon!   Sharper!
Plutocrat!   Diddler!
Gambler!   Rook!
Huckster!   Dick Turpin!
Higgler!   Foot-pad!
Haggler!   Welsher!
Chafferer!   Thimble-rigger!
Scorse!   Shell-man!
Cambist!   Slave-driver!
Stickler!   Card-sharp!
Greedy-gut!   High-wayman!
Shark!   Bill Sykes!
Robber!   Jack Sheppard!
Fleecer!   Jesse James!
Bloodsucker!   Cormorant!
Plunderer!   Stickup and gun man!
Pirate   Prowler!
     Crook!

P.O. Box 181
Los Angeles
Calif.

Jan 26—1921

Dear Mencken:

In regard to Forts book. I consider Fort one of the most fascinating personalities I have ever known. He is a great thinker and a man of a deep and cynical humor. To dub him enormously ignorant of anything is to use an easy phrase without correct information   Fort is not enormously ignorant of anything. He is so far above any literary craftsman now working in the country—your own excellent self excluded—that measurements are futile. I dont know what Liveright put on the cover of his book. I wrote nothing but said much. He is probably quoting my verbal praise. But to me no one in the world—so far—has suggested the underlying depths & mysteries and possibilities as has Fort. To me he is simply stupendous & some day I really believe he will get full credit: If ever I do another book of men—in he goes—life size & he will be fascinating. I have read "X" and "Y" and they are marvellous. I have the sickening feeling that in some bitter mood he will some day destroy them and they are so wonderful to me that it would be like destroying Karnak   In regard to Heliogabalus[1]—I think it is a scream. Delicious. Its a wonder the Comstocks dont descend on it. As for Cabell—well—all I can say is that I hope something horrible happens to this country. It is the realm of smug, contented insects of the Wilson-House-Creel-Palmer brand. I hope they rot.

Th D

1. The farce written by Mencken and Nathan.

[NYP-T]

P.O. Box 181
Los Angeles,
Cal.

Feb. 1, 1921.

Fairest Scribe:

Thanks for the pages from the Baltimore Sun.[1] I note the place accorded the Titan, et seq. The poor old "Genius" remains in outer darkness, as twere. Well, he can stand a little cooling, I admit. A letter from Barrett H. Clark[2] not so long since enclosed a clipping or statement credited to you which said, citing A Hoosier Holiday, pour exampe, that I shared with George Sylvester Vierick the distinction of providing the vulgarest voice yet heard in America. I thought it was Stewart P. Sherman who said that. Which gentleman has the honor of getting me right?

Also, thanks for the latest Smart Set. My attention has been called to your objection to my features. I cannot blame you, upon my word. I object to them myself, and have this long time. They have served no good purpose. But what interests me more is this. Who is it that saith the kind word for The Hand of the Potter? These little unexpected kindnesses will be the death of me yet.

Word comes to me that you are picturing my local life with an accuracy which defies competition. My clothes, purse, car, bungalow and female

Maecenas are touched off with a delicacy Vermeerish in flavor. Well done, oh, Plutarch. But wait until I begin a certain picture of my own. The roars of pain! The lacerated nerve ends! Let us see, now.

What I really wish to know is, did the ms. of A Novel go to Liveright as per my telegram.[3] And will you accept my thanks and kindly report the charges.

I saw your name in print here again the other day.

You grow apace.

Otto Kahn

N.B. Please forward the Nobel prize at your earliest convenience.

1. "More Book Talk: List of 100 Recent American Books Worth Reading," Baltimore *Evening Sun*, 22 January 1921. Mencken included *The Titan*, *Plays of the Natural and Supernatural*, *Twelve Men*, and *A Hoosier Holiday*.
2. Barrett H. Clark (1890–1953), literary historian, critic.
3. On 14 January 1921, Dreiser sent Mencken a telegram asking him to send the book to Liveright.

[UPL]

H. L. Mencken
1524 Hollins St.
Baltimore.

February 2nd [1921]

Dear Dreiser:-

Fort may be a fine fellow, as you say, but nevertheless his book is full of stupid stuff. His standing in astrophysics is exactly that of Dr. Stillwell, the osteopath, in pathology. The mystery he makes no such of is not a mystery at all, and his theory of a celestial Saragossa Sea is very flabby. But let him go on. The more, the merrier.

I don't know what can be done for Cabell. The courts always rule out professional opinions. My feeling is that Comstockery is bound to succeed—that the only remedy for a civilized man is to get out of the country.

Yours,
HLM

[UPL]

H. L. Mencken
1524 Hollins St.
Baltimore.

February 4th [1921]

Dear Dreiser:-

1. I am having a man here cast Kirah's¹ plaque of you in bronze. If it turns out well I want to give a copy to Boyd. He is a good friend of yours and will like it. I assume that I have your permission.

2. A fearful mass of work makes my progress with Newspaper Days very slow. I find many things in it—small details—that jar me. As I go along I am changing them. If you disapprove it will be easy to have them disregarded.

3. God help us all.

Yours,
M

1. Kirah Markham.

[UPL]

H. L. Mencken
1524 Hollins St.
Baltimore.

February 7th [1921]

Dear Dreiser:-

The MS. went to Liveright long ago, as I reported at the time. As usual, he has not acknowledged it.

I can't understand the Clark business. Certainly I never wrote your name on the same page with Viereck's, or accused you of being vulgar. Your crimes are sufficient without that. I constantly get clippings crediting me with statements that I have never made. No doubt Sherman is to blame.

When you begin to lie about me, don't forget to say that I am a pretty fellow, and one who loves God. Every tourist coming back from the Coast has some tale about your Roman levities. Yesterday I heard that you have gone over to the Theosophists, and are living at Point Loma in a yellow robe, with hasheesh blossoms in your hair and two fat cuties to fan you. My congratulations.

If I remember rightly, I put <u>five</u> of your recent books in that list, and the editor of the Sun, noticing the number, added the view of you and the matter under it. I'll revise it and add "The 'Genius'" and "Hey-Rub-a-Dub-Dub".

I am going to Washington to see the inauguration.[1] My taste for the politically obscene grows. Ah, the joy of being an American!

I am up to my arse in the revision of "The American Language", a colossal job. Let me have your prayers.

In Xt.,
Jesus Mencken

1. Warren G. Harding's inauguration.

[NYP-T]

P.O. Box 181
Los Angeles,
Cal.

Feb. 10, 1921.

Dear Mencken:

Glad to hear that Kirah's effort is to be bronzed. If copies are not too expensive I would like to get one for her and one for myself. I have but one of the plaster things left and it is sure to get broken in time. Perhaps, if the things are not too costly, it might be wise for me to order six. Friends have been asking for clay copies for lo these many days.

It's all right about the book. I may have something in connection with that to report to you soon. I wish you would edit it to the extent of being able to ok it from every angle, as you see it. I would like very much to look over your finally stamped version.

Tell me. Is Harding pro English or where does he stand. Is this a strictly Wall Street administration?

Dreiser

By the way. Who is Sol Kann, of Balto the Beautiful.

[UPL-H]

SMART SET
A Magazine of Cleverness
George Jean Nathan
and   } Editors
H. L. Mencken

[after 10 February 1921]

Dear Dreiser:

Six bronze casts of the medallian would cost $50 or $60. Bronze casting is infernally expensive. In N.Y. a foundry wanted to charge $15 for one. I got it for $10 in Baltimore. I'll have one made for you.

God knows I wish I could make better progress with "Newspaper Days", but I have been worked to death—12 @ 14 hours a day. Such work takes time. Meanwhile, the other MS. can be used for negotiating with publishers, etc.

Poor old Huneker![1]

Yours
M

P.S. Harding is simply a damned fool. The very efficient British press bureau will get him under its thumb. In other matters Wall St. will run him.

Sol Kann of Baltimore is an autograph grafter.

M

1. James Huneker died on 9 February 1921.

[NYP-T]

P.O. Box 181
L.A.

Feb. 15, 1921.

Dear Mencken:

Can you see articles fitting the following captions in A Novel About Myself.

1. Newspaper Days, -a- Chicago, 1892.
2.   "   "   -b- St. Louis, 1893.
3.   "   "   -c- Pittsburgh, 1893.
4.   "   "   -d- New York, 1894.
5. Revisiting an Old Worlds Fair.
6. A Great St. Louis Editor.
7. A Vanished New York Summering Place.

8. The Roaring Thirties. (Old Broadway—20th to 39th.)
If not what papers, if any, do you see?

Dreiser

[UPL]

H. L. Mencken
1524 Hollins St.
Baltimore.

February 23rd [1921]

Dear Dreiser:-
I think that all of the articles you suggest are feasible. I am writing to Tom Smith, of the Century, to find out if he can use some of them.[1] My apologies for making such slow progress with the book. The fact is that I have been worked to a frazzle—12 and 14 hours a day on absolutely necessary stuff. I am a wreck, and fall asleep immediately I leave off work.

Yours,
Judas Mencken

1. The Century Co. did not take any of the book; Dreiser published five pieces from his autobiography in *Bookman* during 1921 and 1922.

[NYP-T]

P.O. Box 181
Los Angeles

Feb 28, 1921.

Dear Mencken:
I would not let you pay for a bronze copy of the plaque. It is sufficient to be able to get one. Send it on and I will send you a check. Will it be possible to get other copies at a later date or is this the last call?

Thanks for your words about the articles though I doubt whether Smith will be interested. He has never manifested any interest in anything that I ever sent him so far.

You are wrong as to murder. It is a mortal sin.

I have good reason to believe you have received the Nobel prize recently awarded to me and are withholding it. Kindly forward the same by freight.

Jacob the Fat

[UPL]

H. L. Mencken
1524 Hollins St.
Baltimore.

March 4th [1921]

Dear Dreiser:-

1. Herman George Scheffauer has an article on "American Literature of the Present Day" in the Deutsche Rundschau (German Review) for February. He says of you:

"The novelist who offers us the most veracious and significant picture of the new America is Theodore Dreiser, a man of German origin . . . If one sought European parallels he would be called "the American Zola" because of his courageous handling of erotic themes and his photographic realism. In his longer romances there are some banalities and some violations of good taste, but he is an honorable delineator of his time and of the people he lives among, and neither he nor his art is under the hoff of Puritanism, nor does he sacrifice anything to financial success. His best-known works are 'Sister Carrie' and 'Jennie Gerhardt', studies of women and their destiny; the long novel, 'The "Genius"', 'The Financier' and 'The Titan'—studies of a society dominated by Mammon."

2. I saw Harding inaugurated this morning. His speech was inconceivably asinine.

M

[UPL]

H. L. Mencken
1524 Hollins St.
Baltimore.

March 7th [1921]

Dear Dreiser:-

I am having two more copies of the bronze medallion made. It will be an honor to offer you one for your boudoir. If you say so, the other will go to Kirah. A new mold must be made for each one that is cast, and in the course of time, I suppose, the original plaster model will wear out. If you ever want any hereafter, there is a good man here who will cast them at $10 apiece flat. This is cheap. In New York they asked $15. The bronze case looks very dignified. I'll send you yours the moment it comes in, with my prayers.

I am retaining the new firm of Wilson and Colby to represent me legally.

Yours,
Ignatius von Mencken

[NYP-T]

P.O. Box 181
Los Angeles, Cal.

March 10, 1921.

Dear Mencken:

I have been intending to tell you for sometime past that several years before I ever wrote Newspaper Days I wrote and laid aside for personal and family reasons volume one of what is to be, when completed, a four or five volume <u>History</u> <u>of</u> <u>Myself</u>. Of this series <u>Newspaper</u> <u>Days</u> is, of course, volume two. Volume three, <u>Literary</u> <u>Aspirations</u> was started by me some time ago, but I laid it aside for other work.

The thing I am trying to get to is this. I sent the volume you have to Harpers and at once, upon reading it, they assumed that there was, or should be at least, a volume one, and wrote me a long letter to this effect. That is, if I would give them my next novel, whatever it might be, and would finish volume one of this personal series, and would contract to do a third volume, they would undertake the publication of the entire series and would advertise it in a large way. They seem to think that the set should make a fine piece of literary property. They also suggest that they may be willing to buy up all of the books as soon as printing prices re-adjust themselves.

This is all very fine and I would be glad to do it if it were not for the fact that volume one concerning as it does my extreme youth, is closer to the family than anything I have ever penned and since a few of my rela-tives are still around, it makes it a little difficult. Not that I have roasted anyone. I haven't. I have merely interpreted them and myself. That makes it all the worse, of course. Still, I think that if I could interest you in it, the thing might be taken and whipped into a publishing state. To my way of thinking it is a better thing than volume two. I believe you would like it better. It is more poetic, I am sure. Also, one of these days, I would like to turn over to you the unexpurgated versions of volumes one and two and three and four, if you are still here when they are finished—(I personally have no intention of dying)—to be done with as you will. I would also like to send you, one of these days, the uncut and unexpurgated version of A Traveler At Forty,—a somewhat different thing to the book now in print.

Question: Would you be willing to take volume one of this personal record and examine it with a view to issuing the entire history in the next year or so. Liveright, who has read the second volume and only knows of it, is anxious to publish it as it stands. But the enthusiasm of Harpers for the series as a whole makes me feel that I may be making a grave mistake and that I had better start with volume one. They predicate a stir. I hope they are right.

Dreiser

[UPL]

SMART SET
A Magazine of Cleverness
George Jean Nathan
and   Editors
H. L. Mencken

March 12, 1921.

Dear Dreiser:-

I have marked out seven or eight articles in the manuscript and sent the whole thing with my suggestions to Tom Smith of the Century. He says that he is much interested and will give it an early decision. Some of the articles can be lifted out of the book bodily. Others will have to be made up of extracts from different places. If Smith orders anything, and you want me to do it, I'll be glad to attempt this shoemaking. Obviously, it would save time for me to do it here.

In case the Century crowd can't agree on any of the articles, what do you think of submitting the whole proposal to Lorimer?[1] What are your relations to him? I myself do not know him, but I think it would be all right for me to approach him.

Yours,
M

1. George Horace Lorimer, editor of the *Saturday Evening Post*.

[UPL]

H. L. Mencken
1524 Hollins St.
Baltimore.

March 15th [1921]

Dear Dreiser:-

I incline to think that the Harpers are right, but for God's sake don't tie up with them. I hear constant rumors that the firm is—about to sell out.

They may be quite untrue, but undoubtedly it is a far from healthy condition. You ought to be in the hands of some first-rate publisher, say Harcourt. I think it might be managed—that is, provided Harcourt is not scared to death by the claims and pseudo-claims of Jones et al. I hesitate to mention the matter to Harcourt or Spingarn without your authority. Of course, all publishers, at the moment, are in a hell of a hole, but the printers' strikes have begun and there is hope that they may end in a great reduction of wages. To hell with the proletariat.

Certainly I'll be glad to tackle Vol. I—that is, as soon as I get The American Language off my hands. I have been frightfully overworked—12 and 14 hours a day. I stand it pretty well, but it leaves me no leisure. When I finish I am half dead. No word yet from the Century regarding the articles.

I'd be delighted to have the unexpurgated version of A Traveler at Forty. What is in it? I suspect that you diddled some fat woman on the boat. Well, don't boast. I have done it too. I offer to match you in that department. I once went to bed with aunt and niece and made them both happy. The incident will be described in my autobiography, to be published in 40 volumes in 1999.

Vol II needs some cutting. I have tried the business with the first 10 or 15 chapters; it goes very well. I have a feeling that the book is weak in structure as it stands. It peters out at the end. Undoubtedly it would be more effective with a volume ahead of it and another following.

If you mention me in any later volume, all I ask is that you say I was one who loved God and strove to keep His Commandments.

The Boni questionaire is idiotic. I hope you haven't wasted that letter on him. I never answer such things. Some time ago a fair wench in Pittsburgh sent out the question "What should be done with the Kaiser?" I answered: "Holland should be given to him". I forbade her to use it, and yet she did it twice—in some lousy newspaper and then in a book.

I am at work revising The American Language—a fearful job. I saw Gloom in New York the other day and gave her a bottle of cocktails. She looked very well, but she said she wanted to reduce. I think she is thin enough.

The Smith article in the Bookman seems to me to be excellent stuff. Also, I like Van Doren's article in this week's Nation.[1] I don't think you need to bother about the future. The ground is solid under you.

Yours,

M

1. Carl Van Doren, "Contemporary American Novelists: Theodore Dreiser," *Nation* 112(16 March 1921), 400–401; repr. in Carl Van Doren, *Contemporary American Novelists, 1900–1920* (1922), 74–83.

[NYP-T]

P.O. Box 181
Los Angeles,
Cal.

March 19, 1921.

Dear Mencken:

Thanks for the news in regard to the articles. You may be able to interest Smith but I doubt it. A long time ago I submitted a short story to him—Love, I think,—and he offered me three hundred dollars which sum I promptly rejected because the story was worth six hundred and that sum I took out of it about six months later. After that, as I recall it, he proved rather distant. If he will make a fair offer for the articles I would be very glad to have him use them. I have always paid Lengel a ten percent commission for selling my things and I would be glad if you would accept that plus whatever additional sum you would think fair for your time in editing the same. Personally I think it is a mistake to submit that manuscript as a whole to any editor. Certain of the wandering views are certain to run smack into one or another of his private predjudices and then he cannot view the particular bits offered him with an unpredjudiced mind. I have found that in handling the other copy. This book, as a whole, appears to have something in it which infuriates them. I am curious really, to know just what it is.

My relations with the S.E.P.[1] are most cordial. They paid me $1.000 for Free and $750.00 each for two other stories. From time to time they have commented editorially and otherwise, and always in a kindly way on my work. The same friendly attitude has characterized The Public Ledger. If anything has come up to change this I am not aware of it.

If you will take my advice however, you will not submit the book as a whole, but will let them see only such articles as you are able to extract. If you do the other I fear me much that you will queer the chances of the series with them. And if they take them I am sure they will be perfectly willing to pay $750 per installment. Years ago the Century paid me $1.500 for three articles lifted out of A Traveler.

All my best wishes. And luck to the enterprise. As for the bronze medallion I refuse to hold you up for a replica of the same and shall send ten. If Kirah gets one free that is courtesy enough. Serve God and do no wrong.

St. Theodosius

Harding's speech! I read your dissection of it.[2] He looks to me like the bunk.

1. *Saturday Evening Post.*

2. "A Short View of Gamalielese," *Nation* 112(27 August 1921), 621–22; repr. in Edmund Wilson, *The Shock of Recognition* (1943), 1233–37.

[NYP-T]

P.O. Box 181
Los Angeles
Cal.

March 21, 1921.

Dear Mencken:

Thanks for the word about vol. 1. The same will reach you in due course. I am enclosing a copy of the letter from Harpers concerning this series.[1] Would send the original but Liveright has it at present. As you may see they are very keen for it on the strength of the volume you have. I am rather sorry now that I did not show you volume one when I finished it. It is a more poetic work and will make a good introduction. I think you might like volume two better for having seen volume one. After reading the two and thinking them over I will be glad to know what your general impression of the series is. I know that volume three will be fascinating to many for it concerns a wonderful period of New York that has now vanished like a cloud.

Sorry to hear about Harpers, especially since they are so friendly to me. I know what the trouble is. They lack initiative and daring. Times have changed and they haven't managed to keep step.

As for Harcourt, there is small hope there. Quite without my consent Lengel sent the volume you have to Harcourt.[2] Also to the editor of the Metropolitan,—to the latter to see if he could see the articles I suggested to Lengel in it. Both flew up in the air and denounced the book as this that and the other,—very different to the thing Harpers seemed to think it was. I can't get it. But that is why I said I think it is a mistake to send out the entire mss. Whatever you do, don't send the ms. to the S.E.P. Either let Gloom lift out the stuff under your direction, or let me send it to Grove Wilson, a friend of mine and he will lift out the things and send them back to you for your consideration. Then they can be sent to the S.P. If some assistant editor there sees that thing as a whole, he is certain to take offense and kill that market,—the best I have. If you talk to Harcourt sometime, perhaps you can find out what irritated him so much.

As for Jones, I can't see what any alleged claim of his has to do with the publication of a set of my books. He is willing to sell out for a reasonable sum. He has offered to do before, and I think he will again. Aside from the sum due him there is no other claim of anykind. I don't quite understand the et al.

Saw The Nation article several days ago. It is very good but after all another individual viewpoint with all the theories of the writer spread out to view. Its interesting to discover that I am a peasant.[3] Next I will be written down as having a slaves point of view. The thing in criticism, always apparently, is to write the other fellow down and yourself up as the sum and substance of wisdom. It is so rare that anyone writes a really generous notice of even a meritorious thing. I am not striking at you in anyway. When you praise, as I have often noticed, you do it handsomely.

Dreiser

1. At this time, Dreiser was negotiating with his past publishers either to release the rights to books they printed or to bring all his books together in a set. Harper and Bros. said it would release *Jennie Gerhardt* and *The Financier* if Dreiser had a definite commitment from a publisher for a collection of his books.

2. A letter of 25 February 1921 from Lengel shows that he sent Harcourt the manuscript of *A Novel about Myself* [UPL], but there is no evidence that he did this without Dreiser's consent.

3. Carl Van Doren described Dreiser as a "peasant," that is, a great folk-artist.

[UPL]

SMART SET
A Magazine of Cleverness
George Jean Nathan
and   } Editors
H. L. Mencken

March 25, 1921.

Dear Dreiser:

Smith wires that the articles are receiving consideration, but so far there is no verdict. In his case, I doubt that any harm is done by letting him see the whole book, but if it turns out to be impossible to come to terms with him and the manuscripts go to Lorimer, I shall saw out the chapters before sending in the copy. In any case I am sure that Smith will not pay the prices you mention. The Century is short of money and running very close to the wind. I shall not sell Smith more than one of the articles. As for a commission, send it to the Baptist Foreign Missionary Society.

As you will note, this letter is dictated. My misfortunes continue to pile up. My sister-in-law is ill here in the hospital and I have to go to see her every day. Besides, I am nursing a sprained arm; it is done up so tightly in bandages that I can scarcely sign my name. Meanwhile my work has gone to pot, and I am one more week behind. I begin to believe that in the end, as the hearse approaches the crematory, I shall rise up and give three cheers.

The medallion is not yet delivered. I insist upon sending it to you as a small tribute to your Christian piety. If you had your just deserts, you would be appointed to the "red hat" in succession to Cardinal Gibbons. However, do not pin your hopes to this possibility. Your enemies here would prevent your appointment if I suggested it.

I wrote an article on Huneker last week for the Century.[1] In part it tells the truth about him—especially about his curious timorousness. He was always afraid of his own stuff.

The net result of three months' work is that I have got nothing done, and I am in a low state of mind.

Yours,
M

1. "James Huneker," *Century Magazine* 102(June 1921), 191–97.

[UPL]

H. L. Mencken
1524 Hollins St.
Baltimore.

March 27th [1921]

Dear Dreiser:-

I'll be careful about sending the MS. to Lorimer. Perhaps the best thing will be for me to saw out the articles here, and have my own girl copy them. This will save time. Schmidt still has the whole MS. I'll see him in New York during the coming week.

I have a notion that you are unduly sensitive to criticism. Van Doren's article was certainly in the best of humor. What if he did call you a peasant? In a sense you are. I see nothing opprobrious in the charge. It is like saying that a man is a Swede or an Italian or an American. I am myself partly a peasant, and glad of it. If it were not for my peasant blood, the Mencken element would have made a professor of me. I always tremble on the brink of pedantry, even as it is. This heritage from the Gelehrten[1] is my worst internal enemy. Thank God that my mother's grandfather was a Bauer, with all of a Bauer's capacity for believing in the romantic. Without him I'd have been a mere intellectual machine.

It seems plain to me that the most valuable baggage that you carry is your capacity for seeing the world from a sort of proletarian standpoint. It is responsible for all your talent for evoking feeling. Imagine Sister Carrie written by a man without that capacity, say Nietzsche. It would have been a mess. You say you are not striking at me when you complain of Van Doren. Well, why in hell <u>shouldn't</u> you strike at me, if the spirit moves you? When I write about you as an author I put aside all friendship and try to consider you objectively. When as an author, you discuss me as a critic, you are free to do the same thing, and ought to do it. In this department I am a maniacal advocate of free speech. Politeness is the worst curse of the world.

Why don't you do an article some time on your critics, discussing them absolutely honestly and in detail? Young Farrar would be delighted to have it for the Bookman. It would make a sensation. Every idiot would be offended, but I believe that all competent men would like it. Or the thing might make a good chapter in your autobiography.

How long are you going to stay among the swamis? I wish we could have a palaver. I am in a mad state mentally, and begin to believe that I'll never do the books I want to do. One obligation after another keeps me penned in the brothel. I feel like a poor whore.

This Harper letter seems to me to be mainly slobber. The Harcourt business is too complex to discuss by letter. Harcourt simply saw an impossible MS. He is not idiot enough to lay his head on the Comstockian block. But why ask him to do it? Dell, in his "Mooncalf," gets away with an episode much worse than anything in "Newspaper Days". But he does it discreetly, without flinging the thing into their faces. The Comstocks are baffled by such tactics. But you simply play into their hands—bait and set the trap and then walk into it with hosannahs. They were never more active than they are today. A publisher who takes any unnecessary chances is not brave; he is simply silly. But, as I have said, "Newspaper Days" can be denatured without changing 500 words. This is the United States, God's favorite country. The fun of living here does not lie in playing chopping-block for the sanctified, but in outraging them and getting away with it. To this enterprise I address myself. Some day they may fetch me, but it will be a hard sweat.

My arm is still crippled, but I can use the machine again. Stenographers always drive me crazy.

Yours,
Mencken

1. The world of learning.

[NYP-T]

P.O. Box 181
Los Angeles,
Cal.

April 2, 1921.

Dear Mencken:

You say the Harper letter is mainly slobber. Very good, but I asked you what you thought of the series idea. You stated that you thought Newspaper Days should be preceded by a volume and possibly followed by another. Wouldn't it be all right to start the publication of such a series after the publication of the next novel. And if you think Harpers are N.G. whats the matter with Liveright. He's willing to undertake it and make a very special effort to sell the books. As for Harcourt, I fancy that is done for.

They tell me T. R. Smith has been bounced from the Century. Is that karect? I'm more than sorry to hear of your indisposition and if you will take sane advice you will drop things for a bit and get out of Baltimore. Go and live in Boston for a little while. Or, try ze graund Chicago, a very tonic burg. It always sets me up quite a bit. Or, here is that dear Frisco. Would that I might move up there to oncet. To ease matters I suggest that you drop that article stuff and even the editing of the volumes. I can get Grove Wilson to cut out those articles and you can look them over afterward, assuming you are in shape and in the mood. Better knock off my stuff and some of your other things and take a change. Go up to Nova Scotia. The pines might bring you round. I am one who believes in the value of change. Try a long sea trip to Asia, Africa or the northern Norway coast. You of all people should be benefited by it. You are much too immersed in Balto and N.Y.

All my best wishes. I should resent much the news of your cashing in. You ought to have twenty more brisk years yet and your influence will grow faster each year, so much so that I hope to see you stoned by 1924 at the very latest. Please think up and memorize a fine dying speech or phrase, at least.

Dreiser

Here is one:
Shakespeare, I come.

H. L. Mencken
1524 Hollins St.
Baltimore.

April 7th [1921]

Dear Dreiser:-

1. I think the Harper scheme is excellent, but I rather believe that a new novel should precede the three-decker. My suggestion is that the three volumes come out at close intervals.

2. No news yet from Smith.[1] I'll be glad to saw out the articles. It will not be any labor. What oppresses me is the damned editorial routine. We have had a lot of business difficulties, and I have to listen to them. I hate all talk of business. The sight of a circulation manager always curdles my milk.

3. Smith says he is leaving voluntarily. I never doubt the word of a man who is so liberal with cocktails.

4. A man told me in New York the other day that he heard Louise Dresser make a speech in a vaudeville theatre claiming to be the sister of Paul Dresser.[2] She even warbled one of her dear brother's songs. What is this?

5. A trip to Nova Scotia would kill me. If I ever get a few days off I'll spend them at Eigenbrodt's Brewery.

6. Your dying speech is superb. If I die before you I'll steal it, but change it to "Pontius Pilate, I come."

Yours,
Noah Mencken

1. On 3 April 1921, Mencken wrote saying he had met Tom Smith of *Century*, who said the magazine "would probably make you an offer for two or three of the articles. Let us see if he lies." [UPL]
2. The vaudeville singer Louise Kerlin became Louise Dresser in 1899, when Paul Dresser allowed her to be billed onstage as his sister (see Thomas P. Riggio, "Notes on the Origins of 'Sister Carrie,'" *The Library Chronicle* [Univ. of Pennsylvania] 44[Spring 1979], 7–31).

P.O. Box 181
Los Angeles
Cal.

April 9, 1921.

Dear Mencken:

Thanks for the bronze medallion which came to hand last night. They made a most excellent reproduction, better than I had hoped for. Certainly Kirah will be grateful to you. The only address I can give you in her case is care of Howard Scott, 23 West 35th street, New York, care The Technical Alliance of which he is the chief engineer. She and Scott have or had a private alliance of their own. Better write him and ask him if you can reach her through him. By the way, he is a fine fellow, really charming. He reminds me very much of Boyd and I think you would like him. He has a splendid technical mind and his theories have been written up in the Nation and other papers. As I understand it Kirah has helped him no little and unless I am mistaken she is still with him. I wish you would look him up some time. Take breakfast with them. They would be delighted.

By the by, if you have a lawyer friend who would do me a favor I wish you would have him draw up some sort of a will for me by which I could leave all my books, mss and the royalties from the same after my death in such form that the eventual proceeds shall go to form a fund the proceeds from which, if it should amount to enough could be paid out in the form of a prize to the writers of good novels. I cant see anything else to do with the same. All my publishers report that the sales of my books are on the rise. If this goes on the sum total may eventually prove a fair amount. I own Sister Carrie, Twelve Men, Free, The Hand of the Potter, Hey, Rub-a-Dub-Dub and all of my unpublished things outright. If I win this Genius suit I will own that. I am now dickering with Harpers for the sale to me of The Financier and Jennie Gerhardt. If that goes through my plan is to lease the books to some publisher on a twenty per cent basis. Once I become blue mud or thin air some library might handle the works for the purpose in view. I would like to confine my prize to American writers. If you could get the right sort of paper drawn I would sign it at once. If I don't the works, like Pauls songs, will be hashed around among dizzy relatives and finally drift into the hands of Jew publishers. I find for instance, that in five years from now I will be entitled to renew my Sister Carrie copyright for a second period of twenty years. So you see. In addition there will be the foreign royalties. By the way I have 2.500 marks to my credit in Der Disconto Gesellschaft, Berlin and 1.000 francs in the Banque Nationale de Credit, Paris. If you ever want any foreign exchange, call on me. (Just like that.)

Suggested dying words for you: "I grieve, America, that I had but one life to live for you."

Dreiser

[NYP-T]

P.O. Box 181
Los Angeles.

April 14th., 1921.

Dear Mencken:

Louise Dresser, in her youth and when she first blew into New York was one of Pauls seven hundred and thirty two separate flames. To help her along or reward her, as thou wiltest, he allowed her to pose as his sister, afterwards. That is all there is to the relationship stuff. She always sang his songs and does to this day.

All right, live and die in Baltimore.

Jim the Penman[1]

Last and famous words of the late Henry L. Mencken of Mosquito Point, Maryland.

"Euripedes, recieve thou my spirit."

These words are much cherished by his bereaved children and relatives.

1. A notorious nineteenth-century London forger who became the archetype of the gentleman criminal. Sir Charles L. Young wrote a melodrama called *Jim the Penman*, which played successfully in England and America in the 1880s. The name entered popular culture and was alluded to by writers of the period (Joyce's character Shem the Penman in book 1, chapter 7 of *Finnegan's Wake* is an obvious example). Dreiser is probably simply trying to be clever here.

[UPL]

H. L. Mencken
1524 Hollins St.
Baltimore.

April 14th [1921]

Dear Dreiser:-

1. Glenn Frank, the new editor of the Century, decides against the articles. He is polite, but won't play ball. Smith has left the magazine. I shall now tackle Lorimer.

2. The will you propose would probably be illegal. You still have a wife, and it is my impression that under the New York law she is entitled to one-third (or maybe one-half) of all your estate. You would have to get a release from her. Better look into this matter before you go further.

3. I am informed by Mme. Violet Johnson, the most gifted colored psychic in Maryland, that you will live to be 86. She says that the senile

changes visible in the functioning of your private parts are of no significance. Your heart, lungs, kidneys, etc., are perfectly sound.

4. I adopt the dying words that you propose with enthusiasm. They are very nobby, and will impress the sheriff.

5. I am writing to Kirah. Scott I met at your house, the night he bound up your sprained back.

6. I am surrounded by illness here, and full of troubles.

Yours,

M

[NYP-T]

P.O. Box 181
Los Angeles.

April 18th, 1921.

Dear M:

Reading your screed in this months S.S. today I noted the stuff about the University of Mich. prof. Also the dope on the other highbrow's english.[1] It seems to me that just here is the best and most useful vein opened by you. A few such lascerating attacks will not only bring about the critical and professorial demise of a number of these straw men but it will cool the heels and brows of a number who have a slightly better claim to places in the ranks. I wish you would make it your business to single out a thick-wit here and there, being sure to keep them well apart, geographically and burn them to a crisp. Nothing that could be done now could do more real good. The idea is so interesting to me that I hasten to speak of it. More than likely you have the thing in mind, but if not, put it there and oblige yours,

Billy the Oysterman

I may resume my Tenth Street abode next month. If so we must get together for a talk.

1. In the March 1921 *Smart Set*, Mencken reviewed *American Writers of the Present Day, 1890–1920*, by T. E. Rankin, a professor of rhetoric at the University of Michigan. He ridiculed Rankin's misuse of the language and then went on to mention the ugly prose of other academics.

[UPL]

H. L. Mencken
1524 Hollins St.
Baltimore.

April 23rd [1921]

Dear Dreiser:-

1. It is Euripides, not Euripedes. I blush for you.

2. I wrote to Kirah, but have had no reply from her.

3. Lorimer, the ass, says that the Newspaper Days chapters are not for him. Ditto Hovey of the Metropolitan: he says he is using practically all fiction, save for Hard's stuff. The Hearst outfit looks unpromising. I am rather stumped. What do you suggest?

4. Hark, hark, thou comest back! I'll be delighted. When do you start?

5. I shall tackle the professors as they bob up. The fact is, they already show signs of demoralization. Most of them are now very polite to me. I had my best fun with them 6 or 8 years ago, when they were all full of gas.

6. Letters continue to come in as a result of the false report of my marriage, printed last week. Everybody laughs. But why should my marriage be ridiculous? I begin to grow indignant.

Yours,
M

[UPL]

H. L. Mencken
1524 Hollins St.
Baltimore.

May 17th [1921]

Dear Dreiser:-

I have not sawed out the articles.¹ The plan was to submit outlines of them and then make them fit, as to length, etc., the desires of the nibbling editor. But all the shoe-drummer magazines, while very polite, pleaded previous engagements. It occurs to me that you may do better tackling them yourself; some of them don't like me much. I'll be glad to do the sawing out, if—you want me to do—it.

This Titan letter is very interesting. Sometimes I think that the lowbrow Americano has more sense than he seems to have.

When are you coming East? I hear you are cutting up in society in San

Francisco. At least five of my women agents there mention your silk shirts and gaudy neckties, and hint that you tried to loose their girdles.

If you ever get back to New York you had better give out that you are down with prostatitis. Otherwise you will lose your health.

I am worked to death, and feeling very rocky.

Yours,
Aloysius Hohenzattern

1. Dreiser wrote on 10 May 1921, asking whether Mencken had cut articles out of the manuscript of the autobiography; he also included a fan letter that praised *The Titan*.

[NYP-T]

P.O. Box 181
Los Angeles.

May 30, 1921.
Lincolns' Birthday.[1]

Dear Mencken:

I hear that Kirah is now connected with the Provincetown Players in N.Y. so that you can reach her there. Their Playhouse is in MacDougall Street I think.

Dreiser.

Don't forget Andrew Jackson, on this his natal day.[2]

1. It is hard to know what Dreiser means by this.
2. Jackson's birthday is 15 March.

[NYP-T]

[before 31 May 1921]

Have you heard of Albert Abrams,[1] 2135 Sacramento Street, San Francisco? And what have you heard about him. I hear marvellous things in regard to his scientific achievements especially in the matter of diagnosis and the treatment of consumption, cancer, tumors, syphilis and the like. Do the medical sharks of Baltimore know anything about him?

D

He has titles enough. A.M., M.D., LL.D., F.R.M.S.

1. George Sterling introduced Dreiser to Dr. Albert Abrams, an eccentric who invented what he called an "oscilloclast," an electrical device that the doctor used to treat Dreiser for what he diagnosed as tuberculosis.

[UPL]

H. L. Mencken
1524 Hollins St.
Baltimore.

May 31st [1921]

Dear Dreiser:-

I met Abrams in San Francisco. He made a rather indifferent impression on me—the usual Jew doctor. Sterling admires him greatly. But he can't do the things that Sterling says he can do; no one can.

Judging by the encomiums of you that reach me from the San Francisco fair, you must have employed your private parts to great advantage while you were there. I warn you against such excessive veneries at your age.

I'll be glad to send the specifications of the proposed articles to Wilson. The difficulty is to make self-contained pieces. The book hangs together very tightly.

I ran across the following in an anonymous pamphlet lately.

Democracy: the theory that all pricks are the same length.

Yours,
M

[NYP-T]

P.O. Box 181
Los Angeles.

June 7, 1921.

Henry Hollins Baltimore, Esq.,
Dear Mr. Baltimore:

Your kindly, if excessive, interest in my private parts moves me greatly. Let me explain. At the age of thirty a prediction, almost identical with yours, i.e. that unless I controlled my then excessive veneries I would find myself impotent at forty, carried me most safely and comfortingly to that prescribed age. At forty another well-wisher volunteered that unless I controlled my then excessive veneries I would most certainly find myself impotent at fifty. At fifty, God bless you, dear Mr. Baltimore, you arrive,—a most comforting omen, I feel sure now, dear Mr. Baltimore, that I shall come safely through to sixty, anyhow, at which period, let me hope, some other heaven sent prophet will see me through until seventy, at least. At that dangerous period, and Christ aiding me, I feel sure that I will be able to restrain the ardours against which you now caution. Such at least, dear

Mr. Baltimore, is the wish and prayer, even, of your affectionate and ad-
miring beneficiary——

Thomas A. Edison

[NYP-T]

P.O. Box 181
Los Angeles.

June 7, 1921.

Dear Mencken:

Do me this good turn. Get in touch with W. C. Lengel, now managing
editor of Hearst's, 119 West 40th Street, N.Y. and have him put Grove
Wilson on the job, sending him the pencilled ms. if you can. He has a
copy of the ms. From yours he can transfer your indications to his and then
send yours back to you. In the last six months he has written me at least
six times saying that if he had your tips he could work the thing out,—that
is Grove Wilson could. If I can get hold of the roughed out articles I think
I can shape them up so that I can find a publisher for them. I hate to
trouble you but if you can do this it will get the business done, I am sure.
Send this letter to him or advise him of what I say. Will is an old friend and
will be only too glad to handle the thing as above.

Dreiser

Abrams via the Oscilloclast claims to be able to cure hay fever. Why not
give it a trial if you are still hopelessly afflicted.[1]

1. The postscript is handwritten.

[UPL]

SMART SET
A Magazine of Cleverness
George Jean Nathan ⎤
and ⎬ Editors
H. L. Mencken ⎦

June 15, 1921

Dear Dreiser:

I have at last got hold of Grove Wilson through W. C. Lengel. Unfortunately, Wilson tells me that he is so busily occupied at the moment that it
is impossible for him to undertake the articles. He says that he is keeping

your manuscript and will be glad to do the work if the chance offers later on. My own feeling is that it is rather unwise to produce definite articles until some friendly editor has been sounded out. He may have ideas of his own and may want them executed—that is, ideas as to length, subject and so on. I am rather stumped myself. All the editors I have approached have failed to show proper interest in the enterprise. However, a chance to sell the articles may bob up at any minute. My ears are always open. If you get a tip yourself, let me know and I'll fall on it. My excessive work is sloping off and I'll soon have plenty of time.

Every letter I receive from San Francisco announces that Abrams is able to cure some other incurable disease. It now appears that he has a sure specific for cancer, hay-fever, diabetes, high blood pressure, small-pox and katzenjammer. I begin to suspect either that his friends are overly enthusiastic or that he himself is trying to kid us. Certainly any man living today cannot honestly say that he knows how to cure a cancer.

Yours,
Mencken

What is the state of your new novel? If possible, please let me hear from you on the following points at once:

1. When will it be finished?
2. How long will it be?
3. What do you want for the magazine serial rights, America and England?[1]

1. The postscript is handwritten.

[NYP-T]

P.O. Box 181
Los Angeles.

June 23, 1921.

Dear Mencken:

Do not care to say anything about the novel in hand until it is done. If it were only ready I would be only too glad to discuss it. In re Newspaper Days. I suppose you know that Rascoe is now managing editor of McCall's Magazine. I just sold him an article entitled <u>Hollywood</u> <u>Now</u> for four hundred. He is also considering a short story. I do not care to pester him with anything else for some little time, but in a month, maybe he might be interested to look at the ms. and see if he sees anything in it for him. But please don't say anything to him about it yet. I will sound him out and then let you hear from me.

Gloom reports that you bring her the best of cocktails or wine. Would I were there to share. I have so much respect for Gloom as a man and a gentleman and a scholar that I would gladly contribute a hogshead of booze to her upkeep if I only could. Observe a very poor snap of yours humbly.

Dreiser

[NYP-T]

P.O. Box 181
Los Angeles.

July 14, 1921

Dear Mencken:

I have a letter from Burton Rascoe saying that he would like to look at "Newspaper Days". I don't know whether to ask Lengel to send him the copy he has or you yours. If yours were edited completely, I would prefer that he see it. But I assume that it isn't, as yet, so will you decide which copy should go and see that it is sent him. His address is c/o McCall's Magazine, 236–250 West 37th Street, New York City. I'll write him to get in touch with you.

The studio in West 10th is no more. The house was sold and the new owner, via due process served notice. All my belongings are now in storage with the Chelsea Storage Warehouse until I can find out what I want to do with the tag end of my sinful life. Such, as you see, is the latter end of the unregenerate.

I hear you are doing an article on Maryland for the Nation.[1] And that in the face of the fact that they might have had it done by a real writer.

Timotheus Penobscott.

1. "Maryland: Apex of Normalcy," *Nation* 114(3 May 1922), 517–19.

[UPL]

H. L. Mencken
1524 Hollins Street
Baltimore.

July 20th [1921]

Dear Dreiser:-

I'll send my copy of the MS. to Rascoe, together with my notes regarding possible articles. It is a good idea. I never thought of him.

Gruening tells me that you are to do Indiana for his series.¹ Then God help the poor Indians! I shall treat Maryland in a mellow manner, and surprise the boobery.

I am in the last stages of "The American Language". My ambition is crowned: I have written a book longer than "The 'Genius'". It will be at least five inches thick. You are mentioned with veneration in eight places.

It is too bad about the 10th street house. When are you coming back? My notion is that the best part of Manhattan is Harlem. Quiet streets and relatively low rents. The town is in a state of financial collapse. Rents will go tumbling in the fall.

The weather here is unbearable.

In Xt.,

M

1. Ernest Gruening edited *These United States, a Symposium* (1923), in which Mencken's *Nation* essay on Maryland and Dreiser's on Indiana appeared.

[NYP-T]

The Theodore Dreiser's Widows and Orphans
Relief and Aid Association.
Rev. Henry Van Dyke, secy.
Stuart P. Sherman, Treas.
Los Angeles

Sept. 26, 1921.

Dear Mr. Mencken:

Your letter of inquiry in regard to the last resting place of the late Theodore Dreiser has been referred to us. Mr. Dreiser died without visible means of support of any kind and his body now lies in row eight, grave number seventeen of the present L.A. Gas Works extension of what was recently the old St. Ignatz cemetery. Unless his remains are removed and properly marked within the next ten months they are in danger of being completely obliterated.

In accordance with his request at the time of his death the pine board which was placed at his head was only marked with the cryptic numerals 181. There has been much speculation as to the exact meaning of these. Prof. Silas Carriagewasher of Alfalfa University and long a friend of the late author is of the opinion that they relate to the ancient Coptic ⟨ : ʃ⟨ ʒ⟨ ℒ⟩ of which language Mr. Dreiser was a profound student and are equivalent to "the angels". Freely interpreted, Prof. Carriagewasher explains, these might humorously refer to the modern phrase "gone to join the angels", though he adds that such may not have been his intention.

However, since your letter indicates an intention to contribute a floral offering of some kind we suggest that in view of the many unsettled obligations of the author and his numerous widows and dependents that you make your testimonial, however slight, in cash. As far as at present ascertained Mr. Dreiser left seventy-nine widows and three hundred and fifteen children, all destitute. These need to be looked after in some way and in consequence a sub-committee of the Southern California Authors League has been appointed to gather such means as it can. Thus far seven dollars and eighty-three cents have been acquired but the sub-committee is in hope that more will be forthcoming shortly. Anything that you have to offer will be gratefully received. All sums contributed are immediately divided pro rata, each child and widow counting as one.

> Respy.,
> The Theodore Dreiser's Widows
> and Orphans Relief and Aid
> Association.
> Per Henry Van Dyke, Secy.

Stewart[1] P. Sherman, Treas.

1. Dreiser usually misspells Stuart Sherman's name; his use of Sherman and Van Dyke plays on the distaste of the conservative critics for his writing.

[UPL]

> H. L. Mencken
> 1524 Hollins St.
> Baltimore.

September 27th [1921]

Gentlemen:-

The news of the tragic death of the late Mr. Dreiser fills me with sorrow and indignation. I hope you do not rest until justice has discharged its thunderbolts upon his murderers. If it is not too much trouble, I should be grateful for a memorandum of his last words. I am aware that it was his plan to say "Shakespeare, I come!" But I am informed that, at the last moment, just before he passed away, he fell into a delirium and muttered, "Otto, nachmal ein Seidel Helles".[1]

> Yours truly,
> H. L. Mencken

1. "Otto, after this, a good glass of beer."

[UPL]

H. L. Mencken
1524 Hollins St.
Baltimore.

October 2nd [1921]

Gentlemen:-

I have to acknowledge your letter of September 26th, in re the death of the late Theodore Hermann Dreiser. Permit me to call your attention to the fact that you fail to give me his last words. If I am to write an obituary of him for the New York <u>Times</u> I must have them. Common rumor has it that he said "Shakespeare, I come!" But my extensive experience with moribund great men inclines me to doubt that he actually pulled such words. You will recall the case of the late Walt Whitman, another literary man. For years he practised the following last words: "My one regret is that I could not die on the field of honor, fighting for democracy". But his actual last words were: "Lift me up, Horace; I want to s——t".

A woman calling herself Delphine Hogan has gone into deep mourning here, and announces that she is one of M. Dreiser's widows. She says he overcame her maiden reluctance in the year 1893, and left her with twins. She is not destitute, but has made a fortune keeping a rooming house. She wants to erect a bronze equestrian statue to the memory of the late lamented.

Sincerely yours,
H. L. Mencken

[UPL]

H. L. Mencken
1524 Hollins St.
Baltimore.

October 8th [1921]

Dear Dreiser:-

Knopf sends me the MS. of a book about you by one Burleigh C. Rodick, 38 Moore place, Brooklyn, N.Y.[1] It is too long and it contains a few errors in fact, but on the whole it seems to me to be a very solid piece of work. However, Knopf is scarcely the publisher to do it: Liveright is the man. I am going to New York on Monday, and shall probably take it along and tackle Liveright with it. I believe that such a book would do you a lot of good.

I enclose a portrait of you from a Hun paper.[2] The name under it is "Johannes Riemann". This is obviously an error. As a matter of fact,

Riemann is the owner of a cigar-box factory in Brooklyn, and has never written a line in his life. You may recall him. He married Elfrida Scharnagel, whose sister Wilhelmina you used to entertain in the barn.

God help us all!

Yours,
Mencken

1. The book was never published.
2. Mencken enclosed a sketch of a Dreiser look-alike, Johannes Riemann.

[NYP-T]

P.O. Box 181
Los Angeles.

Oct. 15, 1921.

Dear Mencken:

I know the Rodick book. He sent it to me. Also, Liveright has been familiar with it for some time. I doubt if he will publish it at present. It would really be better if some outside firm did it. At least the critics would have more respect for it. However, while I think it is a creditable piece of work it is nothing that I can do anything for. I wish I were in a position to help him place it because he has spent a great deal of time on it, I know.

As soon as the armistice conference is over, all will be right with the world.

Dreiser

[UPL]

H. L. Mencken
1524 Hollins St.
Baltimore.

November 15th [1921]

Dear Dreiser:-

The performance will have my prayers.[1] Nathan is very much interested in it, and will do whatever he can for it.[2] As you know, he greatly admires the play. As for me, I am certainly no dramatic critic. All plays seem to me to be feeble. More and more, my interests are centered in religion.

How long are you going to stay out there among those swamis, actors, tourists, and whores? Why not move back to Christendom, and give connoisseurs a chance to look at you? I believe it would be a good thing for you to show up in New York again; you are so damned securely buried that thousands of boobs are growing up who have never heard of you. And what of the new novel? I hear conflicting reports of it.

Let me have a letter telling what you are up to.

Yours in Xt.,

M

I enclose a copy of the private appendix to the American Credo.[3]

1. *The Hand of the Potter* opened on 5 December 1921 at the Provincetown Playhouse in New York City.
2. George Jean Nathan wrote an unfavorable review: "Humor Lost in New Play by Kummer; Dreiser's Play Is Poor," St. Paul *Pioneer Press*, 8 January 1922, 2d sect., 6.
3. The appendix to Mencken and Nathan's *The American Credo* (1920), which contains many obscenely funny epigrams, is in the Dreiser Collection at the University of Pennsylvania.

[NYP-T]

P.O. Box 181
Los Angeles.

Nov. 23, 1921.

Dear Mencken:

Well, at last, after about eighteen years, I welcome a slight suggestion of affection. So you would like to see me back in New York and safely beyond the clutches of these local whores. I wish I were, to tell you the honest, God's truth. And I expect to be, one of these hours. I have a certain iron in the fire, which if it goes through—but we won't talk. But I may get a decent studio if rents are not too exorbitant and we'll get some home brew and a baked ham and demolish every human aspiration from pole to pole. I would like nothing better than a Mencken-Nathan-Dreiser dinner with plenty of beer. Will the latter ever be again, I wonder.

If you and Nathan could arrange it I wish you would drift down to a rehearsal of The Hand of the Potter, 133 MacDougall Street, and tell me how the thing goes. I hear that it is being rehearsed and George Cram Cook[1] swears that he has a wonderful cast.

But has he?

Oh, Lord.

Oh, Lord.

Have a mass said for the repose of my nerves.

D

1. Cook was a founder and director of the Provincetown Players.

[UPL]

SMART SET
A Magazine of Cleverness
George Jean Nathan
and   } Editors
H. L. Mencken
25 West 45th Street
New York

November 30, 1921

Dear Dreiser:

Nathan says that the cabots will probably ruin the play but that the production should attract a great deal of attention. You know my own Freudian complex against the theatre. Whenever I look at an actor I begin to reach for my revolver. It is a pity that the old law, allowing one to chase them with dogs, was ever repealed. However, when the play is finally put on, I shall buy a gallery seat and applaud like the devil.

If you come back to New York, I agree not only to get you a Maryland ham that will drive you crazy but also to produce an unlimited supply of excellent beer. The town was never more wet than it is at this minute.

My agents in San Francisco report that Fatty is bearing up like a hero.[1] Let us not slacken in our prayers.

Yours,
M

1. Roscoe ("Fatty") Arbuckle (1887–1933), the film comedian, was being tried for manslaughter. The trial, which resulted from the death of a young actress during a party at his home, ended in acquittal.

[NYP-T]

[after 30 November 1921]

Dear Mr. Mencken:

Reference to Maryland ham with Baltimore cellar Culmbacher is apt to produce dolorans agitatans in the fourteenth cervical cantata to say nothing of a swelling in the secondary coating of the Sempter sphinxoborax, resulting in eliphantiasis of the corbular biloxi. So, in the presence of those with an innate tendency toward these ailments it would be best not to speak too freely.

Oswal McMenamy. M.D. Ph.D.

[UPL]

H. L. Mencken
1524 Hollins St.
Baltimore.

December 12th [1921]

Dear Dreiser:-

You will be rejoiced to hear that bacteriologists at the Johns Hopkins have succeeded in growing yeast from the Löwenbräu laboratories at Munich, and that brews made with it will be available in unlimited quantities by January 15th. A fact.

Don't be afraid to come back to New York. I enclose some circulars that should reassure you.[1] Get a pound or two of the tablets and take them every hour on your way East. You will then be fit for society when you arrive.

Once you have discharged all such duties to the nation, let us have a palaver. I want to take your advice on certain pious matters. When do you land?

Yours,
M

1. These have disappeared.

[UPL]

H. L. Mencken
1524 Hollins St.
Baltimore.

December 17th [1921]

Dear Dreiser:-

Who is Hume?[1] Your lawyer? I doubt that he is able to introduce expert testimony, but if he is it will be easy to round up half a dozen men, say Lawrence Gilman, Hackett, Carl Van Doren, Broun, and so on. But you surely ought to be present. The John Lane American branch seems to be down and out. Its goods are for sale, including its contracts. I believe that, as a matter of law, you are perfectly free to print The Genius whenever you please. Jones broke the contract in ceasing to sell the book.

I am writing Hume. I'll call him up when I get to New York.

Yours,
M

1. Arthur Carter Hume, Dreiser's New York attorney. In the novelist's name, Hume had brought a $20,000 suit for breach of contract against John Lane. Among other things, Dreiser was trying to gain control of his past book publications in order to sell them to a publisher as a set.

[UPL]

H. L. Mencken
1524 Hollins St.
Baltimore.

December 22nd [1921]

Dear Dreiser:-

I had a long gabble with Hume by telephone yesterday and he told me the whole story. The legal situation is very complex, and I doubt that he succeeds in his effort to get the two cases amalgamated. But it is certainly worth trying. When the business comes to trial you ought to be here. Hume is evidently unfamiliar with the matters lying behind the case. I offered to help him with information at any time. If he calls for expert testimony it should be easy to get it. But so far the courts have always ruled it out.

I did not see "The Hand of the Potter". I am in bad shape physically, and was in no mood for it. Nathan tells me that several of the parts are well played, but that in general the performance is second class. He says that the coroner's inquest scene is ineffective theatrically, but that some of the other scenes play capitally. In the main, he believes that the thing does you credit. There is a good deal of talk about it in New York, generally to the same effect.

I am on a very strict diet, and most miserable. My stomach has gone to pot.

Yours,
M

[NYP-T]

P.O. Box 181
Los Angeles.

Dec. 22, 1921.

Dear Mencken:

In so far as I can make out this man Lange [1] is a Milwaukee Mfg. who has been sued by a young girl there—or by her guardian, for seduction.

They are trying to mannact him, I judge. At any rate the gaurdian of the girl found three of my books inscribed by this fellow Lange and presented to this maid of seventeen with high encomiums and blether. Gaurdian takes said works into court and asks the mannactor judge to say, judicially, whether said works are fit volumes for an mfg to present to a maid of seventeen and whether, on the face of them, it doesn't prove that the mfg had designs on her virtue. So much for The Titan, The Financier, Jennie Gerhardt and my priceless reputation. I gather all this from reading press clippings at five cents per clip.

Evidently it is up to the mfg to prove that not only am I, personally, a man of probity and virtue and standing, but that the said works are compositions of the highest biblical character. He has to do it to save his own skin. Hence his industry. He is bombarding every magazine, critic and literarian with demands for testimony as to my standing and purity. Hearst, The Nation, The S.E.P., yourself, The Cosmo, Harpers, Liveright and God knows how many others have been assailed. A fine collection he must have. Would that I might see it.

But, as thou seest, evil in mine own case turns and returns as good unto me. Having led him into the shadow of the pen he squawks and I am heard of once more in all the editorial officers of the land, and elsewhere. And then they say there is no God. Well, I'll be damned. What more proof does even the most Thomasy of Thomases need. I hereby declare that Christ lives and reigns. Not only that, but he looks after me, personally. You should have given me a snowy character. The learned J. might hand down a decision to the effect that said works, handed to a girl of seventeen are the equivalent of one hundred and seventy eight Our Fathers and one hundred and twenty-two Hail Marys, plus fourteen works of mercy. Why didst thou fail me at the one great moment. Haste and hand him a good character of me, while the light yet shines. A character in time saves mine.

Meanwhile, Merry Christ mass. And may your socks be full of saw dust. I hear that Sir Charles Chaplin now looks upon you as the formost critical intellect of the day. Remember him in your will.

Dreiser

1. W. W. Lange, who collected Dreiser's books.

[UPL]

H. L. Mencken
1524 Hollins St.
Baltimore.

December 30th [1921]

Dear Dreiser:-

I have this day made a will appointing you my literary and military executor. At the moment of my decease, even before you glue my eyes shut, I hereby instruct you to buckle on my old sword, put on my cocked hat, go to the open window, and discharge the following speech upon the waiting throng:

"His last words were: 'I leave my Arschloch to my country!':

If any fail to hear it the first time, say it again.

Yours,
M

[NYP-T]

[December 1921]

[To Mencken]

Last and famous dying words of the late
Henry L. Mencken,
sheriff-poet of Mosquito Landing, Maryland.

"O, Scotus Erigena, lead thou thy desciple on."

These words, hand-painted on
alabaster and signed by the author
are to be had from the Secretary of
the Mosquito Landing, (Maryland)
Y.W.C.A.
Price, ten cents.

[NYP]

[Undated, 1921]

[To Mencken]

A little kiss, a little smile,
A hand clasp every little while;
A little whisper in your ear

That no one else must ever hear
A little pressure of my foot
Upon your dainty buttoned boot—
A scribbled note, a little date,
To meet you when the hour grows late—
A little room in some hotel,
A little pressure on the bell,
A little supper just for two,
A little drink before we're through,
A little fussing in the chair
A little mussing of your hair,
A little shirt waist laid aside,
A little breast that tries to hide,
A little skirt laid on the chair
A little suit of underwear—
That comes off with a little teasing
And shows a rosy form most pleasing.

[NYP]

16 St. Lukes Pl
N.Y.C

Jan. 2nd 1922

[To Mencken]
I am resolved to date my letters correctly from now until Mch 1 next.
The executorship is accepted. Kindly see that a drum and a megaphone
are left in trim for the occasion.
Nothing would give me greater comfort than a visit to Baltimore in due
season, providing and stipulating that I be treated with respect as a godfearing hyphenate and not as an author or an American. Also I must have a
tick full of fresh straw, two blankets and at least two eggs for breakfast. I
find that I cannot keep up my humor on less.
    These details being accepted—yes.

Sincerely,
Frank Crane, M.D.

I presume you note that the Wabash monument stuff has at last got by.
Paulonius is to have a $35,000 staff placed on his chest. Providing I die
beyond my means, I'll go out there and ask him to move over a few inches.
He doesn't need a whole bed to himself anyhow.

[UPL]

H. L. Mencken
1524 Hollins St.
Baltimore.

January 3rd [1922]

Dear Dreiser:-

The matron at the Almshouse promises you a clean bed in her best ward. It is never used save in case of great epidemics. Edgar Allan Poe died in it 1849. Name the day and I'll have the firemen parade.

Phil Goodman[1] suggests a change in my Last Words, thus: "My only regret is that I have but one Arschloch to leave to my country". Please make a note of it. I shall arrange to have your announcement broadcasted by radio.

A friend of mine here has just perfected an invention for liquifying ice. Stock is for sale at 70 cents a share. Verbum sap.

In God's Name,
H. L. M.

1. Goodman was a close friend of Mencken and an advertising man, publisher, and producer of plays.

[UPL]

H. L. Mencken
1524 Hollins St.
Baltimore.

January 4th [1922]

Dear Dreiser:-

The "psychological effect on tourists passing thru Terre Haute on the National road" is immense! All I ask is the privilege of attending you as camerlengo when you go out there for the unveiling. Let us invite Debs,[1] and make a night of it. I am writing to Governor McCray, calling attention to the fact that you are also mortal and cannot hope to escape the arms of Jesus for more than 40 years. I have suggested that your memorial take the form of an heroic equestrian statue in the public square of Warsaw, with the simple inscription: "To the Unknown Slacker".

Sinclair Lewis made a fearful hole in my cellar night before last. Well, all things pass.

Yours,
M

Mencken in the backyard at 1524 Hollins Street (Enoch Pratt Free Library)

1. Eugene V. Debs (1855–1926), American Socialist leader who was born, as was Dreiser, in Terre Haute.

[UPL]

H. L. Mencken
1524 Hollins St.
Baltimore.

January 14th [1922]

Dear Dreiser:-

I take no stock in La Kenton's conspiracy tosh.[1] It sounds very Greenwichy. The dramatic critics of New York are simply imbeciles; nothing worse. The Dawson woman, of course, is against you, but she is not a dramatic critic.[2] The real truth is that the Providencetown Players devote more attention to posturing as martyrs than they do to producing plays. I hear from perfectly fair men that their production of the play, in large part, was very bad. I wish you had let Hopkins[3] do it. So far as I can make out, there is absolutely no general rising against you in New York. On the contrary, all sane men regard you with respect, and even many of the numskulls speak of you in a Christian manner. What they all want to know is why you intern yourself in Los Angeles. I seriously believe that it would be greatly to your advantage to come back.

I had an engagement with Hume in New York last week, but had to break it on account of illness. I have been unable to do any serious work for weeks. My stomach is in a hell of a state, with constant discomfort. Result: my desk is piled mountain high, and I fret and fume. Chirurgy seems ineffective. God knows what the end will be.

Yours,
M

1. Edna Kenton, the Chicago critic, suggested that there was something other than objective criticism behind the bad reviews of the New York production of *The Hand of the Potter*.
2. N. P. Dawson of the New York *Evening Globe* did not like any of Dreiser's work.
3. Arthur Hopkins (1878–1950), a producer who had wanted to stage *The Hand of the Potter* in 1917 but later decided against it.

[NYP-T]

[before 23 February 1922]

[To Mencken]

As you know, I never like to rub anyone's fur the wrong way. So I am sending you this letter.[1] Willst return it?.

There is a woman in jail here convicted of murder in the first degree for shooting a tenant who would not be gouged into paying more rent because he had a lease at a fixed rate. From her cell she now issues a sad plaint. Someone has charged that a number of years ago she lived with a man without being married to him. It is a lie,—a base etc. She never did. She may have killed a man but that is a different thing. Previous to this incident she was always a good woman and so remains. Now that she is in trouble her enemies are trying to slander her.

1. The letter has disappeared.

[UPL]

H. L. Mencken
1524 Hollins St.
Baltimore.

Feburary 23rd [1922]

Dear Dreiser:-

Brown[1] is quite right. I believe the play would do well in Germany and Russia. But as he says, one can't expect much money from those quarters in these days.

I am surprised that you should spread scandal about that poor woman. Murder is lawful in more situations than it is unlawful. Have you ever thought of that? Think of war, legal executions, self-defense, repelling burglars, chasing criminals, useless operations, etc. But frigging, as you must know, is invariably unlawful, save under ecclesiastical permit. I am amazed that you should set up a defense of an adulteress. True enough, she denies it. But you certainly know enough about ethics to know that a woman needs only be accused. The accusation is overwhelming evidence.

God help us all.

Yours,
H. L. Mencken

Why don't you sign your letters. I sell your autographs to a dealer for 50 cents apiece.

1. Probably Curtis Brown, Dreiser's literary agent.

[UPL]

H. L. Mencken
1524 Hollins St.
Baltimore.

March 2nd [1922]

Dear Dreiser:-

I have a letter from Hume, asking me to see him when I get to New York again, in about ten days. He says that he and Edward H. Dodd, of Dodd, Mead & Co., are personal friends, and that he hopes to settle the Jones case at last. He does not state the terms, but says he wants to consult me about "one phase of the matter".

What should I do? If you have any instructions, let me have them at once. Send them to the Smart Set office, 25 west 45th street, so that they will be there when I get in.

It seems to me that the important thing is to release "The 'Genius'", and get it into print again. If necessary, I advise making a few discreet cuts, but I don't think it will be necessary. I doubt that it will be possible to get any substantial damages out of John Lane. His American house was apparently bankrupt when he sold out.

Yours,
M.

[UPL]

H. L. Mencken
1524 Hollins St.
Baltimore.

March 16th [1922]

Dear Dreiser:-

It is too bad that you are not in New York. All of your difficulties, I believe, could be adjusted in an hour.

I had a long palaver with Hume and Dodd on Tuesday. No need to go into the arguments. Here are my conclusions:

1. Dodd is eager to have "The Bulwark", and if you can free it from all claims by Liveright it will count heavily in all future negotiations.

2. Dodd is willing either to do "The 'Genius'" with the reasonable cuts you yourself suggest, or to free it so that you will be able, if you want to, to bring it out yourself.

3. Dodd can be induced to withdraw his suggestion of a cut in royal-

ties. If you offer to waive his offer of a cut of $1,000 in the Lane claim he will agree to let the royalties stand as they are.

4. He regards you very highly, believes that your adventures with suppressed books have had injustices in them, and is eager to put some diligent effort behind you.

5. The question as to whether the Lane claim applies to "The Bulwark" or to all your Lane books is, after all, largely academic. What do you care, so long as you can free "The Bulwark" and settle the whole matter? I believe that Hume can settle it out of court if you give him a free hand. He is disinclined to go before a jury, and for sound reasons. To a jury Lane's claim of actual cash advanced would probably weigh more heavily than your counter-claim of damages suffered by the suppression of "The 'Genius'". Suppose the jury decided that Lane was justified in suppressing it? You would then have a judgement against you—in brief, a lien on all your future work. It seems to me far preferable to settle the business amicably, and without a trial in court. As Dodd's offer shows, Jones is willing to compromise. True enough, Dodd did not buy the Lane suit—it was specifically set aside in the contract—but his offer proves that he is willing to be a party to the settlement.

6. Hume is a very honest man, and eager to aid you. Dodd is no literary critic, but a business man. But he wants to have you on his list, and I believe that he would handle you competently.

7. In case you and Dodd come to terms about "The 'Genius'" I shall be glad to tackle Sumner and dispose of him. It should be easy to do so with a few cuts.

8. I suggest that you send a release from Liveright to Hume and a complete statement of what you would be willing to accept in the way of an arrangement with Lane and Dodd, in detail. Send this last either to Hume or to me.

I need not point out to you the difficulties that beset Hume. He is doing his damndest, and he is helped by his personal friendship with Dodd, but he is constantly impeded by the fact that he can't consult with his client—that is, quickly and frequently. During the conference with Dodd the disadvantages of this were constantly evident. The only solution that I see is to give him a very free hand. If he wrote to you every time some minor point came up both of you would go crazy.

All this for your private eye. Let me know confidentially what the ideal arrangement would be, from your standpoint, and I'll see how near we can come to it. I don't know what Liveright's claims are, if he has any. If I asked him he would not tell me. But they must be disposed of if they exist. Dodd would not enter into any arrangement which would involve a combat with Liveright. But in his present frame of mind he seems willing to go a long way toward an agreement.

Yours,

M

[NYP-T]

P.O. Box 181
Los Angeles.

March 22, 1922.

Dear Mencken:

For the life of me I cannot see that there is much to be gained by dickering with Dodd. His tenders, so far, are all to the bad. He begins by a tricky offer to knock off one thousand of the alleged Lane debt, as though it were a bit of publishing generosity and then suggests a reduction of royalty as though the same had nothing to do with the thousand. The Dodd people are not publishers of liberal books. They approach me about as a Baptist snouts a pervert. I am to alter my books. I am to let them pick and choose. They will see whether I can do anything worthy of them. They do not want "The 'Genius'" unless it is properly pruned around the vitals. And, all being arranged, they will make me an advance against "The Bulwark" of $1,000 when, on presentation of the ms. to Harpers or Liveright I can carry away a check for three thousand. You may not be able to see my point of view but I swear I cannot enthuse over that amiable concern. At heart they are Baptists and there is no real cure. Only consider the history of the <u>Bookman</u> under their care,—a watery bit of high-browery that was as safe as the last Methodist conference.

Pardong. I will consult Liveright and let you know. But I see small hope. If I can't release "The 'Genius'" I can't. But I can do other books which they can't touch and that is what I shall have to do, I presume. But I am obliged to you for the trouble you have taken, are taking and suggest that you will take, if I prove tractable. Thou art a noble scout. But ah, for a decent publisher.

St. Theodore the Surbian

Take my word for it the noble Lane has not let go of his catalogue. He has merely put it in care of <u>Dodd</u>, <u>trustee</u> <u>Fashion</u>. The prokous Jones remains his mealy mouther gaurd.

[UPL]

H. L. Mencken
1524 Hollins St.
Baltimore.

March 29th [1922]

Dear Dreiser:-

The thing grows hopelessly complex. When I met Hume and Dodd the chief thought in my mind was that it would be a good thing to get rid of your suit against Lane and his counter claim. But I agree with you that Dodd is certainly not an ideal publisher for you. However, who is? Liveright? I doubt it. As for the Harpers, they seem to be in decay. If you could liberate all of your books, and take them to some new publisher, the whole business would be settled. But that seems to be impossible. In any case I doubt that you'll ever get anywhere sitting in Los Angeles. If you were in New York you could carry through the four-cornered negotiation far more easily. Hume seems to me to be quite helpless as it is. He is doing his damndest, but he doesn't know precisely what you want.

How are you, anyhow? As for me, I am in a low state, and making heavy weather of my book.

Yours,
M

[NYP-T]

P.O. Box 181
Los Angeles.

April 18, 1922.

Dear Mencken:

Don't worry about the Dodd matter or anything else in connection with the books. Have been intending to write you this for weeks, it seems. I am fairly well satisfied that the Dodd Co and myself will never hit it off. But no harm. We can live without each other. As for Liveright he is certainly a poor fish but a port in a storm. He has rendered me one service and another and I am not ungrateful. One of these days I may be able to finance my own works and then they can all kiss my royal standard, such as it is.

Your noble words about the demise of the puritans makes me laugh.[1] No doubt for others the ban may have been lifted, for yours humbly it seems to hold up fairly well. The Dodd gentlemen seem to teach you nothing. And the enduring attitude of Mr. Sumner, nix. You forget that from time to time I attempt to market various things in places other than the S.S. and that even through a Los Angeles fog I can discern certain things, albeit, dimly. The critical reception of the Hand of the Potter proves clearly that all the old time puritanic rage has been blown out of the land and that we have a body of liberal critics capable of viewing all serious things at least tolerantly. The notices of the play in The Freeman, The New Republic, The Dial, The Independent and such like liberal critical institutions prove as much.[2]

Hail to the new day. Darwin wins by fifty-one to forty-nine in the Ky. state legislature[3] and the Atlantic Monthly announces that it would not publish Sister Carrie even now. You certainly have sound reasons for your optimism.

Dreiser

However I have all the bootleg I need[4]

1. This letter is missing.
2. The *New Republic* (8 October 1919) and *Dial* (20 September 1919) reviews praised Dreiser's intent but questioned his ability as a playwright.
3. The Kentucky House of Representatives had recently rejected a proposed law to prohibit the teaching of Darwinism by a vote of 42–41.
4. The postscript is handwritten.

[UPL]

H. L. Mencken
1524 Hollins St.
Baltimore.

April 22nd [1922]

Dear Dreiser:-

With all due respect, Tush! Even Doubleday would print Sister Carrie today; Briggs, of Harper's, told me not two weeks ago that they would be glad to have The Titan. Some progress has been made, and maybe a damned sight more than you suspect. You are shut off from human society, and apparently read nothing. Worse, you are befogged by your weakness for The "Genius". I could get it past Sumner easily, with not a dozen changes, all of them unimportant. But while it was on the stocks I'd be hot for cutting out whole reams of words. There we would quarrel.

The air is again filled with rumors that the Second Coming of Christ is at hand. Once I thought that Woodrow was the man, but this seems to have been an error. Maybe it is Will H. Hays.

Yours,
M.

[UPL]

SMART SET
Edited By
George Jean Nathan
and
H. L. Mencken

April 25, 1922

Dear Dreiser:

I'll be glad to see Sumner and to arrange the cuts.[1] I doubt that he will insist on any of much concern. He is disposed, of late, to be rather conciliating. But, to be frank, I want to be sure in advance that after the work is done you will not buck. Are you willing to let Dodd do the book with the cuts? If there is any impediment in your mind to this plan, what is the use of going on? I doubt that any other publisher would do the book as it stands. It would simply invite an expensive law-suit. Even if he won, he would lose money. I have just called up Hume by phone and he agrees to this scheme—that is, I am to see Sumner, try to come to some terms with him and then turn the revised book over to Dodd or to whatever publisher you designate. I think it will be easier for me to do the work myself than to call in Lengel and Rascoe.

Lengel was in my office a few weeks ago and told me about his short version of "The Genius".[2] I think it would have been a good scheme to have printed this short version serially before the book came out, but to do it now would be an anticlimax. It is only half the length of the original.

I believe that Lengel agrees with me and my scheme to get "The Genius" past Sumner. Let me know how you feel about it, and I'll go ahead.

Yours,
M

1. On 18 April 1922, Dreiser wrote asking if Mencken would meet with Sumner to help cut *The "Genius"* for a Dodd publication. [NYP]

2. Lengel had made a 100,000-word short version of *The "Genius"* for magazine publication. Dreiser wrote Mencken suggesting that Dodd might want to publish this and thus avoid having to deal with Sumner. (18 April 1922 [NYP])

[NYP-T]

P.O. Box 181
Los Angeles,
Cal.

May 1, 1922.

Dear Mencken:

Of course I am willing that you should purify the Genius and grateful to you for being ready to perform that service. My willingness only extends to what must come out to satisfy the Boy Scouts, however. In your last letter but one you announced that in case you set to cut it at all that you should proceed to cut reams and reams or words to that affect. Hardly. And as much as I may pretend to love you. Your approach to the book is not mine and while I respect your zeal I reserve all rights and prefer to hold the work as it stands. Don't forget that the book is already established as it stands, and such cuts as are now made will be but temporary anyhow.

I was about to polish you off in a screed of great delicacy and point but now prefer to rack my lance for the present. As in the case of the story of the English lock man, I will say one thing: you stand at the head of the class for making assertions and then trusting to the bass drum to silence the reply. We shall see.

I wish you would let me see exactly (seratim) the changes demanded by Sumner. I have his old list,—some seventy-seven in all.

Dreiser

[UPL]

H. L. Mencken
1524 Hollins St.
Baltimore.

May 1st [1922]

Dear Dreiser:-

Hume writes to me again about the Sumner business. How do you feel about it? Let me know precisely.

I believe that I could induce Sumner to lay off the book by making relatively few cuts, none of them fatal to it. But I don't want to negotiate with him unless I am certain of two things:

1. That you want to bring out the book with such cuts.
2. That you are willing to let Dodd publish it.

Your letters, re-read, leave me in doubt. In one of them you seem to be willing to go through with this scheme, but in another you indicate that you don't want to have anything to do with Dodd.

I'll be in New York in two weeks. Let me hear from you in the meantime.

Personally, I have no positive opinion in the matter. My first impulse is to say, Let the thing stand as it is. But that, of course, cuts off all revenue from the book.

Yours,
M

[UPL]

H. L. Mencken
1524 Hollins St.
Baltimore.

May 6th [1922]

Dear Dreiser:-

I'll see Sumner the next time I get to New York. I am up to my ears in my book, and it may be ten days or two weeks. Certainly I have no desire to chop the text unnecessarily. If Sumner will do business at all, it should be possible to get rid of him with relatively few cuts. If he demands too much I shall adjourn the meeting sine die. A pox upon all the camp-followers of Christ!

Has Hergesheimer shown up? He is somewhere in the West, giving the bootleggers the time of their lives.

Yours,
Pontius II

[NYP-T]

P.O. Box 181
Los Angeles,
Cal.

May 16, 1922.

Dear Mencken:

The situation is a little complicated. I am perfectly willing to have Dodd-Mead publish an expurgated edition of the "Genius." But whether they will publish it unless I contract to publish the next novel, I don't know. I am writing Hume herewith to sound them as to this. I am willing to turn in the next novel providing some complications connected with it can be removed. I feel that they can be and am writing as to that. You might ask Hume over the phone in N.Y. if he knows whether Dodd will take the Genius alone or whether it is conditional. If the latter you will need to wait until I advise you further, which will be soon.

Am as sick as a dog to day. Have taken Calomel and—oh, me poor entrails.

Dreiser

I tried to read the other day Al Jennings on O. Henry.[1] What swill.

1. Dreiser is referring to *Through the Shadows with O. Henry* (1921), by Alphonso J. Jennings.

[UPL]

H. L. Mencken
1524 Hollins St.
Baltimore.

May 22nd [1922]

Dear Dreiser:-

I have an engagement with Sumner for May 31st. He makes the usual preposterous demands, but I hope to talk him out of most of them. If he sticks to them I'll simply tell him to go to hell. Whether or not Dodd does the book is, after all, a small matter. Once it is released it will be easy to get a publisher for it. I'll see Hume after the negotiation is completed.

The news that calomel is ever taken in California surprises me. I thought that eating fresh figs kept the bowels loose. If you are troubled again, avoid drugs and read the preamble of the League of Nations. It will give you a very pleasant passage.

I am booked to sail August 8th.[1] I shall stop off in England a week; then for Germany!

Yours,
M.

1. In August Mencken sailed to Europe for a three-month tour.

[NYP-T]

P.O. Box 181
Los Angeles,
Cal.

May 22, 1922.

Dear Mencken:

Enclosed is a list of required changes in The "Genius" furnished by Sumner to Liveright.[1] Last fall Liveright wrote me that he was taking the matter of necessary changes up with Sumner,—that is, he had written him. Later he told me that he had not had a reply. I assumed that he was not following the matter up. But today comes this. Do you suppose Sumner's minimum could be shortened? If not why wouldn't it do to publish the short version. Surely there is nothing in that. Yet he might descend on that for one thing and another, just to be descending I presume. When I think of One Arabian Night and what they get away with in the movies without a squeak from these fellows and then how ardently they check up the commas in the current novels it gives me a very large pain. But the question now is how to get around this damned fakir. I wish you would return this to me, or, if you chance to want it, a copy of it.

Dreiser

1. The list has disappeared.

[NYP-T]

P.O. Box 181
Los Angeles,
Cal.

June 3, 1922.

[To Mencken]
Well, a pleasant sea and land journey and here's hoping you bring back an honest picture of Germany. I am going abroad myself one of these days, belikes to Spain.

Ignatius Loyola.

[UPL]

SMART SET
Edited by
George Jean Nathan
and
H. L. Mencken

June 1, 1922

Dear Dreiser:-
I went to the mat with Sumner yesterday afternoon and finally succeeded in getting him to agree to reasonable cuts in the book. He receded from probably four-fifths of his demands. I am preparing a schedule show-

ing the agreement reached and shall send you a copy from Baltimore tomorrow. Another copy will go to Hume.

Sincerely yours,
M.

[UPL]

H. L. Mencken
1524 Hollins St.
Baltimore.

June 1st [1922]

Dear Dreiser:-

I enclose a copy of the agreement made with Sumner.[1] As you will
note, two whole chapters, which he proposed to cut out bodily, have been
saved, and in many other places substantial changes have been made in
his original demands. In a few cases it was necessary, in order to preserve
the sense, to make small cuts not demanded.

A copy goes to Hume and one to Gloom. If you agree to the scheme,
let Hume know of it. As for the difference between Dodd and Liveright,
you will have to settle that direct.

I spent the whole afternoon with Sumner. He was very polite.

Yours,
M

1. Mencken enclosed a six-page, typed agreement between John S. Sumner and
himself as Dreiser's representative. On one side of each page he listed "Original demand of Sumner" and on the other, "Compromise of Sumner and Mencken." In addition, Mencken had Sumner waive his complaints against "blasphemous, profane and
bar-room language." The following day, 2 June 1922, Mencken sent along Sumner's
original list of demands. [UPL]

[NYP-T]

P.O. Box 181
Los Angeles

June 8, 1922.

Dear Mencken:

Well, I have just finished checking up the solemn labors of yourself
and Sumner. To many of the cuts I make no objection since if cuts must
come I think you have done as well by me as could be. The items which

strike me as fantastic are those which relate to the conversations between Suzanne and Witla—pages 534, 539, 541, 553, 557.[1] Also the cut which explains why Angela wanted a child and why.[2] Since this is a definite point in the dramatic structure of this tale,—the one thing that gives it real point in view of her death afterwards by reason of this wish and effort I cannot see how, logically, it can come out. And I cannot see how it can be written so very differently if the same point is to be made. As for the thing being immoral that is too crazy for words. The discussion of child-bearing and the reasons there fore is almost a commonplace today. I cannot see this and I feel that this point ought to be rediscussed. If the thing is taken up as definitely elsewhere in the book I do not know it. And just now I haven't time to reread the work to see. But there is certainly nothing prurient or salacious about that and I should like to have it stay in. Will you talk to Sumner about this.

Now as to Liveright and Dodd. The matter of The Bulwark has been adjusted. Liveright waives any claim as I knew he would. He never had anything to do with The "Genius". Hence, he has no claim and makes none. Whether it is worth while to reissue The Genius cut remains to be seen. I wonder if any one will want a clipped copy.

Just the same I am once more your debtor for your work in connection with this. I can see that you went carefully into the matter and saved a very great deal that was asininely doomed. It surprises me to know that you could make him accept such intelligent suggestions. I think I shall have to send you a can of pork and beans for christmas.

To be definite here is how I feel and where I stand. If you can save the cut on pages 445–446 above referred to I will accept this revised version and will see if I can induce Dodd to reissue it. I would like it if he would merely black out the offending lines and use the present plates as they run, numbers and all. If you talk to Dodd or Hume, suggest this.

Dreiser

Important—thanks[3]

1. To check Dreiser's references, see *The "Genius"* (New York, 1915).
2. A cut beginning with "I was at this time" on p. 445 and including all but the last line of p. 446.
3. The postscript is handwritten.

[UPL]

H. L. Mencken
1524 Hollins St.
Baltimore.

June 12th [1922]

Dear Dreiser:-

I am writing to Sumner, proposing that he agree to let pages 445 and 446 stand. I incline to think that he'll agree. The other small cuts that you mention represent the currency with which the trading was done. I had to yield in small things in order to save larger things. As it stands, cut, the book is not seriously damaged. In fact, I believe that some further cuts would improve it.

Dodd is apparently willing to reissue the book, but I doubt that he'd do it from the present plates, with the cuts blank. In fact, I have a feeling that this would be rather unfair to Sumner. If it had been done when I first suggested it, with the full cuts, it would have been fair enough. But now that Sumner has met us more than half way it would be a bit thick to kick him in the pants. Dodd could save most of the plates. Whole chapters are uncut. But you had better negotiate with him direct. I doubt that the book, reissued, would sell more than a few thousand. But it ought to be on your list.

I shall be in New York next week, and see Hume.

Yours,
M

[UPL]

H. L. Mencken
1524 Hollins St.
Baltimore.

June 16th [1922]

Dear Dreiser:-

As I expected, Sumner agrees to let pages 445 and 446 stand. But in order to give him something I have suggested cutting out one sentence. It is unimportant. I enclose a memorandum;[1] please attach it to the other list. It is highly important that when the resetting is done every cut agreed upon be observed strictly.

Nathan is laid up with a sprained back. A few weeks ago he read Andre Tridon's new book on the art of love,[2] and was much impressed by some of the novel postures described in it. Accordingly, he sent for a Rentz-Santley girl, put her on his work-bench, and proceeded to pleasure her in the manner advocated by Tridon. But inasmuch as he had not done any Turn-verein work for 16 years his muscles, like Angela's,[3] were very stiff, and so he lacerated one of them and is now heavily bandaged.

Yours,

M

1. This has not survived.
2. *Psychoanalysis and Love* (1922), by André Tridon.
3. Angela Blue, the character in *The "Genius"* whose muscular paralysis contributed to her death in childbirth.

[NYP-T]

P.O. Box 181

Los Angeles

June 24, 1922.

Fairest Ludendorf:

Grateful, grateful, grateful. Herewith my Gastonian compliments and an Alphonsian bow. I think you are right as to the probable sale of the book. Any chance that it had of selling was done for long ago.

I see where two of my old employes,[1] Mrs. Oliver Harriman, now running the Campfire Girls and James M. West, head of the Boy Scouts are to be two thirds of a committee to regulate the morals of the movies. The Boy Scouts and The Camp Fire Girls. It serves that noble art just right.

As for Sir George Nathan and his woes, well——these Englishmen, you know. They will never stay away from the servants.

Dreiser

I have written Hume & Dodd[2]

1. Judge James B. West and Mrs. Harriman worked for the Butterick firm at the time Dreiser was chief editor of its publications.
2. The postscript is handwritten.

[UPL]

H. L. Mencken

1524 Hollins St.

Baltimore.

June 29th [1922]

Dear Dreiser:-

Ed. Howe, who is close to the heart of Kansas, makes the definite announcement in this month's issue of his paper that the Second Coming of

Xt is at hand, and that Will H. Hays is the Man.[1] Tell all the hoors at once! The post of Mary of Magdala is not yet filled. I nominate you for Judas. The role of Pontius Pilate I reserve for myself.

I shall see Hume in New York next week. Dodd is a hollow fellow, but it might be a good idea to let him do The Genius. I doubt that there would be a large sale, but he might get rid of 5,000 or 10,000.

I had dinner with Kirah in New York last week, along with Scott,[2] a German and a Frenchman. She is still an excellent cook, and looks younger than ever. The day before she got news of the death of her mother.

Pray excuse me, my dear Sir. A bootlegger has just come in.

Yours,
M.

1. E. W. Howe (1853–1937), journalist, novelist, editor. Mencken is referring to *E. W. Howe's Monthly* and, mockingly, to the Republican politician Will Hays.
2. Howard Scott.

[UPL]

SMART SET
Edited by
George Jean Nathan
and
H. L. Mencken

[after 20 October 1922]

Hail, Christian![1]

1. To this Mencken appended an unidentified newspaper clipping that reads: "Theodore Dreiser, the novelist, has returned to New York from California and is occupying a studio next to Sherwood Anderson in St. Luke's place. Dreiser is one of the most picturesque figures today in American literature. He has written honestly against the bitterest odds and altho his hair is thatched with gray and he shows the strain of the discouraging years, he never lifts his voice in complaint. Dreiser has never touched tobacco or liquor." Dreiser had returned to New York from California in early October, and Mencken returned from Europe on 20 October 1922.

[NYP]

16 St. Lukes Place
New York City

Oct 23rd 1922

The Henry L. Mencken Detective Service
1524 Hollins St. Baltimore, Md.
Dear Chief:

I hear that Theodore Dreiser is at large in New York & that he has already pulled several crooked deals. Better turn your best men loose on him.

I Spy.

[UPL]

H. L. Mencken
1524 Hollins St.
Baltimore.

October 28th [1922]

Dear Dreiser:-

I hear from New York that you are thinking of doing an unexpurgated edition of "The 'Genius'" next year. Is this true? If it is, I'd like to know it in advance, so that it may not appear to Sumner that I was fooling him about the cuts. He acted very decently and I don't want to him to think that I was stringing him.

What are you doing?

Yours,
M

[NYP]

16 St. Lukes Place
New York City

Oct. 29—1922

Dear M—

You will recieve shortly I am fairly sure an inquiry in regard to the Sister Carrie ms. The gentleman will want to know your selling price. He is one who desires to buy in all of my mss. & gather them under one roof. I have nothing to say—no desire to interfere—as to any use or disposition you choose to make of the mss. But if you do decide to sell will you be good enough not to ask <u>less</u> than $2,000. The ms. will be cheap to him at that price and unless you do ask it you will be underselling me and some others—cutting the price. "Free" brought $300. The Blue Sphere $300. Laughing Gas—$300. The Girl in the Coffin is now held at $800 by the owner. I have recieved a record price for the original of Jennie Gerhardt & it will be no hardship to you to recieve $2000 in case you decide to sell. This is the only favor I ask in connection with that ms.

Yes, I am at the above address. Painters, paperhangers & floor men are on the job. When it becomes presentable—say in 8 more days or so I will be glad to have you look in on me. 7th ave Subway to Houston Street— walk back two short blocks. It faces Hudson Pk. No telephone as yet.

The Author of the Gospel of St. Luke

[UPL]

H. L. Mencken
1524 Hollins St.
Baltimore.

October 30th [1922]

Dear Dreiser:-

I received a letter from Lang,[1] but answered, of course, that the MS. of "Sister Carrie" was not for sale. However, if you think it would be a good thing to let him assemble all your MS. I might be induced, by suitable arts, to hand the MS. back to you. Let us be frank. If you are short of money, it is yours, now or at any time. But no other scoundrel ever gets it. I hate to think of it going to Milwaukee. When I die my kidneys go to the Municipal Museum of Altoona, Pa., and my liver to Oberlin College, but it would take much eloquence to make me leave even my thyroid gland to Milwaukee.

I have almost got through my accumulated mail: a fearful job. I'll be back in New York in a week or two. Do we meet then?

Yours,
H. L. M.

1. W. W. Lange, who collected Dreiser books and manuscripts.

[NYP]

16 St. Lukes Place
New York City.

Nov 5—1922

[To Mencken]

Parding, Captain, this long delay in answering your several courteous notes & inquiries. I have been slaving—unpacking barrels, boxes & crates & rearranging them as is our human way. In another week I hope to have this accursed joint presentable.

In re Sumner. Various discussions here with Hume, Dodd, Briggs, Liveright & others have led me to know that if I publish an ex-purgated version of The "Genius" I will not sell. Expurgated versions of anything do not sell at all and I will have had the mealy pleasure of seeing the book issued & forgotten in that secondary form. Besides Liveright is now having certain lawyers & other vultures of the local District Attorneys staff look into the possibility of defeating Sumner in a fight which is to begin with the publication of the book as it is. I did not ask him to do this. He asked me if I would not prefer to have the book re-issued as it stands. Of course. Then he asked permission to look into the chances of winning via a process of fixation—I believe I have given that permission. If he weakens I may let Dodd Mead proceed. Hume knows my point of view. I went to his office & told him what I had heard & how I felt. You can tell Sumner as much of this as you think is wise—giving my chances as much consideration as you please.

In re Sister Carrie. I do not ask you to sell the book. As a matter of fact if approached again—even with an offer of $2,000 I wish you would rest until you hear from me. Certain things have developed here which make a high priced sale entirely possible. If I should arrange a deal such as you personally could not effect and it meant a round sum & you wanted to take over some ready cash would you split the returns. Your share should be over $2000. Same to me & something to a third mysterious grafter.

Glad you are back & hope to hear that Germany is feeling better. N.Y. to me is a scream—a Kyke's dream of a Ghetto. The lost tribe has taken the island. I plan to return to Chicago permanently I believe next year. There is a Spaghetti joint over this way. Drop down & I will have them weave a spaghetti overcoat for you

Simon—called Peter.

[UPL]

H. L. Mencken
1524 Hollins St.
Baltimore.

November 11th [1922]

Dear Dreiser:-
Can you lunch with me on Tuesday? If so, will you meet me at the office, 25 west 45th street, at noon? I want to show you our objects of art. If you can't will you call me up at the office Monday afternoon or Tuesday morning? We can victual alone and discuss the issues of the day.

Yours,
M

[NYP]

16 St. Lukes Place
N.Y.C.

Nov 14—1922

Listen, Menck:
Why not go to one of the representatives of Abrams   Either here or in Baltimore & have him submit a sample of your blood to Abrams for a diagnosis.[1] Or, do this. Prick your arm with a clean needle & wipe the drop of blood off with a clean sheet of paper & send the paper to me. I saw several remarkable things done by his wave machine & I think once you knew where the complaint lies it could be reached. Don't fuss & don't shout nonsense. I wish you would let me get this diagnosis for you anyhow. I'll do it with affection for my old college friend—Sing Sing college

Dreiser

1. See Dreiser to Mencken, before 31 May 1921, n.1.

[NYP]

16 St. Lukes Pl.
New York City

Dec 6—1922

Dear Mencken:
Yes, I received Prejudices III & read in it several hours. Such things as Spangled Men, Memorial Service, Five Men at Random and Advice to

Young Men—or a part of it—I had read before. I like such things as <u>On Being an American</u>, <u>Huneker</u>, your defense of the critic as an artist[1] and <u>The Novel</u>. All of the stuff is really vastly entertaining   You always muster a fresh and refreshing style & brisk and refreshing thoughts. That the people you openly attack in On Being an American dont retaliate is a marvel to me. I assume that your aim is to goad them into action.

In regard to the critic as artist—You never were a critic really. You have as you say—a definite point of view & philosophy & you have used the critical role to put it over   Your comments on life have always been vastly more diverting to me than your more intensive comment on books. I notice the freer brush strokes the moment you set forth your direct observations on men & things.

Its a good book & ought to sell. I presume all of your things do. But I still think you ought to do a cynical slap-stick political farce with all our stuffed figures galvanized into action. If you want to dine with me call me up when you come—Telephone Spring 8376. I have one now. Dont give my address to a soul

Dreiser

1. "Footnote on Criticism."

H. L. Mencken
1524 Hollins St.
Baltimore.

December 16th [1922]

Dear Dreiser:-

This is by long odds the best view of you that I have ever seen.[1] It would do honor to my house if you adorned a copy of the original with some chaste thought from Holy Scripture, and sent it to me to frame at a cost of $7 and hang on the wall. I'll put it between Joseph Conrad and Bismarck. Hoch, hoch, dreimal hoch![2]

I was pallbearer for an old friend this afternoon. A funeral far in the Maryland hinterland: 30 miles by motor. Two widows showed up and there was a hell of a dramatic moment. Sin pursues a man to the very threshold of Hell.

In Xt.,
HLM

1. The picture has not been identified.
2. Three cheers.

[UPL]

H. L. Mencken
1524 Hollins St.
Baltimore.

December 21st [1922]

Dear Dreiser:-

My obeisance for the picture. A most noble likeness. I'd be delighted to have the large one. If I don't spend $6.25 framing it, and then hang it between Conrad and Bismarck, then put me down a liar forevermore. I am redecorating my office here, and hope to make it one of the sights of the Western World.

Let me know of it when you finally decide to do "The 'Genius'", so that I can get rid of Sumner without laying myself open to the charge of double-crossing him.[1]

I shall spend the Geburtstag[2] gradually engulfing two bottles of Brauenberger 1917.

Hume telephoned me that he had found you through the Children's Aid Society after he wrote to me.

Yours,
M

1. On 18 December, Dreiser wrote Mencken that he had demanded that Dodd-Mead publish the unexpurgated *The "Genius"* or Liveright would get the book; and that Liveright had fixed it so that the district attorney's office would not back Sumner in the case. [NYP]
2. Birthday.

[NYP-T]
[December 1922]

To
My faithful and virtuous son
HENRY L. MENCKEN, S.J.
from his spiritual
guide and present
gaurdian,—now at rest
in the bosom of Abraham

John
Cardinal Gibbons
Pax

[UPL]

H. L. Mencken
1524 Hollins St.
Baltimore.

December 29th [1922]

Dear Dreiser:-

My best thanks for that noble effigy. It goes to the framer at once. I have ordered a frame of Egyptian ebony, with an inner rim of light green velvet. This will fit precisely into the Early Norddeutcher Lloyd style of my studio.

The drinks in New York grow worse and worse. Why not come down here some Saturday, sit through a refined evening with me, and then attend divine worship with me on Sunday, or not, as you say? Nothing but pre-war stuff. A few members of the crowd speak English.

Yours,
M

I shall retire from the turf on January 1st, I hope with honor. No more fornication.

[UPL-H]

H. L. Mencken
1524 Hollins St.
Baltimore.

[before 11 January 1923]

Dear Dreiser:

I'll be in New York next week. What do you say to a session Wednesday evening? Let us victual together, and then hold a patriotic soiree. I suggest meeting at your house at 6³⁰. If this is all right, let me know as above.

Yours,
M

We might get in Anderson¹ or some other fellows later in the evening.

1. Sherwood Anderson.

[NYP]

16 St. Lukes Pl.

Jan 11—1923

Yes, next Wednesday evening at 6:30 here is ok. I know a one-arm lunch stand around the corner where we can get bean soup for a dime. (Rolls &

butter free). T. R. Smith[1] with whom I lunched the other day said the next time you were over he was going to try to arrange a session at his place—that he had—or was installing a two burner gas stove. However he may have been caught in adultery by you and hence be off your list for life. As dreadful things have happened before. Sherwood Anderson lives 3 doors from here. The crown-prince of Bavaria only 5 doors. He travels under the name Essensprisen and is the 2nd assistant janitor here. A. A. Brill, M.D.[2]—a fine, jovial fellow & one of the crack Freudians of this side lives at 1 West 70th   If you would deign to go up there he keeps good food & booze. Ditto Jacques Loeb.[3]

Make up your list.

Choose your poison early

Heinrich Heine

1. T. R. Smith, an editor at Boni and Liveright.
2. A. A. Brill, psychiatrist, author, translator of Freud.
3. Jacques Loeb, biologist whose theory of animal tropism influenced Dreiser.

[UPL]

H. L. Mencken
1524 Hollins St.
Baltimore.

January 13th [1923]

Dear Dreiser:-

I suggest that we dine at the one-arm lunch together and then have a refined session at your atelier and invite in the neighbors. If you ask Smith, tell him to bring along a few cases of beer. I'll bring a bottle of Schnapps containing not more than 4% of wood alcohol. I suggest: Smith, Anderson, Brill, Boyd. Time: 9 P.M. If any new cuties have showed up in the Village, send for 9 or 10 head of them. I'll present myself in white gloves at 6.30. There are some matters of state that I want to lay before you before the populace assembles.

Have you enough hymn-books to go 'round?

Yours in Sso. Corde Jesu,
Has und Bier,
Das rat ich Dir.[1]

1. My advice to you is, have a beer. In place of a customary closing, Mencken pasted in these lines from an unidentified source.

[UPL]

H. L. Mencken
1524 Hollins St.
Baltimore.

March 4th [1923]

Dear Dreiser:-
What do you make of Anderson's Many Marriages?[1] To me it seems to be pretty much a muddle—a mass of ideas that are not worked out. Let me hear your view, pianissimo.

I am laid up with laryngitis, unable to speak, and full of sinful thoughts. Your prayers would be appreciated.

Yours,
M

1. Sherwood Anderson's novel was published in 1923.

[UPL]

H. L. Mencken
1524 Hollins St.
Baltimore.

March 9th [1923]

Dear Dreiser:-
I agree with you.[1] Anderson's short stories often give me a great kick (as Scott Fitzgerald would say), but his novels usually seem a bit confused and muddy. I doubt that he has the sheer power needed to swing a long book. But his details are often superb.

I am laid up with a severe laryngitis, and can't speak. It is a mercy. I am in training for my last days as a Trappist.

Yours,
M.

1. Dreiser's letter is missing.

[NYP]

[before 20 March 1923]

Dear Mencken:
Liveright is running this ad—or is going to—in a number of magazine. If he hasn't contracted to put it in the Smart Set—I wish you would let

me know as I want to see it in there. What would it cost for one, two &
three months.

Dreiser

Do you think it is a really good adv. Return the adv.

[UPL]

SMART SET
Edited by
George Jean Nathan
and
H. L. Mencken

March 20, 1923

Dear Dreiser:

There is a special publishers' rate for advertisements in The Smart
Set. I enclose a rate card. It is 36c an agate line a month straight. They tell
me here that your advertisement would work out to about $75 a month. In
addition, we run a page of small book advertisements. A one inch space
on this page costs $12.50 a month straight.

I think your advertisement is very effective typographically, but some
of the text seems to me to be rather silly. For example, the paragraph beginning "Mr. Dreiser is the only American novelist who rises to heights of
cosmic sublimity." This is nonsense. Again, under the title of "The Bulwark", I am credited with the following sentence: "In 'The Bulwark' especially the big power of Dreiser's massive impetus is evident." I never
said anything of the sort. If I did, I was drunk. The fact is, as you know, I
have never seen the manuscript of "The Bulwark". Otherwise, it seems to
me the advertisement is very effective. I enclose the proof.

Sincerely yours,
M

[NYP-T]

16 St. Luke's Place.

March 21, 1923.

Dear Mencken:

This matter of crediting you with praise of the Bulwark springs from
rank carelessness on the part of some one as you will see for yourself in a

moment. Take a look at the enclosed slip printed for me by Liveright several years ago. You will see, I am sure, where the crazy statement comes from. Because something that you did say is coupled with an additional statement made by the prospective publisher the two, taken together, are carelessly credited to you by whoever was putting the adv. together. I have but now called Liverights attention to this error and he has promised, with various apologies, to eliminate it in the future. But since that doesn't make good for the past I rise to inquire what else you think should be done. And I am sorry.

As for cosmic sublimity,—well, I have been accused of many things but not just this particular thing before. Plainly I grow worse and worse. The truth is until a half hour before I mailed you this page I had never seen it and I did not even read it carefully, merely taking in the general effect. It came with a note from Liveright in which he said that it had already appeared in the Dial, New Republic and I believe, The Nation. I have been so pushed by other things in hand that I have not tried to follow all the publicity being sent out. And, as is usual in such cases, it has not been put before me. Curses on all ad. writers.

I note, by the way, that you most carefully and even painfully spell out the word advertisement. By way of rebuke? I fancy adv. and ad. sandpaper your aesthetic soul. With me all advertisements deserve to be referred to as ads. or advs. The less of them the better.

Dreiser

[UPL]

H. L. Mencken
1524 Hollins St.
Baltimore.

March 23rd [1923]

Dear Dreiser:-

I'm sorry if you thought I was peevish about that matter of "The Bulwark". The fact is that I scarcely ever pick up one of the weeklies without finding an advertisement crediting me with something I have never said. I long ago gave up protesting. As for Liveright, I shall punish him by having 20 anonymous letters written to Sumner, complaining that "The Story of Mankind" [1] is obscene.

The "cosmic sublimity" stuff is simply garbage. What in hell does it mean, if anything. I hope you make Liveright cut it out. If you don't, some comedian will notice it and poke fun at it. Incidently, I discovered in

New York after writing to you that the Smart Set could not print the advertisement. A complex and unintelligent matter, too long to explain. In brief, an idiotic contract with a wholesaler of advertising prohibits the magazine selling any book advertising direct save the small $12.50 boxes that I mentioned. Every full page advertisement must go into all of this wholesaler's magazines, not the Smart Set alone. Who made this contract I don't know. It seems insane to me.

My whole family has been ill, but everyone is now recovering. I met Gloom on the train coming down this afternoon. She was on the way to New Windsor to see her mother, who has had a stroke of paralysis and is very ill.

The word "ad" is one of my abominations, along with "alright". I pray God every night to send the great pox to every man who uses either. It is a harsh prayer, but that is the way I feel about it. God knows why. A silly prejudice, that is all.

Liveright called me up the other day and said he was hatching another bawdy lunch-party. I told him that I'd be delighted to honor him. He gives good parties.

Look at the enclosed (which please return).[2] The old boy seems to be much disturbed. It goes without saying that I never said what I am accused of saying. Who starts such imbecile lies? In this case I suspect a woman who has vowed to have me deported from the United States because I once refused to pander to her baser appetites. As a matter of politeness I would have been glad to roger her, but at the moment I happened to be too drunk.

Yours,
M

1. *The Story of Mankind* (1921), by Hendrick Van Loon (1882–1944), journalist and historian.
2. This has disappeared.

[NYP]

16 St. Lukes Pl
N.Y.C

April 2nd 1923

Dear Mencken:

If you are so greivously pained by alright how do you endure already? This is not to trouble you unduly. I want to know how I may procure a few decent prints or proofs of the libellous drawing of me in your April issue.[1] I want them for my lawyer.

Dreiser

1. The "libellous drawing" by Hans Stengel shows the massive figure of Dreiser surrounded by Lilliputian-type women in lewd positions or hanging from Dreiser's pockets or being crushed in his grip. It is included in a series of four drawings entitled "The World as Seen by Four American Novelists" and includes Anderson, Cabell, and Hergesheimer.

[UPL]

H. L. Mencken
1524 Hollins St.
Baltimore.

April 3rd [1923]

Dear Dreiser:-

How can I endure already? I can't. I always write it all ready, which is correct.[1] Would you convert all aboard into alaboard, or all night into al-night? You shock me.

I am having 10,000 copies[2] of the Stengel drawing struck off. It makes you a very handsome fellow.

Yours,
M

1. Dreiser circled "which is correct" and wrote:
"See Webster's International Dictionary
  The Standard   "   "
  Starmouth English "   "
Are you getting up a dictionary of your own?"
2. Dreiser circled "10,000 copies" and wrote "I want 100,000."

[UPL]

H. L. Mencken
1524 Hollins St.
Baltimore.

April 16th [1923]

Dear Dreiser:-

Thanks very much for the French version of "Twelve Men".[1] I had no idea that so many of your books had already got into French. I only hope they help to civilize the Frogs. See that you get your royalties promptly. By 1928 Hindenburg will be in Paris, and it will be too late.

I don't know French well enough to judge the translation. I only hope it is better done than Franz Blei's German version of my "In Defense of Women".[2] Blei farmed it out to one of his wenches, and she done me dirt.

Not only is Harding to run again, but also Coolidge. God works in a mysterious way, His wonders to perform!

Yours,
M

Alright: have your way! I hate the word, but refuse to get alhetup.

1. *Douze Hommes*, trans. Fernande Helie (Paris: F. Rieder, 1923). Dreiser inscribed the book, "For Mencken from Dreiser. Bows Genuflections Hand-Kissings. N.Y. April 13–1923."
2. *Verteidigung der Frau*, trans. Franz Blei (Munich: Muller, 1923).

[UPL]

H. L. Mencken
1524 Hollins St.
Baltimore.

May 10th [1923]

Dear Dreiser:-

Will you join me on a committee to raise a fund for a statue of Benedict Arnold, to be presented to the British nation for deposit in Westminster Abbey? It won't cost you a cent; the money will be raised in St. Bartholomew's parish. The plan is for the whole committee to accompany the statue to London, and there get horribly drunk. Let me have your views.

Yours,
M

[UPL]

H. L. Mencken
1524 Hollins St.
Baltimore.

May 12th [1923]

Dear Dreiser:-

I take it that you will sit on the committee. I have also invited Rex Beach, as a sop to his feelings for your insults.[1] You Village authors can't understand the red-blooded fellows of the wild West. Beach has balls as big as Indian clubs.

Incidently, how would you like to put in an evening drinking beer in Union Hall, N.J. I am privy to a noble place there, with real beer. On the wall is an elegant picture of Heidelberg Castle by moonlight. The place will delight you—a fossil surviving from the Christian era. Say the word, and you are invited.[2]

Yours in Xt.,
M

1. Rex Beach (1877–1949), novelist. On behalf of the Authors' League, Beach had asked Dreiser to support a plan to improve moving pictures, and Dreiser publicly criticized him and the League for not fighting against the Clean Books Bill recently before the New York state legislature (see Dreiser to Beach, 5 May 1923, in Elias, *Letters*, 2:408–410).
2. On 14 May 1923, Dreiser sent a note accepting the invitation.

[UPL]

H. L. Mencken
1524 Hollins St.
Baltimore.

May 31st [1923]

Dear Dreiser:-

I think you waste your time quarreling with such a hollow fellow as Burgess, or with the Authors' League.[1] The organization is frankly devoted to protecting the business of movie authors, and has no possible concern with artistic questions. I resigned from it five or six years ago, and have since exposed its stupidity several times, notably in Prejudices II. You might as well carry on a debate with the American Legion or the Lambs' Club. Some time ago Beach asked me to sit on his movie committee. I, of course, refused instantly. But my name was published, nevertheless, as a member of the committee. A gang of cads.

You say in your letter to Burgess that you have always fought "The 'Genius'" battle single-handed. With all due respect, you lie like an archbishop. Young Hersey[2] sweated for you like a bull, and there was a critic in Baltimore who, as I recall it, laid out $300 in cash to round up the authors of the United States on your side. Most of them true enough, ratted, but that was surely not his fault.

How are you, anyhow? I am thinking of giving up literature and returning to the cigar business.

Yours,
M

1. The humorist F. Gelette Burgess. When Dreiser published his letter to Rex Beach, Burgess publicly replied to Dreiser and referred to him as the author of "dubious sex-fiction" (New York *Telegram*, 19 May 1923). In reply, Dreiser also went public, attacking the Authors' League and alluding to Burgess's requests that he read the fiction of Mrs. Burgess (see Dreiser to Burgess, undated, in Elias, *Letters*, 2:410–17). In the letter, Dreiser says in passing: "I fought the 'Genius' issue single handed for five years. And I am still fighting it—single handed"—a comment that Mencken challenges in this letter.
2. Harold Hersey.

[NYP]

16 St. Lukes Pl.

June 2nd 1923

It is true.

I admit that I am a victim of the archepiscopal failing.

However I have this to offer in extenuation.

I plan to do you full justice in a later work.

But in case this terrifies you I will make you this offer. You say you have already spent $100 in my behalf.

Send me $400 more and I will agree not to do you full justice in any later work.

Carpe diem

Hart Schaffiner Marx

[UPL]

H. L. Mencken
1524 Hollins St.
Baltimore.

June 4th [1923]

Dear Dreiser:-

Goodman, Boyd and I are planning to go to Union Hill next Tuesday night, the 11th, to drink the waters. Why not come along? Let me know as above. We'll probably start at 8.15.

Yours,
M

I made a mistake: the exact amount was $417.22. Knit me a necktie, and we'll call it square. Are you going to the Liveright dinner? If so, we'll meet again there. I am practising the following limerick:

There was a young lady of Bray
Who bought her a new whirling spray;
   She said, "Ah, that's better
   Now I've found the French letter
That I lost on Armistice Day."

[NYP]

16 St. Lukes Pl

June 6—1923

[To Mencken]
    Tuesday is not the 11th but the 12th. Dost mean Monday or Tuesday.
Union Hill—yea.
Boyd—yea.
Goodman—well—don't know him
Mencken—nay.
8.15—yea.

Ben Kuppenheimer

[UPL]

H. L. Mencken
1524 Hollins St.
Baltimore.

July 11th [1923]

Dear Dreiser:-
    Dr. Franz Blei writes that a German publisher wants him to put you
into German, and suggests beginning with "The 'Genius'". His address is
Luitpoldstr. 41, Berlin. Blei, of course, is an important man, but I don't
know what arrangements you have made in Germany. Will you please
write to him? My own feeling is that it would be better to start with a
shorter book, say "Sister Carrie" or "Twelve Men".

Sincerely yours,
M

[NYP]

16 St. Lukes Pl.

[after 11 July 1923]

Sure I'll write Blei. Thanks. But isn't this a rotten time to publish in Germany.

I'll buy you a dinner at Lüchows any summer night—if I'm still here

Enrico Caruso.

[UPL]

H. L. Mencken
1524 Hollins St.
Baltimore.

July 13 [1923]

Dear Dreiser:-

Done! Let us do it the next time I am in your fair city.

Regarding Blei, I have no recommendation. He did my "In Defense of Women" and it seemed all right to me, but experts tell me that he lost 9/10th of the flavor of the book. The report in Germany is that he is too lazy to do any actual translation himself—that he farms it out to women. He is regarded as the premier copulator of the empire. At last accounts he was living with 8 women. But I shouldn't tell you this: it will make you jealous of him.

Foreign rights are never worth much. Van Loon, I believe, got an average of not much above $100 from Sweden, Holland, France, Italy, etc., for "The Story of Mankind". The French who have done "Twelve Men" will probably swindle you.

I am printing here on Monday the first of a series of articles tackling the Anglo-Saxon head-on. I'll send you a copy.

Yours,
M

[UPL]

H. L. Mencken
1524 Hollins St.
Baltimore.

July 28th [1923]

Dear Dreiser:-

The Berlingske Tidende is one of the leading papers of Copenhagen, with a large circulation.[1] George Brandes often writes for it. I think you can trust the editor to get a good translation. It often prints translations, and must have a good staff.

Confidentially, I am at work on plans for a new review[2]—something far above anything hitherto seen in the Republic. Knopf is to be the publisher. It will probably come out toward the end of the year. Have you anything in hand or in mind that ought to be in it? Or do you know of any other stuff that is likely? I hope to line up a gang of very good contributors. It will horn into politics, economics, the sciences, etc., as well as into beautiful letters.

Keep this quiet for the present.

Yours,
M

1. In an earlier, undated note Dreiser had asked whether "this is really a good Scandinavian paper. And how am I to assure myself of a decent translation [of a section of *Sister Carrie*]." [UPL]
2. *American Mercury.*

[NYP]

Monticello, N.Y.
General Delivery

July 31—1923

Dear Helen L. Menken[1]:

In case you wish to file charges against me before Sept 1 you may send decoy letters to the above address. I am hiding in the woods just east of here.

Fatrick Arbuckle

1. Dreiser is here referring to Helen Menken (1901–1966), stage and radio actress noted for her flamboyant performances and fiery temper. In doing so, he playfully casts Mencken in the role of the "outraged woman" and himself in the Fatty Arbuckle role.

[NYP-Pc]

Monticello, N.Y.

Aug 4 1923

Dear Mr. Menckhorn:

If you want to run up here I agree to give you bed & board in a lovely greenwood undisturbed save by blue-jays, horse-flies & deep sea going mosquitos   Farm hands are the principal export. Rates on application—and up.

Percy Bysshe Gray

[UPL]

H. L. Mencken
1524 Hollins St.
Baltimore.

August 2nd [1923]

Dear Dreiser:-

All I have to say is that you will be very foolish if you credit the common superstition that country girls are free of microorganisms. The fact is that they fairly swarm with gonococci. Certainly it would be a hell of a scandal for a man of your years and dignity to come down with such a malaise. Be very careful, and don't spare the bichloride. Better still, try to restrain your baser nature until you get back to the city, where sanitary science flourishes.

I am hard at work on the new review. Why don't you do a piece for it? You may attack the Methodists by name, and call the Baptists the Sewer Rats of God if you please.

Yours in Xt.,
M

[NYP]

Monticello, N.Y.

Aug 8—1923

Dear Mencken:-

Your plan for a critical weekly—after the format of Nation or New Republic I presume—interests me not a little. You will have no trouble in making it vital & arresting I am positive and I will be glad to do what I can for you. A thing that I would rather like to write would be a comparative study of what the average American thinks he wishes & what he really wishes; what he thinks he is like and—what he is like. But I also think that you are one better fitted to write that than I am. Other subjects will occur to me & I will suggest them.

By the way in the last two years I have pencilled down some one hundred & fifty free verse poems in the vein of those I once showed you & four of which you published. Liveright & his group think rather well of them as do some other individuals to whom I have shown them. You wouldn't be interested I presume in a small group selected from these for your new publication   I have tested them out & find that they have more of an appeal than I thought they would have. Let me know.

Jesus Marie Jose Manganillo

[UPL]
August 9th [1923]

Dear Dreiser:-

President Coolidge has asked me to nominate six men to constitute a committee to write and compile the Harding Memorial Volume.[1] It will include selections from his speeches and state papers, copies of his baptismal, confirmation and marriage certificates, a series of snapshots of him, and half a dozen or more tributes to him by eminent literati. I have suggested your name and those of Nicholas Murray Butler, Harry Kempf,[2] Edward W. Bok, Alfred Kreymborg and Bugs Baer. You will receive your badge and press-card direct from the White House. Pray do not fail me.

The tears shed here have raised the Patapsco river 4 feet and spoiled the crabbing.

Yours,
Henry Van Dyke

1. On 2 August 1923 Warren Harding died and Vice-President Coolidge succeeded him.
2. Mencken means Harry Kemp.

[UPL]

H. L. Mencken
1524 Hollins St.
Baltimore.

August 10th [1923]

Dear Dreiser:-

The new one is not to be a weekly, but a monthly along the lines of the Mercure de France and the London Mercury, but very much more violent, and, I hope, amusing. Its main aim will be to shake up the Anglo-Saxon. Physically, at all events, it will be very fine. Knopf is spreading himself. God knows when the first number will be out—probably toward the end of the year. I must first get rid of the Smart Set, which has been a fearful nuisance for five years past, what with its narrow field, smelling history and lack of money.

Let me see the poems, by all means. It is not yet decided finally whether the new monthly is to print poetry, but I am eager to see the stuff anyhow. The article you mention embodies an excellent idea. Why not write it? My agents report that you have some unpublished woman sketches. What do you want for them? May I see them?

Yours,
M

[NYP]

16 St. Lukes Pl.
N.Y.C.

Aug 21—1923

Dear Mencken:

Back here again, temporarily anyhow. Shall I forward poems to you here—care S.S.—or Knopf,—or to Baltimore? Is Nathan to be co-editor? Of the studies of women only twelve are so far done & two sold. The most difficult ones I have been reserving for the last. Expect to do four more[1]   Can let you see the unsold ones. But are you paying any thing or just nominally paying. Let me know.

Dreiser

1. These became part of *A Gallery of Women* (1929).

[NYP]

16 St Lukes Pl.

Aug 31—1923

Dear Mencken:

Did you get those alleged poems? I sent them by express. You usually acknowledge so I'm wondering. Don't want to lose them

Dreiser

[UPL]

H. L. Mencken
1524 Hollins St.
Baltimore.

September 1st [1923]

Dear Dreiser:-

The Polizei are intercepting your mail again. I wrote to you about the poems at least a week ago. I am going to New York tomorrow, and then talk out with Knopf our policy regarding poetry, which is now very vague. Could we use part of the stuff, say four or five poems in a group? If so, what do you want for it? Let me know at the S.S. office. This, of course, is for the American Mercury. I am leaving the S.S. as soon as possible.

Yours,
M

[NYP]

16 St. Lukes Pl
N.Y.C

Sept 4—1923

Sire:

I never recieved the letter about the scribblings. Will you repeat. As for using 5 in the Mercurie de Amerique, sure. And you may fix your own price. It will save haggling. Got your screed anent the American novel. Thanks.

D.

[NYP]

16 St. Lukes Pl
N.Y.C

Sept 9—1923

Dear Menck:

Please change the title of <u>Neuvaine</u> to <u>Proteus</u>.[1] I like that better and am changing my copy accordingly.

The more I think of the name <u>American</u> <u>Mercury</u> the less I like it. It sounds tame and colorless. Why not <u>H.L.M.</u> as a name for the paper or <u>Menckenathan</u>   If you could find something with the ring of <u>K.K.K.</u> or <u>One</u> <u>Hundred Per Cent</u> or <u>Oh</u>, <u>Hell</u> or <u>Haw Haw</u> you'd have something. It need not be quite so raw—but you get the idea. Or is it all set and advertised

Dreiser

1. This refers to one of the poems Dreiser had sent to Mencken.

[UPL]

H. L. Mencken
1524 Hollins St.
Baltimore.

September 10th [1923]

Dear Dreiser:-

1. The title is changed to Proteus.

2. Phil Goodman writes that his first week's takings with his new piece were $19,000. I am suggesting to him that he give us a bang-up party in gratitude for God's beneficence.

3. The names you suggest would give the thing away. What we need is something that looks highly respectable outwardly. The American Mercury is almost perfect for that purpose. What will go on inside the tent is another story. You will recall that the late P. T. Barnum got away with burlesque shows by calling them moral lectures.

Yours,
M

[NYP]

118 West 11th St.
N.Y.C

Sept. 20—1923

Dear Mink:
Please note my new address. The telephone number is Chelsea 2631
Dreiser

[NYP]
[1923]

[To Mencken]
I suggest an American Pantheon in London to house the entire Wilson official family—with unusually florate columns for Admiral Sims, Herbert Hoover, David(?) W. Gerard, Mr. Palmer, Mr. Creel, Ambassador Page, Brand Whitlock, etc. The grand central sarcaphagus must contain the man who abolished war. An elevated and enshrined ark of gold & silver & Precious stones should house the 14 points. To this edifice and result I hereby subscribe fourteen marks or rubles as the subscription committee may decide

Ralph Waldo Emerson

[UPL]

H. L. Mencken
1524 Hollins St.
Baltimore.

October 4th [1923]

Dear Dreiser:-

My best thanks. I am forwarding your subscription to Knopf at once. He reports that he already has 39,450[1] paid-up subscriptions. I fear he exaggerates.

He'll probably begin to pay for MSS in a week or two.

Yours,
M

1. Dreiser circled this, wrote "Do you believe this," and returned the letter. Mencken returned it, writing below Dreiser's question, "I do <u>not</u>—12,000 to start with would be wonderful, but I <u>do</u> think Knopf a very able hustler."

[UPL]

H. L. Mencken
1524 Hollins St.
Baltimore.

December 8th [1923]

Dear Dreiser:-

My best thanks for "The Color of a Great City".[1] Liveright has made a very sightly book. An excellent idea.

I note, by the way, that Liveright is announcing an edition of "Free" in the Modern Library with an introduction by me. For the life of me I can't remember writing any such introduction. I am asking Smith what it is about.

As one Christian to another, I wish you a wet Christmas.

Yours,
HLM

1. Dreiser inscribed *The Color of a Great City* (1923): "For Henry L. Mencken—his first editions. Theodore Dreiser."

5

In Brief, Go to Hell!
(1924–1926)

"Dear Heinrich: As my oldest living enemy I venture to offer you this little pamphlet. Don't mind if it emits a destructive gas. Us Germans—you know."
TD to HLM, inscription to An American Tragedy *(1925)*.

"Here we have the effects of reading 'The "Genius"' upon the American mind. In brief, go to Hell!"
HLM to TD, inscription to Americana *(1925)*

By 1924 Dreiser was nervously absorbed in a long novel. For *An American Tragedy*, which would run to one million words in manuscript, he concentrated his energies in ways he had not for over ten years. In addition to his studio at St. Luke's Place in Greenwich Village, he rented a working office in the Guardian Life Building. Finding Manhattan too distracting, he moved to a flat in Brooklyn, where he spent nearly a year completing the book. Helen Richardson joined him there, and later recalled the intensity of his work: "The story tracked him everywhere he went. He could only return to his desk as helplessly as a man under sentence."[1] His living habits changed, as he now alternated between long periods of seclusion and sporadic moments of release in play. To Mencken he said little about the novel, and they did not meet often.

When they did come together, they avoided intimate encounters, choosing instead to roar loudly in proverbial twenties fashion. After a few late-night sprees in mixed company, however, they concluded that "sex and beerparties do not agree" and abandoned the speakeasies for more discreet gatherings at Dreiser's place. In public, at least, they once again displayed mischievous high spirits, as when they exchanged inscriptions on a costly antique Bible on show at the Gotham Book Mart; and, to the dismay of the shop clerks, Mencken wrote "If it wasn't for me, Dreiser would be raising chickens in Kansas." In the company of Nathan and others, Mencken took to stuffing Dreiser's mailbox with gag items—

among other things, risqué notes, religious cards, bogus love letters, American flags, and pamphlets on spiritualism.

They had good reason to celebrate. Seventeen years after their first meeting at Butterick's, they were able to send each other books written about them. Burton Rascoe's *Theodore Dreiser* and two books on Mencken— one by Isaac Goldberg, the other by Ernest Boyd—were published in 1925. All assumed the importance of their long association. Novelist and critic were so closely linked that Mencken was asked before Rascoe to do the monograph, and Goldberg approached Dreiser for a piece on his friend. Mencken turned down the offer, saying he had already written too much about the novelist; Dreiser's reminiscence appeared in Goldberg's book (see Appendix 2, pp. 738–40).

Their triumphs did nothing to strengthen the friendship. An edge of defensiveness and caution was seldom missing, even in the festive moods. There was nothing new in this. But now that they were famous and the old survival tactics were no longer needed, mere personal differences were exaggerated. Mencken grew more intolerant of Dreiser's Greenwich Village friends, his gaucheries, and his uneven prose. In his writing, he still solemnly applauded Dreiser's past achievements, but in the *American Mercury*, contumely began to replace reasonable criticism. "Dreiser's heroes imitate the colossal adulteries of a guinea pig," he wrote there in 1924,[2] sounding very much like the puritans he once berated. In turn, Dreiser needled him about becoming a moralist, began letters to him with "Dear John Wesley," and asked about the state of his "Methodist soul."

The result was that they became more peevish, arguing over everything from the ethics of receiving advances on royalties to the sexual habits of "strong men." Whatever the pretext, they were most often talking about themselves. Mencken's editorial control of the *American Mercury* led to a replay of the old *Smart Set* bartering of editor and author, only this time Mencken could not use Nathan as a decoy. "Let us be business-like," Mencken pleaded, knowing how touchy Dreiser could be when negotiating a paycheck for work submitted. But the occasions for quarreling were too numerous, and both men were by now quick to see insult. The situation was made worse by the general unwillingness on either side to forget past injuries. Mencken, in particular, was coming to feel the need to reassess old alliances. Paraphrasing Dr. Johnson, he characteristically turned personal preference into general law:

A prudent man, remembering that life is short, gives an hour or two, now and then, to a critical examination of his friendships. He weighs them, edits them, tests the metal of them. A few he retains, perhaps with radical changes in their terms. But the majority he expunges from his minutes and tries to forget, as he tries to forget the cold and clammy loves of year before last.[3]

Mencken stuck to his rule, and his most notable friendships—with George Jean Nathan and Dreiser—were stricken from his ledgers by the middle of the decade.

The irony of their hostilities, at this point in their careers, must have impressed them at times. Yet it was difficult for either man to articulate the deeper causes of discontent. As a result, by late 1925 they were both smarting over imagined wounds. There was a misunderstanding over a visit to Sing Sing arranged by Mencken to allow Dreiser to gather material for the prison scenes in *An American Tragedy*. There was another misunderstanding over Dreiser's alleged negligence during the final illness of Mencken's mother. (The incident took place after Dreiser had finished his novel and had stopped for a few hours at Hollins Street on his way to Florida. Mencken informed him of his mother's condition, and Dreiser, in his haste to move on, offended Mencken, who, known for his vigils at the sickbeds of even casual friends, read callousness into Dreiser's manner. His mother's death the following day, 13 December 1925, fixed the incident in his mind; and despite Dreiser's moving letter of condolence [2 February 1926], Mencken could not bury his resentment.)

Then there was the matter of Mencken's response to *An American Tragedy*. The reviews that preceded Mencken's were, with few exceptions, spectacular. Joseph Wood Krutch called it "the greatest American novel of our generation"; Abraham Cahan wrote that its appearance "is an event of first-class importance in the history of American letters"; Carl Van Doren found he could compare it, for sheer compelling power among American novels, only to *Moby-Dick*; even Dreiser's and Mencken's old nemesis, Stuart Sherman, published a detailed and intelligent review and found it "massively impressive," one of the few great American novels.

In light of such notices, Mencken's *American Mercury* piece, "Dreiser in 840 Pages," was a little short of devastating. He introduced the book as a "shapeless and forbidding monster—a heaping cartload of raw material for a novel, with rubbish of all sorts intermixed—a vast, sloppy, chaotic thing of 385,000 words—at least 250,000 of them unnecessary!" After a summary of the story line (which he likened to "the plot of a three page story in *True Confessions*") and an extended attack on Dreiser's style, he summed up his position: "As a work of art, it is a colossal botch, but as a human document it is searching and full of a solemn dignity, and at times it rises to the level of genuine tragedy" (see Appendix 2, pp. 796–800).

What sense, as critical statement, can be made of the division Mencken maintains here? Surely the strained personal relations with Dreiser guided him in his appraisal, just as good feelings in the past had led him to soft-pedal the novelist's defects. Yet the review was not simply a cheap shot or an anomaly. Rather, it was one of many signs of Mencken's general decline as a critic of literature by the mid-twenties—a falling off that was signaled by, among other things, his campaign against various forms of literary modernism, his case for *This Side of Paradise* as a better book than *The Great Gatsby*, his preferences for Joseph Hergesheimer and James Branch Cabell over Hemingway and Faulkner, and for Lizette Woodworth Reese and George Sterling over T. S. Eliot and Robert Frost. By 1925 even a close friend like Ernest Boyd could note, in his book on Mencken, that the Sage of Baltimore was now more a publicist than a power in critical circles, and, as Edmund Wilson lamented, "the youngest of the younger literary generation . . . have thrown Mencken overboard."[4]

The literary commentary now coming from his desk—eccentric essays like "The Novel" and "The Poet and His Art"—as well as pieces like the review of *An American Tragedy*, suggest the reasons for this falling off. They highlight Mencken's regression as a critic, which stemmed not only from his growing indifference to fiction, but also from a type of criticism that, by this time, had raised prejudice to the level of principle and the critic to the level of the artist. It was criticism with a distinctive voice, which could expose, amuse, dazzle, and even inspire; but it always ran the risk of degenerating into hollow caricature when faced with ideas and expression outside its sympathies. And Mencken had lost sympathy not only with Dreiser but with much that was valuable in contemporary writing.

With this review, the personal and critical balance that Mencken had struggled so long to maintain finally gave way. So did the friendship. Mencken's subsequent comments about the novel in 1926 did nothing to help matters. In an essay on Edgar Lee Masters, for instance, he points to the deficiencies of the dialogue in Masters's novel *Mirage* (1924): "What is one to make of such inconceiveable banality? Is there worse in 'An American Tragedy'?"[5] Later in the year, Mencken's editorial assistant, Charles Angoff, met Dreiser, who complained about the critic:

"That boss of yours ought to stay in Baltimore on the *Sun* and keep out of writing about books. . . . [Eugene] O'Neill is luckier than the rest of us. He has George Nathan to write about him. Now, Nathan knows playwriting. I can feel it inside me. But Mencken—oh, well. What does it matter, anyway?"[6]

Mencken's opinion did matter, of course, more than any other's to Dreiser. As late as two years after the review, Mencken could complain that Dreiser was still "going about New York saying that I rushed my review of 'An American Tragedy' into the American Mercury in order to get ahead of

Sherman, and so poison the wells."[7] Mencken's response to the book badly hurt the novelist, who tried unsuccessfully to dismiss it without rancor: "As for your critical predilections, animosities, inhibitions,—et. cet. Tush. Who reads you? Bums and loafers. No goods. We were friends before ever you were a critic of mine, if I recall. And,—if an humble leman may speak up—may remain so—despite various—well—choose your insults." When the break came, the two men intuitively understood the extent of their alienation, and for over eight years they maintained a guarded silence.

Notes

1. Helen Dreiser, *My Life with Dreiser* (Cleveland and New York: World, 1951), 113.
2. "Clinical Notes," *American Mercury*, June 1924, 186.
3. "Types of Men: The Friend," *Prejudices: Third Series* (New York: Alfred A. Knopf, 1922), 277.
4. Edmund Wilson, "The All-Star Literary Vaudeville," in *American Criticism* (New York: Harcourt, Brace, 1926); repr. in *The Shores of Light* (New York: Farrar, Straus and Giroux, 1952), 236.
5. "Four Makers of Tales: Masters," *Prejudices: Fifth Series* (New York: Alfred A. Knopf, 1926), 60.
6. Charles Angoff, *H. L. Mencken: A Portrait from Memory* (New York: Thomas Yoseloff, Inc., 1956), 101.
7. Mencken to Irita Van Doren, 22 May 1928, in Forgue, *Letters*, 309.

The Correspondence
(1924–1926)

118 West 11th St.
N.Y.C.

Jan. 13, 1924.

Dear Menkhorn:

Certainly we can meet.[1] Fix your date beforehand.

Like the new Mercury very much but think it needs a certain touch now wanting. Will explain later. Don't publish too many of your own articles under assumed names. Your writing identifies itself about as a foghorn identifies itself. It bawls to heaven.

Boyd's article is simply delicious.[2] And how deftly he wields the scalpel. I also like the Santayana sketch.[3] That is the type of thing that might be used quite regularly. If I had time there is a series of studies I could do that would be well worth your while. I believe you would think so. But this novel is holding me.[4]

By the way isn't there some one in Baltimore whom you could induce to find out for me what the sales of the Genius to Jan. 1, last, was in the two or three leading book stores there. I have a feeling that the statement I have is off and would like to verify it up to a certain point. This statement is confidential.

Regards. Luck.

Dreiser

1. In a letter of 8 January 1924, Mencken invited Dreiser to meet him in New York on 24 January to talk over "some American Mercury matters." [UPL]

2. The first number of the *American Mercury* (January 1924) included Ernest Boyd's "Aesthete: Model 1924," a parody of the avant-garde.
3. Margaret Munsterberg's memoir, "Santayana at Cambridge."
4. *An American Tragedy.*

[UPL]

H. L. Mencken
1524 Hollins St.
Baltimore.

January 14th [1924]

Dear Dreiser:-

I fear that if I inquired about the sales of "The 'Genius'" here it would cause gabble, and that the gabble would get to Liveright instantly. I am on good terms with only one bookdealer in the town. The others hate me on account of rows that went on during the war, and the two principal ones refuse to put any of my books in their show-windows.

I'd like very much to hear your impressions of The American Mercury. What do you say to lunching with me on Wednesday the 23rd? I suggest the Astor at 12.15. Is this all right?

Yours,
M

[NYP]

118 W. 11th St.
N.Y.C

Jan 15—1924

Please dont rush me. I was 52 last August according to what appears to be an erroneous birth registry.[1]
As for the date Wed. 23—12:15 Astor—it is upon my calendar.
Just the same you are uniformly an unobliging soul. It seems to be in the blood.
Abrams is dead.[2]
The Astor—the trashiest hotel in N.Y.
news-stand[3]

1. Dreiser was fifty-two on 27 August 1923.
2. Dr. Albert Abrams, who treated Dreiser in California (see Dreiser to Mencken, before 31 May 1921).

3. Dreiser wrote "news-stand" at the top of the letter to indicate where they would meet in the hotel.

[UPL]

H. L. Mencken
1524 Hollins St.
Baltimore.

January 16th [1924]

Dear Dreiser:-

My apologies. I somehow confused you with Chauncey M. Depew.[1] I'll meet you at 12.15 Wednesday the 23rd at the news-stand in the Astor lobby. You will recognize me by the fact that all the gals will be staring at me. Let us victual in the Hunting Room. It is full of Elks and movie magnates, but the sauerkraut is far from bad. Nick, the headwaiter, has given away 35 copies of "The 'Genius'".

When did Abrams die? It is news to me. Only a few months ago he was still trying to get a sample of my blood.

Last week there was a plebiscite in Baltimore to elect a new boss for the town. I was elected by a large majority. Maybe you will now respect me.

Don't miss the Democratic national convention, to be held in New York. It will be the greatest show you ever saw. New Mexico will be nothing like it.

In Sso, Corde Jesu,
M

1. Chauncey Depew (1834–1928), U.S. senator from New York, lawyer, memoirist. A friend of railroad magnates, Depew was famous as an apologist for the large corporate interests of his day.

[NYP]

118 W. 11th St.
N.Y.

Jan 16—1924

Dear Stanwood:

My telephone is as before—Chelsea 2163—My work room—118 W. 11th. You can send the money by truck or express—

Gene Stratton

H. L. Mencken
1524 Hollins St.
Baltimore.

March 5th [1924]

Dear Dreiser:-

Copies of the January issue are very scarce; I have but one myself.[1] But I am asking Nathan to try to find one, and if it is obtainable you will get it.

What of the second volume of your autobiography? Have you sold the serial rights? If not, and you care to sell parts of it, I'd like very much to get a crack at it. I mean the volume dealing with Street & Smith, etc.

Yours in Xt.

M

1. On 4 March Dreiser wrote asking for a copy of the January *American Mercury*. [NYP]

118 W. 11th St.
N.Y.

March 15, 1924.

Dear Menck:

Apart from chapters one and two of that work—Literary Experiences there is nothing done. The stuff however is serial. I could just as easily do the section relating to Mr. Mc Clure, Mr. Wilder, Mr. Hampton or the brothers Smith[1] as I could that relating to one Henry L. Mencken, and tramp on as many corns in the process. Incidentally it would fit into the main work about as three links of a chain can be fitted into the main cable. So, if it weren't for the novel which now grinds my honorable nose I could do you a chapter or two and make George Smith want to run for a gun.

But as for price I suppose it would be marjorem gloriam Dei. Or, for the repose of the soul of one H. L. M. soon destined for the griddle.

Am I right or wrong?

Dolgorourki.

1. For his projected autobiography, "Literary Experiences," Dreiser thought to include portraits of the well-known publishers with whom he had worked: S. S. McClure, George W. Wilder, Benjamin B. Hampton, and George and Ormond G. Smith.

H. L. Mencken
1524 Hollins St.
Baltimore.

March 30th [1924]

Dear Dreiser:-

The publisher, Kurt Wolff, to whom Scheffauer refers, is now in New York, stopping at the Plaza Hotel. He will return to Germany at the end of the week. I met him the other day and he mentioned "The Financier". Without knowing that he planned to do it, I told him that I thought "The Titan" would probably sell better in Germany.

Yours in Xt.,
M

118 W. 11th St.
N.Y.

May 7, 1924

Dear Mencken:

Will you give me an opinion as to this.[1] It was written by W. C. Lengel. Since the last paragraph relates to me I feel out of it—favorably or unfavorably. He insists that he has a new idea treated in a new way. And since in addition to my opinion he wanted me to pass it on to you, I am doing so. But I guarantee not to trouble you with many things of this or any kind.

Th. D

1. This has not been identified.

118 West 11th St.
N.Y.C.

May 12—1924

Dear Menckhorn:

Just as soon as I get the time I'll be glad to try my hand at such an article.[1] I hesitate to criticize the younger group even though I dislike some of their efforts, because they are working in the right direction. I like Evelyn Scott's trend though not her bitterness. I dislike a book like

Paint² because it is pretentious—grandiose   The writer is thinking more
of himself than he is of life. I like Weeds.³ Also Rose Suckow's⁴ things. But
she isn't half as significant as Sherwood Anderson of whom I heartily
approve—the most original of them all. Ben Hecht thinks more of his
phrase & Ben Hecht than he does of the spectacle of life itself. So it goes
in regard to many. But I'm afraid I would make many useless enemies.
And I haven't any now.

Did you ever read a short story of mine entitled The Mercy of God   It
is right out of life & should have appealed to you

Sorry your ill. And I hope its nothing serious. I wont mind your dying
in 1935   But as yet tis bissell geschwindt.⁵

I have two very large rooms here now and am thinking of staging a
high-brow feast. Do you & Nathan want to come.

Dreiser

1. Mencken had asked for an essay on contemporary novelists.
2. *Paint* (1923), by Thomas Craven.
3. *Weeds* (1923), by Edith Summers Kelley.
4. Dreiser means Ruth Suckow.
5. A little too soon.

[NYP-T]
[before 13 May 1924]

H. L. M.
What would you do about this?¹ You know I am not a joiner. I did refuse
this charter membership. Am opposed by temperament to such things.
On the other hand would I appear inconsiderate in this instance. My
deepest desire is to stay out of it and all such things.

Dreiser

1. Dreiser received an invitation to join the international literary club P.E.N.,
which is said to stand for poets, playwrights, editors, essayists, novelists.

[UPL]

H. L. Mencken
1524 Hollins St.
Baltimore.

May 13th [1924]

Dear Dreiser:-

1. My prejudices against literary clubs is so violent that what I say
about the P.E.N. outfit probably must be discounted. I can only tell you

that I refused absolutely to join it myself and have since refused to go to any of its dinners. It contains some excellent fellows, notably Carl Van Doren, but I believe that most of its members are selling-platers. It has a strongly Anglomaniacal tinge. It would do you no good to join, and it might embarass you greatly. All sorts of third raters would use you as a stalking horse to get publicity.

2. What you say about the young novelists would make a capital article. You would offend no one save the fakes, and they are against you anyhow, and ready to devour your carcass the moment you founder. Simply take them up one by one, setting forth your ideas about them simply, and then finish with some general observations on the present state and probable future of the American novel. Certainly, the article should be written. The novel is constantly discussed, but very seldom by a novelist. I hope you tackle it.

3. My best thanks for the Haldeman-Julius[1] first edition. Julius is a truly amazing fellow. I met him some time ago with Upton Sinclair. He talks and acts like a Rotary Club go-getter, but he prints many good books.

4. I don't know "The Mercy of God".[2] Has it been published? If not, I'll be delighted to get a whack at it.

5. Name the day and I'll be on hand for your soiree. All I ask is that you invite a few clergymen.

6. My hoof is still lame, and the quacks apparently don't know how to cure it, but I have not yet lost my faith in divine Providence. I have just finished "Prejudices IV", in which you appear in the light of a patriot and a Christian. Now I must do a great mass of writing for the Mercury against my absence in June at the two national conventions.

Yours,
Mencken

1. Emanuel Haldeman-Julius (1889–1951), editor, author, publisher.
2. Dreiser's short story would appear in *American Mercury* 2(August 1924), 457–64; it was republished in *Chains* (1927) as "The 'Mercy' of God."

[NYP]

118 W. 11th St.
N.Y.C.

May 24—1924

Signor:

Claude Bowers[1] (Evening World) would like very much to confer with you. He is a man of ideas—large <u>practical</u> political experience & can write. He is in personal & friendly contact with such people as Will Hays,

Tom Taggart, C. Bascom Slemp, Ralston, McAdoo, and others.[2] And he knows the puritanic American mind   For political reasons of his own he is not always willing to attack directly but rather present in such a way as to compel inferences. I like him & think he will prove of value.

I cannot devote time to lunches and neither can he. His job is rather exacting. If you will suggest an evening (barring Thursdays) I will try & have him on hand—or advise further.

Will you show me how, if at all, you intend to reduce that opening quotation.[3] With all due reverence to your insistence on it as an article it chances to be a story after the De Maupassant formula and is to be so classified if you bother to classify in any announcement. And what are you going to pay for it, oh Maecenas! 50 cents.

I suggest to you that some time it might be worth your while to let me do a series of literary characters. I could serve picture paint.

Septimus Severus

I am having the article on Shakespeare written.[4] You are not obligated to even look at it unless you are interested

1. Claude Bowers (1878–1958), historian, diplomat.
2. Political figures of the time: Will H. Hays, the postmaster-general; Thomas Taggart, U.S. senator from Indiana; C. Bascom Slemp, secretary to President Coolidge; Samuel Moffett Ralston, U.S. senator from Indiana; William Gibbs McAdoo, former secretary of the treasury and the unsuccessful candidate for the Democratic presidential nomination in 1920.
3. Mencken objected to the long opening quotation from Keshub Chunder Sen that Dreiser used in "The Mercy of God."
4. Article by John Maxwell (see Dreiser to Mencken, 21 July 1920, n.1).

[UPL]

H. L. Mencken
1524 Hollins St.
Baltimore.

May 26th [1924]

Dear Dreiser:-

Give yourself no concern. The opening quotation is preserved by God's will. You will get a proof in a week. A check will also go to you, lavish and good at the bank. The Literary Portraits scheme looks excellent. I only hope you don't forget De Witt C. Talmadge.[1] But I certainly hope you do the article on the current novel. It would be a very valuable criticism.

Let us see Bowers by all means. I probably won't be in New York again until after the Cleveland convention. But I'll surely be there the whole week of June 22nd. I suggest that it would be a good idea to meet some night at Maennerchor Hall. The beer is excellent. I'll probably be stuck in Madison Square Garden, at the Democratic convention, all day.

Yours,
Mencken

1. T. De Witt Talmadge (1832–1902), popular clergyman and editor of the *Christian Herald*, was a strong advocate of prohibition.

[NYP-T]

118 West 11th St.
N.Y.

June 5, 1924.

Oh, Maecenas:

It will gratify you, I know to learn that your munificence is to be embalmed in not only song but story.

In the meantime I am constrained to hint that the English rights to the tale remain with me. I can sell such things direct and prefer to select me own medium.

Ni how muh?

Ludwig Lewisohn
Per
D

[NYP]

118 W. 11th St.
N.Y.

July 21—1924

Dear Mencken:

If the leaving off from the end of The Mercy of God of the short quotation brought forward from the opening quotation was purely accidental I can only lift my hands & bewail that I was so damned careless as to fail to demand for final inspection the final proofs. I distinctly marked it in.

I cannot believe that it could have been intentional   It is certainly hard enough at best to forgive oversights that bring to nothing ones best intentions

Dreiser

[UPL]

H. L. Mencken
1524 Hollins St.
Baltimore.

July 22nd [1924]

Dear Dreiser:-

My sincere apologies. There was a jam at the end, and quick work was necessary. Our printer was moving his composing-room, and we had a hell of a time. Certainly you are not going to let God outdo you in forgiveness.

I note that you have joined the La Follette Committee.[1] As for me I shall vote for Cal,[2] the Scourge of God. The country deserves him.

Yours in Xt.,
M

1. Dreiser disliked the positions of the Democratic and Republican parties and was supporting Senator Robert La Follette's Progressive Party.
2. Calvin Coolidge.

[UPL]

H. L. Mencken
1524 Hollins St.
Baltimore.

September 5th [1924]

Dear Dreiser:-

Demigod is the word. It is two ranks higher than an archangel. I am a candidate for Patriarch of Venice in the Dreiser church. I only hope you add the parole system to the Ten Commandments.

I am just out of the hospital, and on crutches. I had a tumor on the sole of my left foot. The operation was small and I'll be all right in ten days. Let me have your prayers.

I hear from the West that you are bound there, but I don't believe it.

Yours,
Mencken

[NYP-T]

118 West 11th St.
N.Y.

Sept. 10, 1924.

Dear Mencken:
Wrong again.
I am Elijah III.
The only positions open are those of Press Agent and Bonded Collector. Line forms at the south.
I am also Treasurer.
I am not heading for the west,—yet.
But my plan is to build Zion II next to Hollywood.
Sorry about your foot.
But if you will guzzle continually the swollen big toe must come.

Fraternally,
Elijah III.
Per Moses Jacobs, Secy.

[UPL]

H. L. Mencken
1524 Hollins St.
Baltimore.

September 14th [1924]

Dear Dreiser:-
I suppose you have read in the Staats-Zeitung of my troubles. After growing lamer and lamer for six months I finally landed in hospital, and had a tumor cut out of my left foot. For ten days I was on crutches, but now I am navigating again, somewhat limpingly. Prayer, I hope, will complete the cure. But it seems to have no effect against hay-fever, which is damned bad this year.
These troubles I ascribe to the menopause. I was 44 on Friday and already have the classical symptoms: hot flushes, delusions, etc. One of them is a terrific thirst for beer. Fortunately, there is still plenty of it in the Maryland Free State. I have 80 head of pupils in brewing, and visit them regularly, testing their brews. It is a difficult but agreeable science.
I only hope you are weller.

Yours in Xt.,
Mencken

<u>118 W. 11th</u>

Oct. 24—1924

Dear Mr. Menkhorn:

What evidence have you that no one of the <u>average</u> (very) strong, successful men listed on pages 117–118 of your celebrated work Prejudices—4—[1] ever strayed from the bosom of—ahem!—of his sanctioned spouse? Or is this a shining example of that sublime faith in our fellow men & their intentions that so markedly inspires all right-thinkers and the children of light & truth in general. Or, perchance a special revelation from God. I thought it was generally understood in the case of Tolstoy that Anna Karenina was rather personal. Ditto Ressurection. And in the case of John D. Sr. I thought I was privy to some data that a more ruthless vice crusader than myself would denounce.

However—God willing—and at your sublime ease, let us hear.

Earnestly
Edgar Guest

How did you come to overlook Mark Twain.

1. Dreiser is referring to Mencken's "Reflections on Monogamy," in which he attacks a point in Dreiser's "Hey Rub-a-Dub-Dub": "Does the average strong, successful man confine himself to one woman? Has he ever?" Mencken lists, among others who do not follow this rule, Tolstoy and John D. Rockefeller.

THEODORE DREISER

Oct. 25—1924

Dear Menck:

This is to acknowledge the receipt of the book—but more particularly the inscription.[1] It must be the Spirit of 76 nestling fraternally in our respective hearts that maintains this relationship intact.

Nevertheless, when I consider all the Hunnish stuff in this volume and recall my own Nordic blond and untainted Anglo-Saxon extraction—as well as my present close affiliation with the KKK I question whether I should not protest. Left standing, as is—it may bring back the sack for me.

If you want to see how a right thinking Nordic of Constitution defending & flag kissing propensities can eventually triumph among his fellow Kiwanis read the enclosed.[2] Unfortunately other duties will prevent, I fear.

Dr. Frank Crane.

This long, flossy envelope was wished on me & frugality forbids its destruction.[3]

1. Mencken had sent a copy of *Prejudices: Fourth Series* with this inscription: "Theodore Dreiser, Friend after all these years!"
2. This is missing, but it probably refers to a letter from the Arts Association mentioned by Mencken in his letter of 27 October.
3. Dreiser placed this in the top left-hand corner of the letter.

[UPL]

H. L. Mencken
1524 Hollins St.
Baltimore.

October 27th [1924]

Dear Dreiser:-

All right; I withdraw John D. But what, then, of General William Booth, of the Salvation Army? Again, there is Rabbi Stephen S. Wise. Yet again, William Jennings Bryan. Yet again, Horace Liveright.[1]

This Arts Association arouses my suspicions. Look at the names: Stahl, Junge, Warner (i.e. Wärner). Even Dudley was probably Dinckelmann in Suabia.

I am in my usual low state, worked to death and full of uneasiness about my soul.

Yours,

M

1. Mencken humorously includes Liveright, known for his less than chaste lifestyle.

[NYP]

Oct. 31—1924

Dear Stanwood:

You say "but what, then, about General Booth, Rabbi Stephen Wise, William Jennings Bryan, Horace Liveright? What indeed? I ask more solemnly. But why should you, whose left ear opens directly upon the supreme sanctuary, ask? Did not the voice of God inform you as to the inmost secrets of the first list? The truth is that the sun stood still in Avalon, Christ walked on the water, the mountain—in spite of Mohomet's sly deception, came to him. (He was just kidding us.) Elijah ascended to heaven in a chariot of fire and Balaam's faunal possession spoke loudly in undefiled Hebraic.

I myself am as pure as driven snow.

Dr. Frank Crane.

N.B.

For your celestial ear. Ada Lester who with her sister Eunice (the Everleigh sisters) once conducted the Everleigh Club of Chicago[1] (of glorious memory) and died rich personally told me that Wm H. Taft, Theodore Roosevelt and Supreme Court Justice White were among her private suite guests. Ask your heavenly adviser if this is truth or a lie. I dont know.

1. The Everleigh Club of Chicago was a famous house of prostitution.

[UPL]

H. L. Mencken
1524 Hollins St.
Baltimore.

October 31st [1924]

Dear Dreiser:-

It is true as to Roosevelt, but not as to Taft or White. Both of the latter were too fat for such sports. But I myself met Coolidge in the place. Did you know that Ada Lester became a Christian on her death-bed? I once had the honor of a private session with her. She was somewhat mature, but an excellent performer.

Some time ago, in New York, I met Edgar Lee Masters for the first time. He struck me as a capital fellow. Why not a party for the three of us some day? I have a bottle of genuine elderberry wine, made by Mrs. Emil Gunderhausen, of Kitzmiller, Md.

To my list I add Brander Matthews, Alec Woollcott, John W. Davis, General Pershing and the late Gustav Lenin.

Yours,
Mencken

[NYP]

118 W. 11th St

Nov 6—1924

Mine Herr:

I'm a little off Edgar Lee. Ask me not! Years ago when he had written nothing & was thinking to kill himself he was exquisite   It was I who persuaded him to crystallize his bitter broodings into the Spoon River Anthology. He sent most of them to me & I took them to Lane who rejected them. Reedy began to publish them after they were sent to me. You do not recall my writing to you of him I suppose—in 1913 or 14?[1]

There is an amusing follower of yours whom you should know. Allen Benson. (Very able in a purely practical unpoetic way)   He has a charming house & good car in Yonkers. Any day, on demand he will get it out & cruise us all over lovely Westchester—among the lakes. I will arrange for the luncheon & dinner. Bring the walled-in Nathan & we will make a day of it—showing him a few brown November leaves   Benson will be delighted to put us up for the night. And these are the perfect days in which to go.

D

1. See Dreiser to Mencken, after 19 February 1913.

[UPL-H]

THE AMERICAN MERCURY
730 Fifth Avenue
New York

[after 6 November 1924]

Dear Dreiser:

I can remember the Masters matter very well. And also your very early advocacy of Sherwood Anderson. Some day I must get all the facts in detail, and write an article about it.

God knows, I wish I could go to Benson's house with you, but at the moment I am worked to death. I am writing this at the Algonquin at night, after a dreadful day's work. But all this will pass, I hope, very soon. I see you far too seldom for the good of my soul. Let me write again when I am clear, and then let us have a session.

I met Masters lately for the first time. He spoke of you in a very polite way. I have not seen him since.

Yours,
HLM

P.S.—My brother Gustav is in jail again for bootlegging.

M

[UPL]

THE AMERICAN MERCURY
730 Fifth Avenue
New York

November 11th, 1924.

Dear Dreiser:

I think that Scheffauer made an excellent bargain for you.[1] But I still maintain that advances on royalty are immoral. They burden the publisher and in the long run produce no profit to authors whose books actually sell. The net result of them, in fact, is that the authors who sell have to carry those who do not.

Ullstein is a very prosperous publisher. He not only prints many books but also owns a dozen or more magazines and a chain of newspapers. He is, in fact, a sort of German Hearst.

Yours,

M

---

1. Herman G. Scheffauer negotiated for Dreiser with the Berlin publishing house of Ullstein to buy the German translation rights to *The Titan*.

[NYP]

THEODORE DREISER

Nov 14—1924

John Wesley, Esq.,
1524 Hollins St.
Baltimore, Md.

Dear John:

I know your Methodist soul resents the immorality of it but all my literary life I have worked on <u>advance</u> royalties. If I hadn't been able to trick the moral publisher out of the immoral money—and to the prejudice of such writers as—well as—whose books sell—I wouldn't have been able to work at all—or I wouldn't have worked—(lacking the means therewith)   Major Leigh[1] would testify that he died—my owing him $3000. The Century will testify that I stung them for an advance of $2000. John Lane closed his house here with $2000 due from me. I am ahead of B&L to the extent of $3000 & I would God it were more.

But dear John, you will never get it. Neither will you ever get certain other devices by which I have lived & moved. And I do not even pray your moral God to enlighten you.

Salathiel

1. F. T. Leigh was vice-president of Harper and Bros.

[UPL]

THE AMERICAN MERCURY
730 Fifth Avenue
New York

January 14, 1925.

Dear Dreiser:

I tried to call you by telephone yesterday, but found that the number you gave me some time ago had been transferred to a drug store. The clerk there told me that he had never heard of you. He said, in fact, that he read no Yiddish books. What is your correct telephone number?

Sincerely yours,
Mencken

[UPL]

H. L. Mencken
1524 Hollins St.
Baltimore.

January 16th [1925]

Dear Dreiser:-

The mystery clears. I had your number as Chelsea 2631. You missed a very agreeable party. I had to accomodate them both, and was in a low state the next state.

I am sending you a case of champagne as consolation.

Are you going to Ben Huebsch's lunch to Anderson? If so, we meet Thursday a week.

God help us all!

Yours,
M

[UPL]

H. L. Mencken
1524 Hollins St.
Baltimore.

March 4th [1925]

Dear Dreiser:-

I propose forthwith that we meet at the Algonquin at 5.30 on Wednesday, March 18th, there guzzle a couple of cocktails, and then proceed to Union Hill, where the beer was never better and excellent victuals are to be had. I suggest Boyd and Rascoe as companions.

What do you say?

Yours,
Mencken

[NYP]

THEODORE DREISER

Mch 7—1925

Dear Mencken:

I've been down with near-pneumonia and at this writing am not so sure whether I'll be in good shape or even in the land of the living. If I am I'll come along. Have moved to the fair city of Brooklyn.[1] Pro Tem. It's very nice—churches, schools, water, lights. Helen[2] is keeping my shack for me & if you want to come down some evening for dinner—you may. Its 1799 Bedford Ave. Take B.M.T. Times Square or elsewhere & get on a Brighton Beach Express. You can get the train at 60th or 59th & 5th Ave. Get off at Prospect Park Station (Lincoln Rd. End of the platform) & turn to your left. Walk one block. Presto. About 30 minutes from Times Square. My telephone is Flatbush 3467 J.

Dreiser

1. Dreiser was working on *An American Tragedy*, and he moved to Brooklyn to avoid the interruptions of his Manhattan apartment.
2. Helen Richardson.

[UPL]

H. L. Mencken
1524 Hollins St.
Baltimore.

March 9th [1925]

Dear Dreiser:-

Bad news, indeed. I had heard nothing of it. I surely hope that you are on your legs again, and making good progress. I'll get to New York on Tuesday the 17th—St. Patrick's Day—and call you up. If you can't come over for the Union Hill soiree on the 18th—St. Cyril of Jerusalem's Day—I shall come out to wait on you on the 19th—St. Joseph's Day. But I hope you can come.

Good news mingles with the bad, i.e., that you have moved to Brooklyn. I am always glad to see any man move out of Manhattan. The older I grow the more I am convinced that the island is accursed. Life there is always uncomfortable, and work is extraordinarily difficult. I believe you will find it easier to work in Brooklyn than it ever was in Manhattan.

My chaplain has his instructions.

Yours,
Mencken

[UPL]

H. L. Mencken
1524 Hollins St.
Baltimore.

March 14th [1925]

Dear Dreiser:-

I hope you can come on Wednesday. Rascoe, De Kruif[1] and Boyd will be on hand. The time: 5.30 P.M. The place: The Algonquin. Come direct to my room. We take ship for Union Hill at 6.30.

Baltimore is in the throes of a revival. My Uncle Emil has been converted. He has discharged his beautiful serving maid, Elfrida, and put in a colored woman of 65 years, and has gone on the water-wagon.

Yours,
Mencken

---

1. Paul De Kruif, scientist and author. De Kruif provided Sinclair Lewis with the background material for *Arrowsmith*.

THEODORE DREISER

[NYP]

Mch 16th 1925

Dear Menckhorn:

I will show up at the Algonquin Wednesday, Mch 18—at 5 ^{30} I'm not in the swellest condition but may be—at that hour. I'm glad Rascoe is coming along

Dreiser

THEODORE DREISER

[NYP]

Mch 31—1925

Dear Mr. Menkhorn:

The bierstube[1] in Brooklyn that I had in mind is in Lawrence Street & has just succumbed. Too many snooping Volsteaders.[2] In connection with that you will like the spirit of the enclosed.[3] The Brooklyn joint failing, I suggest a return to Union Hill. The bier is excellent—& I felt 100% better the next morning. But this to be my party. I have taken a writing office—Room 1516 Guardian Life Bldg. N. East corner Union Sq. (17th & 4th ave)   I have even a telephone connection of sorts. (Stuyvesant 8344). Suppose we meet there some day this week. We can then depart from there and I agree to furnish ample cocktails to start with. You round up the animals & direct them here. How about Nathan

D.

But keep the room & telephone number to yourself.

1. Beerhall.
2. Enforcers of the Volstead Act, which made Prohibition the law of the land.
3. This is missing.

[UPL]

H. L. Mencken
1524 Hollins St.
Baltimore.

April 3rd [1925]

Dear Dreiser:-

Your letter has just reached me through the office, forwarded by ox-cart as usual. It appears that de Sanchez has already arranged for a return to Union Hill next Wednesday night, the 8th. Let us go, shouting hosannahs.

I'll be delighted to wait upon you at your new office. If you are not using it in the evenings I may have a suggestion to make about it. Let us go to the Schaefer Brewery, by all means. It is years since I have been in a brewery cellar. The atmosphere there is exactly to my taste.

Yours,
Mencken

[NYP]

THEODORE DREISER

April 4—1925

Fairest Menkhorn:

As I understand it you are coming here—Wed. 8th—at say—anytime from 5^{30} on. Charming view here—and I'll have the drinks. Next—from here—via deep sea going taxis to 42nd St. Bring de Sanchez or any other. I have a guy—a painter friend[1]—a good one—whom I may ring in. If there is any change as to this write—or call up Stuyvesant 8344. If I'm not in leave word—or phone Flatbush (after 9 in the AM.) 3467 J.

R. J. Schaefer of the F. M. Schaefer Brewing Co writes that if we will fix an evening—he will "prepare properly for the occasion." Also he agrees "to manufacture the German Beer Hall with all its essentials will be our aim." And he adds—to see that the cellars are good & damp. Then when we meet—we shall endeavor to annihilate an absurdity and show that dampness can create sunshine.

The 100% German spirit. Bismark himself could do no more.

I move we fix a date

What say

Dreiser

1. Kenneth Hayes Miller.

[NYP]

Room 1516
Guardian Life Bldg.

[before 14 April 1925]

Dear Menck:

Do you know anything about these people?[1]

Sex and beer parties do not agree. We should have gone to Union Hill.

I volunteer to lead the next group in the right path—first to meet here. But when?

D

I'll rent you this place nights for $3 a night. Attendance extra.[2]

1. This item is missing.
2. Dreiser wrote this along the left-hand side of the page.

[UPL]

H. L. Mencken
1524 Hollins St.
Baltimore.

April 14th [1925]

Dear Dreiser:-

I know nothing of Hardon save that he is a hack author in the Village and came to see me a month or so ago. I have not seen his alleged book. It is probably crap. I shall suggest that he ask Rabbi Stephen S. Wise to write a preface for it.

You know my prejudices: I am strongly against taking the fair ones on booze parties. I got lost when we left the restaurant and presently found myself in a taxicab alone. Not remembering where de Sanchez lives, I went back to the hotel.

Let us, the next time, go to Union Hill.

Ever in Xt.,
Mencken

[NYP]

THEODORE DREISER

April 18—1925

Dear Menck:

Friday April 24 is ok. We meet 6 P.M. sharp in the studio of Kenneth Hayes Miller—6 East 14th St. 3rd floor—front. A very admirable artist & fellow. I am trying for Boyd and Ed Smith of the World. Thence by taxi into the wilds. A few drinks before

Dreiser

[UPL]

H. L. Mencken
1524 Hollins St.
Baltimore.

April 20th [1925]

Dear Dreiser:-

Unluckily, Friday is impossible for me. I must be here to keep an important business engagement, and shall have to leave New York in the afternoon. Thus God continues to afflict me. If you could change it to Thursday I'd be full of hosannahs.

I am glad you sent me Frau Hardy's letter.[1] I was about to denounce her as an idiot.

Yours in Xt.,
Mencken

Let me know at the office.[2]

1. On 1 April 1925, Florence Hardy, the wife of Thomas Hardy, wrote Dreiser that she was "horrified to find attributed to me a statement that 'The Genius' ought to be suppressed." [UPL] The statement appeared in Ernest Brennecke's biography of Hardy, *The Life of Thomas Hardy* (1925).
2. The postscript is handwritten.

[NYP]

THEODORE DREISER

May 6—1925

Fairest:

I notice that you gave my telephone number to Goldberg.[1] It's ok in this instance. But its very private for me and if you'll give it to as few as possible it will be better for the work I'm doing. I couldn't get up to Tom Smiths, worse luck, although I heard you were to be there.

Dreiser

I stand ready to finance another beer party to Brooklyn or elsewhere

1. Isaac Goldberg, who published *The Man Mencken, a Biographical and Critical Survey* in 1925.

[UPL]

H. L. Mencken
1524 Hollins St.
Baltimore.

May 7th [1925]

Dear Dreiser:-

My apologies. I did it unthinkingly. I have been very careful in the past. At least once a week some one asks for your address. Sometimes they are of the female sex, and beautiful. But I'll be discreet.

By the time I got to Schmidt's party he was too drunk to recognize me. Two of the women put him to bed.

If you forget me the next time there is a brewery party God will punish you.

Yours,
M

[UPL]

H. L. Mencken
1524 Hollins St.
Baltimore.

[before 22 August 1925]

Dear Dreiser:-

Here you are.[1] Sign it with a nom de plume if you want to.

I hear that Boyd and Red Lewis[2] have come to fisticuffs.

Hay fever has me by the snout.

Yours,
Mencken

1. Mencken enclosed a query, published in the "Notes and Queries" section of the *American Mercury*, asking for information on Dreiser's "Studies of Contemporary Celebrities." The inquirer noted that the item has been included in *Who's Who* up to 1911 and that it was dropped after this date.

2. Sinclair Lewis.

[UPL]

THE AMERICAN MERCURY
730 Fifth Avenue
New York

August 22, 1925.

Dear Dreiser:-

This is very interesting.[1] It is a pity that you have not the original advertisement. If you went out to Sullivan[2] and searched the files of the local newspapers, you'd probably find a lot more such stuff.

I am sorry that so many scoundrels showed up the other night, and one of the girls, name unknown, threatened to be violently ill in my bedroom. I gave her three bichloride tablets and I have no doubt that she is already in the hospital and half way to heaven.

I hope you send in a note about "Studies in Contemporary Celebrities." The query was bona fide. What the writer wants is the exact title of the book, and the time and place of its publication together with the name of the publisher.

God help us all.

Yours,

M

1. This item is missing.
2. Sullivan, Indiana, where Dreiser spent a number of his childhood years.

[NYP]
[before 5 September 1925]

[To Mencken]

This sentence in Hansens letter is what interests me.[1]

Did you ever say anything even approximately like this. Arthur Henry—as the type ms. in which the cuts are indicated cut about 30 thousend words out of Carrie[2]—no more.

Did you cut A Hoosier Holiday

I have found good beer in Hoboken—fine

Ertel Fritz

Please dont stir up any argument with Hansen[3]

1. Harry Hansen, literary editor of the Chicago *Daily News*. Along with this note, Dreiser sent Mencken a letter of 7 August 1925, written by Hansen to Selma Lincoln, a friend of Dreiser. The sentence he is referring to reads: "Mr. Mencken, who once cut

something like 100,000 words out of one of the Dreiser manuscripts at the author's request, so he told me." Dreiser circled this and wrote in the margin, "To what book does he refer?" [UPL]

2. Arthur Henry edited the typescript of *Sister Carrie* for the 1901 Heinemann edition.

3. Dreiser put this in the top right-hand corner of the page.

[UPL]

H. L. Mencken
1524 Hollins St.
Baltimore.

September 5th [1925]

Dear Dreiser:-

God knows what book Hansen refers to. Certainly I never told him any such nonsense. I have, in fact, seen very little of him, and don't recall ever discussing you with him. He is a damned ass. I seem to recall making a few cuts, at your request in "A Hoosier Holiday", but am not sure. I remember very well proposing cuts in "The Financier" and "The Titan", and I believe most of them were made. In the matter of "The 'Genius'" I remember that we discussed cuts at your house one cold Winter night and got into a friendly row, and that Kirah Markham apparently horrified by the thought of two Christians murdering each other, rushed out of the house. But "The 'Genius'" was not cut.

Hansen and his gang of Chicago swine denounce me every week, and frequently lie about me. Some time ago one of them, Preston by name, printed an alleged conversation with me about Hergesheimer—wholly imaginary and most embarrassing. I wrote in, calling him a liar. But otherwise I never pay any attention to such vermin. Certainly I shall not write to Hansen.

A few weeks ago, by the way, I received a furious note from Kirah,[1] bawling me out for printing an article about Roger Baldwin. It appears that Baldwin is in bad odor among radicals. I was glad to hear it. I did not reply to Kirah.

Liveright has not yet sent me "An American Tragedy". I'll stir him up when I get back to New York next week—if I actually get there. Hay fever has me by the snout, and I am suffering from the phenomena of the menopause, including melancholia. I have aged 40 years in 10 days. If you are agreeable, I suggest that we exchange the Boyd and Rascoe books,[2] with suitable embellishments. Our heirs will rejoice.

Again by the way: the American Mercury is gradually getting into easier waters, and I can get more money for worthy literati. So if you have anything in hand I hope you give me a chance at it. Let me know what you want for it and I'll try to meet it. Let us be business-like. Getting the magazine on its legs has been a harder job than it looked on the surface. I almost went crazy the first year, for reasons that you may suspect. To this day I have got no salary, and have paid my own expenses. But as I say, there is now deeper water under the ship, and so it is possible to reward the virtuous. Don't blab this around. I don't want to be beset by the noble birds who, in the first days, refused to lend a hand. I have a list of them.

Yours in Xt.,
Mencken

1. Kirah Markham.
2. Ernest Boyd's *H. L. Mencken* (1925) and Burton Rascoe's *Theodore Dreiser* (1925). In Boyd's Book, Mencken wrote:

> To Theodore Dreiser—war hero and Christian in memory of our days together in the field

Appomattox	Chateau Thierry
Sedan	Santiago
Port Arthur	Union Hill, N.J.
New Windsor, Md.	Tannenberg

H. L. Mencken

[UPL]

THE AMERICAN MERCURY
730 Fifth Avenue
New York

September 10, 1925.

Dear Dreiser:

Robert L. Duffus, who has been doing some excellent articles for <u>The American Mercury</u> wants to do one on you. You'll find him a very charming fellow and I am confident that he'll write something worth printing. When he presents a note from me, will you please designate some time to see him. I think you should be able to dispose of the business in half an hour. I want to print the article in <u>The Mercury</u>. I have deliberately chosen Duffus to do it because he is not a literary critic. He used to be an editorial writer on the New York <u>Globe</u>. He will present a note from me sometime during the next month. That is, he will send it to you by mail.[1]

Your letter has just come in. I greatly fear that a short story of 6500 words is rather too long for us, as it is for Leach, but why not let me see it anyhow? I may be able to suggest a cut. The length won't affect the price. What do you want for it?

I'll send you a copy of the Boyd book as soon as I get back to Baltimore.

Yours,
Mencken

1. Dreiser received Mencken's note introducing Duffus. [UPL]

THEODORE DREISER

[NYP]

Sept 11—1925

Dear Menck:

Here is the story.[1] Price 350^{00} As for Mr. Duffus—his fate awaits him. Let him draw near the sacred divan. I'm glad the Mercury waxes apace even though I may not share the drippings

My compliments
My regard.

D.

1. "Convention" was published in *American Mercury*, December 1925, 398–408, and republished in *Chains* (1927).

[UPL]

H. L. Mencken
1524 Hollins St.
Baltimore.

September 15th [1925]

Dear Dreiser:-

The mazuma will reach you at the end of the week. Also a proof. My best thanks. I have long predicted that you would one day become a talented author and get into the best magazines.

I suggest that simply "Convention" would be a more effective title than the somewhat too literal "The Power of Convention". Give it your prayers.

I like the piece very much. There is a good idea in it and it is well carried out.

Yours in Xt.,
M

THEODORE DREISER

Sept 16—1925

Sire:

The title was for the skull of the dub. If you hold said skull to be less resistent than I hold it to be—"Convention" may do

Once more I note that in the face of the persistent assertion—(could you possibly guess whose)—that I cannot write a short story, a magazine of your editing leaps to embrace and publish—number 3. I stand—well—curious

Sir John Chrysostom.

H. L. Mencken
1524 Hollins St.
Baltimore.

September 18th [1925]

Dear Dreiser:-

Some one has been lying to you again. You give too much credence to the literary shit-bugs who infest New York. As a short story writer I put you above Thomas Edgelow. No doubt I begin to decay as a critic, but I thought "Convention" was very good stuff.

Your check will go out tomorrow. All I ask out of it is a glass of beer. Why don't you come down here some week-end and forget your sorrows? Boyd and Goodman¹ are coming tomorrow. Boyd will be belching like an archbishop for a week after he gets home.

Yours in Xt.,
Calvin

1. Philip Goodman (see Mencken to Dreiser, 3 January 1922, n.1).

THEODORE DREISER

Sept 19—1925

All right, my darling. Shitbugs there may be but I was quoting from the old Smart—and your own private column. (How brief is thy memory, O Lord God of Israel.)

As for Baltimore. Certainly. I occasionally go even there. But who is to meet me. The Lord Mayor? Or his Eminence the archbishop? These little details—including the keys of the city—?!!!?

I bow—

I kiss your hand

I prostrate myself utterly

The Duke of Argyle

[UPL]

H. L. Mencken
1524 Hollins St.
Baltimore.

September 21st [1925]

Dear Dreiser:-

Many of those articles in The Smart Set were forgeries. English spies wrote them. Nothing issuing from my actual hand has ever failed to make three things plain: that you have an adept and lascivious style, that you are a baptized man, and that you are the handsomest book author in the Republic. If anyone tells you otherwise, call him a shit-bug in my name, hand him the enclosed card, and notify me to meet him at dawn of the next day on the vacant lot behind Alt Heidelberg at Union Hill. I have spoken.

Yours,
Gustav of Magdala

[NYP]
[before 23 September 1925]

[To Mencken]

Will you be gracious, O Son of Heaven, and see that <u>all</u> of these corrections are entered into the body of the text[1]

The 38th Thief

And—will you let me have a set of the <u>revised</u> proofs for my files

---

1. "Convention."

[UPL]

THE AMERICAN MERCURY
730 Fifth Avenue
New York

September 23, 1925

Dear Dreiser:

Your corrections will be made with the most meticulous fidelity. Your every wish is a command, not to say a curse. May God prosper you in your public-spirited work.

Yours,
M

[UPL]

THE AMERICAN MERCURY
730 Fifth Avenue
New York

September 24. [1925]

Dear Dreiser:

Your corrections have been copied upon the office proof and I herewith return your own proof for your file.

I met Rabbi Stephen S. Wise yesterday and he was full of flattering words about you. He regards you as a very talented and promising fellow.

Yours,
Mencken

[UPL]

THE AMERICAN MERCURY
730 Fifth Avenue
New York

September 26, 1925.

Dear Dreiser:

This Allied Arts Association is apparently an organization of amateurs. Stahl¹ broadcasts invitations to his dinners and then apparently postures in the newspapers as a literary man. Let me hear of it if you decide to go.

I can then take proper measures to have you confined in a sanatorium for the insane.

Yours,
Prof. H. L. Mencken

1. On 29 August 1925, John M. Stahl, the president of the Allied Arts Association, had written Dreiser asking him to be the guest of honor at a dinner in Chicago. [UPL] Dreiser sent this and two later letters to Mencken for his opinion.

[NYP]
[after 26 September 1925]

[To Mencken]

I gave this guy no hope. I said that dinners were cynical affairs concocted mainly to rack the poor scribe—show him or blow him up. It is the one bit of pyrotechnics in the poor wit's life before as a slick he descends to the sewer. No pyrotechnics—no—(at least public)—descent to les suer. Would you like to disguise yourself in green whiskers and go as me. Or would Boyd do it? He has the whiskers already

The Maharajah of Kapur Thala

[UPL]

THE AMERICAN MERCURY
730 Fifth Avenue
New York

October 7, 1925.

Dear Dreiser:

I assume that you have read "God's Stepchildren" by Mrs. Sarah Millin. It is one of the most remarkable novels done by a woman in recent years. Mrs. Millin lives in South Africa.

This morning I received from her a letter containing the following:

"I think Dreiser is the greatest of American novelists. He comes along—step, step—inexorably, irresistibly, over everything—like a wartank. Not shiny, not elegant: and he musn't be."

This encomium should materially relieve the qualms of your autumnal rheumatism.

Yours,
M

[UPL-H]
[after 15 October 1925]

[To Dreiser]

The music stirring in my very soul and then the mention of your name—
oh my darling, how long? how long?[1]

1. Mencken wrote this on the program of a New York Philharmonic concert given
on 15 October 1925 at Carnegie Hall. He placed it beside a program note that mentions
that the Don Juan of Richard Strauss's tone poem is in the same tradition as Eugene
Witla, Dreiser's character in *The "Genius."*

[NYP]

THEODORE DREISER

Nov 4 1925

Dear Mencken:

Thanks for the Sherman clipping[1]   It <u>is</u> interesting. Smith[2] tells me
he furnished you & Sinclair Lewis proofs of parts 1 & 2 of An American
Tragedy. This is not fair to me. Those very proofs have since been cut and
revised in such a way as to eliminate many weaknesses. If the book is to be
read for criticism it should be read from the final page proofs which should
be available in about a week. Final page proofs of parts 1 & 2 are ready
now—but just ready, now

Dreiser

1. Interviewed by *The Literary Digest International Book Review*, Stuart Sherman
listed Dreiser's forthcoming novel as a candidate for the best book of the year. At this
time, Sherman was literary editor of the New York *Herald Tribune*, and he was beginning to modify his early, hostile criticism of Dreiser.
2. Tom Smith, an editor at Boni & Liveright, worked with Dreiser on *An American
Tragedy*.

[UPL]

H. L. Mencken
1524 Hollins St.
Baltimore.

November 7th [1925]

Dear Dreiser:-

Tom Smith is mashuggah. He never sent me any proofs of the book,
and I have not seen them. I want to read the thing as a whole, and shall
wait until it comes out.

I have just had the melancholy pleasure of getting a lady out of jail—
the old girl of a friend, now dead. Mark well the effects of sin. She began
with a few light-hearted acts of coitus. Then she took to strong drink.
Last night she was incarcerated by the Polizei. This morning it cost me
$6.45 to spring her—and the cops gave me a close inside rate at that. Men-
tion the case in your sermon next Sunday morning.

Yours,

M

[NYP]
[before 14 November 1925]

Dear Menck:

To be accurate in regard to various statements I want to see the inside of
the Death House (Sing Sing) not the Execution room.[1] These letters show
several efforts to date.[2] I hear Al Smith or Jimmy Walker[3] can fix it. I hear
that Herbert Swope[4] can fix it with either. I hear that you can fix it with
Swope. Can you hear me.

Dreiser

1. Dreiser wanted to visit the Sing Sing death-house to confirm details in part 3 of
An American Tragedy.
2. Dreiser tried unsuccessfully to get the warden of Sing Sing, Lewis E. Lawes, to
permit him to see the death-block.
3. Al Smith, governor of New York state, and Jimmy Walker, mayor of New
York City.
4. Herbert Swope was the executive editor of the New York *World*.

[UPL]

H. L. Mencken
1524 Hollins St.
Baltimore.

November 14th [1925[

Dear Dreiser:-

I am writing to the World office by this mail to find out what can be
done. Did you know that Tom Smith and Walker are great friends? Maybe
Tom can fix it at once. The cops are always pedantic. The other day here
in Baltimore I put up $26.45 to procure the release of a lady locked up for
disorderly conduct. When she came to trial her fine and costs amounted to
$6.45. The cops then locked her up again because they said they had no
proof that my deposit was to pay her fine—it might be mere bail. So I had

to turn out in the middle of a busy morning, and get her out again. I hear you are an author. If so, you should put them into one of your books.

Yours,
Mencken

[UPL]

H. L. Mencken
1524 Hollins St.
Baltimore.

November 21st [1925]

Dear Dreiser:-
I have a letter from James M. Cain, of the World, saying that the city editor there can get you into Sing Sing and the death-house, but that he finds it impossible to locate you. It might be a good idea to get into communication with him.

Yours,
Mencken

[NYP]

THEODORE DREISER

Nov. 24—1925

Dear Mencken:
Just received word from Mr. Barrett of the World that they can arrange the Sing Sing business   Obesiences, genuflections,—strange yet significant signs and gestures

Dreiser

I am sending you by slow freight a 415 pound Thanksgiving turkey grown on my estate—Swellheim-on-the-Harlem.

[NYP]

N.Y.

Nov. 27—1925

Dear Mencken:
I am off on a walking tour—itinery not definite as yet. 1799 Bedford Ave. Brooklyn and Room 1516—Guardian Life are no more.[1] Any last fatal words should be addressed—c/o Boni & Liveright—61 W. 48th

When I come back—(sometime) or when I can get a copy of An American Tragedy—I will inscribe same & send it

Th.D

1. Dreiser had completed *An American Tragedy* and no longer needed the privacy provided by these addresses.

[UPL]

H. L. Mencken
1524 Hollins St.
Baltimore.

November 28th [1925]

Dear Dreiser:-

I only hope you are heading Southward—first because you will freeze your glands if you start on a Northward walking tour in this weather, and secondly because I crave the honor of seeing you in this great city. It is, indeed, a horribly long time since we have had a quiet palaver. It seems like years and years. When will you return?

The Goldberg book has just reached me, much delayed. Where shall I send you a copy? Needless to say, I look forward to "An American Tragedy". Despite Schmidt[1] and all other such liars, I have not seen the proofs. I'll review it in a höflich[2] and able manner, God giving me help.

When you get to Sing Sing ask for my uncle, Emil Goetz. He is serving 10 years for a statutory offense. The complainant has since married a respectable colored man.

Yours,
Mencken

1. Tom Smith.
2. Polite.

[UPL-Tel]

Baltimore Md

Nov 28 1925

World complains that after getting you permit with great difficulty by saying you represented it you now demand money this puts me in a nice hole indeed.

H L Mencken

[NYP-Tel]

Brooklyn, N.Y.

Nov 28 1925

The world lies your telegram is an insult

Theodore Dreiser.

[UPL]

H. L. Mencken
1524 Hollins St.
Baltimore.

December 1st [1925]

Dear Dreiser:-
The episode has a classical finish. The innocent bystander is belabored by both sides. On the one hand the <u>World</u> bawls that I let it in for trouble, and on the other you denounce me for libelling you. May the great pox consume you both.

Where shall I send the Goldberg book?

Yours,
Mencken

[NYP]

Hotel Empire
Broadway at 65th St.
New York City

Dec 3—1925

Dear <u>HLM</u>
The ways of the Honorable—the American Press. I ask you as favor to me to use your influence with the World to aid me in getting the physical lay of the Death Block at Sing Sing. You ask the World as a favor to you to do what it can. Presto—the World sees a 5000 word signed article by me—<u>for nothing</u> which it can <u>syndicate</u>. But no word of this in the courteous preliminary negotiations. I am to be permitted to look into the Death Block. Incidentally—(and I wonder why at the time) I am to be permitted to interview Mr. Pantano.[1] <u>But I have no need to interview Mr. Pantano!</u> Nevertheless I am being sent two bundles of clippings relating to the Pantano case, which I am to read. Also a court order permitting me to see

him. Why—I finally & distinctly ask. Because I now hear—the World wishes to know whether he is ready to confess—or how he feels <u>now</u>. Maybe I will be good enough to tell them—or write something. When I hear write (—<u>I</u> <u>am</u> <u>in</u> <u>the</u> <u>midst</u> <u>of</u> <u>packing</u> & <u>moving</u> <u>an</u> <u>office</u> & <u>an</u> <u>apart-</u> <u>ment</u>) I reply—very good—but I cannot say. I will see Mr. Pantano. If anything important appears I will report—come & talk to Mr. (The City Editor)   <u>Tell</u> <u>him</u> (not write) what I have seen. I have no time to write now. I go. See Pantano. The material is fairly interesting. I report by telephone. Presto. Enthusiastic interest. I am to write a 5000 word article for the <u>Sunday</u> <u>World</u> to be used at once and <u>syndicated</u>. Excellent. But I have no time now. Such an article will take a week at least. My price will be $500. "<u>But</u> <u>we</u> <u>had</u> <u>the</u> <u>idea</u> <u>you</u> <u>would</u> <u>do</u> <u>it</u> <u>for</u> <u>nothing</u>." "You are mistaken. Nothing was said about my writing anything. I will be glad to see you—or a reporter & tell you all I heard & saw." Silence. A telegram from you <u>charging</u> <u>me</u> with extorting money from The <u>World</u>. Upon my word. And when I asked this as a favor. Have I ever exacted anything from you— for a favor. The thing makes me laugh. The editors of the World give me a large pain   Why couldn't they have said in the first place—"so much for so much." At that they got a feature. And as for myself—my imagination was better—(more true to the fact)—than what I saw.

My regards—

I touch the floor with my forehead.

Th.D

1. Anthony Pantano, a convicted murderer.

[UPL]

H. L. Mencken
1524 Hollins St.
Baltimore.

December 4th [1925]

Dear Dreiser:

Obviously, what started the row was lack of a definite understanding. In such cases, take your lawyer and pastor along, and a notary public. At the first mention of writing anything—that is, before you went to Sing Sing—you should have thrown a faint and yelled for the police. I'm glad the business was settled amicably.[1] The story is very interesting. I have attended nine men in the last sad scene. They all died in the hope of a glorious Resurrection. What is more, they all looked innocent. For a long while I was a violent opponent of capital punishment. But of late I have begun to believe that we must have it. It doesn't discourage crime, of course, but it at least comforts the populace.

I'll send you the Goldberg book tomorrow.[2] It weighs two pounds.

Yours,

M

1. The matter was settled when the *World* sent Dudley Nichols to interview Dreiser about his experiences in Sing Sing and published the story as "Dreiser Interviews Pantano in Death House: Doomed Man Avows Faith in a Hereafter," 30 November 1925, pp. 1, 14.
2. Mencken inscribed the book, "For Theodore Dreiser, Enemy for 18 years! H. L. Mencken."

[NYP-Pc]
[14 December 1925]

Recent great contest between friends and enemies of the saloon, witnessed by myself. Flag marks last stand of heroic bootleggers.[1]

T.D.

1. The postcard picture shows a scene, complete with a waving flag, from the Battle of the Crater (Petersburg, Virginia), fought between the armies of Lee and Grant on 30 July 1864.

[NYP-Pc]
[12 January 1926]

[To Mencken]

The six people in this gold plated gondola are myself and guests grandly at ease under Cerulean skies.[1] I have brought along my solid silver zither and for their delectation am emitting sweet strains. Rockefeller, Hagler, Morgan are among those present. Don't presume to do more than admire.

Harry F. Sinclair

1. The postcard picture is of the Flamingo Hotel as seen from Biscayne Bay in Miami Beach, Florida. In the foreground is a gondola filled with tourists.

THEODORE DREISER   [NYP]

Jan 14—1926

Dear Menck:

Greeting. How is your mother? I've been so torn & troubled by all sorts of crazy ills since leaving Washington that I haven't had the heart to write. This is really a real estate mad house down here—Signs, blaah! Ta-rah!—from one end of the state to the other. Sickening really   All country jakedom from Wyoming East & Maine south is moving in. The state is all ready completely sub-divided in to lots 50 × 80—and being sold off at from 150$^{\underline{00}}$ to 50,000 per lot. A bigger & brighter & purer Riviera is being constructed with Christ in charge I think. All the awnings, water piles & lanterns—domes & lattices of Venice, Sorrento, Capri—and Spain & Italy are being copied in plaster & papier-mache and sold to crackers as romance, gayety—liberty but not license et cetera. I'm leaving here for the cold & chilly world in about 10 days—and praise God from whom all blessings flow.

I'm 30 miles north of Miami—at Senator Watson's old house in Ft. Lauderdale.[1] Very beautiful—A cocoa-nut grove surrounding a South Sea type of bungalow. But cold. Ass that I was, I left my fur coat at home. Helen has hers—and is comfortable in it right now. Have toured the whole state but to escape another look at it am returning by boat. France—I think—the south of France will be good enough for me.

I meant before this—also—to thank you for that booze.[2] My earnest wish was to pay for it. It still is. However, I'm sending you a signed & numbered & personally inscribed copy of the special edition of An American Tragedy[3] whether you want it or not. If you dont want it—give it to your worst enemy. My regards. My Pontifical indulgence.

De Riser

Leaving N.Y. I forgot to subscribe for the Am. Merc. and I have no permanent address. Will you persuade them to set aside my copies—subject to my order, later.[4]

1. U.S. Senator Clarence Wayland Watson.
2. When Dreiser visited Mencken on his way to Florida, Mencken gave him a bottle of scotch.
3. Dreiser's inscription reads: "For Henry L. Mencken. Dear Heinrick: As my oldest living enemy I venture to offer you this little pamphlet. Don't mind if it emits a destructive gas. Us Germans—you know. D."
4. Dreiser wrote this in the top left-hand corner of the page.

[UPL]

THE AMERICAN MERCURY
730 Fifth Avenue
New York

January 20, 1926.

Dear Dreiser:

My poor mother died the day after you were in Baltimore. I suppose that you noticed I was rather disturbed when we met. At that time, however, I still believed that she might get well, but the next day she died, very peacefully and painlessly.

I am returning your check because it will be easier, once you get settled, to send you all the back numbers—that is, if you still want them. If they were stored here, the chances would be very good that they'd be lost. Whenever you want them hereafter, let me know and I'll see that you get a complete file.

I am writing to you in care of Liveright because you do not mention any other address.

What do you mean by your reference to the south of France? Do you actually contemplate going to live among the Frogs and their cockroaches? I certainly hope not.

Needless to say, I'll be delighted to have a copy of "The American Tragedy."

After you left, I discovered to my horror that I had given you a bottle of Stokes' Liniment instead of whiskey. I certainly hope that the stuff did not incommode you.

Yours,
M

[UPL]

H. L. Mencken
1524 Hollins St.
Baltimore.

January 28th [1926]

Dear Dreiser:-

My best thanks for the hand-painted copy of "An American Tragedy". Schmidt has made a very beautiful pair of books, and I am delighted to have them. I have always argued that you were a talented fellow, and would some day make your way in the art of letters. Let us now see if the so-called critics recognize you.

I have taken a dreadful hack at the book in the Merkur for March, but there is also some very sweet stuff in the notice.¹ I am sending a proof to Schmidt.

Where are you? And when are you coming back?

Yours,
Mencken

1. "The Library: Dreiser in 840 Pages," *American Mercury* 7 (March 1926), 379–81 (see Appendix 2, pp. 796–800).

[NYP]

THEODORE DREISER

Feb. 2nd 1926

Dear Mencken:

It was only this morning that Liveright told me of your mothers death. Lost in the wilds of Florida I never heard. I recall when my own mother died that the earth seemed truly black and rent. The ground shook under me. I dreamed sad, racking dreams for years. These things are in the chemistry and the physics of this immense thing and "wisdom" avails not at all. Yet fortitude is exacted of us all whether we will or not. I offer— understanding.

Dreiser

[UPL]

H. L. Mencken
1524 Hollins St.
Baltimore.

February 5th [1926]

Dear Dreiser:-

Thanks for your note. I begin to realize how inextricably my life was interwoven with my mother's. A hundred times a day I find myself planning to tell her something, or ask her for this or that. It is a curious thing: the human incapacity to imagine finality. The house seems strange, as if the people in it were deaf and dumb. But all life, I begin to believe, resolves itself into a doing without.

Are you back in New York for good? If so, let us have a session very soon. I am performing upon you without anaesthetics in the March Mer-

Mencken at home in Hollins Street (Enoch Pratt Free Library)

kur, but <u>with</u> reservations. I think the trial and execution of Griffiths goes beyond anything you have ever done. But the first volume made me shed some sweat.

I hear the book is selling very well.

Yours,

M

[NYP]

Hotel Empire
Broadway at 63rd St.
New York City

Feb. 8—1926

Dear Mencken

As you see we are here—Helen & I—at this Hokum while I adjust a number of things before a second move. If you are over here & want a free meal call me up and we can dine here in this room. I'll find booze and a policeman to keep order. Better Helen thinks you are handsomer and more intelligent than I am—which goes without saying.

We might get Boyd. I hear he has artistically translated a fine French comedy—Also Abraham Cahan [1]—if you like—who seems to want to dine with me.

Dreiser

As for your critical predilictions, animosities, inhibitions,—et. cet. Tush. Who reads you? Bums and loafers. No goods. We were friends before ever you were a critic of mine, if I recall. And,—if an humble leman may speak up—may remain so—despite various—well—choose your insults.

1. Abraham Cahan (1860–1951), novelist, editor of the Socialist daily *Vorwaerts* ("Forward"), the leading Yiddish journal in America.

6

*Just a Realist Contemplating
Things Realistically
(1934–1945)*

"You should be a revolutionary, an advocate of social justice, an ironer-out of social in-equalities, like myself and some others. But alas you are not,—just a realist contemplating things realistically."
—TD to HLM, 4 October 1936

"It thus appears that the thirty-fifth anniversary of our correspondence is only a few weeks ahead. I shall celebrate it by hanging out the papal flag and inviting the policeman on the beat to join me in thirty or forty rounds of sound malt liquor."
—HLM to TD, 23 July 1942

The two men had not seen each other or corresponded for over eight years when, on 20 November 1934, Dreiser abruptly resumed the exchange with a letter defending himself against Burton Rascoe's remarks in the *Smart Set Anthology*. Rascoe had written in his introduction that "Mencken broke with Dreiser, because Dreiser would not contribute to a fund to defend *The American Mercury*." They admitted this to be nonsense and planned, with high expectation, to meet again. At the outset, Dreiser established the tone for these last years by acknowledging—or rather, exaggerating—their differences: "fundamentally we never agreed on anything." For the most part, they agreed to accept this half-truth, which relieved them of the burden of having to work out past conflicts.

The years had made a difference. Mencken had settled late, at age fifty, into married life. Though Sara Haardt Mencken was eighteen years younger than Mencken, she was plagued with bad health, and she died in 1935, after only five years of marriage. The couple had taken an apartment at 701 Cathedral Street in Baltimore, the only address other than Hollins Street that Mencken was ever to have. He returned to Hollins Street within a year of his wife's death and lived there with his brother August until his death. There were other changes. Mencken was now known more for his coverage of political conventions than for literary criticism. By 1933, he had given up the editorship of the *American Mercury*, and he was no longer the power among intellectuals that he had been for two decades.

On his part, Dreiser had gotten used to fighting his literary battles—he had gone to court to defend *An American Tragedy* against the censors—without Mencken. He was prosperous and famous, but he could not forget how much his present status owed to Mencken's earlier crusades. Past service, however, could carry them only so far. If they had once mirrored each other's interests and needs, now they were left mainly with inverse images. Intellectually and emotionally, they had grown apart with age. Dreiser's social activism, his association with the Left in the thirties, and his scientific and quasi-religious research were far from Mencken's beliefs. The problem was exacerbated by the different receptions given the two men during the Depression. Mencken appeared reactionary to most intellectuals, while Dreiser, though he wrote little fiction, was well known for his progressive politics. Mencken's *American Mercury* did not survive the decade, partly because of his politics. In the early thirties, his following dropped to a small band of Tories, while the Marxist press attacked him and liberal critics nervously avoided him.

Both men tried not to let politics stand in the way of their friendship, though they clearly disagreed about the social and political future of the country. Mencken vigorously opposed Franklin D. Roosevelt's New Deal policies and supported Alf Landon in the election of 1936; Dreiser met with Roosevelt to plan relief for the victims of the Spanish war. Mencken solidified his conservative position and saw the Depression as a snag in a basically sound economic system; Dreiser published an anticapitalist tract, *Tragic America* (1932), and lectured on communal amelioration and care for the underprivileged masses. In Mencken's eyes, Dreiser had become a world-saver; Dreiser felt his friend had isolated himself from the world at large. Dreiser probably approached the truth when he concluded that their social conflicts were rooted in the prejudices they had brought with them from childhood: "You see, Mencken, unlike yourself, I am biased. I was born poor."

In addition, Mencken found it hard to absorb Dreiser's philosophical interests, which had become increasingly more mystical in nature. The author of *Treatise on the Gods* (1930), who could write "I can no more understand a man praying than I can understand him carrying a rabbit's foot to bring him luck"[1] bristled at the novelist whose study was leading him to other conclusions:

I am moved not only to awe but to reverence for the Creator . . . his presence in all things from worm to star to thought. . . . at long last, [I have] profound reverence for so amazing and esthetic and wondrous a process . . . of which I might pray—and do—to remain the infinitesimal part of the same that I now am.[2]

Mencken thought these the ideas of a crackpot. In this respect, Dreiser felt that Mencken had narrowed intellectually; and he wondered that his friend had not outgrown his youthful materialism. They found, as a result, that they had little to say to each other on such questions. Yet, with the exception of the issue of Dreiser's infatuation with Russia, they managed to avoid open conflict. In fact, given their views, both men succeeded admirably at maintaining a surface calm.

Even the prospect of war with Germany, once the spur to a united front, left them simply with sympathetic points of view. The anti-English bias remained, and they both favored American neutrality. In 1938 Mencken visited Germany and, impressed with its growing economy, saw no possibility of war or violent social upheaval. For a short while Dreiser imagined that Germany might be the agent of a needed new order in western Europe. Because of their loyalties to Germany, they shared the same ambivalent reactions to the Nazis. Mencken called them a "gang of lunatics"; Dreiser, whose books the Nazis banned in 1935 as "subversive to the idea of social progress," turned against them after Germany invaded Russia; yet they viewed Hitler as, at worse, a kind of German New Dealer—"a crook and a high finance stool pigeon," said Dreiser—and they failed to see clearly the plight of the Jews in Europe.[3]

By 1936 they had become aware that Hitler's treatment of the Jews had made many intellectuals sensitive to racial slurs. Hutchins Hapgood and Michael Gold publicly criticized Dreiser after he printed some racial comments, supposedly made for comic effect, by him and his fellow editors of *The American Spectator*—Eugene O'Neill, Nathan, Cabel, and Ernest Boyd. Mencken had for years displayed obvious, though not obsessive, anti-Semitic overtones in his writing. Their language had always been spotted with the standard epithets of petty bigotry—nigger, kike, wop—that were part of the world in which they grew up. Much of this was rooted in the populist mentality of their youth and had little of the virulence, and none of the programmatic aims, of European fascism. Like many Americans, they were not forced to reconsider the implications of their attitudes until after the Allied troops had opened the German concentration camps and released photographs of the Holocaust. Until that time, they seemed painfully uninformed and confused, as their earlier biases came up against the harsh realities Europe offered in the thirties.

The confusion was not limited to the Jewish question. While Mencken attacked the Nazis privately in letters to Dreiser, his anti-English stance forced him into an isolationist posture that was interpreted as pro-German. As in 1915, he felt compelled to stop writing for the Baltimore *Evening Sun* until the war ended. Dreiser too found himself once again in a minority position. The last book he published in his lifetime, *America Is Worth*

Saving (1941), showed an Anglophobia as intense as that of the teens, but now he yoked a pro-Russian and anticapitalist thesis to his isolationism. This, of course, did not sit well with Mencken: "The news that Dreiser has succumbed to the Stalinists is not surprising," he wrote James Farrell. "His political ideas are those of a child of seven, and he always succumbs to plausible quacks."[4]

There were other reasons for their inability to come to terms. First, they no longer wrote to each other often. There are long pauses in the correspondence, especially in 1937 and 1938. Internal evidence suggests that they now misplaced or lost letters they received. After 1938, when Dreiser moved to California, they did not see each other again. Moreover, they appear, in important ways, to have been as isolated from world events as from each other. To some extent, this stemmed from their tendency to view current events as a replay of past history. They saw Roosevelt simply as a latter-day Wilson, the New Deal as puritanism in fresh clothes, Churchill's England as a reincarnation of the old imperialist empire. As late as March 1943, Mencken could ask, "What, precisely are your ideas about the current crusade to save humanity? . . . Are you supporting the war, and if so, to what extent? I recall that during the last great struggle for democracy our ideas were virtually identical, but I somehow gather the impression that you have changed your mind this time." Time had indeed changed Dreiser. His response took away, for Mencken, the need for any further comment. "You ask: 'What, precisely, are your ideas about the current crusade to save humanity.' Personally, I do not know what can save humanity unless it is the amazing Creative force which has brought 'humanity,' along with its entire environment into being."

World events did not alter their writing schedules. Though his health weakened, Dreiser managed to work on two novels in the forties and to continue his bouts with publishers. The psychological effects of aging are more noticeable in Mencken, who concerned himself with the minutiae of medical details, exaggerated the changes in his appearance, and showed psychosomatic symptoms. Yet he wrote his memorable Days books in the war years, and by 1948 he had completed two supplements to *The American Language*. His last joint effort with Dreiser was the disposition of their papers, including the decision to make copies of their letters and divide them between the New York Public Library and the University of Pennsylvania. In addition, Mencken had the manuscript of *Sister Carrie*, a gift from Dreiser years before, treated for preservation and handsomely bound.

In the end, they could agree only on one thing: the importance of their work for posterity. In this, for all the many differences throughout the years, they had been consistent. They continued, in these final years, to place loyalty to each other's best talents above personal affection. This was especially true of Mencken. When the American Academy of Arts and Letters offered Dreiser a medal and a cash prize in 1944, he chose to travel to New York to accept the honor, along with Willa Cather, S. S. Mc-Clure, and Paul Robeson. He wrote Mencken, pleading with him to join him for friendship's sake—and to set the record straight. Mencken declined, citing the hostility of academy members to Dreiser years before. Marguerite Tjader, who was with Dreiser when Mencken's letter arrived, recorded his only response: " 'Old Menck'—grumbled Dreiser, affectionately." [5] It was, to be sure, a golden moment lost. What better emblem of the fading literary history of the first half of the century than a reunion of Dreiser and Mencken? The photographs of the ceremony show instead Cather arm-in-arm with McClure while Dreiser stands stiffly by Paul Robeson.

During the few weeks Dreiser spent in New York, he had long meetings with old friends, like Edgar Lee Masters and Richard Duffy, whose friendship with Dreiser went back to the *Sister Carrie* days. Newer disciples, notably Richard Wright and James T. Farrell, also gathered in his rooms. There was an air of finality about the moment, a feeling that this might be what in fact it was—the novelist's final stay in New York. He visited family, his remaining siblings, and helped bury his sister Mame, who died soon after he arrived. When Dreiser boarded a train for California on June 5 he had touched base for the last time with many of the most important people in his life. The one exception was Mencken. The two men managed, once again, to miss each other.

Dreiser's last years were spent putting his house in order. He was eager to have his biography written and gave Robert H. Elias access to his papers and friends. An important part of this summing up included trying to come to terms with Mencken. From his home in California, he sent emotionally charged letters to Baltimore: "But for all the bull-headed faults and ironic conclusions of said Heinrich—I love and always will love him—be the final estimate of said Dreiser or said Mencken what it may." Such appeals gained no response in kind from Mencken. There is pathos in the final letters, as Mencken appears only more perplexed by the road Dreiser has taken, particularly his late membership in the Communist party. Increasingly, the tone on both sides became that of two survivors grown old, tired even of personal battles.

When Dreiser died, on 28 December 1945, Helen Dreiser immediately telegraphed Mencken, adding "He loved you" to the announcement. To himself Mencken noted, almost as if it surprised him, that the news was causing him to feel depressed. For a commemorative service in 1947, he wrote a belated eulogy, in which he referred to Dreiser's intellec-

tual credulity and his lifelong disregard of the "mot juste." On the positive side, he stuck by the argument he had been making for thirty-five
years: despite Dreiser's flaws, "the fact remains that he was a great artist,
and that no other American of his generation left so wide and handsome a
mark upon the national letters. American writing, before and after his time,
differed almost as much as biology before and after Darwin. He was a man
of large originality, of profound feeling, and of unshakeable courage. All of
us who write are better off because he lived, worked and hoped."[6]

As was his habit, he kept from the public eye any hint of his personal
feelings for the novelist. Which makes all the more surprising a series of
letters to Helen Dreiser, written largely in 1946, in which he reflects on
the friendship. In these letters he allows himself a freedom of expression
that he held in check while Dreiser lived.

Theodore's death leaves me feeling as if my whole world had blown up. We had
met only too seldom in late years, but there was a time when he was my captain in
a war that will never end, and we had a swell time together. No other man had a
greater influence upon my youth.[7]

He remembers Dreiser "at his best, and his best was incomparable." He
also recalls old resentments: "I could never, of course, follow him into his
enthusiasms for such things as spiritualism, Communism, and the balderdash of Charles Fort, but they never made any difference between us, for
some of my ideas were just as obnoxious to him."[8] On a more personal
note: "I resented likewise his aloof indifference to my mother's illness. It
was a long time afterward before I ever felt close to him again. But I
should have known him better. There was a curiously inarticulate side to
him, and it often showed up when he was most moved. If I had another
life to live I think I'd attempt a long study of him, trying to account for
him. But now it is too late."[9]

Notes

1. Mencken, "Sabbath Meditation," in *A Mencken Chrestomathy* (New York: Alfred
Knopf, 1949); repr. in *On Mencken*, ed. John Dorsey (New York: Knopf, 1980), 133.

2. Dreiser, "My Creator" (1943), in *Theodore Dreiser: A Selection of Uncollected Prose*,
ed. Donald Pizer (Detroit: Wayne State University Press, 1977), 329.

3. Mencken stated quite early on that he was "entirely out of sympathy with the
method used by Hitler to handle the Jewish question," and he was aware that "intolerable brutalities have been practiced" against the Jews in Germany (Mencken to Herrn
Netzer, 6 January 1936, in Bode, *Letters*, 370). But as he and Dreiser became more
involved in their opposition to the war, they tended to underplay the problem.

4. Mencken to Farrell, 20 November 1940, in Forgue, *Letters*, 450.

5. Marguerite Tjader, *Theodore Dreiser: A New Dimension* (Norwalk, Conn.: Silver-mine Publishers, 1965), 130.

6. Some time in February 1947, Mencken sent this piece to Helen Dreiser, who wrote him that it had been read at the Lecture Hall of the Los Angeles Public Library on 7 March 1947 (Helen Dreiser to Mencken, 2 April 1947 [NYP]). For some reason, it has been assumed by Dreiser and Mencken scholars alike that Mencken wrote it im-mediately after Dreiser's death to be read at his funeral service. (See Appendix 2, pp. 805–6 for the full text.)

7. Mencken to Helen Dreiser, 30 December 1945. [UPL]

8. Mencken to Helen Dreiser, 4 February 1946, in Forgue, *Letters*, 496.

9. Mencken to Helen Dreiser, 30 January 1946, in Forgue, *Letters*, 494.

The Correspondence
(1934–1945)

[NYP-T]

Theodore Dreiser
Hotel Ansonia,
New York, N.Y.

Nov. 20, 1934.

Dear Mencken:

I am enclosing copy of a letter I received from Knopf this morning.[1] My first reaction to it is that Rascoe has lost his mind. As you know, no such request, either from you or the American Mercury or anybody else was made of me. I haven't the faintest idea where Burton got this nonsense.

There's nothing in connection with it that I ever said to him. I think I may have said to him at one time or another that fundamentally we never agreed on anything and I am sure that with that you will heartily agree. I may have confessed, I do not remember whether I did or not, that once the Smart Set asked me to make some statement in regard to it and I did not do it,[2] but that any feeling arose from that would be countered by the fact that it was followed by publication in the Smart Set of some of my best work. There is nothing else that I ever said to Rascoe or anyone else that could cover this particular charge.

I am writing to Rascoe,[3] mailing him a copy of this letter to you and also sending one to Knopf. Regardless of Burton's feelings, and I care for him very much, I am in common decency bound to address Reynal & Hitchcock, his publishers, in regard to it. In their case also I am enclosing a copy of this letter with a request for a retraction in some form.

Cordially
Dreiser

1. On 19 November 1934, Alfred Knopf sent Dreiser a letter in which he quotes a paragraph from the "Smart Set History," a pamphlet written by Burton Rascoe that was to serve as the introduction to *Smart Set Anthology* (1934), edited by Rascoe and Groff Conklin. Rascoe wrote that "Mencken broke with Dreiser, because Dreiser would not contribute to a fund to defend *The American Mercury*" when the magazine was banned in Boston after it published Herbert Asbury's story "Hatrack." Rascoe added that Dreiser confirmed this story and his decision not to support Knopf and Mencken. [NYP]

2. Dreiser to Mencken, 20 April 1915, and Mencken to Dreiser, 22 April 1915.

3. On 20 November, Dreiser wrote Rascoe a letter asking him "What the devil do you mean by imagining things and putting them in my mouth? . . . I can't be angry with you because I care for you too much. But I must be just to all concerned, and so must you." [NYP]

[UPL]

H. L. Mencken
704 Cathedral St.
Baltimore

November 21st [1934]

My dear Dreiser:-

It goes without saying that I never suspected you for an instant of saying anything of the sort. Putting aside the wanton libel on Alfred Knopf and the distress I knew it must have given you to be involved in it, the pamphlet gave me a loud laugh, rare enough in these last days before the Second Coming. The source of some of Rascoe's more grotesque statements is only too obvious.[1] The poor fellow is himself a ridiculous object. He got a stout kick in the pants, and now he is running around rubbing his backside and complaining that it hurts. He has been silly before, and he will be silly again.

I am seriously thinking of doing my literary and pathological reminiscences, probably in ten volumes folio. This is my solemn promise to depict you as a swell dresser, a tender father, and one of the heroes of the Argonne.

My best thanks for your letter. It was decent of you to go to the bat so promptly. The libel on Knopf—perhaps the squarest man in money matters ever heard of—was really filthy and disgusting.

Yours,
Mencken

1. Mencken thought that Willard Huntington Wright, who edited *Smart Set* in 1913, was the source of Rascoe's statements (see Mencken to Dreiser, 24 April 1939).

[NYP-T]

THEODORE DREISER

Friday, Nov. 24, 1934

Dear Mencken:

Thanks.

It pleases me that my rating is no worse, and I doubt that I need reassure you of my unchanging respect and good will.

I assume that you are not often in New York, but if and when you are—we might meet, white flags in hand. A genial, if visibly armed neutrality, I find permits and achieves as happy a social exchange as any other—love feasts with all knives under the table to the contrary notwithstanding.

Helen and I still hold together. Mt. Kisco is a very lovely place[1]—guest rooms and all conveniences. Three days a week—sometimes four, I am here at the Ansonia—sometimes alone, sometimes with Helen. Whether alone or with your wife you are welcome. And to assemble a congenial half dozen is no trouble whatsoever.

Cordially.

Dreiser.

I still feel that there must have been some much more innocent yarn—told by me possibly—and sticking in Burton's mind which led him astray. Never previously that I recall has he misrepresented me.[2]

1. Dreiser spent his time between "Iroki," the house he built at Mt. Kisco, New York, and the Ansonia Hotel in Manhattan.
2. The postscript is handwritten.

[UPL]

H. L. Mencken
704 Cathedral St.
Baltimore

November 26th, 1934

My dear Dreiser:-

Thanks for your note. My wife, unluckily, is laid up here, recovering from pleurisy. But she is not seriously ill, and I'll probably be in New York myself the early part of next week. Will you be in town on Tuesday the 4th, or on Wednesday morning? If so, I'll be delighted to wait on you. You will hardly recognize me. I have grown very bald, and what remains of my hair is simply a few white tufts à la Uncle Tom. Also, I am doubled up by my old war wounds.

Yours,

M

[NYP-T]

Theodore Dreiser
Hotel Ansonia,
New York City

Nov. 28, 1934.

Dear Mencken:

Yes, I will be in town Tuesday evening, December 4, but I am not sure of Wednesday morning.

On Monday next a possibly three-day court case of mine comes up. If it holds until Wednesday I won't be here, but if you can't make it Tuesday try calling me Wednesday A.M. I may not be in court.

The telephone number is
Susquehanna 7-3300.

Incidentally, bring me a hand painted white flag.

Dreiser

[UPL]

H. L. Mencken
704 Cathedral St.
Baltimore

November 29th [1934]

My Dear Dreiser:-

I'll call you up at the Ansonia Palace Hotel as soon as I get in on Monday, probably shortly before 2 P.M.[1] If you are reported in the hands of justice I'll call again the next morning. I'll be at the Algonquin Palace Hotel in 44th street. No doubt you have often dropped in there to peep at Heywood Broun, Alec Woollcott and other such great writers.

I enclose a recent portrait, so that you may recognize me.[2] Since it was made I have cut off the moustache and lost a little more hair.

Yours,
Mencken

1. For an account of their meeting, see Swanberg, *Dreiser*, 425–26.
2. Mencken enclosed a photograph of a portly, balding gentleman with a walrus mustache.

Mencken celebrates the end of Prohibition
(Enoch Pratt Free Library)

[UPL]

H. L. Mencken
704 Cathedral St.
Baltimore

December 8, 1934.

My dear Dreiser:

Under another cover I am returning your memorandum in the Edwards case.[1] Needless to say, I have read it with the greatest pleasure. As always, you make the drama of the courtroom extremely vivid. The newspaper stories of the trial were naturally confusing and misleading, but as you present it I can see the issues clearly and also gather something of the drama.

In general I agree with you, though a couple of doubts suggest themselves. For one thing I question that the social forces which shape such a boy as Edwards are peculiar to America. As a matter of fact, exactly similar crimes occur in England and on the Continent. In the second place I have some doubt that setting up special courts to try such fellows would accomplish much good. Our whole system is so corrupt that in a little while such courts would be monopolized by professional gangsters. The truth is that society is probably fundamentally wise in putting its Edwardses to death. After all, they are decidedly abnormal, and when they live their careers are commonly very costly to the rest of us.

Hundreds of boys confront a situation exactly analogous to that which faced Edwards, yet they do not resort to murder. My guess is that Edwards himself, if he were liberated tomorrow, would turn out to be incurably unfit to live in the society he was born to, and that soon or late he'd be in the hands of the cops again.

As for the peculiar prejudices of Wilkes-Barré, I see no way to dispose of them. After all, every community is entitled to its own mores. In such matters I am in favor of local self-government. Edwards was born in the place and knew what the penalties were for his acts. I don't think anyone would have molested him if he had simply seduced a few town girls. The thing, in fact, goes on all the time and at a wholesale rate. But he went a shade too far, and so the local morons fell back upon their theology and sent him to the stake. If he had not killed the girl they'd have been proud of him for his prowess. Here I seem to describe a lunatic moral system, but I needn't argue with you that most moral systems are precisely that.

You may recall that you showed me the other night a Japanese book in which there was a chapter on me.[2] I'd like very much to get a copy of it, but I assume that it would be impossible to make a memorandum of the title page inasmuch as it is in Japanese. Could I bother you to lend me the book long enough to have a photostat made? I could then send the photostat to a Japanese book-seller and get the book. My apologies for bothering you, but I'd like to have the book for my files, if only in the hope of impressing the coroner.

My apologies also for a too long letter. Your manuscript should reach you along with this.

Sincerely yours,

M

1. Robert Edwards of Wilkes-Barre, Pennsylvania, murdered his pregnant girl-friend, Freda McKechnie, after he began dating another girl. Because of its similarities to the events in *An American Tragedy*, Dreiser was asked to do a series of articles for the New York *Post* and a piece for *Mystery Magazine*. As Mencken's analysis suggests, Dreiser thought Edwards less a criminal than a victim of American social pressures.

2. This has not been identified.

[NYP-T]

Theodore Dreiser
Hotel Ansonia,
New York City

Dec. 10, 1934.

Dear Mencken:

Under separate cover I am having mailed to you the Japanese book you were looking at. I am enclosing a typewritten copy of a hand-written list of contents which explains itself.

You, O'Neill, Floyd Dell, and Hawthorne come off with individual chapters.[1] Anderson and Lewis and Lanier and Whitman are joined in single chapter discussions. I can see Anderson and Lewis, but not Whitman and Lanier.

Needless to say, I enjoyed our talk and dinner. By the way, what are you and your wife doing around the holidays? Are you likely to be in New York?—particularly at Christmas. If so, let me know.

Dreiser.

As for Edwards—you see how eye to eye we are.[2]

1. A separate chapter was given to Amy Lowell also.
2. The postscript is handwritten.

[UPL]

H. L. Mencken
704 Cathedral St.
Baltimore

December 15, 1934.

Dear Dreiser:

The Japanese book came in yesterday afternoon, and I am having the title page photostated today. It should start on its return journey early next week.

If there is a delay, blame it on the fact that my mother-in-law is very seriously ill down in Montgomery, Alabama. If she dies I'll have to go down there, for my wife, who is also ill, can't travel. This is my usual Christmas experience. My house is always in trouble in December.

Thanks for the loan of the book. And thanks also for the translation of the table of contents. My command of Japanese is of the most meagre.

Yours,
Mencken

[NYP-T]

Theodore Dreiser
Hotel Ansonia,
New York City

Jan. 3, 1935

Dear Mencken:

You are more familiar with this Association than I am.¹ I wish you would tell me what you think of this request and whether my rejection of it will do more harm than good. I ask that because in some instances where I felt fully justified in ignoring a request of this kind I have aroused a fairly lasting bitterness that shows itself in the public as well as the personal reactions of some when I encounter them.

Has the Institute of Art and Letters any respectable value, and what, if any, representative American writers and artists are members of it?

I certainly wish you the best for the coming year.

Dreiser

1. The National Institute of Arts and Letters. Henry Seidel Canby, who edited the *Saturday Review*, wrote Dreiser that he had been proposed for membership in the Institute. [UPL]

[UPL]

H. L. Mencken
704 Cathedral St.
Baltimore

January 4, 1935.

My dear Dreiser:

Canby's letter offers you a great honor, and if you were a man properly appreciative you'd bust into tears. The National Institute of Arts and Letters includes all of the greatest authors of the country. Prominent among its members are: Louis Bromfield, Stephen Vincent Benét, Struthers Bart, Owen Davis, Edna Ferber, Herman Hagedorn, Don Marquis, Ernest Poole and Agnes Repplier. One of the most eminent members is Hamlin Garland, whose efforts to put down "The 'Genius'" you will recall. These great men and women now propose to lift you up to their own level, and I think you should be full of gratitude.

Seriously, I can't imagine any sensible man joining any such organization. When Red Lewis was elected five or six years ago he refused instantly. Masters, so far as I know, has never been a member, and neither has Anderson nor Cabell. The chief hero of the club ten years ago was Stuart Pratt Sherman.

There is a superior branch of the Institute, known as the American Academy of Arts and Letters. You must yet go a long way, of course, before you are eligible to it. Its leading light is Robert Underwood Johnson, and among its other luminaries are John H. Finley of the New York Times, the aforesaid Garland, Judge Robert Grant of Boston, Owen Wister and Paul Elmer More.

Here's hoping that you are lucky in 1935. Christmas in my house was a horror. My wife's mother died on December 23rd and was buried down in Alabama on Christmas morning.

Yours,
HLM

[NYP]

How about a week end at Mt. Kisco. Agree to transport you & Mrs. Mencken—or you to and from New York City: ie The Hotel Ansonia.[1]

1. Dreiser wrote this on a copy of a letter he had sent to Henry Canby, refusing membership in the National Institute of Arts and Letters. (7 January 1935 [NYP])

[UPL]

H. L. Mencken
704 Cathedral St.
Baltimore

January 8, 1935.

Dear Dreiser:

Thanks very much for your note. Unluckily, my wife's illness makes it rather impossible for me to think of going to Mt. Kisco. She has no symptoms and is in good spirits, but in view of her history the faculty insists that she remain in bed a while longer.[1] I hate to leave her any more than is necessary, but toward the end of the present month I'll have to get to New York on business. Are you likely to be in town on, say, January 24th? If so, I suggest that we have dinner together. The National Institute business deserves a talking out. Offering you membership was really a kind of insult, and I am glad that you replied with very precise politeness. Certainly you couldn't afford to join an organization containing so many bounders.

Yours,
Mencken

1. Sara Haardt Mencken had been treated for tuberculosis.

[NYP-T]

Theodore Dreiser
Hotel Ansonia,
New York City

Jan. 9, 1935

Dear Mencken:

Yes, I'll be here on the 24th after five o'clock and shall be pleased to have dinner with you as you suggest.

Dreiser

And don't mind the secretarial "shall be pleased."[1]

1. The postscript is handwritten.

H. L. Mencken
704 Cathedral St.
Baltimore

January 10, 1935.

Dear Dreiser:

Very good. I suggest that we meet, say, at 6.30 or 7 on the evening of January 24th, and then proceed to some convenient eating house. If it will be convenient, I'll drop in at the Ansonia at that time. Let me know if these arrangements meet your convenience.

Yours,
M

Theodore Dreiser
Hotel Ansonia,
New York City

Jan. 11, 1935.

Dear Mencken:

The arrangement you suggest is fine.

Dreiser

Theodore Dreiser
Hotel Ansonia,
New York City

Jan. 14, 1935

Dear Mencken:

The INQUIRER here has reported that the German government has barred my works, emphasizing THE "GENIUS" and AN AMERICAN TRAGEDY among others as being subversive of their idea of social progress.

I wonder if they are under the illusion as so many people seem to be that I am Jewish. I know that impression is abroad because I get it from many sources. One of the things that may have given them this impression is the HAND OF THE POTTER, which, as you know, is a purely Jewish Tragedy.

What procedure could I employ to disabuse the authorities over there of the notion that I am Jewish? Wouldn't a word from you to them or whoever it is that has reached this decision, at least clarify their minds on that score? I will be very much obliged to you for advice in this matter.

Cordially,
Dreiser

Will send you the clipping when I get it.[1]

1. The postscript is handwritten.

[UPL]

H. L. Mencken
704 Cathedral St.
Baltimore

January 15, 1935.

My dear Dreiser:

I suggest that the easiest way to deal with the German business will be to write to Karl von Wiegand, Hearst correspondent in Germany. I think he can be reached at the Adlon Hotel, Berlin. If he is not there the New York American office will tell you where he is. I assume that you know him. If not, it is immaterial. He'll be glad to be of any service to you. If for any reason you hesitate to tackle him, I suggest Guido Enderes, Berlin correspondent of the New York Times. He, too, may be reached at the Adlon.

God knows what the Nazis are up to. They seem to be a gang of lunatics to me. I hear that I am also on their Blacklist. Whether they suspect me of being a Jew I don't know. Every now and then I am listed among Jews in some European paper.[1] When this happened a year ago I had the enclosed cards printed and circulated them at large.[2] I have, of course, no means of reaching the Nazis directly. I don't know a single man among them, and all of my friends in Germany seem to be in opposition—that is, all save a few damn fools whom I'd hesitate to approach.

Let us discuss all of this when we meet. I'll wait on you at the Ansonia at about 7 P.M. on Wednesday, January 24th.

Yours,
M

1. Mencken enclosed a notice from *L'Action Française* of 14 September 1933, which listed "le Juif Mencken" as editor of the *American Mercury*.
2. These cards have not been identified.

[UPL]

H. L. Mencken
704 Cathedral St.
Baltimore

January 18th [1935]

My dear Dreiser:-

Lewis' acceptance doesn't surprise me.[1] There was a time when he would have refused, but that time ain't no more.

The whole business will make an amusing chapter for your autobiography. I'll be undertaking mine, if I am still alive, in a couple of years. I renew my promise to depict you as a swell dresser, a true patriot, and a faithful Dunkard.

We meet, God willing, on Thursday. I have heard nothing more from Schuster about your letters.

Yours,
M

1. Probably a reference to Sinclair Lewis's association with the American Academy of Arts and Letters.

[UPL]

H. L. Mencken
704 Cathedral St.
Baltimore

February 4th [1935]

My dear Dreiser:-

You will recall that we had some talk the other night about the disposition of our papers post mortem, and I suggested that probably the best thing to do with them was to leave them to the Library of Congress. When I got home I wrote to Herbert Putnam, the librarian. In his reply he thus refers to you:

"Most certainly Mr. Dreiser's papers and manuscripts would be valued here, and the deposit of them with us highly welcome. Nor would there be any objection to the proviso that they should not be accessible to the public without his permission during his lifetime".

I am planning to go to Washington in the near future to talk to Dr. Putnam about my own papers. Many of them I'll have to hold for the present, for use in a possible autobiography, but soon or late they will reach the Library. If you say so, I'll suggest that Putnam write to you direct about yours. He apparently hesitates to do so until he hears from me again. He says: "We hope you will be disposed to pass such an assurance to Mr. Dreiser".

As in duty bound, I ever pray, etc.

> Yours,
> M

[NYP-T]

> Theodore Dreiser
> Hotel Ansonia,
> New York City

Feb. 5, 1935.

Dear Mencken:

Thanks for your note and the picture clipped from PULSE.[1]

O.K. on the Library of Congress matter. Let Putnam write me.

> Regards,
> Dreiser

When do you return to New York? Dinner with me if you will. You should be scheming out a new form of public expression. I have one idea.[2]

1. On 4 February, Mencken sent a photograph of Dreiser published in the Indianapolis *Pulse*, with the caption "Liberator Theodore Dreiser." Mencken wrote "The picture represents an unsuccessful effort to make you look like a Christian." [UPL]

2. The postscript is handwritten.

[UPL]

> H. L. Mencken
> 704 Cathedral St.
> Baltimore

February 6th [1935]

My dear Dreiser:-

I am writing to Putnam, and he will communicate with you. He is apparently greatly delighted. I'll probably see him in Washington next week.

When I get back to New York I don't know definitely, but it will probably be about the end of the month. Let us have a session, by all means. What you say about a new form of expression interests me very much. I have been thinking of it against the end of "The American Language" revision. Yesterday, by the help of the Holy Saints, I finished another chapter of the book.

Yours,
M

[NYP]

Mt. Kisco

Feb 13 [1935]

Dear Mencken:

I'm sick up here & won't be in N.Y. until next week. Had a letter from Washington & will answer it Monday or Tuesday. Will you tell me this— Exactly what varieties of personal material are you depositing in Washington? It will help me think out my own procedure.

Incidentally I am going to trouble you with a question. It relates to the problem of individual mind—as opposed to some form of electro-physical control operative through all minds as mechanisms   Back in 1900 Jacques Loeb wrote a book—"Comparative Physiology of the Brain & Comparative Psychology." In it he dismissed all metaphysical conceptions of mind and presented a mechanistic series of chemical reactions. This dismisses reason—(except the mechanistic semblance of reason)—any such thing as individual creative power—or creative thought etc. Here are my questions. Did you ever read the book? (Published by Putnam) Have his deductions ever been gainsayed. Has Loeb's tropistic data—his demonstrated heliotropisms, geotropisms, galvanotropisms ever been questioned? Have these been brilliantly enlarged upon or summarized by a particular person? I know there is plenty of work pointing in this direction but are you familiar with any one single luminous work?

Regards
Dreiser

Address me
  Mt. Kisco, New York
The Old Road

[UPL]

H. L. Mencken
704 Cathedral St.
Baltimore

February 15, 1935.

Dear Dreiser:

I was in Washington yesterday and had a long palaver with Putnam. He is eager to have anything you choose to send him. In particular, of course, he'd like to have one or more of your manuscripts. He told me that he hesitated to ask for anything specifically, but preferred to have you make your own choice. I think this will be a good arrangement. If you want to send him a manuscript he'll make any arrangement regarding its use that you impose—that is, he'll agree, if you say so, to forbid anyone to examine it without your permission while you live.

In the matter of letters, your own choice should rule also. I suggest that you send him anything that you think ought to be kept in the Library, with any conditions attached that seem proper. My own letter files will go to him in the long run. I can't send them at once because I'll need them for a book of reminiscences that I have in mind. But as soon as that use of them is finished I think I'll send them to him. Many of the letters in them, of course, will have to be withdrawn, for they deal with very private matters. But those that are harmless and have to do with subjects of literary interest I'll deposit as soon as I finish with them.

So far as I know, there has never been any serious refutation of Loeb's books. His discovery that eggs could be fertilized artificially seems to me to be one of the really great biological discoveries of the last fifty years. Old Loeb's agnosticism and irreverence made him many enemies, and so there has been some disposition to pooh-pooh him, but so far as I know no one has ever really disposed of him.

The theology that you will find in such books as those of Jeans and Whitehead is feeble stuff,[1] and without any basis in the known facts. Loeb dealt exclusively with what he could see and measure. Let us discuss all this the next time we meet. The man who knows most about Loeb is Paul DeKruif,[2] who worked with him at the Rockefeller Institute. Loeb suffered a good deal there from internal politics. There was a faction that didn't like his inconvenient plain speaking.

Yours,
M

1. Sir James Hopwood Jeans (1877–1946), British astronomer and mathematician; Alfred North Whitehead (1861–1947), mathematician, philosopher.
2. See Mencken to Dreiser, 14 March 1925, n.1.

[NYP-T]

Theodore Dreiser
Hotel Ansonia,
New York City

Feb 26, 1935.

Dear Mencken:

When are you planning to come over? I wish you would let me know because it looks as though I will have to leave New York very shortly and I am wondering whether it is going to interfere with this meeting. If you are coming within the next few days it will be all right but if it is later than that I am afraid it will. I am planning to go to the coast.

Regards,
Dreiser

[UPL]

H. L. Mencken
704 Cathedral St.
Baltimore

March 1st [1935]

Dear Dreiser:-

I find your letter on my return to Baltimore. I was in New York yesterday and the day before, but assumed stupidly that you were still in the country. I forbear apologizing for this dumbness: it is a talent that creeps on me as I age.

When, precisely, will you be going westward? It may be that I'll be back in New York before you leave. Moreover, it may be that I'll get to the Northwest in the late Spring. I am trying now to induce my wife to make the trip. I have never been North of San Francisco.

Yours,
M

[NYP-T]

Theodore Dreiser
Old Bedford Road,
Mt. Kisco, N.Y.

March 16, 1935.

Dear Mencken:

I don't know whether I told you, but since writing you I closed up my apartment in the Ansonia and moved up here to Mt. Kisco. Reason—ill health. I found myself giving way under grippe and strains of various sorts. I am staying here and will be for the next two weeks anyhow, after which, if I feel physically okay, I will be moving on to Los Angeles where I will continue with the work that I have in hand.

If you are going to be in New York between now and the first and could find it convenient to spend a night or a day up here, I will be glad to have you. There is plenty to discuss. Of course you noticed that the Spectator[1] folded up and you probably read George's[2] bright picture of its profitable history. It did excellently so long as it had the courage to say something, but when I found George too timid to make any radical assertions I withdrew, after which I always anticipated that lack of courage would kill it.— It has.

You know, I still feel that there is room for a very modern light and even gay-mooded philosophic journal, and it was that that I wanted to talk to you about. I feel satisfied that now the intelligensia could be interested in the mystery of life and it could be attacked from so many angles and at the same time relieved, by the way, by purely play-boy material. In such a matter it seems to me that Nathan would probably be useless, but there are some temperaments drifting around that would provide color and gaiety.

Enough of that for now, but if you come up this way before I go I would certainly like to talk the matter over with you. By the way, if I am in Los Angeles and you come down that way, I will be living for the time being with George Douglas of the Los Angeles Examiner.[3] If you do not know him, I can assure you he is one of the most fascinating temperaments I have ever encountered.

Regards and best wishes,
Dreiser

1. *The American Spectator*, a literary newspaper started by George Jean Nathan and Ernest Boyd in 1923. Dreiser was one of the principal editors.
2. George Jean Nathan.
3. George Douglas, Australian-born journalist and critic who encouraged Dreiser in his scientific and philosophic studies in the thirties.

[UPL]

H. L. Mencken
704 Cathedral St.
Baltimore

March 19, 1935.

Dear Dreiser:

My wife is ill here (fortunately, not seriously, as reported) and so it is difficult for me to get away. I surely hope that your own health has cleared up and that we'll be able to meet in a little while. If I can get to New York toward the end of the month or early in April, I'll certainly be delighted to wait upon you at Mt. Kisco.

I have grave doubt that the time is a good one for launching a new magazine. My reasons are somewhat complicated, and I'll have to explain them when we meet. The field has been invaded and polluted by all sorts of quacks, and it would probably be difficult to get any attention for a new-comer of any genuine merit. However, this situation can't last. More of this when we meet.

I am still plugging away at the rewriting of my old book, "The American Language". The new edition will be a really tremendous tome. A great deal of amusing stuff has been accumulated, and I am trying to find room for all of it.

Has it ever occurred to you that if a set of whiskers were hung on Mr. Secretary Ickes[1] he would look precisely like Isaiah?

Yours,
M

1. Harold Ickes, secretary of the interior.

THEODORE DREISER

[NYP]

March 24 [1935]

Dear Mencken:

How about this coming week end? The weather has cleared up and flora if not fauna are beginning to bud. You can get quite convenient trains from Grand Central Station from 915 A.M. On Saturday they sell a low rate round trip ticket good until Monday midnight. If you fix on any train you can write me or when you arrive at Kisco Station you can call up Mt. Kisco 5413 and I'll send a policeman down with a warrant. The calaboose is just around the corner. Furthermore I'll unchain the watchdog, set the alarm clock, run up the storm signals and in other ways undertake to safeguard the community. Needless to say I have fire, life, cyclone and air-accident insurance. My personal body guard is a newly hired Sicilian. With these precautions you should feel safe.

Do come. Helen says she will provide you with your favorite breakfast dish—birds nest soup. What more can you ask.

Kidding aside we meet all trains—yours for a certainty

Dreiser

[UPL]

H. L. Mencken
704 Cathedral St.
Baltimore

March 26, 1935.

Dear Dreiser:

Unfortunately, my wife is still in hospital, and so I fear my next trip to New York will have to be a short one. Would it be feasible for me to come out late some afternoon, sit with you until ten or eleven o'clock, and then return to New York? If this can be managed I suggest Tuesday or Wednesday of next week, April 2nd or 3rd. If getting back to New York would be difficult, then give me a blanket and I'll bivouac in the orchard and return the next morning. Getting to New York on the coming Sunday would be impossible. My wife is apparently making good progress, but she still needs close attention.

I am more and more firmly convinced that the Second Coming is at hand. I used to believe that Nicholas Murray Butler[1] was the Messiah foreordained, but now I begin to look toward Henry W. Wallace, of Iowa.[2] He has a bright smile, he loves humanity, and there is apparently nothing in his head. This is the ideal combination.

Yours,
M

1. Butler, the president of Columbia University from 1902 to 1947, was a favorite-son candidate for the Republican presidential nomination in 1920.
2. Wallace was secretary of agriculture (1933–40) and vice-president under Franklin Roosevelt (1940–44).

[NYP-T]

THEODORE DREISER

March 28, 1935

Dear Mencken:

Next Wednesday is OK but not Tuesday. On Tuesday I am going down to New York to the Rockefeller Institute to look up some scientific stuff that is going on there. On Wednesday you can get good trains from ten o'clock on. I think there is one around 11:15 or 11:30 that will get you here about one and if you can make it I would advise you to take that one. The running time is about one hour and fifteen minutes. If you can stay over night I would prefer it because we can talk longer. If you have to go back, I am sure there is a train about eleven or about that time. In the morning there are trains going down at nine, ten, and eleven.

By the way, you have an old censer swinging admirer out here, Jean Balch. She comes over here occasionally and I know she would be happy to have the chance of joining us for dinner if you have no personal objection. But that is entirely up to you—I am merely mentioning it. I don't know about Wallace but it seems to me that there are Saviours on every hand. New York has some 500 at least. By the way, do you happen to know if it is the Standard Oil Company that is backing Hitler in this anti-Soviet attitude of his? Certainly there is no money in Germany for any such program as he is advocating and I can't imagine who else apart from Rockefeller would have the money to carry out such a program. I know for one thing that the Standard Oil Company is set against not only the Soviet Republic but Japan also until such time as it can bring Japan to obey orders.

I am sorry to hear that your wife is so ill. Please convey my earnest wishes for her quick recovery. Among my various insurances I have taken out $100,000 to cover all Acts of God.

Cordially
Dreiser

[NYP-C]
March 30, 1935

Dear Dreiser:

One million damns! I now discover that next Wednesday will be impossible for me. Tuesday, however, remains open. Is it likely that you'll have any time after you finish your business at the Rockefeller Institute, or before you undertake it, or in the midst of it? If so, I suggest that we have a brief session. We might have lunch or dinner together, or meet in the late afternoon. Will you let me know about this at the Algonquin Palace Hotel, 59 West 44th Street? I'll get there sometime Monday afternoon.

Jean Balch is an old friend and I'd be delighted to see her. Maybe we can arrange a session with her at some time in the future?

I know precisely nothing about the operations of the Standard Oil Company. The allegations constantly made by the New Republic and other such sheets seem to me to be highly dubious. I doubt that Rockefeller would be fool enough to stake Hitler. Most of the Wall Street brethren are violently anti-Semitic, but they are hardly anti-Semitic enough to risk millions on so poor a horse.

Will you write me at the Algonquin as soon as you get this? I'd like very much to see you if you have the time on Tuesday. The Wednesday business was unexpected and I can't duck it.

Yours,
(Signed) H. L. Mencken

[NYP]

Theodore Dreiser
Mt. Kisco, N.Y.

Friday, April 5—1935

Dear Mencken:

Thanks for word as to next week.¹ My schedule runs as follows. Wednesday I am in Connecticut. Back Thursday about 5 P.M. That is the 11th. On Monday the 15th I leave for Chicago. Back the 18th   By the 25th I hope to leave for Los Angeles. If these intermediate dates are too complicated for your affairs don't bother. I'll be back again in the fall. And we can meet then.

Regards
Dreiser

1. On 1 April, Mencken wrote Dreiser that he had bronchitis and would have to delay for a week his trip to New York.

[UPL]

H. L. Mencken
704 Cathedral St.
Baltimore

April 9, 1935.

Dear Dreiser:

The Holy Ghost has been giving me such a run of late that I begin to doubt that I'll be able to get to New York before you leave for the Coast. However, it may be possible, and if it is I'll certainly write to you in advance. In any case, I may see you in the West before the end of the year. I surely hope so.

My illness is not serious, but it floored me for four or five days and left me wobbly for three or four more. This was the first time that I had been actually laid on my back for at least twenty years, and so I was not only surprised but also indignant. However, I have come to the conclusion that it is vain to oppose the decrees of Heaven. You will recall the last words of the immortal McKinley:¹ "Not our will, but God's be done."

The next edition of "The American Language" promises to run to three volumes and 300,000 words. I am trying hard to cut it down, but the job looks almost hopeless.

Sincerely yours,
Mencken

1. President William McKinley.

[NYP]

The
STEVENS
CHICAGO
Michigan Boulevard
Seventh to Eighth Street

Thursday, April 18, 1935

Dear Mencken:

I urged yesterday on the Student Lecture Bureau of Chi. University that they get you to debate with or rather oppose the Rev. Father Coughlin[1] as to the value of his remedies. They want to bring him on then have some Bushman like yourself leap out and club him down. If in the progress of American Humor this scene should be staged here I'll fly out & back to witness it. It would compensate for a vast array of senile pains and limitations

Heaven is my next stop.

Dreiser

1. Charles Coughlin (1891–1979) was a Roman Catholic priest from Michigan who preached a "social justice" message. In books and radio sermons, Coughlin first supported the New Deal's program for recovery, but by this point he was arguing for an inflationary money supply and a more radical nationalization of resources and banking. Later, in 1936, he formed the Union party in opposition to Roosevelt, and his candidate, William Lemke, received about 2 percent of the popular vote.

[UPL]

H. L. Mencken
704 Cathedral St.
Baltimore

April 20, 1935.

Dear Dreiser:

It is tempting, but I think I had better stick to my rule against making speeches. I break it once a year to burble for a few minutes over the radio, but that is something different. If I cut loose before an audience I'd be beset by lecture agents, and so life would cease to be a long, sweet song. They'd come for me no matter how badly I performed, for they are always looking for fresh victims.

In the matter of Coughlin I believe that it would be difficult to stage a really effective debate. It would be impossible for his opponent to deal with some of the real objections to him, for they are theological and ecclesiastical in character. He grounds his whole case on a papal encyclical. It is full of buncombe, but saying so out loud would probably go beyond the toleration of any American university.

I am sorry that we missed our session in New York. My wife is now home from hospital, and I begin to feel fairly well myself. I am still hoping that we may meet on the Coast before you return. I hear that there are some swell bawdy houses in Seattle. We might drop in on the girls some Sunday afternoon and ask them what they think of the More Abundant Life.

Yours
M

[NYP-T]

Theodore Dreiser
Los Angeles

May 17th. 1935

Dear Menck:

Yes, I am sorry that you couldn't get up to Kisco and you're right about not considering a debate with his Reverence the Coughlin. You couldn't introduce the religious question. Isn't it tough?

If you <u>could</u> have your say what a mess you could make of him but you would be stoned by the German Catholics as you came out.

As you see, I am on the Coast, the Pacific mecca. The Holy Shrine stands at the corner of Glendale and Hollywood Blvd. and Iowans come first. I would like to be in Seattle when you make your planned devotions. The mere thought of it causes me to quake as was my wont in eighteen-eighty-six but Heaven guards me and I can not leave here. I am at 232 S. Westmoreland Avenue with George Douglas and shall be here for some time, probably until Fall. This address is private but O.K. for you. If you come down here I will even visit the Temple[1] with you. If you come to Frisco it is possible that they might even set up a new Barbary Coast in which case I would agree not to miss a door. Anyhow, you know where I am.

Regards,
Dreiser

1. The Angelus Temple, a famous religious center presided over by the evangelist-faith healer Aimee Semple McPherson.

[UPL]

H. L. Mencken
704 Cathedral St.
Baltimore

May 25, 1935.

Dear Dreiser:

My guess is that Coughlin is already in collapse, though he apparently doesn't know it himself, and it would surprise most of the newspapers to hear it. Such mountebanks seldom last long in this country. They are tremendous heroes for a little while, and then suddenly the plain people turn elsewhere and they are left standing on a burning deck. I hear that the response to Coughlin's radio harangues is a great deal less enthusiastic than it used to be, and that he is having difficulty raising money. The fact that he can still fill a large hall in New York is of no significance. Any man whose name has appeared in the papers two or three times can do the same. There are thousands of people willing to turn out to see a celebrity.

I am still grinding away at my infernal book. The trouble with it is that new material accumulates almost faster than I can work it into the manuscript. However, I hope to bring the business to an end by August 1st.

My wife, as you know, has been ill off and on for a year past. At this moment she is in the Johns Hopkins with an undiagnosed condition that entertains the medical gentlemen but leaves her in a sorry frame of mind. All this, of course, is somewhat upsetting, but I still manage to work. It is not inconceivable that I may yet see you on the Coast before you return.

Yours,
M

[NYP-T]

232 W. Westmoreland Ave.,
Los Angeles

June 4, 1935.

Dear Mencken:

I read of your Wife's death[1] in the Examiner here. After all you had told me of her continued illness, I was not as shocked as I might have been, but I have felt all along that this was a relationship which meant a great deal to you, and am very sorry that it has had to end so soon. As I see

*Sara Haardt Mencken. Photo by Cecelia Norfolk Eareckson
(Enoch Pratt Free Library)*

it, life furnishes just one panacea, if so much, for all the ills and accidents of life: it is work—and more work.

As ever,
Dreiser

1. Sara Haardt Mencken died on 31 May 1935, at the age of thirty-seven.

[UPL]

H. L. Mencken
704 Cathedral St.
Baltimore

June 11, 1935.

Dear Dreiser:

Thanks so much for your telegram[1] and your letter. My poor wife's health had been failing for several years past, and so I was always under heavy anxiety. I now find myself unable to do anything resembling sensible work, so I am thinking of going abroad for a couple of weeks with my brother,[2] who lately got out of hospital himself. Unluckily, I have so much in hand that I can't stay long.

I may still carry out my plan to visit the Northwest later in the year. If I do so, and you are still in Los Angeles, I'll drop down to wait on you. I have been swamped during the past week with mail, but have at last managed to clear it off. My plan is to go on with the house here.[3] It is very comfortable and convenient, and I suppose that I'll have to learn to endure the fact that my wife is no longer in it.

Yours,
M

1. This has not survived.
2. Mencken's brother August accompanied him on a trip to England; they returned on 12 July.
3. Though Mencken planned to stay on at the Cathedral Street apartment, he soon found that unsatisfactory. He returned to his Hollins Street home in March 1936 and lived there for the rest of his life with his bachelor brother August.

Theodore Dreiser
232 W. Westmoreland Ave.,
Los Angeles

June 24, 1935.

Dear Mencken:

Thanks for the copy of that Harlan County Coal Investigation report. It merely substantiates in part what I found there.[1] I say 'in part,' because while I was there, people were murdered by the operating gang, or their sheriffs and deputies, for collecting food and clothing for the workers who were being robbed and tortured by them. But they did not get away with their plans in connection with me—not by several long jumps.[2]

I am glad your staying on in the old house: it is the sensible thing to do, but if you start wandering soon, wander out this way.

I am planning, one of these days to open an intellectual monastery somewhere in Southern New Mexico. It will have cells and beds, and a long refectory table which will accommodate wandering apostates from normalidy, wherever they may be. But—!!! they must bring with them the minds that will make the refectory table an escape from the humdrum cares of the world.

Thanks again for the report.
Regards,
Dreiser

Top honor is to be hailed as Father-Brother. Unlimited stay (with final honors) come with a unanimous vote. I am looking for charter members or brothers. Brother Heinrich for instance. All personal archives to be safely stored in the monestary. The Glorious George Douglas has signed up.[3]

1. In November 1931, Dreiser had headed a committee to investigate the desperate working conditions of miners in Harlan County, Kentucky.
2. Local officials tried to discredit Dreiser by publicizing his relations with a woman companion while in Kentucky (see Swanberg, *Dreiser*, 387).
3. The postscript is handwritten.

[UPL]

H. L. Mencken
704 Cathedral St.
Baltimore

July 16th [1935]

Dear Dreiser:-

I got in safely, and am resuming my slavery. The damned revision of The American Language will keep me jumping until September. During the month I was away another gallon or two of material accumulated. The thing becomes a pestilence.

Yost,[1] the editor of the Fayette (O.) Review, is a very intelligent fellow, and his editorial was characteristic of him. He has been banging away at the local simians for years past, but has made no impression on them. They still believe firmly that the Kaiser hoped to conquer Ohio, and that a horse hair put into a bottle of water will turn into a snake.

Put me down for a cell with bath in the monastery. I choose the name of Brother Pilsner. It is unhackneyed, and represents my sentiments. I hope you make a strict rule against loose women. It would be scandalous to see a gang of holy men chasing them up and down the corridors, and mounting them in the view of tourists. But no doubt you have already given thought to this matter.

Somehow, the suicide of Ray Long didn't surprise me.[2] He was a completely futile fellow. But the tragedy of such a flamingo is still a tragedy. I can imagine his agonies before he managed to pull the trigger. You and I, I hope, will be spared such a finish. I greatly prefer the electric chair, which the gipsies tell me will probably be my lot.

We had 15 sunshiny days in London—the longest stretch since the reign of Alfred. The temperature went up to 82 degrees. As a result, the English fell like flies. But so far as I could make out, none of them thought to take off his doormat clothes and his heavy sanitary undershirt. It seemed only balmy to my brother and me.

Whether I can keep house remains to be seen. Today I hired a new maid. If she ever spills any really decent wine I'll shoot her on the spot. My brother is staying here for the Summer, but after September I'll have to go it alone.

Yours,
Mencken

1. Charles E. Yost, the founder of the Ohio journal *The Fayette Review*, was a friend of Dreiser.
2. Ray Long edited *Red Book* and other literary journals.

[NYP-T]

Theodore Dreiser
232 S. Westmoreland Ave.,
Los Angeles, Cal.

July 20, 1935.

Dear Mencken:

Herein is copy of letter I received from Theodore V. Brown, dated July 16th, - for your information and attention.[1]

Regards,
Dreiser

I'll be glad to inscribe a book & write a letter if these people are ok.[2]

1. Brown wrote on behalf of the Frank Harris Memorial Exhibit and asked Dreiser for an inscribed copy of one of his books. He mentioned Mencken as one of the other prominent writers who was being asked for his support. [NYP]
2. The postscript is handwritten.

[UPL]

H. L. Mencken
704 Cathedral St.
Baltimore

July 27, 1935.

Dear Dreiser:

It is possible that I had some sort of communication with Brown, but if so I can't recall it. Certainly I am sure that I never made any contribution to the Harris fund. Who Brown may be I don't know. I'd feel easier about the matter if the business were in the hands of some one better known. I don't know Harris's widow, and have never had any communication with her.

My little trip abroad bucked me up physically, but on returning I walked into two weeks of the most infernal heat ever heard of. Here in Baltimore the humidity broke records. Thus anything resembling serious work was impossible. But now a coolish wind is blowing and so I have resumed work on my revision of "The American Language". If all goes well I hope to finish it by the end of October. It has been delayed horribly during the past year.

What are you up to?

Yours,
M

[NYP-T]

Theodore Dreiser
232 S. Westmoreland
Los Angeles

July 29, 1935.

Dear Mencken:

I am glad you are back and settled. I hope and trust you stay put and am pretty sure that you will. I do not see how you expect to keep up with the American language, but there is one comfort in it, you will always have an interesting job.

If you decide to come west, let me know.

As ever,
Dreiser

[UPL]

H. L. Mencken
704 Cathedral St.
Baltimore

August 8, 1935.

Dear Dreiser:

That Los Angeles Times interview was swell indeed.[1] But the head-line somewhat upsets me, for I dislike seeing the work rake used in connection with the name of a man I venerate. It is bound to cause misap-prehension in Christian circles. The photograph shows a startling resem-blance to my Uncle Julius, who passed away in 1894, after devoting 32 years to the retail hardware business in this city. He died worth nearly $11,000. Once a year the Mozart Liederkrantz goes to his grave in Loudon Park cemetery and sings a programme of German folk songs. The mem-bers then move to Adam Dietrich's saloon down the lane and tank up. Julius left no lawful issue, but it is a remarkable fact that all of the servant girls in his employ became mothers, on being married, with a speed which greatly interested biologists.

The weather here has suddenly turned cool, and I am beginning to feel that work will be possible again.

Yours,
M

1. Anon., "Rake Calls to Dreiser," *Los Angeles Times*, 29 July 1935, pt. 2, 1.

[NYP]

4922 Rosewood Ave
L.A.

Oct. 6 [1935]

Dear Mencken:

Are you still in the U.S.A. Suppose you report. I am here but leaving for New York between the 15th–20th of this dear month. Have just been reading a book by Alexis Carrel. If this is his measure, he is smaller than I thought. Have you read it. (Man the Unknown) I wish we could meet and talk. Not finding one to suit me I am constructing (drudgingly and trudgingly I will admit) a life picture of my own.[1] It may not even please me but it will, I hope, please me personally much more than the things I read.

L.A. begins to take on the feel of a city   It has taken 2,400,000 people to approximate this but now one can find some people—some resorts and not feel the weight of either Iowa or the movies. There are too many internationals here. When it reaches four or five million as it will I believe be arrestingly different and perhaps—who knows—intellectually gay. Just now it faintly suggests its future. Drop me a line

Dreiser

1. In the thirties Dreiser collected scientific and philosophic notes for a book that would synthesize his thinking on the nature of human existence. He never completed what he referred to as "The Formula Called Man," but its chapters, fragments, and notes were published as *Notes on Life* (1974), edited by Marguerite Tjader and John J. McAleer.

[UPL]

H. L. Mencken
704 Cathedral St.
Baltimore

October 7, 1935.

Dear Dreiser:

It is good news that you are returning to the East. I surely hope that the chance offers for a meeting soon after you get to New York. I'll be there off and on all Winter and ready for any deviltry, so long as it remains refined in its main outlines.

I have been grinding away at the rewriting of "The American Language" and have come pretty close to the end. I began it a year and a half ago, but my wife's illness and death interrupted it dreadfully, and it has only been since September that I have put in hard licks on it. The book will be enormous in size—indeed, it will probably make "An American Tragedy" look like a college yell. But the material in hand was so interesting that I simply couldn't resist it.

I haven't read the Carrel book, but it is on my desk and I hope to tackle it shortly. I hear from all competent persons that it is dreadful bilge. Carrel has apparently gone over to Holy Church. Well, this is nothing new. There is a kind of scientist who inevitably weakens in the long run. I give you Millikan and Whitehead as examples.[1] Unfortunately, the real scientists seldom write books dealing with religion, so their position is not known. I have been urging some of my friends among them to form a national association for putting down such Presbyterians as Carrel.

Once I clear off "The American Language" and one or two other small jobs, I'll probably tackle the first four or five volumes of my autobiography. There will be very little news in it, but I am hoping to make parts of it at least amusing. The first volume will deal with my sufferings on the immigrant ship coming over from Poland, and the second will describe my career at Harvard.

Yours,
M

1. Robert Andrews Millikan and Alfred North Whitehead.

[NYP]

Mt. Kisco

Sunday, Oct. 27—'35

Dear Mencken:

Arrived last night about 8 P.M. Drove accross the continent for one more look at it. It seems unchanged in calibre mentally though technically it is much more mechanized. Are you coming over soon. Haven't made any downtown arrangement but feel now that such time as I spend in N.Y. will be at the Edison in West 46th 47th. I have several days of work on the place here.

Incidentally I have a letter from my theiving Austrian publisher—Paul Zsolnay—which I cannot adequately translate. It's only a page—double-spaced of type writing. Can I send it to you for translation? I'd be duly thankful.

I hope that that stupendous work of yours draws to a close. Your memoirs may not be very colorful in your eyes but the public is most certain to think differently. Advise me

Dreiser

[UPL-H]

HOTEL ALGONQUIN
56 to 65 West Forty-fourth Street
New York

[30 October 1935]

Dear Dreiser:

Your letter of Sunday has just reached me here, forwarded from Baltimore by Jim Farley's[1] ox-cart. And now, damn it, I must go home at once. But I'll be back shortly, and I hope you'll be in town by then, and free for a session. Let the Zsolnay letter go to 704 Cathedral St., and I'll do my best with it. German is a grand language for a publisher writing to an author—and trying not to say anything.

Yours
M.

1. James Farley was postmaster general.

[NYP]

Mt Kisco

Thurs. Oct. 31 [1935]

Dear Mencken:

Its ok. I decided afterward that I'd rush it down to the foreign department of the Central-Hanover Bank and they made a good job of it. Next time give me fair notice—two days say—and I'll drop down. For the present there are some things I have to do and can do better here than in the worlds largest Hebraic center.

Regards
Dreiser

[UPL]

H. L. Mencken
704 Cathedral St.
Baltimore

November 2, 1935.

Dear Dreiser:

Your hunch was a good one. The translation of the Central-Hanover Bank is probably completely accurate, whereas mine would have been full of guesses. My German, I confess, is not what it ought to be.

When I'll get back to New York I don't know, but it will probably be toward the end of the month. If I could get two clear weeks here I'd finish the book. Unluckily, I am horribly beset by unexpected visitors and all other sorts of interruptions. Yesterday I didn't get to my desk until 7 P.M., and by that time I was so tired I began to drowse at 9.30. I am thinking of pulling down all the curtains of my apartment and putting a smallpox sign on the door.

Yours,
M

[NYP]

Mt. Kisco

1–1–36

Dear Mencken:

On February 22—1821 John Quincy Adams sent a report on Weights and Measures to Congress. I understand it is a metro-logical classic. Have you any idea where I could pick up a copy? Is it possible to get the loan of a copy of it from the Library of Congress? I have canvassed old book stores here but so far in vain. Also I have several document hounds on the trail. It may show up but perhaps you can advise me to greater advantage than these others. If not OK and I will have the comfort of having made one more "try."

I am having the British flag reinforced with concrete so as to preserve it over our front entrance until A.D. 2000. The lacy portraits of Jesus and Mary I am having backed with gold metal cloth and combined back to back Scapula-wise. When finished it will be suspended by a silver chain over my grateful heart.

I join you in prayer for my welfare.

D.

Not a word about the New Year in this issue.

[UPL]

H. L. Mencken
704 Cathedral St.
Baltimore

January 2, 1936.

Dear Dreiser:

I believe that you can get a copy of that Adams report at the New York Public Library. Why not write to H. M. Lydenberg, the chief librarian?

He is a very amiable fellow, and a great admirer of yours. I don't know whether you are familiar with the New York Public Library, but if you ever look into it with any particularity you'll discover that it is one of the really great libraries of the world. Lydenberg runs it with immense skill, and it can answer almost any question you or I could frame. To get a copy of the Adams report for yourself would probably be difficult. It is highly esteemed and probably brings a considerable price.

I have just passed through one of the merriest Christmases ever heard of. You can imagine what a cheerful festival it was in this house. To add to its charms four of my oldest friends died within ten days. Another friend was horribly injured in an explosion, and a fourth, a medical man, had a fire in his office and lost the records of thirty years—his chief stock in trade. I marvel at the continued virtuosity of Yahweh. Human beings, as they grow old, tend to lose some of their bounce and resourcefulness, but He seems to be just as clever an operator as he was in the days of Moses.

I hope to see you soon. I had planned to be in New York today, but a funeral is detaining me.

Yours,
M

Souvenir of the confederacy.[1]

1. Mencken wrote this on an NAACP advertisement that featured a photograph of a Negro being lynched, and enclosed it in this letter.

[NYP-T]

Theodore Dreiser
Mt. Kisco, New York

January 6, 1936

Dear Mencken,

Thanks for the word as to Lydenberg. I am writing him. Naturally I am grateful for the picture entitled Spring Time in the South. I will hang it along side a flower piece by Al Smith.

The pressure of the cataclysmic world in which you live moves me to suggest that you study to be a mortician—the Townsend Plan failing as it may[1]—this would provide comfortably for your old age.

Regards,
Dreiser

1. Francis E. Townsend originated the Townsend Recovery Plan, which proposed a monthly pension of $200 for all citizens over sixty.

Do not look at the Negro.

His earthly problems are ended.

Instead, look at the seven WHITE children who gaze at this gruesome spectacle.

Is it horror or gloating on the face of the neatly dressed seven-year-old girl on the right?

Is the tiny four-year-old on the left old enough, one wonders, to comprehend the barbarism her elders have perpetrated?

Rubin Stacy, the Negro, who was lynched at Fort Lauderdale, Florida, on July 19, 1935, for "threatening and frightening a white woman," suffered PHYSICAL torture for a few short hours. But what psychological havoc is being wrought in the minds of the white children?

Mencken to Dreiser: "Souvenir of the Confederacy"
(University of Pennsylvania Library)

[NYP]

Mt Kisco

[before 26 May 1936]

Sir:

My conviction is that this[1] is a sly and circuitous attack on my impeccable honor and peace of mind. And were I a sinful man it might, I admit, shake an evil conscience. As it is, I remain as ever, confused and content.

One thought holds me. The Rev. Theophilus Brodtgesang Schmitt, the exorcist shown on page two, looks amazingly like the notorious moralist and vice-crusader, Henry L. Mencken, whose pleasure it is as all know to shake the confidence of the suspected. I assure you and him that in this case he is barking up the wrong tree. This long while I have made my peace with the Church and God.

> Peacefully
> Brother Ixion, Pietist in Excelso

1. Mencken had sent Dreiser a pamphlet called *Begone, Satan*, written by the Rev. Carl Vögel, a German Catholic priest. It contained the story of an exorcism of demons by a German-born Capuchin monk named Father Theophilus. The priest was said to have expelled demons that took possession of a woman, a native of Iowa, who was taken to a Franciscan convent in Earling, Iowa, where, with the approval of the bishop of Des Moines, Father Theophilus performed the rite of exorcism.

[UPL]

H. L. Mencken
~~704 Cathedral St.~~
Baltimore
1524 Hollins St.

May 26, 1936.

Dear Dreiser:

Your mocking doesn't shake me. I am still convinced, on the massive evidence brought forth by Father Vogel, that demoniacal possession is still possible on this earth. Moreover, I am convinced that it is rampant in Iowa. The fact explains many other inexplicable phenomena in that great state.

I have lately discovered that the State of Maryland maintains an official board for inspecting madstones. I have procured a specimen passed by it, and shall send it to you in a few days. It is said to be efficacious, not only against hydrophobia, but also against 10,000 other diseases, most of them fatal. The chairman of the board tells me that clapping it on the head behind either ear for two minutes will cure the most frightful headache ever heard of. It is also said to be helpful in cases of impotence, but on this point I offer no opinion.

I have been sweating away here in this lovely weather writing a history of the Baltimore Sun, which will be 100 years old next year.[1] Once the job is off my hands, I'll start for the two national conventions. I surely wish you were coming along. The shows this year will be really magnificent. The worst quacks ever heard of on earth will be assembled, and they'll all be on their toes. I look for such obscenities as the human eye has never hitherto beheld. If you are still collecting postcards I'll be able to send you one from Cleveland and another from Philadelphia. Let me know about this. I don't want to waste the money on the stamps if you have stopped collecting them.

God help us all!

Yours,
M

1. Mencken wrote chapters 11–18 and was general editor for *The Sunpapers of Baltimore, 1837–1937* (1937).

[NYP]
May 28 [1936]

Dear Menck:

I still hold you to be the author of "Begone, Satan". As the Rev. Theophilus—O.M. Cap. you are most thinly disguised. Remove monks cloth, glasses & whiskers & there you are. As for party conventions I have attended four in my time—each duller than the other. I might go to Philly for it but they wouldn't let me in. Besides its very peaceful here—and meditating on my past sins proves very comforting—almost stimulating. I heard you address the Publishers convention (over the radio) and thought you swell. Enclosed is something by Broun[1] which you probably have seen.

Father Damien

1. The piece, apparently by Heywood Broun, has not been identified.

[UPL]

H. L. Mencken
Baltimore
1524 Hollins St.

May 30, 1936.

Dear Dreiser:

If you come to Philadelphia I'll guarantee you a ticket. If I can't get you one as a journalist representing the Moscow Idvesta, I can certainly get you one as a chaplain. In any case, you'll have a gaudy badge, and a chair so hard that it will wear your breeches to the shininess of alabaster. If you want to reach me at Philadelphia I'll be at the Ritz Hotel, in care of the Baltimore Sun Bureau. Despite the fact that Roosevelt is sure of re-nomination, the show will probably be a good one. The Democrats always quarrel, even when they are unanimous.

Broun's account of our meeting on the train is characteristically inaccurate. It is true that a young newspaper reporter barged in on us, but every other detail is false. Broun has even mistaken the name of the boy's paper. He was actually a former reporter on the <u>Wall</u> <u>Street</u> <u>Journal</u>, and he turned out to be an ardent admirer of the literary style of Arthur Brisbane.[1] My belief is that pinks never tell the truth. I can't recall a case in which one of them has actually followed the known facts. I ascribe this to the influence of the Devil.

I hope the madstone reached you safely.[2] Don't handle it carelessly. Treat it as if it were radium. I have known people to be severely burned by carrying such things in their pants' pockets.

Yours,
M

1. Arthur Brisbane (1864–1936), newspaperman, editor; at this time, he was editing the New York *Mirror*.
2. Sending a "madstone" was one of Mencken's famous hoaxes. He took a common rock, wrapped wire around it, and attached a card that listed the stone's powers—everything from a remedy for baldness to a cure for impotence.

[NYP-T]

Theodore Dreiser
Mount Kisco, New York

June 8, 1936

Dear Mencken,

The mad-stone arrived and in the hope of valuable results I rubbed in on the fore-head of my secretary and she achieved an insane complex in regard to my evil life and is now in Bedford Reformatory. And also there was an artist here, Ralph Fabri, who was doing excellent work, but after two rubs he smeared the walls and destroyed a large portion of my art objects. I have notified my attorney to bring suit as you will surely perceive. As for myself I have been saved by these demonstrations, and will have nothing more to do with your criminal tendencies.

I have decided however to accept your invitation to attend the Democratic convention in the hope of being able to rub the heads of some of the leaders of the Democratic party which will doubtless bring on the great American disorder which I so much desire.

Saved by the grace of God, I am yours forgivingly.

Dreiser

P.S. Kindly give details as to how long this intellectual storm is to last and how many meals I may consume at your expense.

[UPL]

H. L. Mencken
1524 Hollins St.
Baltimore

June 15, 1936.

Dear Dreiser:

I'll be at the Ritz Hotel in Philadelphia, along with the Baltimore <u>Sun</u> outfit. If you get to the convention, will you please let me hear of it as soon as you reach town? I'd like very much to introduce you to the notables. To be sure, most of them don't speak to me, but when they see me in your company they'll relax and relent. I'll be in Philadelphia by Sunday morning. The show starts at noon on Tuesday, but will not really get under way until Wednesday. I am informed confidentially that the arrangements are in charge of the Holy Ghost in person. Thus you are sure of seeing something to bulge your eye.

Yours,
HLM

[NYP-Tel]
1936 June 25

CAN YOU GET ME TWO SEATS FOR TONIGHT AT THE CONVENTION HALL IF SO LEAVE AT RITZ DESK.

THEODORE DREISER

[UPL]

H. L. Mencken
1524 Hollins St.
Baltimore

June 29, 1936.

Dear Dreiser:

Your telegram of June 25th seems to have gone astray somewhere along the line, for it didn't get to me until after I had seen you. I might have rustled a pair of seats for you, but that, of course, is not certain. There was a heavy demand for all the good ones, though the bad ones went begging.

I am sorry that our session had to be so short. Such jobs are amusing but very onerous. Covering the notification ceremony on Franklin Field was especially so. The press stands were wobbly, typewriters and copy paper got wet, there was not sufficient light, and the whole place was swarming with ringers. My account of the orgies was sent out in twelve different pieces, and the first two paragraphs were written last. Thus I bespeak your charitable consideration when you read the stuff. It is going to you under another cover.

I may see you on the Coast before the end of the year. Once the campaign is over, I'll have to have a holiday, and I am thinking of taking a look at the Northwest, which I have never seen. If I do so, I'll certainly drop down to Los Angeles on my way home.

Yours,
M

[UPL]

H. L. Mencken
1524 Hollins St.
Baltimore

July 6, 1936.

Dear Dreiser:

My best thanks for "Beyond the Grave." [1] I have read every word of it, and with the greatest pleasure. Ah, that the proletarian authors of New York would give a little time to the study of it, and so learn how to write themselves! Their horrible Yiddish American affects me like a shriek of the damned souls in Hell. But Brother Rutherford is a natural born writer, and would have been contributing to the <u>Saturday</u> <u>Evening</u> <u>Post</u> regularly if he had not taken to good works.

I am off to Cleveland at the end of the week to see the Townsend convention. [2] It promises to be a circus in the grand manner. All the worst nuts in America will be brought together in one hall. You should stop out and help me to laugh.

Yours,

M

1. Along with their letters, Mencken and Dreiser had taken to enclosing religious tracts with names like "Three Great Facts Discovered," "100 Years Young," and "Beyond the Grave."
2. The Californian Francis E. Townsend had organized about three million people into Townsend Clubs, dedicated to national recovery programs financed by a sales tax.

[NYP]

July 7 [1936]

Dear Mencken:

I browsed through your convention comments at my leisure, fascinated as usual by the comic exaggerations & contrasts. I wish you would turn your electric eye on science,—college science. They are trampling on each others feet—actually repeating as new experiments a hundred years old. Loeb is re-cerebrated, Faraday also.[1] Every medic has his eye on the first page of the Times—or the Balto. Sun as the discoverer of something. As a lay reader I get it clearly.

Don't understand the delayed telegram. They told me at the Ritz desk that it had been put in your room. However conventions are conventions. The Times here seems a little dubious as to Landon.[2] I thought it was for him.

Nice and hot. I spent the 4th in Manchester, Vt.—one of the really charming old New England resorts. Here's hoping Townsend wins. I have my eye on my 97th year.

Dreiser

1. Jacques Loeb and Michael Faraday, the nineteenth-century British chemist and physicist.
2. Alfred M. Landon, who became the Republican nominee for president in 1936.

[UPL]

H. L. Mencken
1524 Hollins St.
Baltimore

July 10, 1936.

Dear Dreiser:

The public library here in Baltimore has a fine new building, and along the front of the building are some show windows. In them it gives exhibitions dealing with the life and work of eminent literati. The librarian tells me that plans are under way to give you a window on your next birthday, and I have been asked to supply some of the materials. I promise you to send in nothing that will defame you as a patriot and a Christian. Insofar as I have anything to do with it, the window will make you a shining example to the ambitious youth of this great nation.

I am off for the West in an hour, and this note will have to be signed by my secretary. I am going first to Cleveland for the Townsend convention, and then I shall proceed to Kansas for the Landon notification orgies. God knows I wish you were going along. The Townsend show in particular promises to be magnificent. There has never been such a collection of nuts since the days of the Twelve Apostles.

Yours,
H. L. Mencken
Per RCL[1]

1. Signed by Rosalind C. Lohrfinck, secretary to Mencken.

[NYP]
Tuesday—July 25 '36

Dear Menck—

Thanks for the word about the Library window. It's nice of you to look after it personally and I appreciate that of course. And I would have written but I have been thinking of you as deep in your Townsend & Landon affairs. I wish you would give me the floor level of the Townsend-Coughlin-Lemke[1] affair. Did the dear old doctor sell out his followers—or what. Politics! And the priest apologizes to the pope! So who would rule if a Catholic reigned?

I have important confirmatory news in connection with the madstone. As you know it weighs two pounds. A small dog went mad here last Monday and I applied it at fifteen feet, seven ampheres strength, Eastern Southern time. Result: a complete cure. Am having the hide stuffed by a taxidermist. You are entirely free to use this as a testimonial—on the State of Maryland.

If I had the bus fare I'd come down to look at the window. It would revive my failing literary spirit, I am sure.

Dreiser

If you pass this way on your annual visit to Emerson's shrine, stop in
I am offered a lecture date in Baltimore this winter. I see you are down

for a bout with Ham Fish.[2] What are the lecturing conditions—hall etc—there?

1. Representative William Lemke of North Dakota ran on the New Union party ticket, which was endorsed by Father Coughlin and was committed to a radical anti-bank platform.
2. Hamilton Fish, a conservative Republican member of the U.S. House of Representatives from New York.

[UPL]

H. L. Mencken
1524 Hollins St.
Baltimore

July 29, 1936.

Dear Dreiser:

I don't think it would be fair to say that Old Townsend sold out his followers. He simply succumbed to the blarney of Gerald Smith, who is out to get Roosevelt's scalp and believes that the best way will be to encourage the Lemke third party. The scheme is not without its sagacity. Most of the jobseekers who have Townsend's endorsement were running, of course, on either the Democratic or Republican ticket, and so they violently resisted being sold down the river to Lemke. The result was a sort of compromise, with the Townsend outfit split. My guess is that it has seen its best days. The moron delegates were undoubtedly greatly shocked when they discovered what sort of politics was being played behind the door. Townsend himself, I believe, is a completely honest man, but he was certainly surrounded by porchclimbers.

I carried a madstone to Kansas with me, and had the pleasure of working at least a dozen miracles. Some of the people wanted me to stay in the State and become its archbishop, but I refused.

If anybody tells you that I am to lecture in Baltimore call him a liar, with my compliments. I'd no more do it than I'd jump over the City Hall. If you are invited to address the Baltimore Forum I'd advise against accepting. The weekly audience, I believe, is composed mainly of ninth-rate radicals.

I have been on the jump for more than a month past, and my troubles seem to be far from over. If Coughlin holds a convention in Cleveland I'll have to go back to cover it. How long are you staying at Mount Kisco?

Yours,
HLM

[NYP]
Aug 9—'36

Dear Mencken:

I meant to ask after your personal reactions to Dr. Landon, but I forgot. If you would trouble yourself I would appreciate it.

As to my place here the big house is rented until Oct 1st. I am living in two cabins at the extreme south—or main gate entrance to the place. One of the cabins is visible from the gate—looking straight forward as you enter. You make a complete circle past the big house, (a blue arrow shows you the way in) until you come to an arrow pointing to the cabins. It reads The Cabins. I have the cooking done in one—and sleep in either as I choose. The upper cabin is a true office with a sleeping porch. I have no telephone and a telegram arrives no more quickly than a letter. Just the same, letter or no letter, if you are up this way and will drive in you are likely to find me. If you will stay all night or over a week-end I can house you comfortably in the upper cabin. All you have to do is to drop a note beforehand. However I expect to leave here Sept 1 on a trip. I'll be back in 10 days. But on Oct 1 I move into the big house. There you will be made very comfortable   If are moved by these suggestions act accordingly. I can take you fishing right on the place.

It is very lovely here at any time. And absolutely quiet. I am over 1500 feet from the road & hear only the whistle of distant trains

I have a feeling that the novel is dying not only because of multiplicity but because of the movies, the radio and what is sure to be, television. Not only that but because of the immense development of transportation, advertising and freedom of contact and exchange   Even the numbskull responds to a few stimuli while our one-time readers all turn to doing novels or stories and so gradually drift to Hollywood. My one consolation appears to be Scotch and Soda.

Dreiser

[UPL]

The HOLLENDEN
Cleveland, Ohio

August 15th [1936]

Dear Dreiser:-

Your letter reaches me here. I am doing the Coughlin convention—an inspiring sight to us old sons of Holy Church. Imagine 9000 morons crowded into one hall, and all of them bawling.

I'll probably be engaged on such jobs until October 1st, at the least, and maybe until election day. New ones are popping up all the time, and you know how I enjoy them. Thus, if I wait on you at Mt. Kisco, it will most likely be well after October 1st. More of this anon. My very best thanks.

I have half made up my mind to vote for Landon. He is far less dumb than he looks. I had a long talk with him in Topeka and came away convinced that he is a shrewd fellow and would make a very fair President. He realizes that people will be voting in November either for or against Roosevelt, and he plans to take every advantage of the fact that he is Roosevelt's complete antithesis. Thus he will not attempt any tenor oratory, nor will he pretend to be a wizard. He believes the people are tired of wizards, and I agree with him. He is a Pennsylvania Dutchman, and shows all the stigmata of the race. That is, he works hard, says little, and pays his debts.

Yours,
M

[UPL]

H. L. Mencken
1524 Hollins St.
Baltimore

August 29, 1936.

Dear Dreiser:

By this mail I am sending you a photograph of the show window that the Enoch Pratt Free Library of Baltimore has dressed in your honor. The Nordfeldt[1] portrait, seen through plate glass and at a distance of six feet, really looks pretty good. If you will apply a microscope to the photograph you will find that your humble slave is mentioned two or three times on the cards. They set them out while I was in the Middle West, and so I couldn't prevent it. The Library is always most polite to persons who dig up material for it.

I stood in front of the window for twenty minutes yesterday and listened to the comments of the passersby. An old colored woman, after looking at your portrait intently for two or three minutes, told me that she had made up her mind to vote for you in November. I gave her ten cents to buy snuff, and she went on her way full of patriotic sentiments.

I have just got back from the Landon tour, and feel somewhat dilapidated. The weather was infernally hot during the first few days, and then turned very cold. I had to sit in an open stand for nearly three hours with the temperature scarcely above 50 degrees, and a strong wind blowing. As a result, I picked up something that appears to be epizoötic, and feel somewhat low.

Yours,

M

1. The painter Bror Nordfeldt.

Theodore Dreiser
Mount Kisco, New York

September 9, 1936

Dear Mencken,
Serves you right for tracking around with Landon. Not that I wish you any bad luck, but—bad company, etc. . . !

As you suggested, I applied a microscope to the photograph and found as many as three and four separate signatures per card. This sort of self-advertising is actually prohibited by law in Arizona. Just the same, I am so moved that I am thinking of coming down there and spending a day in front of the window myself. Would you like to join me? If so, wire prepaid. I don't suppose you informed anyone that you selected the worst portrait of me that ever was done.

Affectionately,
Dreiser

P.S. I hear that your advocacy of Landon has injured him enormously in Kansas and nearby states.

H. L. Mencken
1524 Hollins St.
Baltimore

September 10, 1936.

Dear Dreiser:
Your note reaches me just as I am clearing out for Chicago to join the Landon funeral train. Thus this reply will probably have to be signed by my secretary, who has read all of your books, and some of them twice.

You are too late to see the memorial window. It was cleared out at the end of last week. Some one sent me a circular saying that you are to deliver a lecture before a gang of Communists in Baltimore on December 7th.[1] You may trust me to be present in the rear row, along with a couple of reliable cops. If the Hearst bashibazouks attempt to lynch you we'll protect you. We seem to be in for four more years of the New Deal. It will be a circus.

> Yours,
> H. L. Mencken
> R. C. L.[2]

1. Dreiser, believing Mencken was to debate Hamilton Fish, agreed to lecture before the Baltimore Forum.
2. Signed by Rosalind C. Lohrfinck.

Mt Kisco

Oct. 4—'36

Dear Mencken:

Well, I see they've buried you again—in the New Republic.[1] The interesting thing about these funerals of yours is that they are carried out with so much pomp and ceremony. And so regularly—about every year or so now. And it takes so much space to do it,—pages & pages. And invariably they begin with a staggering recital of your achievements which no one could hope to bury in the next two hundred years, and then try to carry out the ceremonies on the ground that you're not a joiner or special pleader. You should be a revolutionary, an advocate of social justice, an ironer-out of social inequalities, like myself and some others. But alas you are not,—just a realist contemplating things realistically. Hence the ceremonies—Ist doch Komisch.[2]

Unfortunately the corpse will not stay put. It is duly buried regularly, the earth even tamped down. But somehow, you louse, you get out again and make for the nearest beer saloon. And then begin the rumors that you are not dead after all. That you are here and there, drunk and disorderly,—the same old irreconcilable   Hence the new pursuits. The four-page obituaries. "Into the grave, you!" Out with him! Down with him! But the chief result, as I see it, is that they celebrate the deathlessness of the creature to be buried. Its true resting place if it would ever condescend to stay there would be the Hall of Fame. Only the body would turn & twist and grow amazing whiskers. So I take it the best place, after all, is hell.

How are you. Your man Landon waxes pale. The real candidate appears to be Knox.[3] Even the N.Y. Times has turned. And the ironic fates have wished Al. Smith on him.

I'm back in the big house—until I leave for N.Y. or the Coast.

Dreiser

I doubt if I will keep that lecture date. Briggs listed you for a debate with Hamilton Fish & I thought the society or club or whatever it is was worth speaking to. I signed a contract but maybe I can get out of it

1. Louis Kronenberger, "H. L. Mencken," *New Republic* 88(7 October 1936), 243–45.
2. Even so, it's comic.
3. W. Franklin Knox was the Republican nominee for vice-president in 1936.

[UPL]

H. L. Mencken
1524 Hollins St.
Baltimore.

October 6, 1936.

Dear Dreiser:

I have been through so many burial ceremonies that I am beginning to feel like a veteran. I'll never believe I am actually dead until they stuff me beautifully and deposit me in the National Museum at Washington. I long ago arranged with the curator for a place there, and at the same time I took the liberty of asking him to reserve one for you. I can imagine no greater felicity than standing beside you through eternity, with you labeled "Roosevelt Man," and me labeled "Landon Man." Millions of school children would come to see us, and all the anthropologists on earth would measure us with their rules and calipers.

I often wonder why the poor Jews are such utter damn fools. All of their so-called leaders seem to devote themselves assiduously to promoting anti-Semitism. Whenever they are confronted with a fair choice between doing a sensible thing and making idiots of themselves they always choose to be idiots. The so-called Jewish intellectuals are in the forefront of this folly. They keep the world Jew conscious at all times, and so pave the way for demagogues. You will observe that a violent anti-Semitic movement has sprung up in England. There will be another and worse one in France before Blum[1] comes to the end of his term.

What are your plans for the immediate future? Are you going to stay in

Mount Kisco until the end of the year? If so, I hope you let me wait on you some time.

Yours,
M

1. Leon Blum (1872–1950), Socialist leader of the Front Populaire and premier in 1936.

Theodore Dreiser
Mount Kisco, New York

October 15, 1936

Dear Mencken,

Posed as you say, and assuming that we are not molested, we should endure for some time. However, these museum pieces have their ups and downs, the same as anybody else. If you are meditating coming to Mount Kisco, now is a good time. The leaves are sticking to their jobs, and they look wonderful. You can even come as the Landon man. I will see that you are not molested at the station or on your way out here, and I will lay in a supply of cans of Schaefer's beer.

I had a letter from Boyd the other day. He seems a little subdued. I don't know whether you ever see him any more but I am thinking, since he asked me, of going down some evening and looking him up. Insofar as this place is concerned, you do not need to give me any particular notice. If you should wire twenty-four hours ahead, it will be ok. I can even get up a Republican evening for you.

Regards,
Dreiser

P.S. What about the Jews? I would like to hear what you have to say.

H. L. Mencken
1524 Hollins St.
Baltimore.

October 17th [1936]

Dear Dreiser:-

Boyd I see once in a great while. What he is up to at the moment I don't know. He seems to have a pretty hard time of it. Why not a joint session of the three of us? I think it would be grand. I suggest some time around the beginning of November—best, perhaps, after election day. I'll probably be on the jump until poor Alf is laid away. I am joining him at Indianapolis next week, and shall continue with him until he starts back to Topeka and the caves of oblivion. Thus I can't come to Mt. Kisco now. God knows, I wish I could.

My belief is that the Jews in this country are diligently preparing for themselves the damndest anti-Semitic movement ever heard of. They handle themselves incredibly badly. But it is useless to talk to them on the subject. They assume that every man who raises it is a Hitler agent. Hitler has driven them all crazy.

The National Museum authorities have two styles of stuffing—with ordinary excelsior and with reinforced concrete. I can't make up my mind. Let me hear your wishes.

Yours,
M

[NYP]
Oct. 31—'36

Dear Mencken:

Boyd is pleased with the idea of meeting. He suggests joining us for dinner or our coming to his place afterward. No date is fixed. It can be whenever.

I expect to be passing through Balto. either Saturday or Sunday & may call you on the phone merely to say hello. Be sure to caution all that you are not in.

Dreiser

[UPL]

H. L. Mencken
1524 Hollins St.
Baltimore

November 9, 1936.

Dear Dreiser:

I find that I'll be in New York on December 2nd, which is a Wednesday. Will that be convenient for our proposed session with Boyd? I surely hope so. I am writing to him by this mail. I propose that we have dinner at

Lüchow's, and then put in the evening discussing the horrors of human existence in Utopia.

The débâcle of poor Alf, of course, didn't surprise me, nor did it altogether grieve me. I am looking forward with great pleasure to four more years of the New Deal.

Yours,
M

[NYP]

Mt. Kisco, N.Y.

Nov. 15—1936

Dear Mencken:

Thanks for the note in regard to Boyd   I have written him and, if it is agreeable to him, it will do for me.

As for Landon—as I see him, he was a mere small-town hall boy for the gang of nobles I know who are egotistically convinced that nothing is too much for them & nothing too little for the other guy until they are licked. Then it has another look.

We're all the same man—or ass—or ham. When we're driving the car the pedestrian is an encumbrance on the face of the earth. When we're walking the man in the car is a selfish & inconsiderate bastard. Fortunately time & circumstance does for all of us.

With due bows and genuflections I am yours—statistically—

Dreiser

When Coolidge died I desired—after a diplomatic lapse of time—to run a black-bordered death box in which was printed

In
Memoriam

———

Mickey Mouse

But my associates seemed to think we'd be Spectatorially destroyed.[1]
Well it died   But not for such reasons as the above

1. Dreiser is playing on the name of the journal he helped edit in the thirties: *The American Spectator*.

[UPL]

H. L. Mencken
1524 Hollins St.
Baltimore

November 18, 1936.

Dear Dreiser:

Very good. I have heard from Boyd, and he tells me that he has been laid up by the flu. I am suggesting that the three of us meet at Lüchow's at 7 P.M. on Wednesday, December 2nd. I surely hope that that will be convenient for you. I shall ask Eddie Fink, leader of the orchestra, to play nothing but patriotic music during the evening.

Poor Landon was punished by the Holy Ghost for his sins—especially profanity, Sabbath breaking, and tobacco chewing. I warned him earnestly, but he refused to listen.

Yours,
Mencken

[UPL]

H. L. Mencken
1524 Hollins St.
Baltimore

November 23, 1936.

Dear Dreiser:

The other day I had a letter from you dated October 31st (apparently an error), saying that you expected to pass through Baltimore on either Saturday or yesterday, and would communicate with me by the Bell telephone. I kept my ear glued to the receiver both days, but no word from you came. I also had the Sun's police reporter search the hotels, but he reported that you were non est. I surely hope that you didn't perish on the way.

I am counting on seeing you at Lüchow's Wednesday night, December 2nd, at 7 P.M. Boyd says he'll be on hand. Lüchow's cook has sobered up of late, and is reported to be surpassing himself. The beer, of course, is fabulous.

Yours,
M

[NYP]
Nov. 25—'36

Dear Mencken:

OK. Dec. 2nd (Wed.) Lüchows—7.30   As for the letter—you were on a cold trail. It refers to an earlier visit. Here, by us giffs ice and snow. Also Scotch & soda. For a man who rarely reviews books I am the subject—object—of a library down pour. Publishers must have books to throw away. So I contemplate a book fair of my own. After which comes California.

Want to buy a small lot in Florida? Ft. Lauderdale-by-the-Sea. One block from the Ocean. 100 × 100. Price $500. No commissions—nothing.

Dreiser

[UPL]
THE JOHNS HOPKINS HOSPITAL
Baltimore, Md.

December 24, 1936.

Dear Dreiser:

I am laid up here with an infection of the trachea. It doesn't seem to be serious, but it is somewhat uncomfortable, and the chiropractors tell me that they'll probably keep me on my back until the end of the week. For the first time in my life I'll miss Christmas altogether—a magnificent escape.

Do we meet before you retire to the Western wilds? I surely hope so. I enjoyed our session in New York immensely.

Yours,
H. L. Mencken
R.L.[1]

1. Signed by Rosalind C. Lohrfinck.

[NYP]
[December 1936]

To
    Menck
        from
            Dreiser
And no rocks, Please[1]

1. This was placed on a Christmas card that included a song sheet for "Hark! The Herald Angels" and "God Rest Ye, Merry Gentlemen." Next to the conventional card inscription, Dreiser wrote "Ho, Hum!"

[NYP]

THEODORE DREISER

Jan 4—'37

Dear Mencken:

Yes, it was stimulating and agreeable, the entire evening. I was sorry not to be able to stay but not to catch that evening train meant no train at all. For the remainder of my stay here we have moved down to N.Y.—the Park Plaza—50 West 77th Street   The telephone number is Endicott 2-3700. I have suite 623. If your over here and will be my guest I'll do the rest.

We seem to be centered in alarms. I take it the Universe is about washed up. Homo sap seems as insubstantial and meaningless to me as all of my pet theories. I think along one line in order to head off the possibility of thinking along many lines and winding up in a knot. Yet the sun blazes pleasantly through my windows. If God had only made me a George Abbott.[1]

I'm sorry your sick. I had five days of flu and then was let off. This week I'm in court—or will be—the old Liveright case.[2] But this winds it up except for a possible appeal if I lose. After that peace and quiet for me I hope. Health for you, sir.

I hear they're slowly poisoning the Pope.[3] Thus Science dispels the encircling gloom.

Regards
Dreiser

1. George Abbott was a successful producer of Broadway plays.
2. The Liveright Company was trying to recover monies for unearned advances and for book purchases Dreiser had made. Dreiser countersued but lost the case and was forced to pay $16,393.69.
3. Pope Pius XI, who was ill at the time.

[UPL]

H. L. Mencken
1524 Hollins St.
Baltimore

January 6, 1937.

Dear Dreiser:

Thanks be to the mercies of God, I seem to be making a slow recovery. My doctor wants me to go southward for a couple of weeks, but I am so enmeshed in unfinished business that I can't do it at once. My brother[1] is also ill, and if I take the trip he'll go with me. Precisely what happened to me I don't know. It was violent while it lasted, but it didn't last very long. I was laid up in hospital ten days.

It must be manifest to every judicious man that His Holiness is being poisoned. At first I suspected the Jesuits, but my thoughts are now running toward the Trappists. They are silent fellows—and silent men are always dangerous characters. If you have any confidential information on this subject, let me know. I promise not to publish it.

Certainly we must meet again before you go to the Coast. When precisely are you leaving? I may be in New York before I go southward, and certainly I'll be there when I get back.

Yours,
M

1. August Mencken (1889–1967).

[NYP]

Park Plaza
50 West 77th
N.Y.C.

Jan. 12—[1937]

Dear Mencken:

Glad your ok again. I didn't think it was as serious as it now looks. You ask when I'm leaving. The Liveright trial should come up Feb. 1. If it does it may take a week. Besides I'm trying to sell the estate—putting a bargain offer on it and am advised that certain negotiations now under way may run into February. If a sale eventuates it will pay me to wait here. Up to that time any day you are in town, I can be reached and will be pleased to show you a small eating place I know which I have come to like

By the way, the last time we met it was my intention to ask you what you thought of current literary trends, — the new scene or set up: Whether, for instance, anything worth mentioning has appeared in the past ten years and whether you have detected any new worth-while tendencies. I read some—very few novels—mostly science and current sociology & economics. But I'm interested in the novel. Most plays seem piffle to me, though I must say I set store by <u>Tobacco</u> <u>Road</u> & <u>Within</u> <u>the</u> <u>Gates</u>.[1] Other touted masterpieces did not ring the bell for me.

I ought to look up Gloom. But I'm so busy getting an education that I never have an hour any more for idling just to be idling. I see your Language Book[2] is <u>tops</u> in that field. Congratulations

Affectionately

Dreiser.

1. *Tobacco Road*, by Jack Kirkland, based on the novel by Erskine Caldwell; *Within the Gates*, by Sean O'Casey.
2. The fourth edition of *The American Language* (1936).

[UPL]

H. L. Mencken
1524 Hollins St.
Baltimore.

January 22, 1937.

Dear Dreiser:

I'll probably be back in New York before you leave finally. The week in Florida gave me a big lift, and I begin to feel like work again. My desk, of course, is piled mountain high, and it will take me a little while to dig through the accumulation. I suggest that we have dinner alone and go through the matters you discuss. It seems to me that there is a great deal of quackery in literature, as there is in politics. Most of the geniuses discovered by the Communists are simply imbeciles. But I have considerable confidence in young Farrell,[1] despite his political hallucinations. His new book[2], just out, contains some really excellent stuff.

I saw Gloom several times during the Autumn. She came to Baltimore to visit her brother, who was laid up here in hospital. She looked to be in excellent health, and was in her usual depressed but amiable spirits.

I surely hope that you find a buyer for your house. The real estate market seems to be improving rapidly. Down in Florida the realtors are prancing around in their old form. Every one I saw had on a new suit of clothes and a new hat.

Yours,

M

1. James T. Farrell (1904–1979).
2. *A World I Never Made* (1936).

[UPL]

H. L. Mencken
1524 Hollins St.
Baltimore.

February 6, 1937.

Dear Dreiser:

Gloom was in Baltimore early in the week and asked me to give her your address. I gave it to her, and assume that you don't object, for you told me some time ago that you wanted to see her. She looked to be in blooming health. She has been coming down here to look after her brother, who has been seriously ill.

I am still hoping to see you before you shove off for the West. I must return to hospital tomorrow for some minor repairs, but they are not serious and I am counting on being back at work by the middle of the week. If all goes well, I should be in New York again during the last half of the month.

Yours,
M

[NYP]

HOTEL PARK PLAZA
50–58 West Seventy-Seventh St.
New York

Monday [after 6 February 1937]

Dear Mencken:

Giving Gloom my address is ok. What between my trial & some row about my 1931 income tax I'll be here this month out & maybe a little longer—so if your in town & free you can let me know. I've another slight cold & feeling like the roses of yesteryear

D.

[UPL]

The Union Memorial Hospital
Baltimore, Maryland

February 10, 1937.

Dear Dreiser:

This second bout in hospital turns out to be relatively mild, and I should be back home by the end of the week. I am hoping to get to New York about ten days hence. I'll write to you again before I leave here. We must meet before you go to the Coast.

Yours,
H. L. M.

[NYP]

50 W. 7th St.

Feb. 15—1937

Dear Mencken:

I fear the worst. You have probably ignored the necessary prophylaxis as boys in a hurry will. Have a care. Impetuosity in these matters leads— very, very frequently to grief. Remember that a few moments of delay in the bedroom may well save weeks in the hospital. Button up the overcoat. A stitch in time saves doctor's bills. Youthful waste leads to aged want. And not only that but woeful want. I am having done in bright red yarn an excellent motto, the product of ages of experience. Hang it above your desk and meditate on it. I pray you. Affectionately

Old Doctor Dreiser

By express insured goes one gross, XXXXXX Goodyear Prophylactic Overcoats pre-sprayed with Spanish fly. A Xmas present.

[UPL]

H. L. Mencken
1524 Hollins St.
Baltimore

February 16th [1937]

Dear Dreiser:-

My one regret is that I didn't have your advice in time. They wanted to castrate me, but I begged off and so lost my epididymis. Having never heard of it before, I'll probably not miss it. It will be restored at the Resurrection, with new valves.

I begin to feel brisk again, and am at work on a completely useless and hopeless book. Such are the follies of artists! It will cost me six months' work, and sell 200 copies. You get one absolutely free.

I am hoping to get to New York very soon. More of this anon.

Yours in Xt.,

M

[UPL]

H. L. Mencken
1524 Hollins St.
Baltimore

February 26, 1937.

Dear Dreiser:

Very good.[1] I'll be at Lüchow's at 7 o'clock on Tuesday evening. Let us sit down together in a far corner and discuss the sorrows of the world. I have had some uncomfortable adventures since our last session, but fortunately they have turned out very well. There are still a couple of bald spots on my head, and I look somewhat like a man prepared for the electric chair, but you are too old a bird to judge any human being by outward appearance. I hope I can prove to you that I am still a true Christian at heart.

Yours,

M

1. On 25 February 1937, Dreiser sent Mencken a telegram agreeing to a meeting at Lüchow's.

[NYP]
[before 20 December 1937]

To Mencken
from
Dreiser
N.Y. Xmas 1937

And it isn't "just another one of those things."[1]

1. Dreiser wrote this after the Christmas card inscription, which reads:

"To Wish You Happiness at Christmastime
And Joy Throughout the New Year."

[UPL]

H. L. Mencken
1524 Hollins St.
Baltimore.

December 20, 1937.

Dear Dreiser:

My best thanks for your reminder of the holy Christian season. I shall spend the day as usual in pious exercises. When the churches shut down at last I'll move to some convenient saloon and there continue my meditations.

I am uncertain about your address, and am thus sending this to Simon and Schuster. Where are you living? Are you still planning to go to California? Let me hear about this.

I haven't had a holiday for two and a half years, and am thinking of taking one in the near future. If I do so I'll probably go to the West Indies on a brief cruise. The tropical air will clear out my frozen pipes, and a few rounds of Planter's Punches will surely not do me no harm.

Here's hoping that you are lucky in 1938.

Yours,
M

[UPL]

H. L. Mencken
1524 Hollins St.
Baltimore.

October 14, 1938.

Dear Dreiser:

In excavating my interminable archives, I lately came on some copies of early pamphlets relating to you. They include five or six copies of a sixteen-page brochure announcing "A Hoosier Holiday;" the same number of a thirty-two-page pamphlet entitled "Theodore Dreiser—America's Foremost Novelist;" and a couple of copies of a leaflet advertising "Free" and other stories. If you want them I'll be delighted to send them to you.

Yours,
M

[NYP]

THE GEORGE WASHINGTON
23 Lexington Avenue
At 23rd Street
New York

Oct. 19—'38

Dear Mencken:

Thanks. I remember the things and since I haven't any of them any-more I can give them to people who are always wanting items. So send them on. I do hope you are sound in mind and limb. Not a day goes by that I don't think of you—and almost as frequently do I hear of you,—your still unregenerate ways. Don't reform. Die as a criminal should—but in due course, of course. Regards,

> And always affectionately
> Dreiser

[UPL]

H. L. Mencken
1524 Hollins St.
Baltimore.

October 21, 1938.

Dear Dreiser:

The pamphlets are going to you under another cover today. If I find any more I'll forward them. At odd moments during the last year I have been excavating my almost interminable archives. They fill a large con-crete vault in the cellar here. I have unearthed some very interesting stuff, and also a great deal of trash. I'll probably leave the whole collection to the League of Nations when I am hanged.

It would be impossible for a man living in Baltimore to lead a truly righteous life. The town is full of temptations that haven't been matched on earth since the days of the Babylonians. There are drinking dens at every step, and the great Christian vice of fornication is carried on on a colossal scale. I begin to suspect that even the clergy have been corrupted.

Why don't you come down some time and see the town before it finally collapses? It is a literal fact that whole rows of houses are being torn down to save taxes. The vacant lots go into the public domain and become the resort of brigands, and even Indians.

I am toying with the idea of a book that will set forth my final conclusions on the human race. I needn't tell you that it will not be altogether flattering.

Yours,
M

[NYP-T]

Theodore Dreiser
G. Washington Hotel,
Lexington & 23rd St.,
New York City

October 25, 1938

Dear Mencken,

The pamphlets came duly to hand. Thanks. And thanks too for the invitation to visit your corrupt and degenerate heath. I would like to very much but at present I am too pressed with work and changes to do a thing except stick right here. When I am a little freer I will let you know. In the mean time never doubt the clergy or impugn their general character. They are, as you know, the vicars of God on earth.

As ever,
Dreiser

I hope I will be around when your conclusions concerning your fellow travelers here issue. More, I herewith subscribe.[1]

1. The postscript is handwritten.

[UPL]

H. L. Mencken
1524 Hollins St.
Baltimore.

October 31, 1938.

Dear Dreiser:

I have an obscene letter from Edgar Lee Masters proposing that I sit with him on a committee for disposing of your ashes post-mortem. I am telling him in plain language that you'll outlive both of us, and by many years. I am also adding that you will reconcile yourself with Holy Church, and die at last with the holy oils almost suffocating you. If this prediction turns out to be false, I'll be delighted to apologize in Hell.

When I'll get to New York again I don't know, but it will probably be before the end of November. I propose that you and I and Masters have a sitting at Lüchow's. When Eddie Fink sees us he'll undoubtedly order his band to play "Nearer My God To Thee." Masters is busy with a plan to erect an equestrian statute to Minnie Everleigh, the celebrated Chicago lady of joy.[1] I have given him $10,000, and have promised to make a speech at the dedication. It would probably be better if you and I joined in an old-fashioned clog dance. People would come from miles around to see it, and some of them, no doubt, would be tempted to throw money at us.

I surely hope that you are in good health, and full of sin.

Yours,

M

1. Mencken is referring to one of the sisters who operated the Everleigh Club, a famous house of prostitution.

[NYP-T]

Theodore Dreiser
G. Washington Hotel,
Lexington at 23rd St.,
New York City

November 3, 1938.

Dear Chancellor,

Conditions in Europe are certainly dark. Mussolini is an emperor and Chamberlain is (seemingly) a hall-boy. Dr. Hitler is consulting astrologers, male and female. The iced axe seems ready for any neck. In Spain Franconian Catholics are murdering Loyalist Catholics as was made and provided by Christ. In Asia the Jews are being ousted from their own native heath. In China one Chinese Mongolian murders one Japanese Mongolian, and vice versa, which reminds me of my own native heath at its best.

Being in consequence low in mood, your suggestion is not without weight or import. At least you are not an iced axe and Masters is certainly no dispossessed Jew, however he may conduct him. In good sooth I am not Emperor of Abyssinia—yet. But there is hope—for in an asylum to what may not one aspire?

Hence I have decided to consult Dr. Masters. With your $10,000 in his pocket he should be delighted to buy you a dinner—and even me. So—more anon.

However, since I may be gone by November 25th, and have engagements in Indianapolis and Detroit on the twelfth and thirteenth, and one in Boston on the twentieth, I suggest that you suggest a possible hour. Lüchows is ideal.

Profoundly and respectfully,
Dreiser

P.S. As to my ashes, alas, I have already contracted with the N.Y. Ash and Garbage Corporation for their removal.

[UPL]

H. L. Mencken
1524 Hollins St.
Baltimore.

November 7, 1938.

Dear Dreiser:

In all probability, I'll be unable to get to New York before November 25th, save on November 20th, which is the day you'll be in Boston. You speak of being gone by November 25th. What do you mean? Are you moving from New York permanently? If not, when will you return? I suggest that we have a session with Masters when you get back. He tells me that he is bothered by arthritis, and is generally in low state. So am I. It is thus your Christian duty to console both of us.

Once more, I begin to believe seriously that the Second Coming may be at hand. All the signs mentioned in Holy Writ are visible, not to speak of a number that the Twelve Apostles overlooked. Certainly the world is coming to a really magnificent estate. The scare caused by that radio broadcast last week gave me a tremendous thrill.[1] I am more than ever convinced that the American people are rapidly returning to the family of apes. Hitler, I hear, is a very pious fellow. He never does anything without consulting dream books. I am sending him a copy of the Hagerstown Almanac in the hopes that it will help him. Mussolini, unfortunately, is an infidel. I get this from private sources, and believe it.

Let me hear about your movements.

Yours,
M

1. Orson Welles's radio version of H. G. Wells's *War of the Worlds* on 30 October caused many to believe an alien attack was under way.

THE GEORGE WASHINGTON
23 Lexington Avenue
at 23rd Street
New York

Nov. 8th [1938]

Dear Mencken:

I'm moving out to the Coast for an extended period. I'm back from Boston the morning of the 21st. It is just possible that I will be delayed beyond the 25th. If so, and you were here on the 26th or 27th (I can't say for sure—but I'll know by the 23rd)—I can join you. I can wire you of course by the 23rd. Masters, I hear, is buying a new set of teeth for the occasion. Anyhow its fine, as you say, to know that we're all honest men and so at peace with God and the world. Just the same it comforts me to have you repeat it so regularly

Yours in light and truth,
Dreiser

H. L. Mencken
1524 Hollins St.
Baltimore.

November 9, 1938.

Dear Dreiser:

Unhappily, I'll be stuck here on the 26th and 27th, and so I fear it will be impossible for us to meet. I am sorry indeed, for I'd like to discuss with you several spiritual matters before you go to the Coast. You say you'll stay there for an extended period. How long do you mean precisely? Are you likely to be back before the end of the Winter? I surely hope so. I am counting on seeing Masters the next time I get to New York. You are, of course, in error about his teeth. He is still using the set that our Heavenly Father gave him. To be sure, he has lost a few, but only a few. I believe the total number replaced by china artificialities is no more than eight in the upper register and six in the lower.

The election yesterday somehow delighted me. I was especially tickled by the wallop that the LaFollette machine got in Wisconsin. It has had a good press for many years, but it actually operates in a manner hard to distinguish from that of Tammany. I was in Milwaukee a year ago and heard endless stories of its doings. I don't know Phil LaFollette,[1] but I have known Bob[2] for years. He is a very pleasant fellow but, unfortunately, full of a yen to save the world.

Yours,

M

1. Philip F. La Follette (1897–1965), governor of Wisconsin for two terms (1931–33, 1935–39).
2. Robert Marion La Follette (1855–1925), governor and U.S. senator from Wisconsin. He ran unsuccessfully for the presidency in 1924 on the Progressive ticket.

[NYP]

THE GEORGE WASHINGTON
23 Lexington Avenue
at 23rd Street
New York

Nov. 10—'38

Dear Mencken:

I am not planning an early return—maybe no return, except on business. I have a house out there and may live in it or rent another. Besides I like the climate and now know quite a few people. Also in '35 I found that I worked to real advantage and was not bored—far from it. So—But, if you ever get out there I'd love to see you. George Douglas and I ran a great household together—a fascinating group assembled about three times a week. This time I may tie up with Calvin Bridges, the scientist, or Maj. McCord, of the U.S. Army, who lives near my Montrose place. However it works out I'll be thinking of you and wishing you the best of everything. Helen will be with me a part of the time anyhow. She spends a good deal of her time with her mother in Portland. Sorry to miss you. Regards

Dreiser

It looks now as though I will be able to sell my Mt. Kisco place. I have a standing offer for it.

[UPL]

H. L. Mencken
1524 Hollins St.
Baltimore.

November 14, 1938.

Dear Dreiser:

I am delighted to hear that you have a good offer for the Mt. Kisco place. Getting rid of it will relieve you of a burden and a worry. I agree with you thoroughly that Southern California is far better than it is painted. People think of the horrible morons who infest the place, and forget that there are also a good many civilized men and women.

It is quite possible that I may be coming to the Coast before the end of the Winter. In the newspaper business a man never knows where he is headed, but several western enterprises are now formulating and I may undertake one of them. I assume that the supply of malt liquor is adequate. I don't need much, but if you can arrange for two or three gallons a day my health will be secure.

The horrible minor infections that harassed me during the Spring and Summer seem to be passing off, and I am full of eagerness to get back to work. As soon as some routine jobs now in hand are finished I'll probably tackle a book. It will be a defense of international morality, and its heroes will be Lloyd George, Churchill and Hull.[1]

Good luck!

Yours,
M

1. The British statesmen David Lloyd George and Winston Churchill; and the American Secretary of State Cordell Hull.

[NYP]
[18 December 1938]

"MAY CHRISTMAS AND
THE NEW YEAR
BRING EVERY HAPPINESS"

From
"Ten Thousand Original
Xmas Greetings"
by
Theodore Dreiser

[UPL]

H. L. Mencken
1524 Hollins St.
Baltimore.

December 23, 1938.

Dear Dreiser:

Thanks very much for your elegant reminder of the day. I'll spend it as usual, on my back. For some reason that I have never been able to make out—probably the personal enmity of the Holy Ghost—I am almost always floored at Christmas. Worse, this flooring comes on before I have had a fair chance to get down any Christmas cheer. This year it doesn't seem to be serious, but nevertheless it is a nuisance. I'll spend the day drinking milk, eating soft-boiled eggs, and searching the Scriptures.

I had dinner with Masters in New York last week. The two Gish sisters were present,[1] and the old man seemed in fine fettle. He told me that he had had his teeth fitted with special vitamin color screens.

What are you up to? I surely hope that you are full of luck in 1939. I am planning to spit on my hands on January 1st and tackle a new book. I needn't assure you that it will be of an optimistic tendency.

Yours,
M

1. The film stars Lillian and Dorothy Gish.

[UPL]

H. L. Mencken
1524 Hollins St.
Baltimore.

December 27, 1938.

Dear Dreiser:

I must say in all honesty that it seems to me that Rupert Hughes's[1] argument is completely unanswerable. If Shakespeare were alive today, he would undoubtedly be doing movie scenarios for Louis B. Mayer. What is more, if the Twelve Apostles were alive, they would be sitting on Louis's committee for the reception of distinguished visitors. I hope that your conscience has afflicted you sufficiently by now to make you apologize publicly. Hughes offers ample proof in his own person of the truth of his contention. He is the Shakespeare of our time.

I begin to believe seriously that war may be upon us. Roosevelt and his goons are lathering for it in the grand manner. So far, to be sure, they haven't made up their minds whether to tackle Hitler or to confine themselves to the Japs. But they are hot for fighting some one, and they'll probably get their wish soon or late. If war actually comes, I shall volunteer as an orator in the movie parlors. I am, indeed, already preparing a speech.

What is your news? When you print your apology to Major Hughes, let me have a copy of it. I want to present it to the library of the League of Nations.

Here's hoping that you are lucky in 1939!

Yours,

M

1. Rupert Hughes (1872–1956), editor, playwright, biographer, and motion picture producer. The source of Hughes's statement has not been identified.

[NYP]

THEODORE DREISER

Jan 4—'39

Dear Mencken:

I am not sure that war is at hand. There is so much at stake all around. And each one knows that when it begins their enemies may form strange, non-predictable alliances. From what I know of Russia, if Germany & Japan begin they are going to have plenty to do. There are enormous caches of supplies in remote unlabeled spots in Russia—not easily found by aero-planes and not be destroyed by bombs. Taking their cities wont help. It's these caches and the eighteen armies that will have to be met, taken, beaten. And there is the Russian winter—from Oct 15 to May 1. It is their greatest defense. And besides they can live & fight in it. They licked Japan on the Harbin front. And they are quite as crafty

As for this country I never saw such a welter of insolent, brazen graft—really open, political banditry. Here in L.A. they have arrested scores of councilmen & office holders for selling everything from jobs & pensions & privileges to franchises and contracts. There is a city supply department—supposed to cover all official car and other needs—and from it 600 new tires have disappeared—taken by politicians   One firehouse gang sold a good engine and ladder wagon to an outlying town entering them as disabled & then got new ones from a graft-paying fire department supply company. Everything is sold. And the Times here devotes itself to the horror of gangsters and W.P.A. Aliens!

As for myself, good master, I work on my novel & certain other things and praise God that I am not like other men—that he has made me honest, virtuous, kind and of good intent. But you know that of course. I hear that you look to see me canonized—in due course—of course.

Dreiser

Psst! What is Lillian Gish's address.

[UPL]

H. L. Mencken
1524 Hollins St.
Baltimore.

January 11, 1939.

Dear Dreiser:

I suspect that this fellow is simply fishing for an autograph. If you actually wrote that paragraph let me know confidentially, and I'll have you laid away at Matteawan.[1] The tricks of autograph-hunters are really most astonishing. I often get apparently serious inquiries that turn out to be mere dodges for getting a salable letter. This is a penalty that our Heavenly Father lays upon us for our great talents, and even greater virtue. The Twelve Apostles, if they were alive today, would be afflicted in the same manner.

It is good news that you are tackling another novel. I hope that it goes prosperously. I have been trying to horn into a new book for six months past, but so far without success. That is my invariable experience. It always takes me a long while to maneuver into a new book, but once it gets under way it proceeds very smoothly. The new one, as you may imagine, will be of a highly idealistic tendency. It will be devoted largely to proving that the proletariat is clean, virtuous, and industrious, and radiates a lovely bouquet.

Lillian Gish's address at last accounts was 360 east 55th street. I saw her in New York about a month ago, along with her sister Dorothy. She seemed to be in excellent health and spirits. Red Lewis, who was present, told me that he was on the water-wagon. He certainly looked it.

I have a rather low opinion of Russia as a military power. The Japs found it easy in 1904, and the Germans gave it a dreadful beating in 1916. I hear from men who should know that its new army is no better than the old one. It is enormous in size, but the competence of its officers is very low. That was precisely the trouble in the Czar's days. The Russian is a good soldier, but he is hardly more likely to succeed in battle under ward politicians than he was under dancing men.

I was in Germany during the Summer and talked to many Germans who know the military situation. They told me that they believed they could dispose of the Russian air fleet in a month. During the first few days, they said, it would undoubtedly do a great deal of damage, but by the end of four weeks most of its airmen would be quietly buried on German soil. As you probably know, I have a low opinion of the Japs, but I am still convinced that they could beat the Russians, just as they have mopped up the Chinese. I am told by returning newspapermen that the idea that the Chinese are giving the Japs any serious trouble is nonsense. All the Japanese lines of communication are open, and most of those of the Chinese have been cut off. I certainly prefer Chinks to Japs, but the facts are the facts. Read your Bible and you will find many other surprising, if unpleasant, things.

Edgar Lee Masters was here the other day, and there was much pleasant talk of you. I laid him a bet that you will enter Holy Orders before you leave this earth. He refused to believe it, but I believe my arguments shook him somewhat. He is planning himself to give up poetry and become an arctic explorer.

Very little about the Los Angeles scandals gets into the papers here. There is too much competition from other towns. My belief is that democracy is incurably corrupt. The chief thing to be said in favor of it is that it is infallibly amusing.

Yours,
M

1. Matteawan is a New York state psychiatric hospital. Dreiser's letter, to which this is a reply, has disappeared.

THEODORE DREISER

March 6—'39

That KP excerpt from the Congressional Record! Marvelous! [1]
And the late Pope! [2]
And the new one's sweet prayer for Peace & human bliss under the imperial control of the Vicer of Christ!
How come that the Holy Roman Church has no Red Cross. You never see

it stepping up and relieving famine—not in these late prosperous American years. They collect money. But distribute!

Father Damien. Yes.[3]

St. Francis (700 years ago)

Any priests in the starving labor camps all over America?

Public morals? Sure. An easy graft. Gets them into the movies.

Note Dr. La Guardia![4] Any chance for him?

1. On 25 February 1939, Mencken had sent a copy of the *Congressional Record* (23 February, Appendix, p. 2617). He marked for derision a speech by Senator Thomas Connally of Texas, praising the Knights of Pythias on the seventy-fifth anniversary of its founding. [UPL]

2. Mencken also questioned New York Congressman Emanuel Celler's praise of the late Pope Pius XI as a "friend and champion" of the "Jewish faith" (p. 2638).

3. Joseph De Veuster (1840–1888), Belgian-born Catholic missionary priest who took the name Damien in 1840. In 1873 he began to care for the leper colony on the island of Molokai, and after twelve years he himself contracted the disease.

4. Fiorello H. La Guardia (1882–1947), mayor of New York City.

[UPL]

H. L. Mencken
1524 Hollins St.
Baltimore.

March 11, 1939.

Dear Dreiser:

I suspect that you are somewhat prejudiced against our holy Christian religion. To be sure, it doesn't seem to be powerful enough to prevent wars, but you must admit that it is very effective against hurricanes, earthquakes and pestilences. If you haven't a copy of the Holy Scriptures, let me know and I'll send you one.

My guess is that La Guardia's chances of getting the Republican nomination—or, indeed, any nomination—next year are rather slim. He is playing both sides against the middle, and as a result all the professionals suspect him. This includes the Communists quite as much as the Republicans. I have known La Guardia off and on for a good many years, and have a rather indifferent opinion of him. He is a fellow of tremendous energy, but he seems to me to be something of a showman. I suspect that when the accounts are totaled up at last it will turn out that his administration in New York has been extraordinarily expensive. Reformers always manage to get away with a great deal of money.

How are you feeling? And what are you up to? I was laid up last week by some minor surgical repairs, but they weren't painful and I am now fully recovered. I have been plugging away at a new book—a sort of record of my first twelve years.[1] It is pleasant stuff to write, and I may finish it before the end of the Summer. Unfortunately, all sorts of other jobs are constantly breaking into it.

Yours,

M

1. *Happy Days, 1880–1892* (1940).

[NYP]

THEODORE DREISER

Thurs. Mch 23rd [1939]

Dear Mr. Mencken:

It is plain that you are the devil's own. You scoff at truth and right. No soul so good and pure, so self immolating, self-erasing, so thoughtful for the welfare of others but what you scoff! Take Alexander Woolcott,[1] now,—that great man and great writer, and great humanitarian. You scoff! You refuse to see him in his true light! to admire his genius; his immense and tireless services to democracy and to world letters! How can you be so obtuse—or, so unfair—perhaps—yes, I think, jealous? How can you, when his overshadowing merits are so plain to all? Fie! Eleven times <u>Fie</u>. For shame! Eighty-two times for shame! Yes, eighty-nine times, even.

But you will live to awaken and repent. I know it. I feel it. That great, white light of purity and wisdom will yet burst through that thick cranial defense of yours   You will bow your head in shame and regret. I feel it. I know it. Oh, that I might be the one to lead you to a full understanding of that great soul.

With charity & in hope

Luella H. Parsons[2]

1. Alexander Woollcott (1887–1943), journalist, author, radio broadcaster known for his barbed humor. Mencken had sent a page from the *Congressional Record* (14 March, Appendix, p. 3872) containing a radio speech by Woollcott on the admission of German refugee children.
2. Luella O. Parsons, the Hollywood columnist famed for her gossip column about motion picture personalities.

[UPL]

H. L. Mencken
1524 Hollins St.
Baltimore.

March 28, 1939.

Dear Dreiser:

There is unquestionably something in what you say. We literati always yield to secret jealousy. I had always suspected you of having a hate on Alec yourself, but your noble defense of him convinces me that I was wrong. This concentrates all of your venom on Shakespeare, who is happily dead and doesn't know it. As for me, I believe that my real enemy is the late Ludwig van Beethoven.

What are you up to, and how are you feeling? I have fallen into a writing streak, and am making good progress with the new book. It will be a volume of autobiography, running down to 1892. I'll probably sell some of the chapters to the New Yorker, which seems to like such stuff.[1]

The rigors of Lent always leave me flat, and I'll certainly be glad when Easter Sunday dawns.

I suppose you have heard of the death of Professor Alexander Geddes, Baltimore's favorite poet. I enclose his last broadcast.[2] It was written, of course, before he passed away, but it did not come out until after his funeral orgies. I hear that he left a considerable estate—in fact, it is said to run to more than $700.

Yours,
M

1. The *New Yorker* published nine of his autobiographical pieces in 1939.
2. Mencken enclosed a series of six poems on the themes of spring and Easter by Alexander Geddes, who was called the "Poet Laureate" of Baltimore.

[UPL]

H. L. Mencken
1524 Hollins St.
Baltimore.

April 8, 1939.

Dear Dreiser:

Thanks very much for the copy of the Thoreau book.[1] Rather curiously, I know relatively little about Thoreau, and so it will be an especial pleasure to read your selections. For some reason or other, I have always felt a sort of antipathy toward him—probably because he was a New Englander and something of a transcendentalist. Looking through your collection, I am surprised by the range of his ideas. I had always thought of him as a sort of nature lover.

The ignorance of the so-called intelligentsia is really appalling. I encountered a college professor some time ago who had never heard of Sam Blythe.[2] I am told, by the way, that Blythe is living in California. If you ever encounter him please give him my best regards.

I am plugging away at my book, with various longish interruptions. Doing it is a lot of fun, but whether anybody will want to read it remains to be seen.

The idealists at Washington are determined to get us into a war, and I begin to suspect that they may have their wish. The next one will be very much worse than the last one. I am planning to become a spy hunter. If you don't want me to denounce you the first week you had better send me a good box of five-cent cigars.

Yours,

M

1. Dreiser had edited *The Living Thoughts of Thoreau* (1939). He inscribed the book: "For Henry L. Mencken in gratitude for much."
2. Samuel G. Blythe (1868–1947), journalist, memoirist.

[UPL]

H. L. Mencken
1524 Hollins St.
Baltimore.

April 11, 1939.

Dear Dreiser:

That page of religious advertisements from the Los Angeles Times is really almost fabulous. I have read the whole damn thing, and with constant amazement. Here in Baltimore the ordinary churches advertise more or less, but the Rosicrucians, Hebrew Christians and so on are never heard from.

I trust that you went to Mass on Easter Sunday. It is a small politeness to pay to the Holy Ghost, and you never can tell when it may be useful. If I had the time I'd go to Alaska with the Christian Endeavor expedition advertised. Unfortunately, my patriotic duties keep me busy here. I hear from Washington that the New Deal brethren are still hopeful of getting the United States into a European war. They begin to realize that if they don't they'll be licked next year. I don't care much. I enjoyed the last war, and the next one will probably be even better.

Yours,

M

[NYP]

Theodore Dreiser
253 W. Lorraine

April—11—'39

Dear Mencken:

Do you, by any chance, know of a readable digest of Kant's Philosophy—the first and second phases? I waded through the total mass thirty-five years ago. Now I would like to have by me a digest.

I enjoyed your mural of the Maryland State Legislation[1] and can only think of the old song 48 Bottles a hangin' on the wall. "Take one bottle away from the wall leaves 47 bottles a-hangin' on the wall."

Life, Strength, Hope.
Dreiser

1. "The Same Old Gang," Baltimore *Sun*, 2 April 1939.

[UPL]

H. L. Mencken
1524 Hollins St.
Baltimore.

April 17, 1939.

Dear Dreiser:

Off hand I can't think of any good digest of Kant's Philosophy. Those that I am acquainted with are even more difficult than the original. However, I am making inquiries, and if I find out anything I'll pass it on. Kant was probably the worst writer ever heard of on earth before Karl Marx. Some of his ideas were really quite simple, but he always managed to make them seem unintelligible. I hope he is in Hell.

I sent you a few more clippings from the Congressional Record the other day. Please don't indulge yourself in any sneers. The men who contribute to the <u>Record</u> are genuine patriots, and deserve the veneration of all Christian citizens.

Yours,

M

[UPL]

H. L. Mencken
1524 Hollins St.
Baltimore.

April 19, 1939.

Dear Dreiser:

Masters, who knows a great deal about philosophy, tells me that George Henry Lewis's history of it remains one of the best books ever done on the subject. I read it many years ago, but recall it only vaguely. Masters also thinks well of Durant's "Story of Philosophy," but here I dissent. It seems to me that Durant is a very superficial fellow. In general, metaphysics seems to me to be very hollow. Half of it is a tremendous laboring of the obvious, and the other half is speculation that has very little relation to the known facts. Altogether, I think I'd support a law drafting all philosophers into the army.

I am going to Washington tomorrow to harangue a meeting of newspaper editors. It is always a depressing job. They are, taking one with another, a very innocent class of men. They always believe, deep down in their hearts, whatever they hear from official bigwigs.

Yours,

M

[NYP]
[before 24 April 1939]

[To Mencken]

Tell some guy with newspaper publishing sense and at least 1/2 of 1 percent of honesty to come out to L.A. and run a newspaper. A fortune awaits   But it will require not less than 1/2 of 1 per cent of honesty. That is <u>minimum</u>.

[UPL]

H. L. Mencken
1524 Hollins St.
Baltimore.

April 24, 1939.

Dear Dreiser:

If anyone ever started a decent paper in Southern California the natives would lynch him. Now that you are on the scene, I advise you to read the Los Angeles <u>Times</u> carefully. It is really almost incredible.

Thanks for the clipping about the death of Wright.[1] He was a great liar, but nevertheless an amusing fellow. He gave Rascoe a great deal of the blather that Rascoe printed in his introduction to the Smart Set Anthology. Later on he tried to blame it on Nathan, but I know where the stuff came from. I saw Wright only a few times in recent years. Two or three years ago he brought his wife down to Baltimore for surgical treatment.

Yours,
M

1. Willard Huntington Wright died 11 April 1939.

[NYP]

Theodore Dreiser
1426 N. Hayworth
Hollywood
Calif.

June 6—'39

Dear Mencken:

As I read these Congressional Record bursts the thought comes to me that the authors may not be so dumb as they sound.[1] Back in the sticks where they come from are their congressional followers,—their <u>votes</u>. Maybe these same are sufficiently emotionalized by this Edward Guestian[2] drip as to fail to note the gaseous content of the bogs they send to Congress. There are more things Horatio L. Mencken—than—well

Pay attention to the following, regardless of the above. The original script of <u>Sister Carrie</u> is written on such poor pulp that it will soon be dust. It should be treated with some water clear glue, or stickum, so as to fix and give body to the restless atoms & molecules that compose it. Also the pages—beforehand might be photographed. Merely a friendly warning. Otherwise, presently—giffs a quart of dust.

Respectfully

Dreiser

I suppose I forgot to report that I moved. I did it to save 10⁰⁰ a month in gasoline.

1. Mencken had gotten into the habit of sending sections of the *Congressional Record*, often with brief comments beside pompous or thoughtlessly patriotic speeches.
2. Edgar Guest (1881–1959), journalist, poet. Guest's "folksy" newspaper verse became the standard for sentimental and "inspirational" greeting cards.

[UPL]

H. L. Mencken
1524 Hollins St.
Baltimore.

June 8, 1939.

Dear Dreiser:

The script of "Sister Carrie" has been elegantly mounted on all rag paper, and I am informed by experts that it is good for five hundred years at least. I forgot to tell you about this the last time we met. The original copy paper was beginning to disintegrate, but now it is quite safe. If photographs or photostats are ever needed they may be made without the slightest difficulty.

You are quite right about those dreadful speeches in Congress. They make votes by the thousand. Every time one of them is printed it costs the taxpayers five or six hundred dollars.

I have been in Washington all week, attending the congress called by the Workers' Alliance. In all my life I have never seen a more pitiful collection of half-wits. They have been sitting there with their mouths open listening to an endless series of quacks. These poor people are in desperate trouble, but all the help they get is useless. Next week I am going to Indianapolis to attend the orgies of the Townsendites. I only wish you were along. The show is really appalling.

I have spit on my hands and am working on a new book.¹ It is going pretty well, and I hope to finish it by October. I can always work best when the temperature is above 80.

I hear vaguely that you have sold "Sister Carrie" to the movies, and I surely hope it is so. The book would make a magnificent movie.² Has

"Jennie Gerhardt" ever been done?[3] I recall that you sold the rights, but it is my recollection that the production of the movie was held up.

I note your new address.

Yours,

M

1. Probably *Happy Days* (1940).
2. *Sister Carrie* was made into a movie (*Carrie*) in 1952, with Jennifer Jones as Carrie and Laurence Olivier as Hurstwood.
3. *Jennie Gerhardt* was filmed in 1933, with Sylvia Sidney as Jennie and Donald Cook as Lester Kane.

[NYP]

THEODORE DREISER

June 16, '39

Dear Mencken:

I am truly glad to hear that the original ms of <u>Sister Carrie</u> will not be dust for a while, anyhow. It was courteous of you to look after it. Sometime I may want to look over the script and now it is possible. <u>What does a photo-stat copy cost?</u>

Barring the indescribably mental and financial fluctuations of this area Sister Carrie is sold—as a movie   The price is between $40,000 and $50,000, but commissions, income tax etc come out of that, so it isn't so much. Pending the amicable adjudication of certain <u>moral</u> points with the Hays office[1]—(believe it or not the book is still immoral because— harken—Carrie isn't punished for her crime)—a fairly solid binder has been handed over free and clear. And they'll work to get that back if they have to turn it into a comedy. It's total history certainly constitutes one.

I work very hard. Every day. This region is stuffed with hardboiled savage climbers, stuffed and mounted shirts, the lowest grade of political grafter, quacks not calculable as to number or variety, all grades of God-shouters—(now welcoming Heywood Broun[2]) and loafers, prostitutes, murderers and perverts. In the bland sunshine here they multiply like germs in the Canal Zone. What saves it is the wisdom, taste, honor and virtue of the moving picture industry

I am—barring possible incarceration—

As ever

Dreiser

1. The Hays office was the censoring agent for films.
2. Heywood Broun, crusading journalist whose conversion to Catholicism Dreiser may be recalling.

[UPL]

H. L. Mencken
1524 Hollins St.
Baltimore.

June 27, 1939.

Dear Dreiser:

It is excellent news that you have placed "Sister Carrie" with the movies. However much the money may be diminished by fees and taxes, it still remains money found. As you know, I have always believed that "Sister Carrie" would make a really first-rate movie. In the days when it was first discussed the movies were in a crude state; today they are at least better than they were then. My guess is that the Hays office will not make any real difficulties.

The manuscript was mounted by hand at the expense of the New York Public Library. I placed it in the Library's custody simply because I thought it should be taken care of better than I could do it. The understanding is that nobody is ever to have access to it in your lifetime without your written permission. If, by any extraordinary and incredible manifestation of God's grace, I survive you, then they will have to come to me. After we are both in Paradise it will be in the custody of the Library.

My guess is that making a photostat would be rather expensive. The thing, as it stands, is accessible to you, of course, at all times.

I have just returned from Indianapolis, where I spent five days attending the convention of the Townsendites. It was a dreadful show, but somehow amusing.

Yours,
M

[UPL]

H. L. Mencken
1524 Hollins St.
Baltimore.

August 4, 1939.

Dear Dreiser:

I see nothing absurd in the theory that our Saviour on His return will come in the guise of a woman; indeed, there is a great deal of support for it in Holy Scripture. Read the book of Revelation carefully and you will learn a lot. It is very deep stuff, but if you are patient you will be able to penetrate it.

What are you up to? I have been laid up for ten days, but managed to escape under my own steam, and am now feeling pretty brisk again—in fact, I am resuming work on my book. If all goes well, it should be ready by the end of the year. It will be a small volume of a devotional nature, and I am thinking of dedicating it to Harold L. Ickes.[1]

I surely hope that you are in the best of health, and full of sin.

Yours,

M

1. Secretary of the Interior.

[NYP]

1426 Hayworth

Aug 13—39

Dear Mencken:

You ask what I am doing   Better ask <u>who</u> am I doing. The answer is a few. My native state, for one, as this proves. This thing in the paper[1] is a vile reproduction of the brilliant original, which is amazingly definite as to detail, physically and temperamentally accurate and brilliant as to idea and arrangement. I do not know this fellow Lilly[2] but he's having the portraits of various writers of the state either assembled or newly painted. He seems to have commissioned the Schneider-Gabriel Galleries of New York to select different artists to do the job. I picked Chaliapin,[3] having seen some of his other work. He is amazingly good. I suggested that he run you down, chain you to the floor and paint you. He says he will.

Dreiser

1. A reproduction of Dreiser's portrait appeared in the *Los Angeles Times*.
2 Josiah K. Lilly, Jr., of Indianapolis, an Indiana drug magnate, arranged to have Dreiser's portrait painted.
3. Boris Chaliapin painted Dreiser in July 1939.

[UPL]

H. L. Mencken
1524 Hollins St.
Baltimore.

August 21, 1939.

Dear Dreiser:

Judging by the reproduction in the <u>Los Angeles Times</u>, Chaliapin has made a really excellent portrait of you. It shows you in a sober and even

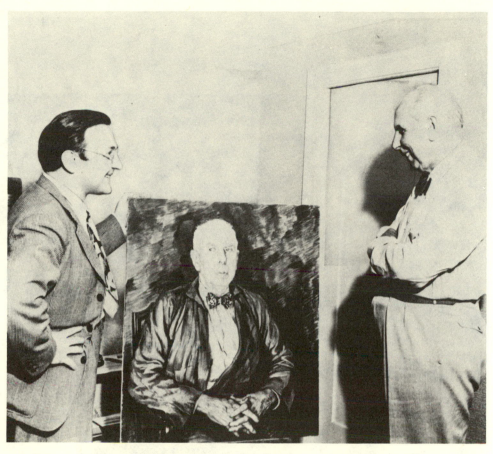

Dreiser viewing portrait with painter Boris Chaliapin
(Los Angeles Public Library)

*Mencken sitting for a portrait with Nikol Shattenstein
(Enoch Pratt Free Library)*

Christian mood; indeed, you seem to be rolling your eyes at the Holy Ghost in person. But the likeness is excellent, and I like the general layout of the portrait.

Why can't portrait painters work faster? Nine two-hour sessions must have been dreadful. I sat to Nikol Shattenstein five or six years ago, and found it a dreadful experience. Altogether, there must have been eight or nine sittings. What became of the portrait I don't know. In the long run, of course, it will go to the League of Nations.

The war talk in the newspapers begins to fatigue me, and I long for actual hostilities to begin. After all, the last war was a great show, and the next will probably be even better. I shall enlist in the Y.M.C.A. at once.

Yours,
M

[UPL]

H. L. Mencken
1524 Hollins St.
Baltimore.

September 6, 1939.

Dear Dreiser:

In these days of idealism my thoughts turn to you frequently. I sincerely hope that you have put your soul in order and are preparing to serve your country in the field. Roosevelt's pretensions to neutrality are so bogus as to be ludicrous. I am convinced that he'll horn into the war much more quickly than Wilson did. The result will be a circus in the grand manner. All the newspapers will be under the hoof of Ickes, who has been denouncing them violently for two or three years. I think I'll try to get a job as a censor of Bibles.

I am putting the last licks on the little book of reminiscences of my first twelve years. It describes my arrival in America from Poland, my early schooling in a Hebrew school in New York, and my gradual conversion to Christianity. You are introduced into it as a boy who was known in the neighborhood for his skill at stealing apples from grocers' baskets.

Yours,
M

[NYP]
[before 18 September 1939]

[To Mencken]

Here you are. I've always been wondering what to do for you: how make you into something. Write Mr. Dingle[1] today   Your hour has struck You can thank me for this.

1. Dreiser enclosed an advertisement for a mind-healing method offered by Edwin J. Dingle, which claimed to free "the mind of the hypnotizing ideas that paralyze the giant powers within us."[NYP]

[UPL]

H. L. Mencken
1524 Hollins St.
Baltimore.

September 18, 1939.

Dear Dreiser:

I have a letter from H. M. Lydenberg, librarian of the New York Public Library, saying that a man giving his name as Robert H. Elias and his address as 111 east 56th street, New York, has been to the library asking for permission to examine the manuscript of "Sister Carrie." Lydenberg says that Elias claims to have authorization from you. Inasmuch as I am apparently the legal custodian of the manuscript, Lydenberg wrote to me for instructions. I told him to let no one see the manuscript without written permission from you. I know nothing of Elias, and assume that if you really wanted him to see the manuscript you'd have given him a note.

My little book is now almost finished, thanks be to God. Getting rid of it will give me time to read the war news, which promises to be very lively during the next three months. My guess at the moment is that Satan will take care of Adolf.

Professor Dingle's theory that "all of us are giants in strength and mind-power" certainly sounds good to me—indeed, I have suspected it for many years, but have always been too modest to mention the fact.

Yours,
M

THEODORE DREISER

[NYP]

Oct. 3rd—'39

Dear Mencken:

The man who wants to see the <u>Sister</u> <u>Carrie</u> ms is Robert H. Elias—111 East 56th St. N.Y.C. He is a Columbia graduate (Literature of course)   Put together a thesis on me and took a degree. He now collects various things and plans biographies—I think. Not a bad sort. I am perfectly willing to have him examine it. I judge his wish is to study the editing and cuts and as far as I am concerned he is at liberty so to do.

I begin to suspect that Hitler is correct. The President may be part Jewish. His personal animosity toward Hitler has already resulted in placing America in the Allied Camp—strengthening Britains attitude and injuring Germany in the eyes of the world   The brass!

But we seem to grow Wilsons on every bush

Dreiser

[UPL]

H. L. Mencken
1524 Hollins St.
Baltimore.

October 2, 1939.

Dear Dreiser:

I needn't tell you that I agree with your answer to <u>Common</u> <u>Sense</u>.[1] All the current talk about the collapse of civilization is mere hooey. What it actually means is that if England gets a good licking the whole world will be ruined. I can imagine nothing more idiotic. The plain fact is that civilization would be improved by taming down somewhat the pretensions of the British imperialists. They have been running this earth long enough.

I enclose a clipping of a piece I printed in the <u>Sunday</u> <u>Sun</u> yesterday.[2] As soon as Roosevelt horns into the war it will become impossible, of course, to tell the truth.

I hope you are in good health and full of sin. As for me, I still feel somewhat rocky, but I have managed to finish my book. It is of an inspirational and idealistic tendency.

Yours,
M

1. Mencken is referring to Dreiser's piece, "The Dawn Is in the East," which he published in *Common Sense* in December 1939. Many were stunned by the Nazi-Soviet

pact, but Dreiser defended Germany and Russia, arguing that the pact safeguarded Russia and was a threat only to England—and that the real threat was not to civilization but to Western capitalism.

2. "Sham Battle" (1 October 1939) discusses the pretense of American neutrality in the war.

[UPL]

H. L. Mencken
1524 Hollins St.
Baltimore.

October 4, 1939.

Dear Dreiser:

For years past, as you may know, I have been assembling quotations for my own use. It is now suggested in my old age that I put this collection in shape for publication.[1] I have, in fact, been playing with it with that idea in mind for some years. In it there are naturally a number of quotations from your philosophical and theological works. Have I your permission to use them? I understand that all of your copyrights are now in your hands. How many of them there are I don't know, but the final editing will probably limit them to maybe ten or fifteen. In every case they will be short, with a maximum of two sentences.

It goes without saying that full credit will be given. Most of them are naturally from your polemical writings; for example, "Life, Art and America."

Yours,
M

1. This was published as *A New Dictionary of Quotations on Historical Principles from Ancient and Modern Sources* (1942).

[UPL]

H. L. Mencken
1524 Hollins St.
Baltimore.

October 9, 1939.

Dear Dreiser:

I note what you say about Robert Elias, and I am writing to Lydenberg at once. Hereafter it will probably be best if you give such men letters. I have told Lydenberg that any order of yours is to be respected. He has spent a good deal of money mounting and binding the manuscript, and so he guards it with a jealous eye.

My guess is that Hitler has at least an even chance of beating the English. If he can do any damage to the English grand fleet he'll have them on their knees. Roosevelt, I hear from Washington, is snorting and fuming to leap in. He figures that taking a hand will make him immortal. I have some doubt about it.

I enclose a couple of clippings[1] that will show you that my wickedness continues into old age.

Yours,
M

1. Mencken enclosed two editorials he wrote for the Baltimore *Sun*: "Sham Battles" and "On a Moral War."

[NYP]

THEODORE DREISER

Oct. 12—39

Dear Mencken:

Sure. Quote whatever you need. No charge. I own all the copyrights.

Dreiser

Is Hitler coming or going?

[UPL]

H. L. Mencken
1524 Hollins St.
Baltimore.

October 19, 1939.

Dear Dreiser:

Thanks very much. I'll be careful to choose quotations that do you credit, both as a patriot and as a Christian.

I hear from Washington that Roosevelt is lathering to get into the war. That he'll be able to do so is probable. My guess is that Hitler is wrecked unless he can destroy the England grand fleet. Whether or not this is possible remains to be seen.

Yours,
M

[UPL]

H. L. Mencken
1524 Hollins St.
Baltimore.

October 30, 1939.

Dear Dreiser:

That Colonel House letter seems to have been a pure fake.[1] If you want to read it nevertheless, write to the Hon. Jacob Thorkelson, House Office Building, Washington, D.C. He is a Scowegian Congressman from Montana, and was responsible for its appearance in the Congressional Record.

I suppose you read Roosevelt's solemn declaration, printed three or four days ago, that he is teetotally opposed to entering the war. When he actually horns in it will placard him as the damndest liar seen on earth since Ananias. It is amazing that the boobs swallow such stuff, but they do.

What are you up to? I have passed the proofs of my little book of reminiscences, and am now figuring on doing a commentary on the Holy Scriptures. I have photographs of Moses, Abraham and Martin Luther to illustrate it, and am now trying to get one of Jack Garner.[2]

Yours,
M

1. On 24 October Dreiser wrote asking if this letter, which appeared in the *Congressional Record*, was authentic. [NYP]
2. John Nance Garner, the vice-president at the time.

[UPL]

H. L. Mencken
1524 Hollins St.
Baltimore.

December 5, 1939.

Dear Dreiser:

Thanks for the clipping, which I have naturally read with great interest.[1] It always amuses me to encounter denunciations of newspaper proprietors by the Newspaper Guild. As a matter of fact, the common run of reporters, copy-readers, and rewrite men are much worse. I think you were wise to avoid a law suit. Such things seldom produce anything more than headaches.

I have acquired for your private reading, at great trouble and expense, a souvenir book reporting the speeches made at the time the heroic statue to Will Rogers was unveiled in Washington. It will reach you anon, along with a little book of my own.[2] Please remember that the latter is not to be released until January 22. Thus it is for your private eye alone. My one hope is that it lifts you to higher realms of fancy and virtue.

Yours,
M

1. This has disappeared.
2. *Happy Days, 1880–1892.*

[NYP]

Theodore Dreiser
1426 N. Hayworth

Dec 17—'39

Dear Mencken:

Thanks for Happy Days—which came three or four days ago. I've been squinting into here & there and have read, so far, the preface, the Universe, the training of a gangster and some odd paragraphs including the last in the book. I keep it beside my bed to read mornings & midnights—mostly—entirely in fact—to cheer myself up a bit. Your angle is certainly <u>your</u> <u>angle</u> and there is no other to compare there with. It's read and chuckle and thats why it will be passed along and read. I see myself reading it all just as I see myself taking another high ball—to lift me up a bit. I hope sincerely you'll go on with other periods—being your critical self all the way. This country needs just such an autobiography.

And your almost 60! Kind heaven! You sound like a racketeering youngster of 27 or 8. Luck. Regards

—Dreiser

Already I've been asked the loan of it!
To hell with Xmas.
All the way through this book I am compelled to note how unlike Henry W. Longfellow you are.

[NYP]

Theodore Dreiser
1425 Hayworth Ave.
Hollywood

Dec. 19—'39

Dear Mencken:

I'd like it if you would write the New York Public Library—its chief. Would he be so kind as to write me a letter saying the Sister Carrie manuscript is there and that in case I wish anyone to see it all I need do is to write and request the favor. I know you wrote me this but it would make the relationship a little more—I wont say intimate but factual. Some one has asked me so to do and I'd feel a bit easier. I know it's all allright.

I'm passing along two clippings from a local daily which throws a light on the Finnish situation,[1] illuminating to me. You may not have seen these. Don't return them.

Regards,
Dreiser

They're quarreling out here (in the movie world) as to which of 84 directors and associates are entitled to the honour of filming that worlds masterpeice—Gone With the Wind. T. S. Stribling's[2] Trilogy—the source of most of it is never mentioned.

1. When war broke out in Europe, Finland declared its neutrality, but the Soviet Union, anxious to secure its eastern border, invaded the country (3 November 1939). The Finns fought back and won some surprising victories, but eventually gave in to the greater Russian power. The clippings are missing.
2. T. S. Stribling (1881–1965), popular southern novelist. Dreiser admired Stribling's fiction (see Dreiser to Stribling, 23 October 1934, in Elias, *Letters*, 2:701).

[UPL]

H. L. Mencken
1524 Hollins St.
Baltimore.

December 22, 1939.

Dear Dreiser:

When you mention Longfellow you touch a tender chord. All of my early poetical work was written in imitation of him, and at one time my admiration for him actually went to the length of growing whiskers. In my later years I have somehow slipped out of his orbit, unquestionably to my damage as patriot and Christian.

Knopf wants me to do a series of reminiscences, each covering a decade, but I shy from the idea.[1] "Happy Days" sets a mood that it would be impossible to keep up in the later years. My teens, for example, were full of loud alarms, and it would sound idiotic to treat them as I deal with my first ten years. In my twenties I was gay again, and also in my thirties, but since the age of forty I have been full of a sense of human sorrow. This sense has frequently taken the virulence of an actual bellyache.

I hope that you are in the best of health, and that you see nothing but good luck in 1940.

Yours,
M

1. Mencken eventually added to his autobiographical "Days" books: *Newspaper Days, 1899–1906* (1941) and *Heathen Days, 1890–1936* (1943).

[UPL]

H. L. Mencken
1524 Hollins St.
Baltimore.

December 27, 1939.

Dear Dreiser:

I am writing to H. N. Lydenberg at once, suggesting that he write to you giving you the general authorization you want. I certainly see no objection to it. I advise you to be careful about issuing such permission. A great many quacks are afloat in this great country, and some of them specialize in literary felonies. You should hear from Lydenberg within a few days after this note reaches you.

The Finns have made a magnificent fight against the Marxians, but I think it would be a mistake to assume that they are wholly innocent. Their politicians have been playing the English-French game for some time past, and the Finns themselves are now paying for it, as the Czechs and Poles paid for it. Obviously, public opinion in the United States is for them almost unanimously.

I seize the opportunity to hope that you are in good health, and that you'll be lucky in 1940.

Yours,
M

[NYP]

Hollywood

[December 1939]

Yes, Sir! No Kidding!

Affectionately
Dreiser[1]

1. Dreiser wrote this on a card that read "Wishing You A Merry Christmas and A Happy New Year."

[UPL]

H. L. Mencken
1524 Hollins St.
Baltimore.

January 19, 1940.

Dear Dreiser:

Your letter to Hoover's agent gave me a loud laugh.[1] I think you put the facts very effectively. Unfortunately, you overlook the wonderful things that Hoover did for the country during his four years in office. As you will recall, it was a veritable golden age. Every one was full of money, and life was a grand, sweet song. To be sure, the dream blew up in the end, but that was not Hoover's fault. He himself kept on dreaming, and is in fact still doing so to this day.

What are you up to? I pray for you regularly.

Yours,
M

1. To Fred Smith, who directed publicity for the Finnish Relief Fund and acted in Herbert Hoover's name, Dreiser wrote in response to a request for a "300-word article on the Finnish situation." Dreiser said that he was not a "propaganda sucker" and added that Hoover did not call for relief of the Spaniards in 1937, the Abyssinians in 1934–35, or the Chinese since 1933; and then he reviewed what he considered Hoover's poor record on relief for needy Americans during the Depression. (See Dreiser to Fred Smith, 9 January 1940, in Elias, *Letters*, 3:864–65.)

[UPL]

H. L. Mencken
1524 Hollins St.
Baltimore.

April 19, 1940.

Dear Dreiser:

I hear vaguely that you have been ill, and I only hope that you have made a complete recovery. Let me hear about it when you feel like it. I am somewhat wobbly myself, but still manage to get through a reasonable day's work.

Among other things, I am putting in some finishing licks on a book of quotations that has entertained me off and on for thirty years. I started it for my own use, and it has now grown to 30,000 cards. I am thinking of bringing it out early next year. Have I your permission to print a few brief quotations from your own works? They come chiefly from "Art in America" and "Hey Rub a Dub Dub," and are never more than two sentences long. I assume that all of the copyrights of your books are now in your hands. I'll write to Max Schuster also, but understand that he has only a license to print.

The New Masses brethren sent me a circular in which you are made to speak of the New Masses as "our magazine." Is this authorized? If so, have you turned Communist? I certainly hope you haven't. It must be manifest to any one that Communism stands in contempt of the imperishable truths of our holy Christian religion.

Yours,
HLM

[NYP]

1426 N. Hayworth
Hollywood.

April 23rd '40

Dear Mencken:

These radicals! Invariably if you give them an inch they take a yard or more. I never spoke of the New Masses or any other publication as "our magazine"   By request I wrote an article on Lenin which they republished.[1] I certainly favor the Soviet economic set up as opposed to lands where work of any kind is wanting for many. I prefer what I saw there—work, or go to jail   The only people I saw loafing were the jobless priests holding out his cups   Anyhow use the quotations. I own all rights to my books and am moving out of S & S[2] presently.

Yes I was sick. First flu and neuritis. Then I thought I had heart trouble but they decided not. I took a long rest—but most days I worked some—1/2 day or I read. Now I'm doing full time again.

Your quotation book should be worth looking over. I think I'll subscribe.

Regards
Dreiser

I wish the Germans would clean up England and Europe.

1. "Tribute to Lenin" was published in *People's World*, 20 April 1940, 5; and republished (as "V. I. Lenin") in *New Masses* 35(23 April 1940), 16.
2. Simon and Schuster publishing company.

[UPL]
H. L. Mencken
1524 Hollins St.
Baltimore.

April 30, 1940.

Dear Dreiser:

I am delighted to hear that you are feeling so much better. The reports about your illness that reached these wilds were somewhat vague, and so I couldn't make out what had floored you. Please don't forget that at our venerable age it is necessary to take more rest than hitherto. I begin to realize that it is no longer possible to work twelve hours a day without feeling bad effects.

Thanks very much for your permission to quote you in my Quotation book. The material is all accumulated, but the job of reducing it to order promises to be a heavy one. I'd like to tackle it at once and push it through, but unhappily I'll be interrupted all Summer by politics. If I am on my two legs I'll certainly go to both national conventions, and also to any other rump conventions that are organized. The Townsendites already announce one in St. Louis for July, with John L. Lewis[1] as chief gladiator.

My experience with radicals has been quite as unhappy as yours. Every time I try to be decent to them they take advantage of it, and meanwhile they seize every opportunity to libel me. The plain truth about them is that they are a bunch of swine.

Yours,
M

1. John L. Lewis (1880–1969) was the president of the United Mine Workers and of the Congress of Industrial Organizations.

[NYP-T]
Theodore Dreiser
1426 North Hayworth,
Hollywood, Calif.

August 22, 1940.

Dear Mencken:

Can you tell me where I am likely to pick up data explaining the financial hook up between big American finance and big British finance,— Threadneedle Street and Wall Street? I know, of course, the streets are mere trade and money mechanisms functioning by reason of powerful fig-

Dreiser surrounded by nature (University of Pennsylvania Library)

ures in and out of government. The question I am seeking to answer for myself is this: Have English and American and Continental Finance cooperated with Hitler to bring about an International control of money, manufacture and trade? Do you chance to know of any books or magazine articles or Congressional reports or speeches that cover or touch on this? If so I'll be grateful for advice.

How are you? You must have had a grand Convention tour. Yet, if you wrote anything, I haven't seen it. Any articles in the Sun paper? If so I'd like to see them.

If you can't advise me don't trouble to write. I'll understand.

Regards.
Dreiser

[UPL]

H. L. Mencken
1524 Hollins St.
Baltimore.

August 24th [1940]

Dear Dreiser:-

Unhappily, my ignorance of the subject you mention is immense. I suggest writing to John T. Flynn, of the New Republic. He is very likely to know where the facts are to be found. All the other financial writers seem to have turned 100% British.

My guess is that Roosevelt will win. If Willkie[1] pushes him hard, he will horn into the war at once and then go on the air and scare the boobs out of their pants. It is an old trick, but it always works.

My political stuff so far has not been worth reading. The heat at Elwood, Ind., was so dreadful that it was almost impossible to work. I may travel with Willkie on one or more of his later tours, but that is not certain. As I have said, I doubt (at least at this writing) that he can win.

I hear vaguely that you have been ill, and hope it was a false report. I am in very fair shape myself, and hard at work.

What are you up to?

Yours,
M

1. Wendell L. Willkie (1892–1944) was the Republican presidential nominee in 1940.

Mencken surrounded by Nietzsche, Ibsen, and Shakespeare
(Enoch Pratt Free Library)

[UPL]

H. L. Mencken
1524 Hollins St.
Baltimore.

November 27, 1940.

Dear Dreiser:

Thanks for the clipping,[1] which I have naturally read with great interest. I needn't tell you that I agree with you thoroughly about England.
Unhappily, I suspect that you overestimate the innocence of Stalin. His
so-called neutrality is probably bogus.

What are you up to? Let me have some news of you. I have been putting
in some licks on my memoirs. You are the principal character in Vol. XI.
I am depicting you as a sincere Christian and a lover of the flag.

Yours,
M

1. This is missing.

[UPL]

H. L. Mencken
1524 Hollins St.
Baltimore.

February 25, 1941.

Dear Dreiser:

Thanks very much for the book,[1] which came in safely yesterday. I
have gone through it with interest, and am hoping to read it in full on Sunday. I needn't tell you that I agree with at least nine-tenths of your argument. Unhappily, my belief is that the time for discussion has passed. We
are in for a circus in the grand manner, and it will unquestionably end in
disaster for this great Republic. I am so far convinced of this that I have
stopped writing in the Baltimore Sunday Sun. It seemed vain and idiotic
to be trying to tell the truth in a newspaper that has gone over to England,
Willkie, and even Roosevelt.

I trust that you are in the best of health and full of sin. I was somewhat
wobbly a year ago, but begin to feel better. At the moment, I have no less
than two books on the stock—one of them a dreadfully long one. If these
are finished by the end of the Summer (as I hope), I may go out to Seattle
to see the Northwest. It is the only part of the United States that I have
never visited. If I do so, I'll certainly drop down to the Los Angeles re-

gion, and so I may have the felicity of viewing you. I trust that your beauty is unimpaired. Every now and then I meet some woman here who speaks of it with her fists clenched and eyes flashing.

Yours,
M

1. *America Is Worth Saving* (1941). Dreiser inscribed the book: "For Henry L. Mencken from—(and with enduring affection of) Theodore Dreiser. In trade, as you might say, for those ten realistic years of your youth. No concealed attempt at proselytizing because of no hope of so doing."

[UPL]

H. L. Mencken
1524 Hollins St.
Baltimore.

March 4, 1941.

Dear Dreiser:

I enclose another circular from the <u>New Masses</u>.[1] As you will note, you are still depicted as a whooper for the magazine. Whether anything can be done about this remains to be seen.

I have read your book with great pleasure. As I have told you in the past, I can't follow you all the way, but nevertheless it seems to me that you put a great many plain truths in very effective language. Unhappily, it is now too late to make any impression on the country. Roosevelt and his fellow-demagogues have sold the war to the boobs, and we seem to be in for it. My guess is that the final cost to the American people will be gigantic. This is not the pushover that the last war was. The English will discover that fact very soon.

Yours,
M

1. This is missing.

[UPL-HPc]

Baltimore

Nov 26 1941

Where are you at? I hope our Heavenly Father guides you, and protects you, and makes His light to shine upon you.

H. L. M.[1]

1. The postcard picture is of the Adam Scheidt Brewing Company of Norristown, Pennsylvania.

[NYP]

THEODORE DREISER

Dec. 2nd—41

Dear Menck—

I am at 1015 N. Kings Road, Hollywood. Moved from 1426 North Hayworth a year ago. Was in New York Nov. 24–25 last but came directly out here.

I see, you scoundrel, you swiped my title <u>Newspaper</u> <u>Days</u>[1] and I am buying a copy of the book so as to prosecute you later.

Otherwise all is ok. Bought out of S & S at last and am making over to Putnam's (I think) this coming week. It was why I traveled east

Just now I wish I were at the Brewery pictured on your card—for it is 80Fh here and the beer would fit me neatly.

Love and good health—Heavenly Father or no Heavenly Father—to you.

Dreiser

If you come out this way I have an extra room for you.

Do you know what Hilters dream of the perfect State is—if any? I cant make out whether he's settled on the perfect formula or not.

1. The second volume of Mencken's autobiography, *Newspaper Days* (1941), has the same title that Dreiser used for one of his autobiographies.

[UPL]

H. L. Mencken
1524 Hollins St.
Baltimore.

December 6th [1941]

Dear Dreiser:-

I hope you forgive me, as our Heavenly Father undoubtedly has. My memory, thanks to a dissolute life and many troubles (some of them deserved), is not as sharp as it used to be. In fact, I didn't begin to notice anything familiar about that title until the book was out, and it was then too late. Naturally enough, I rushed at once to my lawyer, Charles Evans

Gorefine. He told me that it had been used 17 times in the past—the last time by Richard K. Fox, the first editor of the <u>War Cry</u>. A copy of the book is going to you by express today, elegantly embellished and embossed. You get it absolutely free of all charge or expense. Pay nothing at the door.

I hear vaguely that you have sold "Sister Carrie" to the J——s, and are rolling in money. If this is a fact, I am delighted to hear it, and surely hope you don't take to evil courses. I would appreciate a can of lard as a Christmas present. All my revenues are going for taxes, and I begin to wonder if, whether and what I'll be eating in 1942. The salvation of humanity seems to be a very costly business.

But the show is swell, and I am now glad that I was not hanged in 1917. What we are looking at, I suspect, is the suicide of democracy—as clumsy and noisy an affair as the suicide of a whale or a locomotive. Whether or not Hitler has invented anything better I can't make out. But it seems to me to be pretty clear that we are in for some sort of imitation of his scheme in this country. I stand ready to join up with anything that is announced, just as I stand ready to be baptized for a box of good 5-cent cigars.

Maybe I'll see you soon. I am toying with a plan to take a last look at California during the Winter. Unhappily, I hear that the native malt liquor is inferior. Let me have something confidential on that point.

Yours,
H. L. M.

[NYP-C]
December 9, 1941

Dear Dreiser:

The more I think of the Newspaper Days business the more I am convinced that my faculties are failing. Certainly I was well aware that you had done a book of that title. Incidentally, what has become of it? I don't see it in your list of publications. Is it still to be printed? Let me know about this. I may have a third book of reminiscences ready during 1942 and I want to make some reference in the preface to my conscious violation of your chastity.

I sincerely hope that the Japs don't bomb you out. The war promises to be long and bitter. I believe that Roosevelt could have avoided it but now it is on our hands and it is useless to repent.

What are you up to?

Yours,
(Signed) H. L. Mencken

[NYP-T]

Theodore Dreiser
1015 North King's Road,
Hollywood, California.

December 11, 1941.

Dear Mencken:

Your sly attempt to evade my just claim for injury in connection with the use of my title does not go—and I have instructed my lawyer, Mr. Solomon Shinstone, to communicate with you.

Meantime, should you come to Hollywood I will house you in comfort. My hope in so doing is to cause you to reform.

Regards,
Dreiser

By the way my telephone here is Gladstone 2876
As to wealth—it all went to pay up old debts & the income tax & agent's commission.[1]

1. The postscript is handwritten.

[UPL]

H. L. Mencken
1524 Hollins St.
Baltimore.

December 19, 1941

Dear Dreiser:

Let the lawyers fight it out. If Shinstone can make any impression on DeWitt C. Fineberg, then he is a master indeed. They will send us tremendous bills, but I herewith propose formally that we refuse to pay them. You will be rewarded post-mortem for your Christian attitude.

Christmas in this house is always a dismal festival, and so I am glad when it is over. My brother and I commonly devote it to quiet boozing. If I really get to the Coast during the Winter I'll certainly communicate with you in advance. I want to consult you about various difficult questions of theology.

Yours,
M

[NYP]
[before 26 December 1941]
Dear H. L.—
This is as I recall you at the age of four. Remember?[1] Whaddaya know?
Dreiser

1. Dreiser wrote this on a Christmas card, below a picture of a child with angel wings.

[UPL]

H. L. Mencken
1524 Hollins St.
Baltimore.

December 26, 1931[1]

Dear Dreiser:
Those angel pictures take me back to my days of innocence, though I think I should tell you frankly that I lost my wings before I was three years old. The scars are still visible, but they grow less marked every year.
I surely hope that you got through Christmas without too much misery. It is a dreadful festival here, and I am always glad when it is over. I look forward with eager anticipations to 1942. The human race will get what it deserves, and with interest at 200 percent. Meanwhile, the show ought to be swell.
Don't you ever come eastward any more?
Yours
M

1. Mencken meant to write 1941.

[UPL]

H. L. Mencken
1524 Hollins St.
Baltimore.

March 18, 1942.

Dear Dreiser:
Your tract[1] came in just in time to help me through the rigors of Lent. They are always oppressive, and sometimes I emerge from the sacred sea-

son with my withers damn nigh wrung. So far today I have been to Mass eighteen times.

What are you up to? and how are you feeling? I surely hope that the wicked Japs are not putting you to serious inconvenience. Here in the East there are blackouts, but they are not taken too seriously. In Baltimore the saloons are permitted to keep open as usual.

Let me have a line from you when you feel like it.

Yours,
M

1. This is missing.

[UPL]

H. L. Mencken
1524 Hollins St.
Baltimore.

March 27, 1942.

Dear Dreiser:

Thanks very much for that lovely reminder of Lent.[1] As you know, I always go on a strict diet during the holy season, and so get rid of at least a part of my paunch. Unhappily, Lent always coincides, at least in Maryland, with the Bock beer season, and so I am subjected to horrible temptations. Prayer enables me to resist them, though not always.

What are you up to? I asked you that question some time ago, but you did not reply. I only hope that you have nothing in hand of an unlofty and subversive nature. As for me, I am torn between two attractive chances to serve humanity: on the one hand the Archbishop of Canterbury has invited me to England to consult me on a question of pathological theology, and on the other hand I have been asked by General MacArthur to join him in Australia.

In New York the other day I encountered, by chance, your son Julius. He told me that he was still at odds with you over money matters, but that he regarded you with filial reverence and wished you well. I suppose you know that he is now one of the captains at Lüchow's. He tells me that his takings amount to $50 a week, and that sometimes they run up to $60 or $65. Of my 34 living grandsons no less than 27 have been drafted for the army. I begin to feel like a hero.

Yours,
M

1. This is missing.

THEODORE DREISER

[NYP]

April 2nd '42

Fairest Mencken:

In answer to your repeated inquiry. Believe it or not I am working on The Bulwark and doing quite well with it, I think. Also enjoying it   After 8 years I managed to get loose from those lice labeled Simon & Schuster and am now in the hands once more of An American publisher—Putnam's Sons—who look to be fair minded enough in their literary outlook. I am not taking any advance from them worthy of the name—a thousand dollars as a binder. They are taking over all my plates and books—renting the <u>Plates</u> from me for 5 years. Although you do not know it, I spent seven long years solving the peculiar equation called <u>Life</u> for myself and have all the chapter data ready to my hand. I was going to bring that out first—this year—but was persuaded to shift to this. As soon as this is off my hands I'll shape up the other.

By the way the University of Pennsylvania is taking over all my stuff, lock, stock, & barrel. Trunks & boxes of material are leaving here every few days. I have been wanting to tell you that I have a lot of letters of yours that can go back to you or to UP as you choose. They contract in the matter of all letters <u>from</u> <u>any</u> <u>living</u> <u>person</u> not to permit their examination, copying or photostating during the life time of the writer unless he and myself provide our respective consents in writing. So before anyone can look at yours let alone copy them or quote from the same he or she must write you & obtain your consent & mine. Once you are dead I assume it cuts no ice. Certainly in my case—once I am gone they may quote and be—. However, if you want yours back, let me know. Personally I'd like to see the UP preserve them

T.D

They say they're going to devote a fine large fire proof room to the whole business. I have a contract[1]

Too bad you forgot to sign your patriotic burst   It now waves over my liquor case.[2]

1. Dreiser placed these lines in the left-hand margin.
2. Dreiser wrote this on the top of the second page.

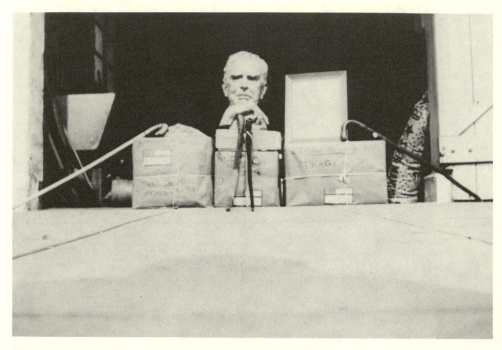

*Manuscripts and bust of Dreiser on their way to the University of Pennsylvania
(University of Pennsylvania Library)*

[UPL]

H. L. Mencken
1524 Hollins St.
Baltimore.

April 11, 1942.

Dear Dreiser:

I needn't tell you that I am delighted to hear that you have resumed work on "The Bulwark". I'll never forget its first days, now so many years ago, and your plans for it. The idea at the bottom of it is one of the best you have ever had, and I think you'll make a swell job.

I see no objection whatsoever to your plan for depositing your memorabilia in the University of Pennsylvania library—on the contrary, it seems to me that it is excellent. As for my own letters, I am glad that you are including them. Some of them, to be sure, contain ribald and even subversive material, but by the time both of us are angels in Heaven no one will care. Incidentally, I wonder if it would be possible for me to get a set of copies of them? I have been at work, off and on, on a sort of record of my own life, and I find that my letters are very helpful. Accordingly, I have been collecting copies of them from various old friends. Have you sent your material to the library? If so, let me know and I'll ask the librarian for permission to have a copy made. If you still have my letters, and care to let me go through them, I'll have them copied here and then forward them either back to you or direct to the library. Let me know about this.

I hope that the uproars of the time are not interfering with your work. Here on the East coast the war seems enormously far away. People talk of it vaguely, as they might talk of the Judgment Day.

Yours,
HLM

[NYP-C]
April 20, 1942.

Dear Dreiser:

Thanks very much for your note of April 6th.[1] I'll write to Mr. David at once. After Mr. Elias has sorted out your papers it should be possible to unearth my letters and then drop in at the library of the University, and maybe it will be possible to arrange to have copies made of them. They would help me enormously in some writing that I now have in mind. My memory is clear enough but I have a bad hand for dates. The letters cover several episodes in my life that I certainly want to write about, and they will help me to get the records straight.

There is no news here. The malt liquor on tap steadily deteriorates, mainly because the supply of Bohemian hops is exhausted. Nevertheless, it remains drinkable and so I manage to survive. I have been putting in a whole year on an enormous newspaper record that will probably never be published. What I now have in mind is a similar record of my adventures in magazines. You will appear in it in the character of a beautiful young hero, with pink cheeks.

I hope that The Bulwark is going prosperously. I am certainly very eager to see it.

Yours,
(Signed) H. L. Mencken

1. This is missing.

[UPL]

H. L. Mencken
1524 Hollins St.
Baltimore.

April 29, 1942.

Dear Dreiser:

Thanks very much for the clipping from Variety.[1] "My Gal Sal"[2] sounds really interesting, and when it comes to Baltimore I'll turn out to see it. My one regret is that you are not among the actors.

I have been floored by my old enemy, tracheitis, and am going to hospital this afternoon for treatment. It is not serious, but simply a dreadful nuisance. It makes speech painful, and so I'll be as silent as a Trappist for four or five days.

Yours,
M

1. "My Gal Sal," *Variety*, 22 April 1942, 8.
2. *My Gal Sal*, a film based on Dreiser's sketch "My Brother Paul" (*Twelve Men*).

H. L. Mencken
1524 Hollins St.
Baltimore.

June 5, 1942.

Dear Dreiser:

I am glad you have challenged Sherwood Anderson's idiotic account of that Scott Fitzgerald episode.[1] I remember it perfectly clearly. Certainly you did not turn Fitzgerald out. On the contrary, I recall how he stalked across the room and said: "Mr. Dreiser, I get a great kick out of your books." As you will remember, he was far gone in liquor, but still able to talk.

There is a statement in the Anderson book about my own relations to him that is completely insane. In substance, it is to the effect that I disliked "Winesberg, Ohio," and yet laid claim to discovering Anderson. Both halves of this are false. I have, in fact, a letter from Anderson thanking me effusively for my review of "Winesberg," and I never made any claim to his discovery. The first time I ever heard of him was through you. Nathan and I debated doing some of the "Winesberg" stories in the Smart Set, but at that time the Comstocks were in violent eruption, and it was obvious that if we printed them we'd only get the magazine suppressed. Later on I printed a great many pieces of Anderson's, both in the Smart Set and the American Mercury.

What are you up to? I fell ill at the end of April and landed in the Johns Hopkins for a couple of weeks. I am still a bit rocky, but manage to get some work done. I have arranged with the Pratt library here to give it all of my copies of your books. It is in a new building, and in the basements thereof are a number of steel-barred rooms that seem to be quite safe from bomb attacks. Your embellishment of the national letters will be incarcerated in one of them for the wonder and instruction of posterity. In all probability, I'll send the books before long. They'll be much safer in the library vault than in my house. So far the Japs have not bombed Baltimore, but there is no telling when they will start.

Yours,

M

1. The incidents referred to in this letter are in Anderson's posthumously published *Memoirs* (1942).

[NYP]

THEODORE DREISER

June 15—42

Dear Mencken:

Thanks for your word concerning Sherwood Andersons statement that I refused to admit Scott Fitzgerald. Your letter settles that nonsense. Lengel wrote me that he also wrote that once, at some weekend gathering where I was a guest, I strolled out naked before the entire company to enter a swimming pool! I never did. It reads more like a literary yarn concerning Oscar Wilde and Lord Sholto Douglas.[1] Although he may be confusing me with you and some of your mad doings. The fact is that I had a large pool at my Mt. Kisco place. It was to the north of the house and down (at the foot of) a sharp slope. (300 feet distant) On the other hand the guest lounging grounds were to the south of the house which concealed the presence of the pool completely. There on occasion I did put on shorts, shoulder a towel and proceed to the pool—guests or no guests—since most of them were on the South lawn entirely out of view. True, they could amble down to the pool—on occasion. Among those that accompanied me,—more than once—was Sherwood—but not naked. I furnished him with shorts and a towel. So—he must be thinking of you somewhere

Love & best wishes—
Dreiser

1. Dreiser is referring to the sexual scandal that resulted from Oscar Wilde's association with Lord Douglas.

[NYP-C]

June 23, 1942.

Dear Dreiser:

Your mention of Lord Alfred (not Sholto)[1] Douglas revived a curious memory. When I was in London in 1930 Douglas began writing me furious letters demanding that I apologize for an article published in New York in which I referred somewhat sniffishly to his habits. I naturally refused to do so, but he kept on banging away and in the end actually argued that his relations with Wilde had always been innocent. He was apparently preparing to sue me for libel at the time I quit London and returned to this great Republic.

I hear from the University of Pennsylvania library that the sorting out of your papers has not yet been undertaken. Thus it is impossible for a layman to get at my letters. Incidentally, Dr. Julian P. Boyd, librarian of Princeton, is planning to do a volume of selections from my letters while (so I hope) I am still alive. Would you object to him looking through those from me to you? If not, will you please notify the proper authorities at the University of Pennsylvania. Boyd's discretion can be trusted. Moreover, I'll have a look at the manuscript before it goes to the printer. If you object, please say so frankly.

I am reassured by your categorical statement that you didn't parade around your Mt. Kisco place in the altogether. It is common gossip in the New York saloons that you wore only a jock-strap from May to November—in fact, I have my own letters from forty head of women who allege that you not only stripped off your own clothes but also theirs, and then proceeded to work your wicked will upon them. I should add that none of them actually complained—in fact, they all hint that they enjoyed it.

I am looking forward with immense interest to the Bulwark.

                    Yours,
                    (Signed) H. L. Mencken

1. Dreiser had given the correct family name of Sholto to Lord Douglas.

                                        [NYP-T]

                    Theodore Dreiser
                    1015 N. King's Rd.,
                    Hollywood, Calif.,

                                        July 14, 1942.
Dear Mencken:

About turning my letters to you over to Mr. Boyd of Princeton, I am perfectly willing to do that after I have looked them over.

Wont you please ship the lot out here for me to look through, and if I don't find anything that will immediately place me behind bars, I will forward them back to Mr. Boyd. I would like to spend my few remaining years in this crazy world outside of jail if that is in any way possible.

Yours to the last drop.

                    Dreiser
P.S. Please send the letters collect American Railway Express.

[UPL]

H. L. Mencken
1524 Hollins St.
Baltimore.

July 16, 1942

Dear Dreiser:-

My apologies for the obscurity of my letter. It gave you an entirely erroneous impression of the proposal. Boyd had not asked for your letters to me, and has no intention of printing them. The request came from Dr. Charles W. David, director of libraries at the University of Pennsylvania. I asked David for permission to make copies of my letters to you, so that I could select some to send to Boyd, and he replied that they were in confusion and that it would help him a lot in sorting them out and dating them if he had copies of your letters to me. I replied that I could not let him see these letters without your permission, and so wrote to you. It was my plan, if you said yes, to offer to give David photostats of your letters to me in return for photostats of my letters to you. That is all. Your letters to me, as your know, are to go to the New York Public Library at your death. I made that promise to H. M. Lydenberg, the librarian there, long before I heard of your arrangement with the University of Pennsylvania.

I hesitate to send the originals of your letters to me to California in these cockeyed times. The express service is very bad, and the mails are worse. For the first time in years I have had packages lost of late. But if you say so I'll be glad to have photostats made of your letters and send them to David. I have been through them with some care and they are quite harmless. Nine tenths of them deal with your work, and the rest are amiable persiflage. In any case, as I understand it, they will not be accessible to anyone until after you have become an angel.

Let me know if this plan is all right.

Meanwhile, God help us all. These are dreadful days for us sinless Anglo-Saxons.

Yours,
M

[UPL]

H. L. Mencken
1524 Hollins St.
Baltimore.

July 21, 1942.

Dear Dreiser:

I hear somewhat vaguely that you are ill, and I surely hope that you are making a good recovery. My own troubles seem to be passing off. I had an operation on my throat week before last, but it is now virtually well.

Let me have a line from you when you feel like it.

Yours,
H. L. Mencken

[NYP]

Theodore Dreiser
1015 N. Kings Road
Hollywood

July 23—1942

Dear Menck—

Those illness rumors are wrong. I'm feeling about as good as usual. Back in the fall of 1940 I thought I had a heart attack but later I concluded a local medic was putting one over on me. I shouldn't have gone to bed at all. Since then I've eaten my three square and worked as usual. If I die suddenly I'll wire you. Meantime put your trust in politicians and advertising and all will be well with you. All else is hokum.

Affectionately if irreverently,

Dreiser

[UPL]

H. L. Mencken
1524 Hollins St.
Baltimore.

July 23, 1942.

Dear Dreiser:

I have your letter of July 20th.[1] Very good. I'll have photostats made of your letters to me at once and send them to Dr. David. He has promised, in return, to send me photostats of my letters to you. They will be of immense use to me when the time comes for me to do the story of my magazine days. My own records are full of holes.

I observe that the first letter from you in my file is dated August 23, 1907. It thus appears that the thirty-fifth anniversary of our correspondence is only a few weeks ahead. I shall celebrate it by hanging out the papal flag and inviting the policemen on the beat to join me in thirty or forty rounds of sound malt liquor.

I find an undated letter, marked "1912" in pencil, as follows:

3609 Broadway

"Dear Mencken:

   This introduces Edgar Lee Masters of Chicago, of whom I spoke and wrote. You may have a few thoughts in common".

This Masters is still living in New York. He is a gambler, and is said to be very prosperous.

Yours,
M

1. This has not survived.

[UPL]

H. L. Mencken
1524 Hollins St.
Baltimore.

August 3, 1942.

Dear Dreiser:

   I am naturally delighted to hear that the reports of your illness were false. If you had actually had a heart attack I'd have offered my congratulations, for people with heart lesions seem to live forever. I could give you a list as long as your arm, but refrain because of the scandal. You will outlive me by years. I have left orders that you are to be asked to address the assembled police and bartenders at my funeral, which will be held at the Yankee stadium in New York. My carcass, as you know, is to be stuffed and then deposited in the National Museum at Washington. I once offered to get you standingroom in the same place, but you made no reply.

   The photostats of your letters to me should be finished tomorrow. I'll send them at once to Dr. David at the University of Pennsylvania. As you know, he has promised to send me a set of photostats of my letters to you. I discovered, in looking through them, that your letters are full of subversive stuff. In one of them you actually indulged yourself in some contemptuous remarks about our holy Christian religion. Naturally enough, I blacked out this passage before having the letter photostated.

The weather down here is infernal, and I am finding work almost impossible. We have had high temperatures for three weeks running now, with very high humidity. Once the heat passes, I'll be floored by hay fever, so I am looking forward to continuous entertainment during the next six weeks.

Yours,
M

[NYP-T]

Theodore Dreiser
1015 N. King's Rd.,
Hollywood, Calif.,

August 14, 1942.

Dear Mencken:

As usual I have to point out to you that your memory is failing. I remember clearly your offer to get me standing room for my embalmed carcass in the National Museum at Washington, D. C., but you appear to have forgotten my reply, which was that one year before your offer, being short of cash, I sold my body to the Rush Medical Dissection Section of Chicago for $8.40, cash in advance. I have the contract in my files. According to you, at the time, the National Museum was demanding a large storage fee. Rush Medical was offering to send, immediately after my departure, a truck for the remains. The $8.40 cleaned up three weeks back room rent and left some change for beer.

I suggest you consult a specialist. You give signs of approaching amnesia.

Theodore Dreiser

[UPL]

H. L. Mencken
1524 Hollins St.
Baltimore.

August 19, 1942.

Dear Dreiser:

I apologize most abjectly. You not only told me that you had sold your carcass to Rush for $8.40; you also asked me to inquire if the Johns Hopkins was willing to pay more. I had to reply that the Hopkins pays nothing whatever, for Baltimore is a great seaport, and the sailors killed in the waterfront saloons every week provide it with an actual oversupply of anatomical material. Such, in brief, is God's will. Let us not repine.

The whole East coast has just experienced a spell of weather so dreadful that not even the oldest inhabitants remember anything worse. The temperature ranged from 80 degrees above, and the humidity was at the saturation point. In New York on Sunday there were five separate downpours, each of them amounting almost to a flood. I got caught in two of them and was soaked. You escaped a lot when you became an actor and went to Hollywood.

Yours,

M

[UPL]

H. L. Mencken
1524 Hollins St.
Baltimore.

February 23, 1943.

Dear Dreiser:

Since the University of Pennsylvania sent me photostats of my letters to you I have arranged them in their places among your letters to me, and have been going through the whole series. It is full of interesting stuff, and will no doubt edify posterity. Here and there I find references that puzzle me, for example, on April 28, 1911 you wrote me about a certain Charles B. De Camp. Who was he? I can't find any trace of him in my own files. Again, on August 8, 1911, you speak of "The Financier" as your fourth book and hint that there was a third running ahead of it, just after "Jennie Gerhardt". Did this so-called third book every have any real existence? Later on in our correspondence you began speaking of "The Financier" as No. 3. Do you happen to recall what the sales of "Jennie Gerhardt" were? My impression is that it did very well—in fact, much better than "The Financier". Certainly it appears to have got better notices. Some of these days a couple of young Ph.D.'s will tackle the Dreiser papers at the University of Pennsylvania and the result will be series of studies so profound no one on earth will ever be able to read them.

I enclose a slip from the latest bulletin of the New York Public Library. There should be copies of your letters to Johnson at the University of Pennsylvania.

I assume that you are still hard at work on "The Bulwark". Are you making good progress? I surely hope so. Let me have some news of you when you feel like it.

Yours,

M

[UPL]

H. L. Mencken
1524 Hollins St.
Baltimore.

[2 March 1943]

Dear Dreiser:

In going through the Dreiser-Mencken correspondence I find that you were hard at work on "The Bulwark" all through 1916, and that the Lane Company announced it for the Spring of 1917. The assumption was that it was finished, but I suppose that that was wrong. When did you abandon it? As I understand it, you have now taken it up again and propose to push it through. Is the time of publication scheduled? If so, what is it?

I also find myself asking some questions about "A Book About Myself". The "Newspaper Days" volume was published in 1922 and "Dawn" in 1931. What became of the third volume? Also, what became of the third volume of "The Financier"-"Titan" triology? My apologies for pursuing you with these questions. If our Heavenly Father spares me, I may undertake soon or late a record of my literary experiences. If I ever do, it goes without saying that you will stalk through the book as a prancing hero.

I trust and pray to God that you are in the best of health and spirits, and making good progress with your work. Down here in the Confederate swamps the rationing business is growing really serious. Food, indeed, has become so short that most of the restaurants are closing at 10 P.M. One of the best is open only from 4 P.M. to 9 P.M., and many others are closed all day Sunday. I am thus reduced to eating at lunch wagons. It would not be so bad if there were any meat left in the hot dogs. As it is, they are mainly composed of wormy cornmeal and second-hand cedar sawdust. This is a hard dose for a man with a delicate stomach to swallow.

Yours,

M

[NYP-T]

Theodore Dreiser
1015 N. King's Rd.,
Hollywood, Calif.,

March 8, 1943.

Dear Dr. Menckhorn:

Charles B. DeCamp, a promising writer and editor who held an assistant editor's job on Everybody's Magazine back in 1904–5 when I was founding and editing <u>Smith's</u> <u>Magazine</u> for that noble pair of brothers— O. G. and George—who constituted Street and Smith. He was from Ohio, a graduate of Yale and a delightful person. However, his father, a well to do man, had cursed him with the outright gift of $100.00 per month for life. The result was that Deacon, as his friends used to call him, and who was of a genial and sociable disposition, soon took to drink and girls, and presently, after a year of work, was fired from Everybody's. Then a friend of mine, knowing I needed an assistant, sent him to me. I was fascinated by him and kept him on until I moved to The Broadway Magazine (Ben B. Hampton's paper). After that the Deacon took to drink again, wrote six really good short stories which, as I recall, were published. Then suddenly came pneumonia and death. A long time ago I intended to present him in <u>Twelve</u> <u>Men</u> because he was really so wise, so sensitive, so esthetic and kind, but $100.00 per did him in. I think of him often to this hour.

As to <u>The</u> <u>Financier</u>, I'm really a little mixed myself. I was always starting something and then finding that for some reason or other I couldn't go on. I was always getting a small advance from a publisher on some one book and then being ordered to make good. Meanwhile I would have become interested in another. For instance, while writing The Financier, I had completed three or four of the studies which were to make Twelve Men. Also at least ten of the sketches that were to make The Color Of A Great City. In 1903, while dreaming of doing <u>Jennie</u> <u>Gerhardt</u>, I wrote 32 chapters of what was to be The "Genius", and in 1907 or 1908, tore them up and burned them in order to do Jennie Gerhardt, etc. etc. Somewhere in there, as a side-line, I began <u>Dawn</u>, and actually wrote a half dozen or more chapters, only to find that at that time it was too soon to be doing it—family reasons. So it was left until much later.

Then came, of course, Jennie Gerhardt and The Financier and, after my trip to Europe with Grant Richards, A Traveler At Forty, because he wanted it done. Then The Titan, for reason of which, Harpers kicked me out. Then The "Genius" and John Lane. They had made me a slight advance but refused to publish the book, as you know. You were in on that. For some reason Jennie Gerhardt sold and I made some money, enough (what with articles, stories and such) to go on for quite a little while, even though Horace (Liveright) didn't show up in my life until about 1918. He took over The "Genius", as well as Twelve Men, finished at that time, both of which sold. Meanwhile The Bulwark idea had come to me back in 1914 or 15 and I did some work on that—now and then. Also, around the same time, A Hoosier Holiday, which was due to Franklin Booth's desire for us to go back and see Indiana. You edited that book for me. Also I finished Plays of The Natural and Supernatural and The Hand of The Potter, which Horace published. Also (in there) having given up Dawn, which was to be volume one of A History of Myself, I decided to work on Newspaper Days, which was to be volume two of my life. Meanwhile, as you know—I decided to remove to Los Angeles and did so. There—between 1919 and 1921 I finished Newspaper Days and sent it to Horace. Without my consent or any word to me he changed the title to A Book About Myself. I didn't like that. It interfered with My Dawn, Newspaper Days, A Literary Apprenticeship series. (Literary Apprenticeship was to be the title of volume three). Later, as you know, I had Horace drop A Book About Myself title and put in its place Newspaper Days. Between 1922–1930—after I returned to New York, I finished The Color Of A Great City, Free and Other Stories, An American Tragedy, Dawn, A Gallery of Women, Chains—a volume of short stories—Tragic America, Dreiser Looks At Russia and God knows what else.

Right after the last of that series I became interested in the structure of Life itself and decided to explain it in a book to be called <u>The Mechanism Called Man</u>. Well, in between articles and stories, I devoted about seven years to that and now have in my store room—collected and separated in labeled folders—all of the data for about 40 chapters, which begin with The Mechanism Called The Universe and end with The Problem of Death. If I don't find time to reduce this mass to book form, someone should look it over. I'll leave it to the University of Pennsylvania. Included in data quoted from many, many authorities and sources, are hundreds of pages of my own deductions.

As for your other questions—<u>The Bulwark</u>, resurrected last fall, is in its 34th chapter. It will come through.

As for the third volume of the History of Myself, which is to be called—A Literary Apprenticeship,—I dream of doing it. It is a scream! Yet it only goes up to Sister Carrie (1900) and her fate. By the way I have a copy of the $35,000 movie script of the same done two years ago by Mr. and Mrs. Spivak,[1] which has been allowed to die. (R. K. O. bought the movie for $40,000 and paid $35,000 for the script. But it is a bad script, and so the whole thing is now as dead as a door nail—if door nails are dead.

As for Volume III of the Yerkes series[2] (A Trilogy of Desire)—the third volume—half done—is here in my store room. After all I am only one man and like to live a little outside the literary jail.

As for what else—well—I am in pretty fair health. Owe no one anything, except the Government which seems to need everything that any or all of us have, and will get it finally unless we finish Dr. Hitler pretty soon.

As for you and your food, you've eaten and drunken so much that I am not deeply moved. You probably are grabbing off right now three times more than is your just due. So

Censoriously and yet affectionately
Dreiser

P.S. I'd like to send all letters from you to me on to the University of Pennsylvania. What about it? I have a good sized bunch.

P.P.S. Moods—my volume of prose poems—which were written between 1914 and 1926, were copyrighted and published by Liveright in 1926. In 1935 Simon and Schuster copyrighted and issued an enlarged edition of the same. All copies are controlled by Putnams.

1. Dreiser means Samuel and Bela Spewack.
2. *The Stoic.*

[UPL]

H. L. Mencken
1524 Hollins St.
Baltimore.

March 12, 1943.

Dear Dreiser:

Thanks very much. You tell me precisely what I wanted to know. The record that I am putting together is hardly printable as it stands. It is rather a collection of notes and documents than a book. If I ever do the story of my magazine days I'll use it as source material.[1] If I am snatched to Heaven before I ever get to the business, I'll leave the record to some library.

I surely hope that you are making good progress with "The Bulwark". I remember you talking about it years and years ago, and it sticks in my mind to this day. The other things can wait.

You are free to send anything of mine to the University of Pennsylvania. My impression is that all of my letters are already there. Have you any left over? If so, let me know, so that I can get photostats of them when they are turned in.

My brother[2] is going to hospital today with a severe head and throat infection, and I am somewhat rocky myself. Thus the place is in a dreadful mess. I'll write to you again when our Heavenly Father lets up on us.

Yours,

HLM

1. Mencken never published such a book.
2. August Mencken.

[NYP]
Mch 13—'43

Dear Mencken:

In my letter concerning my various mss. and the writing and publishing dates of the same I spoke of my proposed third volume of personal recollections which I intend to call "A Literary Apprenticeship" which is or was to follow <u>Newspaper Days</u>. In regard to that I said it was to carry up to the publication of <u>Sister Carrie</u> in 1900. What I meant to say was that it was to carry up to the publication of Jennie Gerhardt in 1911. Also the republication of Sister Carrie—both by Harpers.[1] That is as far as I intended—and now I may add.—"I intend" to carry my recollection. Many of them are in "A Gallery of Women," Twelve Men—and various article & short stories   So please pin this to the other letter.

Dreiser

I assume like myself you are a lover of Dies,[2] the Southern Poll Tax, Beneficiaries, Hoover, Willkie, our dear unpensioned Congress, the American Manufacturer's Association, The Am. Chamber of Congress, our Free Press, and the American Federation of Labor—and so, like myself are happy. <u>Yes</u>?

1. Harpers published *Sister Carrie* in 1912.
2. Martin Dies, congressman, chairman of the House Special Committee to Investigate Un-American Activities.

[UPL]

H. L. Mencken
1524 Hollins St.
Baltimore.

March 19, 1943.

Dear Dreiser:

I note what you say in your letter of March 13th. I surely hope that if you ever finish that autobiographical trilogy you push on to four volumes, and devote the fourth to the period since 1911. It has been full of rich experience.

What, precisely, are your ideas about the current crusade to save humanity? I have seen many statements of them, chiefly in the Communist papers, but most of those statements seemed to me to be incredible. Are you supporting the war, and if so, to what extent? I recall that during the last great struggle for democracy our ideas were virtually identical, but I somehow gather the impression that you have changed your mind this time. Have you ever printed anything on the subject? I observe that the Communists have ceased of late to list you as one of them, and I assume that this has been done in response to your protests. I continue of the opinion, as always, that they are a gang of frauds.

Some time ago, E. H. O'Neill, of the University of Pennsylvania library, came down to Baltimore to see me. He told me that the Dreiser bibliography that he has under way has now reached really formidable proportions. I hope and assume that it will be printed soon or late.[1] O'Neill says that he hopes to make it really exhaustive. It will include not only everything that you have published yourself, but also everything that has been written about you, not omitting book reviews.

Yours,
M

1. O'Neill did not publish a bibliography.

[NYP-T]

1015 N. Kings Rd.,
Hollywood, Calif.,

March 27, 1943.

Dear Mencken:

You ask: "What, precisely, are your ideas about the current crusade to save humanity." Personally, I do not know what can save humanity, unless it is the amazing Creative force which has brought "humanity", along with its entire environment into being. I, myself, have cursed life and gone down to the East River from a $1.50 a week room in Brooklyn to a canal dock to quit. My pride and my anger would not let me continue, as I thought. And yet a lunatic canal boatman ferrying potatoes from Tonawanda to the Wallabout Market in Brooklyn did. Wanting me as a companion to accompany him on his return trip to Tonawanda, he stated as his excuse for his liberality or charity that he "thought maybe I was trying to run away from my wife." And my wife was in the west living on her parents while I struggled and starved on alone. To a guy with a total of 15 cents left and a $1.50 a week room to return to, this brought an ironic laugh, and, in consequence, a change of mood that saved me from going to Tonawanda and instead—the next day—moved me to cross over to Manhattan Island with a new idea. But I will have to write "A Literary Apprenticeship" before you can learn all about that. Incidentally, that is why I said to you that "A Literary Apprenticeship" would be a scream.

For not more than five years from that date I was Editor-in-Chief of all the Butterick Publications at a fat salary. My predecessor as editor had—on being discharged—committed suicide. And you ask me about the "current crusade to save humanity." My answer is that I do not know positively—nor do I think that anyone else does so know,—that is, that it will be saved. It may go under.

And certainly many phases of it—the lunatic rich with their asinine control of billions—should go under, just as did the French monarchists—Louis XIV, XV, XVI—and Charles I in England. And as the Russian Czarist system up to 1917 should have and did go under. For if there is any reason for saving humanity surely it should not be that of starving and murdering it. No life of any kind, in my humble opinion, is better than that. For I do not believe in slavery or starvation. For if, with all that we know through modern science,—agronomy, medicine, economy and education—we cannot do better by the average man than I saw in Russian in 1927—(the left over miseries of the Czarist Regime) also in England in 1911, '12, '26, '28, '38—and Spain, France and Belgium, then I think humanity had better be allowed to pass. For I have pity. And pity suggests that no humanity at all is better than what I have seen here and there,—many fractions of the United States included.

I know you have no use for the common man since he cannot distinguish himself. But I have—just as I have for a dog, a worm, a bird, a louse or any living or creeping thing. The use that I see is contrast and so interest for you and for me. For without these where would either you or myself or humanity, as a whole, be? Where? The interest and charm of life—where would it be? And for whom? Your unsaved humanity? I do not follow that course of reasoning. For without natural universal interest in all phases of created life this night I would take a sleeping potion that would end the argument for me. As for you—you might live on without mental interest of any kind, assuming that you could and also chose to do so. But I cannot even see it as possible.

You see, Mencken, unlike yourself, I am biased. I was born poor. For a time, in November and December, once, I went without shoes. I saw my beloved mother suffer from want—even worry and wring her hands in misery. And for that reason, perhaps—let it be what it will—I, regardless of whom or what, am for a social system that can and will do better than that for its members—those who try, however humbly,—and more, wish to learn how to help themselves, but are none-the-less defeated by the trickeries of a set of vain-glorious dunces, who actually believe that money—however came by—the privilege of buying this and that—distinguishes them above all others of the very social system which has permitted them to be and to trick these others out of the money that makes them so great. Upon my word! To be more specific—for Christ's sake!

As for the Communist System—as I saw it in Russia in 1927 and '28— I am for it—hide and hoof. For, like Hewlett of Canterbury, who wrote that fascinating book on England and Russia,[1] I saw its factories, its mines, its stores, its Kommisars, with at least ten of whom I discussed the entire problem.

On their hands, at that time, they had the recuperation and future welfare of some 100,000,000 people that included millions of Mohamedans, Buddhists, Nomads and God knows what else. And better educated, and higher thinking, and more kindly and courageous men and women, I have never met in my life. In my humble estimation their equals in this country are few indeed. In sum, I conceived a passionate respect for that great people and still retain it,—a people who, in so far as I could see, wished humanity to survive on a better plane than ever it had known before,— not die or starve or be made slaves of. And the love I conceived for them then, and that passionate admiration I also developed there, I still retain, as also, I have for their writers, artists and musicians since ever I became aware of their enormous gifts. If you question my judgment here, show me a Chekhov, a Dostoievsky, a Tolstoy, a Mousorghsky in all the history of American art and American reaction to American life and I will sit up in silent reverence, for their equals I do not know.

As for Doctor, Professor Mencken—to me, of course, he is sui generis. Never has there been in this or any other country before, in so far as I know, one like him! And sadly, I fear, there will not soon be another. He seems to me to lack faith in anything and everything save the futility of everything—which is a Voltairean approach to all that is, and that amuses me. But for all the bullheaded faults and ironic conclusions of said Heinrich—I love and always will love him—be the final estimate of said Dreiser or said Mencken what it may.

Darling—don't forget that I remember how, almost fatalistically, you arrived in my life when, from a literary point of view, I was down and out, and you proceeded to fight for me. Night and day apparently. Swack! Smack! Crack! Until finally you succeeded in chasing an entire nation of literary flies to cover. It was lovely! It was classic. And whether you choose to slam me right or left, as is your wont, in the future, Darling, Professor, Doctor, I will love you until the hour of my death. <u>And don't pull any Edgar Allen Poe stuff in connection with my forgotten grave either</u>.[2] <u>Do you hear me? Or I'll come back and fix you. And how!</u>

Love and kisses from

P.S. As for the American Communists—well there are—or were and still are, I assume,—many fakirs and flies and camp followers who hope to pick up a living out of the cause. They have never interested me and I have never been interested by their gyrations and genuflections. I am— and have been—content to deal with the Russian government direct—its foreign office, its American Ambassador, its consuls, etc. I have written for Pravda often and have answered many cables that have come to me direct. P.P.S. If you really want to bother with my social viewpoint, why not read <u>American Is Worth Saving</u>?

I have now nine extra letters from you. When they reach 15 I'll send you the dates and send them on together with my answers, if you say so the U.P. in Philadelphia.

1. Hewlett Johnson, *The Socialist Sixth of the World* (1940, 1941).
2. Mencken had the habit of taking his literary drinking companions to Poe's grave to imitate the local canine custom of urinating on the tombstone.

[NYP]
Sunday, Mch 28 [1943]

Dear Mencken:

Here is a PPS to my letter to you. Join it up with the same.

I ceased following Hitler when in 1940 he attacked Russia—my pet. At first I thought that he had a progressive program for a United States of Europe—a better intellectual & social Europe. But when I saw Russia being attacked and Italy and the Holy Father and the dear Church going Scot free—even being allowed to pay for the destruction of Democratic Spain, my interest in Doctor Hitler save as a crook and a high finance stool pidgeon, I passed. And that goes for today, tomorrow & the end of time.

T. D.

H. L. Mencken
1524 Hollins St.
Baltimore

April 1, 1943.

Dear Dreiser:

You are far too kind, and I think you exaggerate considerably. What you forget is how we both enjoyed the battle, even when it was going against us. I kept it up on ten or twenty fronts until 1926, and then had the joy of seeing the Comstocks curl up. They have never been the same since, though as a part of the war to save humanity they are now trying once more to enlist the Postoffice. I am half in hopes that they succeed, for if they do it will give some other pair of scoundrels a chance to tackle them all over again.

You need have no fear that I will take up a collection for a monument to you when you become an angel, and for a very good reason: I'll be in Heaven before you are. Naturally enough, the holy saints will ask me about you, and maybe they will confront me with the report made by J. Jefferson Jones. No matter how damning the record I'll insist that you are and always have been a Christian. Is it or is it not a fact that you voted for Harding? Is it or is it not a fact that you once gave a blind man ten cents and urged him to trust in God, to wit, in Tyrone, Pa., in 1904?

I simply can't follow you in your belief in Comrade Stalin. To me he seems to be only a politico like the rest, and if anything worse than most. All the Russian genii you mention flourished under the czars. Since Marxism came in the race has produced nothing above the level of a book of Waldo Frank. Russian music, when not Jewish, is balony, and Russian science belongs to the school of the late Prof. George Washington Carver of Tuskegee[1]—in brief, to the school of the Hearst Sunday supplements.

Moreover, there is the indelible fact that the comrade cut more throats, before 1939, than a dozen Hitlers, and that he was quite willing, for two years, to share Hitler's burglaries. I am no gipsy, but I presume to predict that before this cruel war is over he will be burgling and butchering again. When you were in Russia you saw the show-window, but not much else. How could you communicate with the poor fish at the bottom? Very well: tell me that you learned Russian. I answer that no Russian would dare to tell his troubles to a stranger in tow of officials, or even to a stranger on his own. It was as if you had been taken to the best whorehouse in St. Louis, and then come out saying that all Americans lived like that.

But let us not argue. You seem to have picked up the notion—diligently spread by me, for I know how all Americans respect money—that I have eaten nothing save caviare since leaving the cradle. The fact is that I have paid my own way since the age of 16, and that on my 21st birthday I transferred to my mother my small inheritance from my father, and have never touched a cent of her estate since her death. You knew far worse poverty than I did, to be sure, and you pulled out of it magnificently, but don't forget that when I first met you you were a rich magazine editor with six or eight secretaries. I recall perfectly that you had on a suit of Hart, Schaffner and Marx (not Karl, but Julius) clothes costing at least $27.50, and used a gold lead-pencil. Thus I simply can't think of you as a proletarian. To me you must always be a kind of literary J. Pierpont Morgan.

I have been rather below par physically for two or three years, but still manage to survive, and even to work. If our Heavenly Father spares me for a couple of years longer I hope to do a book that will set you to howling and gnashing your teeth—to be published, of course, after the war: at the moment free speech is suspended. Perhaps it will never be restored: if so, the MS. of my book will go to the Vatican library.

It is a pity that we are so far apart that we can't meet for an occasional palaver. But such appears to be God's will, and I agree with McKinley that objecting to it is vain and probably in bad taste. Let me hear, when you feel like it, what you are up to.

Yours,
M

1. George Washington Carver (1864?–1943). Born of slave parents, Carver became an educator and taught at Tuskegee, beginning in 1896.

[NYP-T]

Theodore Dreiser
1015 N. King's Rd.,
Hollywood, Calif.

April 21, 1943.

Dear Menck:

That article you prepared—What The American High School Graduate Knows—is simply staggering. For me it has about a hundred laughs.

Much as I dislike to admit it, it seems to justify your opinion of the mass. But, of course, High School graduates of America do not constitute the total mass.

Affectionately,
Dreiser

The swinging of the critical ax is an art with you. How the chips fly and the so-called trees fall.[1]

1. The postscript is handwritten.

[UPL]

H. L. Mencken
1524 Hollins St.
Baltimore

April 28, 1943.

Dear Dreiser:

That article I sent you was not mine. It came from the New York Times, and was written by some unknown wizard. As you have probably noticed, it has got an enormous amount of attention in the newspapers. The other day it was debated in the United States Senate for two hours. The facts in it, of course, didn't surprise me in the slightest. I have preached for years that the so-called education provided in most American colleges makes the boys stupider instead of smarter.

I trust that you are in good health and reasonably good spirits, considering the horrors of the times. I have been plugging away at all sorts of dull jobs and, despite my illness during the Winter, have made reasonably good progress. Prayer has helped.

Yours,
M

[NYP-T]

THEODORE DREISER

Aug. 11, 1943

Dear Mencken,

I am interested in helping the writer of the enclosed stories[1] to get either a Houghton Mifflin fellowship or a Guggenheim. She is a draftsman at one of the airplane plants here and is also working on a novel, of which I have seen a small part. I am going to sponser her for a fellowship and I want to ask if you too will do so.

I am sure that these stories constitute an impressive addition to American literature, not only as realistic studies of varying American characters but as humane, tender, wise and socially helpful picturizations of the oddities as well as the weaknesses of all of us. I am sure they rank with the best writing of our day and time and I wish so much to see them in print and being widely read.

If you will make a statement which she can use in an application for a fellowship, would you please send it to me?

Theodore Dreiser

1. The writer has not been identified.

[NYP-C]
August 17, 1943.

Dear Dreiser:

These short stories certainly do not lift me to frenzy, but nevertheless they seem to be competently done and it goes without saying that I'll be delighted to recommend the author to either Houghton Mifflin or the Guggenheim. Tell her to put down my name as one of her subscribers and the usual questionnaire will reach me.

What are you up to yourself? I surely hope that you are diligent in good works and losing no opportunity to strike a blow for humanity.

Knopf is urging me to do a supplement to The American Language. I have accumulated a really enormous amount of fresh material and it seems a pity to let it go to waste. Unfortunately, the business of getting it into order promises to be almost backbreaking. However, I should get some help from prayer and more from my clean life.

How are you getting on with The Bulwark? I hope it is making good progress.

Yours,
(Signed) H. L. Mencken

[NYP-C]
October 7, 1943.

Dear Dreiser:

In New York the other day I dropped in at the public library to see what had been done with the manuscript of Sister Carrie. I had not seen it since it was mounted. These few lines are simply to say that I was genuinely astounded. Lydenberg and his goons did a really magnificent job. The manuscript is beautifully mounted, covered with Japanese tissue and bound in four volumes with the loveliest leather I have seen for years.

Each volume is also in a leather box. It is kept in the manuscript vault under the city level and no one can see it without an order from you or me. The next time you return to Christendom you must certainly take a look at it.

I trust that you are in good health and reasonably good spirits. I have just passed through the worst hay fever season since the year of Valley Forge and am still somewhat dilapidated.

I notice in the Billboard that the authors of America have lately held a three-day congress on the Los Angeles campus of the University of California. I observe that many eminent men were present, including George Jessel, Glanville Heisch, Leo Hurwitz, Sidney Minchman and Allen Rivkin, but I don't find the name of Theodore Dreiser. Can it be that you have retired from good works? If so, I can only lament it. Let me have some news of you when you feel like it.

Yours,
(Signed) H. L. Mencken

[NYP]

THEODORE DREISER

Oct. 13—'43

Dear Mencken:

It was nice of you to send me your word picture of the Carrie ms. sleeping so royally and peacefully in the subterrainean vault of the New York Public Library. What grandeur after her long and poverty stricken beginning! And how pleasant it would be to track down into that royal sanctuary with you and, hat in hand, gaze humbly—maybe, who knows, even genuflect! One can never trust these literary moods that sweep over one on occasion. Remember your Jennie Gerhardt spasm. The good old days!

Well, darling, please thank Dr. Lydenberg for me for his—what shall I call it?—Courtesy? Reverence? Sympathy for that once so bedraggled maid. And I will write him also.

Personally I'm not so well off. Arthritis, nervous depression, little physical strength just now—etc etc. Have just lost 13 pounds but am on a still hunt after them—still gin and still whiskey—good hunting hounds these.

Well, thanks again,—many.

Only yesterday I was reading in your In Praise of Women and laughing. I have a small bedside library.

Dreiser

[UPL]

H. L. Mencken
1524 Hollins St.
Baltimore

October 18, 1943.

Dear Dreiser:

I am distressed indeed to hear about that loss of weight, and hope that it turns out to be only transient. You are, after all, a very bulky fellow, and so you can afford to knock off a few pounds without damage. It may be that the change in the national dietary due to rationing has produced some effect. We all assume that we are getting as much to eat as ever, but we are certainly getting different kinds of food. I notice myself that my corporation seems to be shrinking. I only hope that the supply of decent drinks is holding out on the Coast. Here in the East it has been shot to pieces. It is actually impossible in Baltimore to buy whiskey by the bottle, and the supply of decent beer is shrinking constantly. One of the best brews in America is made here, but it is now unobtainable in its home town. The brewer ships it out because under the ceiling arrangement made by the idiots in Washington he can charge a larger price for beer sent out of the State. As a result, all of his output is going to New York and Chicago. Here in Baltimore we are drinking Pennsylvania, Missouri and Wisconsin beers. I object to this on patriotic grounds, but mainly on the ground that they are bad.

Lydenberg and his agents did a really magnificent job with the "Sister Carrie" manuscript. I only hope you take a look at it yourself some day. It will convince you, I believe, that your soul will never die. The thing not only shows respect and reverence; it even goes to the length of superstition.

What are your political ideas in these days? Let me hear them when you feel like it.

Yours,
M

[NYP-T]

Theodore Dreiser
1015 N. King's Rd.,
Hollywood, 46, Calif.

Nov. 25, 1943.

Dear Mencken:

Do you know anything about the Viking Press-Knopf combination? I hear there is one such. Who is the top dog in there? Knopf or who? I need to find some house that would really be interested in a complete set of my books. So far as I can make out the idea is never to bother about any past work—that is, call attention to the works as a whole—but always to yowl about the next novel, leaving the others to rest as non-existent. I have never been able to see that as a policy, especially when there are so many people looking for one's works, as I find to be the case. Nor have I found a publisher who appeared to be interested in any of his authors past works. Perhaps you know of one.

Apart from that—how are you? This is Thanksgiving but I know that you invariably ignore Turkeys and Cranberries and celebrate with beer and pretzels. Such being the case I use your customary salute "Heil Hitler!" As for me—give me Ham and Heggs.

Dreiser
P.S. Affectionately.

[UPL]

H. L. Mencken
1524 Hollins St.
Baltimore.

November 29, 1943.

Dear Dreiser:

So far as I know (and I'd certainly have heard of it if it were a fact) there is no alliance between Knopf and the Viking Press—indeed, none has ever been discussed, and I am sure that combining the two firms would present almost insuperable technical difficulties to the lawyers. Have you ever communicated with Knopf directly? Or with Ben Huebsch of the Viking Press?

What is the exact present condition of your books—that is to say, are the plates still in existence, and if so, do you own them? I rather suspect that any publisher who brought out a complete set would want to re-set it. At the moment, of course, that would be almost impossible. Moreover, there would probably be difficulties about getting enough paper. However, the war can't last forever, and I think it would be a good idea to begin negotiations at once. If you want me to tackle Knopf on the subject I'll be delighted to do so. My guess, however, is that it will be hard to interest him, not because he doesn't appreciate your books, but because he is horribly badgered by the current rationing.

I spent Thanksgiving day at hard work—the only reasonable occupation for a true Christian. So far the weather down here has been bearable, but there are already some whiffs of Winter, and in a little while I suppose we'll be beleaguered.

My project to be stuffed post-mortem is proceeding apace. I have lately received some very attractive overtures from a first-rate taxidermist. If you want to come aboard, let me know. My plan is to have my carcass deposited in the National Museum at Washington.

Yours,
M

[NYP-T]

Theodore Dreiser
1015 N. King's Rd.,
Hollywood, 46, Calif.

Dec. 4, 1943.

Dear Mencken:

Thanks for the information as to Knopf and Viking. Taking Knopf's situation, as you present it, I prefer Viking.

As to my books as a whole, I own all of them—copyrights, plates and the few copies in stock at Putnam's since these were transferred to them by Simon and Schuster at the time I paid S. & S. all I owed them. The crookedest trick ever played on any author, I hope, was the one handed me when I took an advance from S. & S. against The Bulwark, which was to be turned over to them the year following the acceptance of the advance and the signing of the contract. (You see Liveright, or rather his successor, Arthur Pell, had a stock of my books, as well as my plates, for which I had to pay in order to be able to transfer them to S. & S. S. & S., according to my agreement with them, were to then take those books and market them, paying me my 15% royalty. Instead, the entire lot, which I had already paid Pell for, were taken by S. & S. and dumped into old books stores all over New York, where they were sold at 40 to 80 cents per copy. Out of this money so collected came the S. & S. advance of $5,000 to me! So they were out nothing, had a contract with me and I was out any decent distribution of my books, and, in addition, the 15% royalty on sales which I should have had. So I quit S. & S. then and there, sought another publisher, and finally, two years ago, found Putnam's who were willing to take over and store my plates and such few books as were left unsold to old book dealers.

At that time I again went to work on The Bulwark, which was to have been delivered a year ago. As it worked out, I encountered a psychologic barrage of some kind and have only finished a third of it.

Meantime, Putnam's—a quite honest firm, having advanced me $2,000 against full control of my general works and $1,000 against The Bulwark, cannot see the wisdom of printing and selling a complete edition of my works—so far 23 volumes. Neither can they see any wisdom in reprinting a number of copies of the more saleable books and supplying the current demand which exists. For Grosset and Dunlap, a year or so ago, issued a 10,000 edition of SISTER CARRIE, Random House printed and has in stock what is left by now of an edition of TWELVE MEN, Doubleday Doran several years ago printed a 5,000 edition of The 'Genius' and The Financier. And so on. So I feel that my works as a whole have a steady selling value which should be taken advantage of by someone. Yet, Putnam's, who, as I see it, if they were an up and coming concern, could profitably print and stock a number of my books, for which there is an unchanging demand. Yet still they cannot see the wisdom of it—even though the publicity in connection with me is sufficiently constant and impressive to warrant the same. A book of mine that is coming into demand right now is MOODS—a book that could be easily pushed and sold. But no—all of my works must wait on the completion of The Bulwark, which is counted on to restore all of my works to the sales counters, yet which would never be the case, as you know, unless an intelligent advertising campaign were indulged in, which, in Putnam's case would not be the procedure, I fear. They have not the perspective of a Liveright by any means, nor the money, I think.

So what I am looking for is a publisher who would be willing to restore to Putnam's the $2,000 advance against my general works, paid by them to me (possibly the $1,000 advance against The Bulwark), take over all of my books now extant, publish my next volume, whatever it is, and all future volumes, and upon so doing, advertise my works as a whole. It may be that some publisher can be made to see that, or will see it. On the other hand, it may not be.

What I feel is that a set of my books is sure to sell one of these days—the grave yard route as you see—and whoever has control of them then might profit a little. However, as yet, I have not selected my mausoleum as have you. (Something less than the Washington monument might do, I think). However, in your case, I wouldn't hurry if I were you. You're certain to be missed a lot.

Affectionately,
Dreiser.

[UPL]

H. L. Mencken
1524 Hollins St.
Baltimore.

December 13, 1943.

Dear Dreiser:

On reflection, I am still convinced that this is a bad time to talk of bringing out your collected works. It would be a sheer impossibility for any publisher to get enough paper. Moreover, the labor situation in the printing industry is such that it would be equally difficult to get so long a job set up. I suspect that your difficulties all revolve around the fact that you ask publishers for advances. That always makes them cautious and dries up whatever liberality may be in them. My belief is that it is always better to take nothing until a book earns it. That encourages them, and they give it whatever help is possible. The value of such help, I believe, is always considerably overestimated by both author and publisher. A book really sells itself or it doesn't sell at all. I believe that "The Bulwark," if you finish it, will have an excellent sale.

I wish we were closer together, so that we might discuss the business at length. I really don't know precisely what is in your mind. Your proposition, as you outline it, would probably alarm any publisher in New York. But there is no reason whatsoever why it might not be so modified as to fetch a good one. Sets of books, as a matter of fact, seldom sell. They are brought out as vanity jobs. There have been, of course, exceptions, though not many. I doubt that the collected works of Ambrose Bierce, for example, sold 200 sets, yet they were full of good stuff, and much of it was unavailable elsewhere.

Is there any chance that you'll be in the East in the near future? If so, we must certainly have a real session. I am so hard at work on my supplement to "The American Language" that it seems very unlikely that I'll be able to get to the Coast during the Winter. The accumulation of new materials is so gigantic that I get through it only by working ten hours a day.

I'll be glad to tackle Knopf if you say so, but I know absolutely that he'll refuse to undertake any large enterprise at this moment. He is having a dreadful time getting paper for books already on his list—indeed, it is still doubtful that he'll be able to bring out my supplement to "The American Language," which will probably run to seven or eight hundred pages.

God help us all! Now that humanity is saved once again, the state of the world is worse than ever before.

Yours,

M

[UPL]

Chamber of Commerce
Holland, Michigan

December 22, 1943.

Dear Dreiser:

I have begun to have serious doubts about Santa Claus. So long as he confined his business to Christmas, he was worthy the respect of Christian people, but when he began to work for Roosevelt all the year round he lost a good deal of his old character. I am thus moved to say to hell with him, but am not prepared as yet to go that far.

I certainly hope that you are feeling better, and that 1944 sees you full of luck. I judge by the newspapers that the year will be the most wondrous the human race has ever seen—in fact, some of them predict formally that sin will be abolished in the world before it is over. On this point I have my doubts, but perhaps it may be wise to keep them to myself for the present.

I am plugging away at the projected supplement to "The American Language". It is making fair progress, but it is a really dreadful job.

Yours,
M

[NYP]

1015 N. King's Road
Hollywood 46
Los Angeles

Tuesday, Dec. 28—'43

Dear Menck:

Its nice to hear from you, regardless of whether you do or dont lecture me. And as to advances from publishers I know you are right, particularly when one has the money to work on without an advance. But in my case, in my early years I had so little that where possible I had to extract an advance or go get a job—and in various instances I did so get a job—first as editor of Every Month at 15⁰⁰ a week—later as editor of Diamond Dick and Brave & Bold not to mention Nick Carter and Frank Merriwell—all for the noble sum of 15⁰⁰ a week. That was in 1904–5. And naturally when I found that I could raise some working cash for such an idea as Jennie Gerhardt I took it, even though I was not able to finish that work until much later. So the habit was formed. Actually if I had thought of the advance as a serious deterrent in connection the distribution of all the unsold books now in Putnam's hands, I never would have asked for it. And it may be that I can repay it for they have quite a few of my works that now lie there on their shelves and if I owed them nothing they might get the current book stores to stock them.

Meantime I'm sorry your so overburdened with work on your American Language Supplement   It must be tough, even though the work is so interesting, for I have found in my case that it is possible to bite off more than I can chew and in two cases at least I gave up—dropping two novels—one carried to 33 chapters—the other to 16 if I recall aright. Yet I felt better for doing it and so managed to finish other things   Just now I am going through a period of eye trouble—my one good eye—the left— seems to be losing strength and I am indulging in eye calisthenics. The other I have never used. Its lense is poor and out of focus but perhaps God or Science will come to my aid. I hope so.

But here is no news but movie and war news. Also socializing and concubinage ad lib. Every soldier has to be taken care of in all ways   As for me, poor oaf,—here I sit and work while all the world plays. Do you be kind and pray for me—Or take a trip out here and cheer me up.

Dreiser

Incidentaly I have the shingles! Masters is sick in N.Y. Park East Hospital   I'm writing him.

John Cooper Powys is translating Rabelais into the Welsh language! He just wrote me.

[NYP]
[December 1943]

Dear Mencken:

Here I am heading straight for Hollins Street with Xmas greetings— 1943 brand. Please note what a swell driver I've become. Some class, eh!—With love—

Dreiser[1]

1. Dreiser wrote this on a Christmas card showing Santa Claus driving a sled. Dreiser drew an arrow to the figure and wrote "me" beside it.

[UPL]

H. L. Mencken
1524 Hollins St.
Baltimore.

January 3, 1944.

Dear Dreiser:

I repudiate and protest against the charge that I was trying to lecture you. I was simply trying to answer your questions and offer you the best advice that our Heavenly Father would permit me to formulate. To be sure, you needed advances in your early days, but those we have been talking of date from relatively recent years and, indeed, from a period when you were currently reputed to be bursting with money. The difficulty will be to find a publisher willing to make good the debts to the existing books. However small they are, it will irritate him to have to pay them. The question of paper, of course, is currently even more important, but soon or late that problem will solve itself.

I am distressed indeed to hear that you have shingles. To be sure, it is not fatal, but it seems to be extraordinarily irritating. Some years ago the local Catholic archbishop[1] had a seizure, and as a direct result of it he got into a violent row with the Baltimore Sun. For four weeks during an infernally hot Summer I had the job of negotiating for the Sun with his ambassadors. We came to terms quickly, but the archbishop refused to see reason until his shingles had abated. I hired two sets of colored clergymen to pray for him, one in favor of his quick recovery and the other in favor of his swift death. Neither got anywhere with God.

I certainly hope that you are in good health and spirits otherwise, and that you resume work on the book in the near future. I can well imagine what a nuisance that eye trouble must be. Whether or not the exercise scheme advocated by Aldous Huxley is worth anything I do not know. The experts here at the Hopkins laugh at it, but that, of course, is not conclusive evidence. My own eyes are still holding out fairly well, despite the cruel abuse of them that I carry on constantly. The supplement to "The American Language" is making excellent progress, and so I am not disposed to abandon it. It amuses me as I go along, and in the end it will probably bring me in some money. If so, every nickel will be invested in Victory bonds.

It is difficult to get any accurate news of Masters.[2] His second wife has turned up in New York and seems to be in charge of him. Inasmuch as he dislikes her intensely, this makes for a most complicated situation. I am going to New York next week and hope to see him. I hear confidentially that he is in really low state and barely able to function. He has been visibly deteriorating for a year past. The last time I saw him, in fact, he was almost tottering. I have put in a great deal of time with him in New York during the past ten or twelve years and had many a swell evening with him. More than once we have come close to drinking Lüchow's dry.

It takes no gipsy to prophesy that 1944 will be a bad year. I hope, however, to get through it with reasonable placidity. "The American Language" supplement will keep me occupied, and I am now too old for sin. I even got through Christmas and New Year cold sober.

Yours,

M

1. Archbishop Michael Joseph Curley.
2. The newspapers carried various reports of Edgar Lee Masters's ill health and impoverished state.

[NYP]

Jan. 29—[1944]

Fairest Mencken:

Now I have a letter from New Haven (Yale) asking me to contribute to a fund that is to establish a Memorial Library to the honor and perpetuation of none other than Wm Lyon Phelps[1]—his name and his great service to literature—American and other! Will you contribute a <u>dime</u>? I hate to dig down alone and yet—considering his stupendous services—if no one else will I may have to. My conscience may trouble me. Or, are they kidding me?

Dear Doctor Mencken: do let me have your advice, even though it be dimeless. I will appreciate that.

Meantime here I am still suffering from my <u>allergy</u>. I have tried three prescriptions thus far and my neck & right shoulder and arm are still sore. Hast thou ever heard of a sure cure? No? Well, good morning. I'll call later.

Dreiser

Avoid these allergies. The devil himself is in them.

1. William Lyon Phelps (1865–1943), critic, teacher at Yale University.

[UPL]

H. L. Mencken
1524 Hollins St.
Baltimore

February 3, 1944.

Dear Dreiser:

It is my solemn belief, borne of long and bitter experience, that the quacks know precisely nothing about allergy. I have been suffering from it in the form of hay fever for forty years, and have taken at least twenty cures, but all of them have failed. The thing seems to be a form of witch-craft, and is probably engendered by the evil spirits that swarm in the at-mosphere of this great republic. The only relief I ever get is from alcohol, and that is only slight. Last Autumn I put in a really dreadful time. For-tunately, allergy sometimes passes off spontaneously. I surely hope that yours takes that route.

It seems to me that it is your bounded duty to send a contribution to the Yale fund. The last time I encountered the deceased we fell into talk of you, and I had the privilege and honor of disabusing him of certain mis-apprehensions regarding you. He had been told by your secret enemies that you were talking against the current war to save humanity. I told him that this was a base libel, and that as a matter of fact you were making patriotic speeches on the Coast. I also added that you were engaged upon a life of Uncle Joe Stalin. All this reassured him, and he went away con-vinced that you were a literary artist of high tone.

I certainly hope that your discomforts abate sufficiently to let you get back to work. In all this world there is nothing more unpleasant than the situation of a literary gent who finds writing difficult or impossible. I could give you a long list of such unfortunates, for the East seems to swarm with them. By the direct intervention of our Heavenly Father, I seem to have escaped so far myself. I am plugging away at a proposed supplement to my old book, "The American Language," and making very fair progress. My office is piled mountain-high with material, and some of it is very amus-ing. Fortunately, it is possible in writing such a book to flit from chapter to chapter as the mood suggests. Thus I never get tired of it, though I am putting in a great deal of hard work. If the matter of surnames begins to worry me, I simply turn to soldiers' slang, or the changes undergone by the Polish language in Erie, Pennsylvania.

There is no news here. I gather by the papers that the war will be over in a couple of weeks. I shall celebrate the business by going to the poor-house.

Yours,
M

[NYP]

Theodore Dreiser
Hollywood

Mch 9—44

Dear Henry L—

This is to gravely announce that on May 14th or 15th next I am to be in New York City for reason or reasons which will appear later.[1] The thing which interests me most (in connection with this) is will I be permitted to see your royal highness, have one dinner at least and by reason of the same be permitted to settle the affairs of this world as now is, as well as its certain to be disordered hereafter. As to that, as I know, you are certain to be the final word. Incidentally Helen is coming along (I think) and she craves the pleasure of seeing you and studying your classic form and features. As for me I have degenerated into something not unrelated to a Swift-Armour-Nelson Morris self, mouldered ham intended to be labeled (labeled) and sold as prime ham at 70 cents a pound. So you see how it is. Incidentally I expect to visit in Philly and possibly Washington but I shall—mostly—be around N.Y.C. If I can get a room there I'll be at the Commodore—central and convenient. And, as the guy said about his tombstone—this is on me.

Love and respect—(if they go together)   Sometimes I think not
Dreiser

1. Dreiser had been asked by the American Academy of Arts and Letters to accept an Award of Merit Medal, which carried with it a cash prize of $1,000. [UPL] Dreiser does not mention the reason for his trip east, since he is aware of Mencken's dislike of the academy and all such affairs.

[UPL]

H. L. Mencken
1524 Hollins St.
Baltimore

March 27, 1944.

Dear Dreiser:

Your letter of March 9th has just reached me. You must have mailed it without postage, as the enclosed envelope shows. As you will note, I was put to the expense of 3c to recover it. It will be all right to postpone the refunding of this money until we meet in New York.

I'll certainly be delighted to run up to see you, or if you are in Washington or Philadelphia, to wait on you there. Needless to say, I'll be delighted to see Mrs. Dreiser[1] again. It begins to seem like ten thousand years since we last sat down for Christian communion together.

I hear that you are going to New York to be crowned with a laurel wreath by the American Academy of Arts and Letters. If this is true, I can only deplore the fact that you are having any truck with that gang of quacks. Its members for many years were your principal defamers. If they have actually offered you a hand-out, I hope you invite them to stick it up their rainspouts.

There is no news here. I am somewhat depleted by the rigors of Lent, but I manage to get a considerable amount of work done. My projected supplement to "The American Language" is already more than half finished, and unless our Heavenly Father has at me with some new and extraordinary assault I should be able to finish it by the end of the year.

Yours,
M

1. Dreiser did not marry Helen Richardson until 13 June 1944.

[NYP]
April 22—[1944]

Dear HL

Here more dope for your American Language[1] I'll be in N.Y. on May 12th or 13th. Stopping at the Commodore. I'm going to Philadelphia around May 15th I think. Anyhow hope to see you. I'm taking the thousand and $500 expenses because I need it for some work in N.Y.

Dreiser

1. The enclosure is missing.

[UPL]

H. L. Mencken
1524 Hollins St.
Baltimore–23

April 27, 1944.

Dear Dreiser:

Thanks very much for the clipping. I am delighted to have it for my archives.

Whether or not I'll be able to get to New York on May 12th or 13th remains to be seen. How long precisely are you staying? Let me know, and we can arrange to meet.

Yours,
M

[NYP]

THEODORE DREISER

May 3—'44

Dear Mencken:

I leave here May 10—at noon and am supposed to be at the Hotel Commodore Saturday May 13. I am coming early—(the award doesn't take place until May 19th) because of various personal matters which require my attention. After May 19th I'll leave as soon as various family matters are adjusted. All my living sisters and brother reside in N.Y. But while I'm there I'd very much like to see you. If you can't come over I'll try to get down to Baltimore for several hours, if no more. Beginning May 13th mail should reach me at the Commodore. All my good wishes

Dreiser

[UPL]

H. L. Mencken
1524 Hollins St.
Baltimore—23

May 5, 1944.

Dear Dreiser:

I have your note of May 3rd. If it is at all possible, I'll certainly drop into New York while you are there. I gather that you'll be in town about a week. Let us get into communication as soon as you reach the Commodore.

Yours,
M

[UPL]

H. L. Mencken
1524 Hollins St.
Baltimore—23

May 5, 1944.

Dear Dreiser:

Will you let me hear of it as soon as you settle down? I am hoping to get to New York while you are in residence.

God help us all!

Yours,
M

[NYP]

THEODORE DREISER

May 5—'44

Dear Mencken:

That American Academy of Arts and Letters fracas takes place Friday afternoon, May 19th. And afterwards, at his home, Walter Damrosch the president, is giving a dinner to a number of friends and members of the Academy. As the same is in my dishonor I have been approached by thus and so to discover whether you, being my chief aid and abettor in the perpetration by me of at least a percentage of my various literary crimes, would be willing on this occasion to make one more sacrifice in my behalf,—ie—to not only accept an invitation to said dinner in my dishonor but actually to attend the same, along with yours humbly. No speeches or requests of any kind in so far as you are concerned being involved. Perhaps the great fear is that you, after various and sundry cocktails or straight bourbon might arise and dessicate the whole proceeding as an outrage perpetrated upon decent literature as a whole,—which same I can see as a justified and to be respected conclusion to a decidedly dubious and perhaps even wildcat adventure in the first instance.

However,—there you are. The cat is now out of the bag. Personally, unless I can have your aid and support at my right or left hand I am going to feel—well I can scarcely tell you how—forlorn, deluded, even imposter like! Help! Help! May heaven and HLM protect me!

Meantime let me assure you, I mean you no evil. Nor will I feel otherwise than justly reproved if you refuse. Every man to his principles. Only—seriously—what a pleasure it would provide yours truly if you were

Dreiser with S. S. McClure, Willa Cather, and Paul Robeson at the American Academy ceremony, 1944 (AP/Wide World Photos)

to go with me. And how deleriously gratified they (Mr. Damrosch and his company) would be if you were to attend. Are you willing?

Privately and confidentially as well as affectionately yours—

Dreiser

Think of decent whiskey at $7⁰⁰ a fifth! And I love and need it so.

P.S. I am making[1] any remarks of any kind anywhere. No speeches or comments of any kind other than "I rise to thank you" from yours nervously, TD.

1. Dreiser means to say "*not* making."

[UPL]

H. L. Mencken
1524 Hollins St.
Baltimore—23

May 9, 1944.

Dear Dreiser:

Unhappily, I can't join you in the orgies. Some of the chief members of that preposterous organization made brave efforts to stab you in the back in 1916,[1] and I am not disposed to forget it. I'd be most uncomfortable at the Damrosch dinner, and I incline to suspect that some of the other guests might be uncomfortable also. I only hope the speeches include a categorical apology for the gross injuries sought to be done to you in the past.

Whether or not I'll be able to get to New York while you are there remains to be seen. I worked hard all Winter, but have been floored of late by a series of aches and itches that seem to stump the chiropractors. They prescribe a rest, but resting is one of the things I do very badly.

Let me hear of your plans as soon as you get to the Commodore.

Yours,
M

1. Mencken is referring to the fight over the suppression of *The "Genius."*

[NYP-Tel]
May 14, 1944

WILL BE AT COMMODORE ALL THIS WEEK PLEASE COME OVER LATER TO TALK ABOUT REGARDS

DREISER

[NYP-C]
May 15, 1944

Dear Dreiser:

Unhappily, it begins to seem impossible that I'll be able to get to New York this week. An extraordinary mass of tedious business has fallen upon me, and I am, moreover, in a somewhat shaky state physically. Thus I simply can't fix a date with any confidence. You don't say precisely how long you'll remain. If it turns out that I am able to get loose I'll wire you at once, and maybe we can have at least a brief session. I am sorry for this but can't help it.

Yours,

[NYP]

Theodore Dreiser
Hollywood

June 28—'44

Dear Mencken:

Well I'm back safe and sound (apparently) although almost mobbed by pneumonia en route—an unfumigated berth I suspect, for our railroads are nothing if not licensed germ carriers and breeders these days.

As for the American Academy of Arts and Letters—a really dreary demonstration. The best bet of the whole show was Paul Robeson[1]—an outstanding personality who in my judgement dwarfed all the others. His remarks were truly interesting

As for Masters of whom I saw much—I fear his condition is serious. He has poor control of his legs. Fortunately, however, he is being carefully and lovingly provided for. On the other hand I was told that Boyd had suffered a stroke but I could not reach him and so could not confirm that.

A lot of practical affairs of my own kept me going for three weeks and incidentally my eldest sister Mary died while I was there and that complicated matters not a little.

However by now things have settled into their customary routine—my affairs. I was sorry not to have seen you but I can understand your reactions. Personally, I had to cancel three planned trips—Hartford, Philadelphia & Paoli, but here's hoping that we meet later.

Regards
Dreiser

I fancy the party conventions keep you busy now.

1. The singer and civil-rights activist Paul Robeson (1898–1976) was also honored by the Academy of Arts and Letters.

[UPL]

H. L. Mencken
1524 Hollins St.
Baltimore

July 4, 1944.

Dear Dreiser:

I am sorry indeed to hear about that brush with pneumonia, and I only hope that you have made a really complete recovery. The sad thing about passing 60, as I have discovered to my sorrow, is that all minor malaises of the earlier years tend to become more serious. Fortunately, pneumonia is now an easy nut for the chiropractors to crack. They have developed at least a dozen sulfonal drugs, all of which seem to work pretty well, though some of them are poisonous.

I saw Masters in New York last week, and he seemed to be still somewhat decrepit. He told me that the trouble with his legs, at least in his own opinion, was due to the drugs he swallowed last Christmas. I have some doubt about this myself, but nevertheless he is sure of it. His head seemed to be quite clear, but he told me that he found work next to impossible. His gait as he crossed the room was that of a man 275 years old.

I see and hear nothing of Boyd. He took to drink in a large way about ten years ago and since then, to the best of my knowledge and belief, has done no work of any consequence. How he exists I simply don't know. I heard of his alleged stroke, but later on I was told that he had simply fallen on the street.

I heard nothing of your sister's death until after you had left New York. I can well imagine what a gap it must make in your life. You and I, for literary gents, have always been close to our relatives. My own sister,[1] now 55 years old, seems to be flourishing. She has a little farm in Carroll county, Maryland, not far from the Smith place,[2] and gets a great deal of fun operating it. It is, of course, only a toy, and she comes to town in the Winter, but nevertheless she enjoys the business immensely.

I am still plugging away at my book, but it is making rather slow progress. I have been interrupted constantly by all sorts of minor illnesses, and there are days on end when I can do no work save the simplest routine. I am going down to the mountains of North Carolina next week in the hope of getting a week's rest. If the trip there and back doesn't kill me, I should return somewhat recuperated.

What are you up to yourself. I am sorry indeed that we didn't meet in New York.

Yours,
HLM

1. Gertrude Mencken (1886–1980).
2. The Harry Bailie Smith farm at Westminster, Maryland, where Dreiser and Mencken met in earlier years.

[NYP-C]
November 7, 1944.

Dear Dreiser:

I hear from Masters that you have been ill. I surely hope that you are recovering and that in a little while you'll resume all of your ferocity. I have been in the hands of the chiropractors myself but have somehow survived and am still able to do more or less work—in fact, I have just finished an eight hundred page Supplement to The American Language and hope to bring it out in the Spring. It is full of patriotic stuff and will undoubtedly get me an LL.D. from some colored college.

Let me hear from you when you feel like it. I am sorry indeed that we are living so far apart. There are many things to talk of and it is a pity that two such lifelong Christians can't exchange ideas.

I had a note the other day from Gloom—my first news of her for two or three years. She is living at her ancestral estates at New Windsor, Maryland and seems to be in excellent health and spirits.

The other day a young man named Robert H. Elias, of the University of Pennsylvania, came to see me. He made an excellent impression on me and I promised to give him whatever help I can with his proposed study of you. I told him among other things of your heroic conduct in the Spanish American War and assured him that the story that you were once married to Lillian Russell was a canard. I am confident that he will do the book that will do credit to you and himself.

Yours,
(Signed) H. L. Mencken

[NYP-C]
January 29, 1945.

Dear Dreiser:

How are you anyhow and what are you up to? I'd certainly appreciate a brief note from you. I wrote to you a couple of months ago but you failed to reply. As for myself I can only report that I have finished my long book and it has left me in a state of extreme dilapidation.

Yours,
(Signed) H. L. Mencken

[LIU]

H. L. Mencken
1524 Hollins St.
Baltimore—23

May 25, 1945.

Dear Dreiser:

What is your news? I hear vaguely that you have been ill, and I certainly hope that a good recovery is under way.

Six months ago I completed a long Supplement to my old book, "The American Language," and since Christmas it has been in type. Unhappily, Knopf has been unable so far to find the paper needed to print it. This is an irritating delay, but there is nothing to be done about it, and so I yield myself supinely to the will of God.

About a year ago I gave up sin, and ever since I have led the life of a Christian patriot. I only hope you follow suit yourself. I can assure you that it is no more uncomfortable than an ordinary attack of sciatica.

Let me have a line when you feel like it. If you are too proud and haughty to write to poor people, then please ask Mrs. Dreiser to send me some news of you.

Yours,
HLM

[LIU-T]

Theodore Dreiser
1015 N. King's Rd.,
Hollywood, 46, Calif.,

June 2, 1945.

Dear Mencken:

Where am I? What am I doing with my time? Well this last year—for one thing—I dug out a pet novel of mine—THE BULWARK—which I planned out in 1914, no less, but for one reason or another dropped. Then in 1932 or 3 I took it up again and did quite a little work on it. This last year, I dug it out again and, to my astonishment, finished it—a long book which my agents tell me Doubleday-Doran have accepted for publication this coming Fall.[1]

Then—believe it or not—I dug out that old pet of mine—A Trilogy of Desire—the first two volumes of which—The Financier and The Titan—I wrote and published long ago. Harpers. About 1913. You read both of them. Recently I took up the task of finishing Volume III of the Trilogy which I have entitled The Stoic and have finished it. Now all I need is to find a publisher who will publish the three volumes in a box—and then sell them as a set. My agent in New York—Jacques Chambrun—thinks it can be done. But we will see.[2]

As for myself, I, like yourself, tried giving up sin but it made me very ill—so much so that I had to return to my evil ways, which thank Heaven I found provided instant relief. No medicine, no pills, no diet—just sin— and so—well you can see for yourself.

As for your American Language, I am sorry that you have at last outrun the world's paper production capacity. But I feared that some time ago, as I wrote you. However, when the book is completed wire me its dimensions and I will add a large room to the house—one large enough to contain it. As for us personally, here is Love, suspicion, personal insurance— every possible safeguard, one against the other.

As ever,

Dreiser

1. Doubleday & Co. published *The Bulwark* posthumously on 21 March 1946.
2. *The Stoic* was published posthumously on 6 November 1947.

[NYP-C]

June 8, 1945.

Dear Dreiser:

I am certainly delighted to hear that "The Bulwark" is finished at last. Some time ago, as I was going through the photostats of my letters to you in the University of Pennsylvania library, I found a note indicating that you were at work on the book back in the 1914 era. At that time, I believe, you had actually finished ten or twelve chapters, for I remember distinctly reading some of them. I certainly hope that Doubleday finds enough paper to print it, and that it makes a big success.

"The Stoic" also sounds swell. It would probably be inadvisable, of course, to bring out the two books together. Perhaps "The Stoic" can follow next Spring. By that time the paper shortage should be less pressing than it is now. My own book, if it were done on the usual paper, would weigh seventeen pounds and eight ounces, but the paper now available will probably reduce its weight to no more than three ounces. Thus you can put off building that extra room for the present. If the book is ever reissued on proper paper, I'll send you a Sears Roebuck bungalow to keep it in. I have set up one in my backyard to house my collection of Gideon Bibles. If you ever want a dozen or two, let me know.

It is excellent news that you are well again and restored to your usual industry. Some time ago a report circulated here in the East that you were laid up. I wrote to you at that time, but got no answer. I thereupon concluded that you were either completely non compos mentis or locked up by the police. It is good to hear now that you have escaped.

Have you any plans for coming eastward during the Summer or Autumn? If so, we must certainly sit down together. I had a session in Baltimore a couple of weeks ago with James T. Farrell. He is certainly one of your most sincere admirers—indeed, he carries his admiration to such an extent that he believes that you are a magnificent example of a 100% American Christian. I took the liberty of warning him against you.

Yours,

[NYP-C]
July 21, 1945.

Dear Dreiser:

I have a note from a man named Walt Blazer, P.O.Box 248 Portland 7, Oregon, saying that his father was a friend of yours in St. Louis and that the old man was also a friend of Eugene Field. He wants your address. I have refused to send it to him. It occurs to me that you may want to do so yourself.

Yours,
(Signed) H. L. Mencken

[NYP]

THEODORE DREISER

Sept. 2nd—1945

Dear Mencken:

Just to let you know that I am on earth worthy or unworthy. Have just finished The Bulwark—(final revision) and like it very much. In another week or so expect to conclude The Stoic which is volume 3 of A Trilogy of Desire—(The Financier, The Titan—The Stoic)   After that a period of rest.

How are you? The end of this international fighting makes me feel better if it is really ended. I have often wondered how certain phases of it have affected you? There have been so many tragic angles. Regards, best wishes, affectionately,

Dreiser

[UPL]

September 11, 1945.

Dear Dreiser:

I am delighted to hear that "The Bulwark" is done at last. What a period of gestation! It must have been in 1914 or thereabout that you first told me of it. It will go down into literary history, section embryology, alongside the second part of "Faust". I only hope that you have got hold of a good publisher, and that he reprints all your other books.

The news that you have just been baptized in the Volga really surprises me. I have been thinking of you as a comrade since the beginning of the second holy war against sin.[1] In case you are now approached by a Jesuit or Trappist, perhaps disguised as a Jewish rabbi or a Wall Street customers' man, be on your guard. Remember Heywood Broun.[2] If you are fetched I win $2.

Yours,

M.

1. A reference both to Dreiser's recent membership in the Communist party and his religious speculations at this time.
2. The journalist and novelist Heywood Broun converted to Catholicism.

[NYP]

[December 1945]

Dear H. L. M.

Heres another device for reducing your stay down below. It's going to be hot down there and these hundreds of days off will be welcome I'm sure. Here's your chance to cut down your stay in purgatory. Get busy[1]

1. Dreiser wrote this on a Catholic indulgence card, which offers years of afterlife relief in exchange for a set number of prayers.

[NYP]

[December 1945]

Dear Henry L—

Literature and the alledged arts aside here you are as I not so much see as wish you to be—comfortable.[1] And now if it only weren't for those accursed uranium pocket bombs[2] how well off you would and should be— but—as things are I can only wish you the ease and peace pictured on the other side of this sheet. The peace that goes with your fairly well substantiated skeptical soul. Hence regards and best wishes—

Dreiser

1. The picture on this Christmas card shows a Santa Claus sleeping comfortably before a log fire. Beside a bundle of toys near his chair, Dreiser wrote "The rocket-bomb disguised."

2. Dreiser is alluding to the then new nuclear weapons: the first was exploded in New Mexico on 16 July 1945; and on 6 August 1945 a uranium-235 bomb was dropped on Hiroshima.

[NYP]

H. L. Mencken
1524 Hollins Street
Baltimore 23, MD.

December 27, 1945[1]

Dear Dreiser:-

Your elegant reminder of Yom Christmas reached me this morning, two days late and bearing marks of search and seizure. Well, we Communists must expect to be spied on by the Dies committee. As for me, I do not care, for my heart is pure. But you have been to Moscow, and everyone at the Stork Club believes that you came home loaded with Russian gold. I don't exactly believe it myself, but I am willing to hear the evidence supporting it. I only hope your ill-gotten gains are not a curse to you. Money earned thataway ain't never done nobody no good, as Paul Armstrong used to say.

What are you up to now? I gather that "The Bulwark" is in the works, and will soon be out. I hope it has a roaring sale, and is suppressed by all the comstocks. They show feebleness of late, and need something to feed on. I am thinking of doing a volume of literary reminiscences entitled "Adventures Among the Anthropophagi". If I do, I shall tell in detail how I first met you in 1906—at the Salvation Army's Shelter for Wayward Girls in Cincinnati. What you were doing there I have never been able to figure out. Or what I was doing there.

I trust you are in ruddy health and good spirits. As for me, I grind away at dull tasks and hope for a club-house ticket in Heaven.

Yours,
M

1. Dreiser died on 28 December 1945, and Mencken was relieved when this letter was returned to Hollins Street that day, because he had forgotten to place a stamp on the envelope.

The Mencken Letters
to Helen Dreiser
(1945–1949)

After Dreiser died, Mencken began a correspondence with his widow. These letters provided an opportunity for Mencken to reflect on Dreiser's place in literary history and on their friendship. Mencken discovered that even in death Dreiser made demands on his time and energy: he found himself advising Helen Dreiser on the two posthumous novels, *The Bulwark* (1946) and *The Stoic* (1947); on the disposition of manuscripts; and on the proper administration of the estate. And in writing her memoir of the novelist, she received from Mencken the kind of encouragement and practical advice that he had so often given Dreiser. Even after Mencken's massive stroke in 1948, Helen Dreiser kept in touch with him until her death in 1955.

The Correspondence (1945–1949)

[NYP-C]
December 29, 1945

Mrs. Theodore Dreiser
1015 N. King's Road
Hollywood, Calif.

He was lucky to have you and you were kind to think of me. It is hard to think of his work as ended. What a man he was. I need not tell you of my sympathy or of my distress.

H. L. Mencken

[NYP-C]

H. L. Mencken
1524 Hollins Street
Baltimore 23, MD.

December 30, 1945

Dear Mrs. Dreiser:-

You were very kind indeed to send me that telegram. Are you likely to be in the East in the near future? If so, I hope you let me see you. I am eager to hear more than I can gather from the newspapers. I only hope you are in good health yourself. I won't attempt any consolation, for no man knows better than I do how vain it is.

Theodore's death leaves me feeling as if my whole world had blown up. We had met only too seldom in late years, but there was a time when

Dreiser: In memoriam (University of Pennsylvania Library)

he was my captain in a war that will never end, and we had a swell time together. No other man had a greater influence upon my youth.

Let me hear from you when you feel like it.

Sincerely yours,
(Signed) H. L. Mencken

[NYP-C]
January 12, 1946

Dear Mrs. Dreiser:-

I can well imagine what a dreadful day it must have been for you, with poor Theodore in that cruel agony and nothing to do about it.[1] But there is some consolation in the fact that it did not last long. I assume that what took him off was a coronary attack, and I am sure that there was but little pain after he got into the oxygen tent. From that time onward he must have been comfortable, and his actual end was easy. How fortunate he was that you were by him! You were his mainstay, and you were there to offer the last services.

I am only sorry that I saw so little of him in his later years. There was a time when we were together very often, and had a lot of business in common, but after the two of you moved to the Coast, there were few opportunities to meet, though we always kept in contact. I hope that "The Bulwark" is well on its way, and that "The Stoic" is ready for the printer. It was truly amazing that a man beyond seventy should have pushed two such large works to a finish. But I know that he had both of them in mind for many years. They will probably turn out to be the best books of his whole life.

Some of these days I hope to do my recollections of him, stretching over almost a lifetime. Unhappily, I am now approaching seventy myself, and work is not as easy as it used to be. Nevertheless, I plan to tackle the story as soon as my current book is off my hands—probably by the end of 1946. Some years ago I made a trade with the University of Pennsylvania Library—photostats of all of my Dreiser letters in return for photostats of all my letters to him. Thus I have a pretty complete record, including many documents. My Dreiser books were all deposited in the Pratt Library here in Baltimore, where they are safer than in my house. All of them, of course, are inscribed, and with them are some proof-sheets and other such things. They will not be open to anyone until my death: after that the library will make them available to literary researchers. I have not yet seen the collection of his own papers at the University of Pennsylvania, but I am told that it is comprehensive and excellent.

Edgar Masters, I fear, is in pretty bad shape. He can barely walk, and what is worse, he can't work. Theodore was luckier. If he had recovered from that first attack he'd have been an invalid—and he was certainly not the sort of man to endure invalidism contentedly. The newspaper notices of him have interested me greatly. Even the people who once tried to put him down now admit that he was a great writer.

I hope you let me hear from you now and then. What are your plans? Are you staying on the Coast?

Sincerely yours,
(Signed) H. L. Mencken

1. On 8 January 1946 Helen Dreiser wrote describing Dreiser's last days, including his final collapse and the scene at his deathbed. [NYP]

[UPL]

H. L. Mencken
1524 Hollins Street
Baltimore—23

January 18, 1946

Dear Mrs. Dreiser:-

Thanks very much for your two letters. You tell me precisely what I wanted to know, and I am certainly delighted to have it.[1] I am only sorry that I couldn't get to Los Angeles for the funeral. If I get to the Coast during the year, I'll certainly come to see you. Meanwhile, you must let me hear of it whenever you head eastward yourself. Maybe I can give you some aid with the business of getting all the books brought out in an uniform edition. There are some, of course, that are apparently hopeless. That happens to the work of every author. But there are others that well deserve new editions, and I incline to believe that Doubleday will undertake them. He is certain to do so if "The Bulwark" has a good sale.

I hope you give serious consideration to a book of memoirs. I don't think you should undertake a formal life of Dreiser, but simply an account of him as you saw him. The woman who did a book on him ten or twelve years ago has broken into the papers in New York with what purports to be an authoritative statement of his ideas, and I gather that she is planning to revise her former work.[2] Inasmuch as she seems to be pinkish in politics, she will probably devote herself mainly to Dreiser's relations with the Communists. This was an unimportant detail of his life. He will be remembered, not as a politician, but as a novelist, and I think he'll be remembered for a long, long while. I'll get hold of <u>Life</u> magazine and take a look at the funeral story.[3]

Once my current book is off my hands, I'll probably begin work on a memoir of my own, describing my relations with Dreiser from 1906 onward. It is, however, not certain that I'll be able to tackle this job, and in any case I'll probably not print the result. It will be less a book than a detailed record for the use of scholars of the future.

I surely hope that you are in good health and reasonably good spirits. I have been disabled for a week past by an injury to my foot. It is not very painful, but it makes it impossible for me to wear a shoe, and so I am somewhat handicapped.

Sincerely yours,
H. L. Mencken

1. On 14 January 1946, Helen Dreiser wrote Mencken giving him the details of the funeral service (3 January 1946), the eulogies, and her feelings at the time. [NYP]

2. Dorothy Dudley, *Forgotten Frontiers: Dreiser and the Land of the Free* (New York: Harrison Smith and Robert Haas, 1932). Dudley did not publish a new book on Dreiser.

3. *Life* covered the funeral, but the story did not appear in the magazine.

[UPL]

H. L. Mencken
1524 Hollins Street
Baltimore—23

January 30, 1945[1]

Dear Helen:-

That letter was Dreiser at his best, and his best was incomparable.[2] I remember seeing you in Baltimore at the time the two of you started South together. It was, to be precise, on December 12, 1925, for my mother was desperately ill in hospital and died the next day. I remember how I resented his leaving you sit in the cold car up the street, and how I resented likewise his aloof indifference to my mother's illness. It was a long while afterward before I ever felt close to him again. But I should have known him better. There was a curiously inarticulate side to him, and it often showed up when he was most moved. If I had another life to live I think I'd attempt a long study of him, trying to account for him. But it is now too late.

I have done a preface for "An American Tragedy."[3] It is poor enough stuff and I had some difficulty with it, for I put the book much below some of his others, especially the first half. It must have been back in 1908 or 1910 when he showed me the first sketch of the early chapters—those describing the street preacher. But I hope the preface serves its purpose. So far I have not heard from Zevin.[4] My own copy of "An American Tragedy" is buried deep in the Mencken papers at the library here, and Zevin had to dig up one for me in New York.

I hope you bear in mind your own book.[5] Write it exactly as it comes to you. If I can give it any help let me know. My best thanks for the copy of the letter.

Yours,
H. L. M.

1. Mencken meant 1946.
2. On 27 January 1946, Helen Dreiser sent a copy of a letter she had received from Dreiser in 1924. The letter is not identified, but from her description it is clear that it was a letter full of tenderness and appreciation for her. [NYP]
3. Mencken wrote an introductory essay for the memorial edition of *An American Tragedy* issued by the World Publishing Company in 1946.
4. Benjamin David Zevin, editor and publisher for whom Mencken wrote the preface.
5. Helen Dreiser, *My Life with Dreiser* (Cleveland: World Publishing Co., 1951).

[UPL]

H. L. Mencken
1524 Hollins Street
Baltimore–23

February 4, 1946

Dear Helen:

The introduction I wrote for Zevin does not attempt anything beyond the most superficial criticism. It is mainly devoted to reminiscence of Dreiser and with special attention to his method of work. I sent it to Zevin last week, but so far have not heard from him. Whether or not he likes it I don't know.

It is too late for me to do a book on Dreiser, simply because I have grown old and have too many other irons in the fire. My present schedule will keep me jumping for three or four years at least, and I begin to doubt that I'll be fit for work by the time it is completed—indeed, it will rather surprise me if I don't find myself an angel in heaven.

I remember that December day very clearly.[1] Dreiser parked your car on a hill about a block from my house, and we had been sitting at the fire for some time before I learned that you were in it. I thereupon rushed out to the place, dragged you out of it and brought you in to warm up. We had a drink or two, and then you and he started off for the South. My mother died the next day. I naturally expected some communication from him, but none came in. This irked me considerably, and we were on cool terms for some years afterward. Eventually, however, we came together again, and in his later years we were very friendly. I could never, of course, follow him into his enthusiasms for such things as spiritualism, Communism and the balderdash of Charles Fort, but that never made any difference between us, for some of my ideas were just as obnoxious to him.

I didn't understand from Zevin that his edition of "An American Tragedy" was to be part of a Memorial Edition—in fact, I gathered that he was bringing out only the one book. If he offers to do the others, it seems to me that it will be a good idea to let him go ahead. He is a very enterprising fellow, and should be able to sell a good many copies.

I am delighted to hear that you are going on with your book. If I can give you any help with it, you know that I'll be more than glad to do so. I have a great many records that may be of use to you. All of them will go to the New York Public Library at my death.

Yours,

H. L. Mencken

1. On 1 February 1946, Helen Dreiser had written Mencken that "It is strange about that visit in December, 1925. I don't remember a thing about being out in the car," and she went on to inquire about the details of that day. [NYP]

[UPL]

H. L. Mencken
1524 Hollins Street
Baltimore—23

February 11, 1946

Dear Helen:

I note what you say about the publication date of "The Bulwark,"[1] and I assume that "The Stoic" will follow in due course. It is fortunate, indeed, that Dreiser lived to get through his proofs. You had better see to those of "The Stoic" yourself. It is never safe to trust publishers' proofreaders.

I am engaged in a lawsuit here, and it is keeping me jumping.[2] Fortunately, I am still able to get in a little work.

Yours,

HLM

1. On 8 February 1946, Helen Dreiser wrote Mencken that *The Bulwark* was to be published in March. [NYP]
2. The suit was against a neighbor whose dog was disturbing Mencken's peace with his barking.

[UPL]

H. L. Mencken
1524 Hollins Street
Baltimore—23

February 14, 1946

Dear Helen:

I think you picked up the wrong impression of my Preface to "An American Tragedy."[1] It is by no means an attempt at criticism; it simply presents some reminiscences of Dreiser in the days when I saw most of him. It tells how he worked, and makes a good deal of his constant kindness to young authors. I see no reason why you should object to anything that is in it. What Zevin's plans are for other volumes I don't know. I hope he brings them all out, for he seems to have an extremely efficient machine for selling books.

It is good news that you are proceeding with your own reminiscences. If I can give you any help along the way, it goes without saying that I'll be delighted.

Yours,
HLM

1. On 8 February 1946, Helen Dreiser wrote Mencken requesting that his preface "have a different slant than simply criticism." Clearly, the publisher had sent her a copy of Mencken's essay, and she now asked him to revise it "and put some of that great warm undercurrent that I now see you have into it." [NYP]

[UPL]

H. L. Mencken
1524 Hollins Street
Baltimore—23

February 18, 1946

Dear Helen:

I have a general distrust of the rev. clergy, and so it does not surprise me to hear that Dr. Hunter played what seems to be a mean trick on

Chaplin.[1] Chaplin himself I have met only once. He seemed then to be a very amusing fellow. It amazes me to hear that Dreiser was ever an attendant upon the orgies in Hunter's church. I hope he resisted the blandishments of the pastor.

Needless to say, I'll be delighted to see the galleys of "The Bulwark." I haven't yet received the proof of my Preface to "An American Tragedy," but suppose that it will be coming along very shortly.

I hope you don't stop writing to me. I am always delighted to hear from you. Those two photographs are magnificent, and I am especially delighted with the one showing you and Dreiser together. My very best thanks.

Yours,

HLM

1. Mencken is responding to Mrs. Dreiser's story about Charlie Chaplin, who had read one of Dreiser's poems at the funeral service but was not introduced by the officiating minister, Dr. Allan Hunter. She felt this to be an intentional slight on the part of the minister. (13 February 1946 [NYP])

[NYP-C]
February 24, 1946

Dear Helen:

I still think that this is good stuff and in New York last week I tried to induce Knopf to make a book of it.[1] Unhappily, he told me that he has more books of poetry in hand than he can print during the next two years, so he was reluctant to ask for the manuscript. I'll keep my eye open in New York and maybe I'll find some other publisher.

I haven't heard from Estelle Kubitz for a long while. At last accounts she was living somewhere in the wilds of Carroll County, Maryland. I'll write to a friend there and try to find her address.

I never visited you in West 57th Street or at Mt. Kisco, for the simple reason that I was never invited. In those days there was a sort of coolness between Dreiser and me. It passed off afterward but by that time you had left Mt. Kisco. If I ever come to my reminscences I'll probably have a paragraph or two about that coolness. It amounted to nothing.

Thanks very much for Mrs. Dudley's address.

Yours,

(Signed) H. L. Mencken

1. Helen Dreiser sent Mencken a number of her poems to get his opinion of them and of their marketability.

[NYP-C]
March 11, 1946

Dear Helen:

Doubleday sent me the galleys of The Bulwark but not the book. I read them at once and was extraordinarily delighted. It is really amazing that a man of Dreiser's years should have done so graceful and charming a book. In many ways it seems to me the best thing among all his works. There is a beautiful clarity in it; it is well designed and in detail it shows really first-rate writing. I offered to do a review of it for Irita Van Doren of the Herald Tribune but she told me that she had already selected a reviewer. I'll whoop it up if any way offers.

I think you are wasting that death mask by sending it to Russia.[1] Soon or late there will be a revolution there and it will probably be destroyed. It should really go to the New York Public Library.

I'd be delighted to send you a photograph but, unfortunately, I have no decent one at the moment. I am hoping to sit to a refined artist in the near future. It he turns out anything presentable I'll be glad to send you a copy.

Yours,
(Signed) H. L. Mencken

1. Mencken is responding to the information he received in Helen Dreiser's letter of 6 March 1946: "The death mask of Teddy is a beautiful thing. I am sending one to The University of Pennsylvania, and one to the Russian Government. I am keeping the original. I have never seen a finer mask." [NYP]

[UPL]

H. L. Mencken
1524 Hollins Street
Baltimore—23

March 25, 1946

Dear Helen:

It is highly improbable that the New York Public Library would be willing to lay out $1,000 on a cast of the Simone bust.[1] Libraries are so used to getting presents that they never pay any cash when they can avoid it. I think I'd advise you yourself not to buy a copy. The bust is interesting as a piece of sculpture, but it hardly shows the real Dreiser. The death-mask probably represents him much more competently.

It is good news that you'll be in New York during the Summer. We must certainly have a session. If I can give you any aid with "The Stoic" it goes without saying that I'll be delighted. "The Bulwark" made a really powerful impression on me. To be sure, it lacks the extraordinary persuasiveness of some of Dreiser's earlier books, but on the other hand it is much better designed than any of them, and very much better written. It would be hard to find in literary history a man of his years doing so excellent a job.

Do you want me to return the photographs of the Simone bust? If so, let me know. If not, I'll put them in my file of Dreiseriana.

Yours,

HLM

1. The sculptor Edgardo Simone, who had made the death mask of Dreiser and a cast of his right arm, also did the bust referred to here.

[UPL]

H. L. Mencken
1524 Hollins Street
Baltimore 23

May 13, 1946

Dear Helen:

No one, however plausible, will ever convince me that he or she had anything to do with the actual writing of "The Bulwark."[1] Any one who knows Dreiser's work at all must be convinced instantly that he did the book, and without any outside help whatsoever. It was always his custom to ask friends to copyread his manuscripts, but the changes thus made were never serious. All the ideas were his own, and all the planning. I don't know La Harris, and shall pay no attention to her.

I incline to believe that it is an advantage to keep all of an author's souvenirs in one place, but inasmuch as the University of Pennsylvania has always seemed to me an inappropriate place for Dreiser's, I conclude that you are probably right to scatter the manuscripts. Those that get into private hands will be cherished, of course, but it may be difficult for scholars to obtain access to them. That, however, is a difficulty that time will solve. There will be relatively little writing about Dreiser during the next few years, and that little in the main will be unimportant. But in the long run he is bound to be studied at length, and by competent men.

I am glad he put his literary remains into your hands without tying any strings to them. You are free to decide things rationally, and without paying any attention to the ideas of others. I hope you place all of his manuscripts as soon as possible. There is never any telling when our Heavenly

Father will issue a summons for any of us, and it would certainly be a calamity to leave the job half done on your own departure for bliss eternal. I certainly hope that that departure will be very much delayed.

When you get to the East, let me hear of it by all means. We must certainly have a session.

Yours,
HLM

1. On 11 May 1946, Helen Dreiser wrote Mencken, expressing her fear that Marguerite Tjader Harris, who worked with Dreiser on *The Bulwark*, would claim too much credit for its final shape and content.

[NYP-C]
May 31, 1946

Dear Mrs. Dreiser:

Your letter and the enclosures came in just as I was leaving for New York. I took them along and have since read them. It seems to me that your first chapter is excellent indeed and I certainly hope that you go on with the book.

I had no idea whatsoever how you and Dreiser met, and it is certainly news that you were related. For some reason or other I picked up the notion that you came to New York from Charlotte, South Carolina. I'll be delighted to read the subsequent chapters as you finish them.

My apologies for this unavoidable delay.

Yours,
(Signed) H. L. Mencken

[NYP-C]
December 2, 1946

Dear Helen:

I have made another search of my files but I can't find a single photograph showing Dreiser and me together, nor can I remember one having been made. I am sorry indeed that I can't join in that display of beauty.

What are you up to? Have you heard anything from Doubleday about the sales of The Bulwark? At last accounts it was doing well and without doubt it will continue to sell more or less for years.

If you ever receive any offer to bring out a collected edition of Dreiser's books, I hope you let me hear of it before you accept. Such proposals are often full of snares.

The best of luck in 1947!

Yours,
(Signed) H. L. Mencken

[NYP-C]
December 8, 1947

Dear Helen:

I am sorry that Dreiser didn't live to revise The Stoic. It comes close to being a good book but I think it falls a little short. Certainly it is not as effective as The Bulwark. Will you send me a slip to paste into it with your signature?[1] It will go eventually to the Mencken collection in the public library here, which is already enormously rich with Dreiseriana.

I surely hope you have a pleasant Christmas and a lucky New Year. I am sweating away at the two long indexes to my second Supplement to The American Language. It is a really dreadful job and I'll be delighted when it is over.

Yours,
(Signed) H. L. Mencken

1. Helen sent a copy of *The Stoic* with the following inscription, dated 12 December 1947: "For Henry L. Mencken—a friend of long standing, and a true source of inspiration to many—from Mrs. Theodore Dreiser." [EPL]

[NYP-C]
December 20, 1949

Dear Mrs. Dreiser:

Mr. Mencken sends his best thanks for your Christmas greetings. Unfortunately, he is still ill and unable to write to you. He is making some progress, and it is hoped that he will be very much better in the early part of next year. He surely hopes that you are lucky in 1950.

Sincerely yours,

————[1]

Secretary to Mr. Mencken

1. On 23 November 1948, Mencken had the stroke that left him unable to write or read. His correspondence was carried on by Mrs. Rosalind C. Lohrfinck, his secretary until his death on 29 January 1956.

Reviews and Reminiscences (1911–1948)

THEODORE DREISER

"HENRY L. MENCKEN AND MYSELF"
(in The Man Mencken: A Biographical and Critical Survey, *by Isaac Goldberg [1925], 378–81).*

It was sometime during the Spring or Summer of 1908, and my second year of editorial control of the Butterick Publications, that there came to me a doctor by the name of Leonard K. Hirshberg who explained that besides being a physician of some practice in Baltimore he was a graduate of Johns Hopkins and interested in interpreting to the lay public if possible the more recent advances in medical knowledge. There had been various recent developments, as there always are. Some phases of these he proposed to describe in articles of various lengths. And then it was that he announced that, being a medical man and better equipped technically in that line than as a writer, he had joined with a newspaper-man or editorial writer then connected with the Baltimore *Sun,* Henry L. Mencken. The name being entirely unfamiliar to me at the time, he proceeded to describe him as a young, refreshing and delightful fellow of a very vigorous and untechnical literary skill, who, in combination with himself, would most certainly be able to furnish me with articles of exceptional luminosity and vigor. Liking two or three of the subjects discussed, I suggested that between them they prepare one and submit it. In case it proved satisfactory, I would buy it and possibly some of the others.

In less than three weeks thereafter I received a discussion of some current medical development which seemed to me as refreshing and colorful a bit of semi-scientific exposition as I had read in years. While setting forth all the developments which had been indicated to me, it bristled with gay phraseology and a largely suppressed though still peeping mirth. I was so pleased that I immediately wrote Hirshberg that the material was satisfactory and that I would be willing to contract with him and his friend for one of the other subjects he had mentioned.

And then some weeks later in connection with that or some other matter, whether to discuss it more fully or merely to deliver it or to make the acquaintance of the man who was interested in this new literary combination, there appeared in my office a taut, ruddy, blue-eyed, snub-nosed youth of twenty eight or nine whose brisk gait and ingratiating smile proved to me at once enormously intriguing and amusing. I had, for some reason not connected with his basic mentality you may be sure, the sense of a small town roisterer or a college sophomore of the crudest and yet most disturbing charm and impishness, who, for some reason, had strayed into the field of letters. More than anything else he reminded me of a spoiled and petted and possibly over-financed brewer's or wholesale grocer's son who was out for a lark. With the sang-froid of a Cæsar or a Napoleon he made himself comfortable in a large and impressive chair which was designed primarily to reduce the over-confidence of the average beginner. And from that particular and unintended vantage point he beamed on me with the confidence of a smirking fox about to devour a chicken. So I was the editor of the Butterick Publications. He had been told about me. However, in spite of *Sister Carrie*, I doubt if he had ever heard of me before this. After studying him in that almost arch-episcopal setting which the chair provided, I began to laugh. "Well, well," I said, "if it isn't Anheuser's own brightest boy out to see the town." And with that unfailing readiness for any nonsensical flight that has always characterized him, he proceeded to insist that this was true. "Certainly he *was* Baltimore's richest brewer's son and the yellow shoes and bright tie he was wearing were characteristic of the jack-dandies and rowdy-dows of his native town. Why not. What else did I expect? His father brewed the best beer in the world." All thought of the original purpose of the conference was at once dismissed and instead we proceeded to palaver and yoo-hoo anent the more general phases and ridiculosities of life, with the result that an understanding based on a mutual liking was established, and from then on I counted him among those whom I most prized—temperamentally as well as intellectually. And to this day, despite various disagreements, that mood has never varied.

Subsequent to this there were additional contacts based on this instantaneous friendship. He visited me at my apartment in New York and I in turn repaired to Baltimore. We multiplied noisy and roistering parties. Sometime during 1908 or 9—or whenever it was that the old Col. Mann's *Smart Set*, owning to various scandals in connection with its management, was reorganized and a new editor sought, a managing editor of mine came to me with the news of this thing. He was a capable fellow but not as I saw it suited to the particular work he was doing for me—nor to the editorship of the *Smart Set* for that matter. Yet, because I had been pondering how to replace him without injury to himself, I now encouraged him in the thought with which he had come to me—i.e.—that with my approbation and aid he would apply for the editorship of the same. And why not he as well as another? If they did not like him, they could soon get rid of him, could they not—said I. So I stirred him with the plausibility of the idea and he immediately proceeded to apply for the place, and, to my satisfaction, as well as astonishment, secured it.

But as was the custom of some others whom I had advised in this fashion in times past, he soon returned to me with the request that I aid him in outlining a policy and a suitable staff or list of contributors for his magazine. And, in discussing what regular and permanent features might be introduced and who would be most likely to lend lustre to that magazine by their work, I suggested that as intriguing as anything would be a Book Department with a really brilliant and illuminating reviewer. Instantly the one name that appealed to me as ideal for this work was that of Mencken. I insisted that he could not do better than get this man and that he should engage him at once. This he did. And this was the beginning of Mencken's connection with the *Smart Set*, which subsequently led to its control by himself and George Jean Nathan who was already doing dramatics for the magazine, if I am not mistaken, when my youthful aspirant and assistant moved in.

New York, August 1925

H. L. MENCKEN
"A NOVEL OF THE FIRST RANK"
Smart Set *35 (November 1911)*, *153–55*.

If you miss reading "JENNIE GERHARDT," by Theodore Dreiser (*Harpers*), you will miss the best American novel, all things considered, that has reached the book counters in a dozen years. On second thought, change "a dozen" into "twenty-five." On third thought, strike out everything after "counters." On fourth thought, strike out everything after "novel." Why back and fill? Why evade and qualify? Hot from it, I am firmly convinced that "JENNIE GERHARDT" is the best American novel I have ever read, with the lonesome but Himalayan exception of "Huckleberry Finn," and so I may as well say it aloud and at once and have done with it. Am I forgetting "The Scarlet Letter," "The Rise of Silas Lapham" and (to drag an exile unwillingly home) "What Maisie Knew"? I am not. Am I forgetting "McTeague" and "The Pit"? I am not. Am I forgetting the stupendous masterpieces of James Fenimore Cooper, beloved of the pedagogues, or those of James Lane Allen, Mrs. Wharton and Dr. S. Weir Mitchell, beloved of the women's clubs and literary monthlies? No. Or "Uncle Tom's Cabin" or "Rob o' the Bowl" or "Gates Ajar" or "Ben Hur" or "David Harum" or "Lewis Rand" or "Richard Carvel"? No. Or "The Hungry Heart" or Mr. Dreiser's own "Sister Carrie"? No. I have all these good and bad books in mind. I have read them and survived them and in many cases enjoyed them.

And yet in the face of them, and in the face of all the high authority, constituted and self-constituted, behind them, it seems to me at this moment that "JENNIE GERHARDT" stands apart from all of them, and a bit above them. It lacks the grace of this one, the humor of that one, the perfect form of some other one; but taking it as it stands, grim, gaunt, mirthless, shapeless, it remains, and by long odds, the most impressive work of art that we have yet to show in prose fiction—a tale not unrelated, in its stark simplicity, its profound sincerity, to "Germinal" and "Anna Karenina" and "Lord Jim"—a tale assertively American in its scene and its human material, and yet so European in its method, its point of view, its almost reverential seriousness, that one can scarcely imagine an American writing it. Its personages are few in number, and their progress is along a path that seldom widens, but the effect of that progress is ever one of large movements and large masses. One senses constantly the group behind the individual, the natural law behind the human act. The result is an indefinable impression of bigness, of epic dignity. The thing is not a mere story, not a novel in the ordinary American meaning of the word, but a criticism and an interpretation of life—and that interpretation loses nothing in validity by the fact that its burden is the doctrine that life is meaningless, a tragedy without a moral, a joke without a point. What else have Moore and Conrad and Hardy been telling us these many years? What else does all the new knowledge of a century teach us? One by one the old ready answers have been disposed of. Today the one intelligible answer to the riddle of aspiration and sacrifice is that there is no answer at all.

"The power to tell the same story in two forms," said George Moore not long ago, "is the sign of the true artist." You will think of this when you read "JENNIE GERHARDT," for in its objective plan, and even in its scheme of subjective unfolding, it suggests "Sister Carrie" at every turn. Reduce it to a hundred words, and those same words would also describe that earlier study of a woman's soul, with scarcely the change of a syllable. Jennie Gerhardt, like Carrie Meeber, is a rose grown from turnip seed. Over each, at the start, hangs poverty, ignorance, the dumb helplessness of the Shudra—and yet in each there is that indescribable something, that element of essential gentleness, that innate, inward beauty which levels all caste barriers and makes Esther a fit queen for Ahasuerus. And the history of each, reduced to its elements, is the history of the other. Jennie, like Carrie, escapes from the physical miseries of the struggle for existence only to taste the worse miseries of the struggle for happiness. Not, of course, that we have in either case a moral, maudlin fable of virtue's fall; Mr. Dreiser, I need scarcely assure you, is too dignified an artist, too sane a man, for any such banality. Seduction, in point of fact, is not all tragedy for either Jennie or Carrie. The gain of each, until the actual event has been left behind and obliterated by experiences more salient and poignant, is rather greater than her loss, and that again is to the soul as well as to the creature. With the rise from want to security, from fear to ease, comes an awakening of the finer perceptions, a widening of the sympathies, a gradual unfolding of the delicate flower called personality, an increased capacity for loving and living. But with all this, and as a part of it, there comes, too, an increased capacity for suffering—and so in the end, when love slips away and the empty years stretch before, it is the awakened and supersentient woman that pays for the folly of the groping, bewildered girl. The tragedy of Carrie and Jennie, in brief, is not that they are degraded but that they are lifted up, not that they go to the gutter but that they escape the gutter.

But if the two stories are thus variations upon the same somber theme, if each starts from the same place and arrives at the same dark goal, if each shows a woman heartened by the same hopes and tortured by the same agonies, there is still a vast difference between them, and that difference is the measure of the author's progress in his art. "Sister Carrie" was a first sketch, a rough piling-up of observations and impressions, disordered and often incoherent. In the midst of the story of Carrie, Mr. Dreiser paused to tell the story of Hurstwood—an astonishingly vivid and tragic story, true enough, but still one that broke the back of the other. In "JENNIE GERHARDT" he falls into no such overelaboration of episode. His narrative goes forward steadily from beginning to end. Episodes there are, of course, but they keep their proper place, their proper bulk. It is always Jennie that holds the attention; it is in Jennie's soul that every scene is ultimately played out. Her father and mother, Senator Brander the god of her first worship, her daughter Vesta and Lester Kane, the man who makes and mars her—all these are drawn with infinite painstaking, and in every one of them there is the blood of life. But it is Jennie who dominates the drama from curtain to curtain. Not an event is unrelated to her; not a climax fails to make clearer the struggles going on in her mind and heart.

I have spoken of reducing "JENNIE GERHARDT" to a hundred words. The thing, I fancy, might be actually done. The machinery of the tale is not complex; it has no plot, as plots are understood in these days of "mystery" stories; no puzzles madden the reader. It is dull, unromantic poverty that sends Jennie into the world. Brander finds her there, lightly seduces her, and then discovers that, for some strange gentleness within her, he loves her. Lunacy—but he is willing to face it out. Death, however, steps in; Brander, stricken down without warning, leaves Jennie homeless and a mother. Now enters Lester Kane—not the villain of the books, but a normal, decent, cleanly American of the better class, well to do, level-headed, not too introspective, eager for the sweets of life. He and Jennie are drawn together; if love is not all of the spirit, then it is love that binds them. For half a dozen years the world lets them alone. A certain grave respectability settles over their relation; if they are not actually married, then it is only because marriage is a mere formality, to be put off until tomorrow. But bit by bit they are dragged into the light. Kane's father, dying with millions, gives him two years to put Jennie away. The penalty is poverty; the reward is wealth—and not only wealth itself, but all the pleasant and well remembered things that will come with it: the lost friends of other days, a sense of dignity and importance, an end of apologies and evasions, good society, the comradeship of decent women—particularly the comradeship of one decent woman. Kane hesitates, makes a brave defiance, thinks it over—and finally yields. Jennie does not flood him with tears. She has made progress in the world, has Jennie; the simple faith of the girl has given way to the pride and poise of the woman. Five years later Kane sends for her. He is dying. When it is over, Jennie goes back to her lonely home, and there, like Carrie Meeber before her, she faces the long years with dry eyes and an empty heart. "Days and days in endless reiteration, and then—"

A moral tale? Not at all. It has no more moral than a string quartet or the first book of Euclid. But a philosophy of life is in it, and that philosophy is the same profound pessimism which gives a dark color to the best that we have from Hardy, Moore, Zola and the great Russians—the pessimism of disillusion—not the jejune, Byronic thing, not the green sickness of youth, but that pessimism which comes with the discovery that the riddle of life, despite all the fine solutions offered by the learned doctors, is essentially insoluble. One can discern no intelligible sequence of cause and effect in the agonies of Jennie Gerhardt. She is, as human beings go, of the nobler, finer metal. There is within her a great capacity for service, a great capacity for love, a great capacity for happiness. And yet all that life has to offer her, in the end, is the mere license to live. The days stretch before her "in endless reiteration." She is a prisoner doomed to perpetual punishment for some fanciful, incomprehensible crime against the gods who make their mirthless sport of us all. And to me, at least, she is more tragic thus than Lear on his wild heath or Prometheus on his rock.

Nothing of the art of the literary lapidary is visible in this novel. Its form is the simple one of a panorama unrolled. Its style is unstudied to the verge of barrenness. There is no painful groping for the exquisite, inevitable word; Mr. Dreiser seems content to use the common, even the commonplace coin of speech. On the very first page one encounters "frank, open countenance," "diffident manner," "helpless poor," "untutored mind," "honest necessity" and half a dozen other such ancients. And yet in the long run it is this very *naïveté* which gives the story much of its impressiveness. The narrative, in places, has the effect of a series of unisons in music—an effect which, given a solemn theme, vastly exceeds that of the most ornate polyphony. One cannot imagine "JENNIE GERHARDT" done in the gipsy phrases of Meredith, the fugual manner of James. One cannot imagine that stark, stenographic dialogue adorned with the brilliants of speech. The thing could have been done only in the way that it has been done. As it stands, it is a work of art from which I for one would not care to take anything away—not even its gross crudities, its incessant returns to C major. It is a novel that depicts the life we Americans are living with extreme accuracy and criticises that life with extraordinary insight. It is a novel, I am convinced, of the very first consideration.

After the Fifth Symphony—or any other of the nine, for that matter—it is not easy to listen to a Chopin nocturne, and after Mr. Dreiser's story, by the same token, you will not find it easy to read the common novels of the month.

H. L. MENCKEN
"DREISER'S NOVEL THE STORY OF A FINANCIER WHO LOVED BEAUTY"
New York Times Book Review, *10 November 1912, 654.*

Theodore Dreiser's new novel, "The Financier," shows all of the faults and peculiarities of method that gave a rude, barbarous sort of distinction to his "Sister Carrie" and "Jennie Gerhardt," those arresting tales of yesteryear. The man does not write as the other novelists of his day and generation write, and, what is more, he does not seem to make any effort to do so, or to have any feeling that such an effort would be worth while. You may read him for page after page, held spellbound by his people and their doings, and yet not find a single pretty turn of phrase, or a single touch of smartness in dialogue, or a single visible endeavor to stiffen a dull scene into drama, or any other such application of artifice or art.

For all the common tricks of writing, in truth, he reveals a degree of disdain amounting almost to denial. He never "teases up" a situation to make it take your breath; he never hurries over something difficult and static in order to get to something easy and dynamic; he never leads you into ambuscades of plot or sets off stylistic fireworks; he never so much as takes the trouble to hunt for a new adjective when an old one will answer as well. In brief, his manner is uncompromisingly forthright, elemental, grim, gaunt, bare. He rolls over the hills and valleys of his narrative at the same patient, lumbering gait, surmounting obstacles by sheer weight and momentum, refusing all short cuts, however eminently trod, as beneath his contempt, and turning his back resolutely upon all the common lifts by the way.

But do I give the impression that the result is dullness, that all this persistent, undeviating effort leads to nothing but a confused and meaningless piling up of words? Then I have described it very badly, for the net effect is precisely the opposite. Out of chaos, by that unceasing pounding, order finally emerges. Out of the disdain of drama comes drama stirring and poignant. Out of that welter of words step human beings, round, ruddy, alive. In other words, Dreiser accomplishes at last, for all his muddling, what men with a hundred times his finesse too often fail to accomplish, and that is, an almost perfect illusion of reality. You may say that he writes with a hand of five thumbs, and that he has no more humor than a hangman, and that he loves assiduity so much that he often forgets inspiration altogether, and you may follow up all of these sayings by ample provings, but in the end you will have to admit that Carrie Meeber is far more real than nine-tenths of the women you actually know, and that old Gerhardt's veritable existence is no more to be doubted than the existence of Père Goriot.

If "The Financier," on a first reading, leaves a less vivid impression than the two books preceding it, then that apparent falling off is probably due to two things, the first being that its principal character is a man and that in consequence he must needs lack some of the fascinating mystery and appeal of Carrie and Jennie; and the second being that the story stops just as it is beginning, (for all its 780 pages!) and so leaves the reader with a sense of incompleteness, of a picture washed in but not wholly painted. Final judgment, indeed, will be impossible until the more important second volume is put beside this first, for it is there that the real drama of Frank Cowperwood's life will be played out. But meanwhile there can be no doubt whatever of the author's firm grip upon the man, nor of his astute understanding of the enormously complex interplay of personalities and events against which the man is projected.

This Cowperwood is meant, I suppose, to be a sort of archetype of the American money king, and despite a good many little deviations he is probably typical enough. The main thing to remember about him is that he is anything but a mere chaser of the dollar, that avarice as a thing in itself is not in him. For the actual dollar, indeed, he has no liking at all, but only the toleration of an artist for his brushes and paint-pots. What he is really after is power, and the way power commonly visualizes itself in this mind is as a means to beauty. He likes all things that caress the eye—a fine rug, an inviting room, a noble picture, a good horse, a pretty woman, particularly a pretty woman. There is in him what might be called an aloof voluptuousness, a dignified hedonism. He is not so much sensual as sensitive. A perfect eyebrow seems to him to be something worth thinking about, soberly and profoundly. The world, in his sight, is endlessly curious and beautiful.

And with this over-development of the esthetic sense there goes, naturally enough, an under-development of the ethical sense. Cowperwood has little more feeling for right and wrong, save as a setting or a mask for beauty, than a healthy schoolboy. When a chance offers to make a large sum of money by an alliance with political buccaneers, he takes it without the slightest question of its essential virtue. And when, later on, the buccaneers themselves lay open for pillage, he pillages them with a light heart. And as with means, so with ends. When Aileen Butler, the daughter of his partner and mentor, old Edward Malia Butler, the great political contractor—when Aileen comes his way, radiant and tempting, he debauches her without a moment's thought of consequences, and carries on the affair under old Butler's very nose.

The man is not vicious: a better word for him would be innocent. He has no sense of wrong to Aileen, nor of wrong to Butler, nor even of wrong to the wife of his youth. The only idea that takes clear form in his mind is the idea that Aileen is extremely pleasing, and that it would be a ridiculous piece of folly to let her charms go to waste. Even when he is the conquered instead of the conqueror, not much feeling that an act of conquest can have a moral content appears in him. Old Butler, discovering his affair with Aileen, knocks over his financial house of cards and railroads him to prison, but he shows little rancor against Butler, and less against the obliging catchpolls of the law, but only a vague discontent that fate should bring him such hardships, and take him away from beauty so long.

This term in prison is a salient event in Cowperwood's life, but it cannot be said that it is a turning point. He comes out into the Philadelphia of the early seventies with all his old determination to beat the game. He has been defeated once, true enough, but that defeat has taught him a lot that easy victory might have left unsaid, and he has full confidence that he will win next time. And win he does. Black Friday sees him the most pitilessly ursine of bears, and the next day sees him with a million. He is now on his feet again and able to choose his cards carefully and at leisure. With the utmost calm he divorces his wife, tucks Aileen under his arm, and sets out for Chicago. There, where the players are settling down for the wildest game of money ever played in the world, he will prove that luck in the long run is with the wise. And there, in the second volume of this history, we shall see him at the proving.

An heroic character, and not without his touches of the admirable. Once admit his honest doubts of the workaday moralities of the world, and at once you range him with all the other memorable battlers against fate, from Prometheus to Etienne Lantier. The achievement of Dreiser is found in this very fact: that he has made the man not only comprehensible, but also a bit tragic. One is conscious of a serene dignity in his chicaneries, and even in his debaucheries, and so his struggle for happiness becomes truly moving. I am not alluding here to that cheap sympathy which is so easily evoked by mere rhetoric, but to that higher sympathy which grows out of a thorough understanding of motives and processes of mind. This understanding Dreiser insures. Say what you will against his solemn and onerous piling up of words, his slow plodding through jungles of detail, his insatiable lust for facts, you must always admit that he gets his effect in the end. There are no sudden flashes of revelation; the lights are turned on patiently and deliberately, one by one. But when the thing is done at last the figure of the financier leaps out amazingly, perfectly modeled, wholly accounted for.

So with the lesser personages, and particularly with Aileen and her father. Old Butler, indeed, is worthy to stand just below the ancient Gerhardt, by long odds the most real of Dreiser's creatures, not even excepting Carrie Meeber and Hurstwood. You remember Gerhardt, of course, with his bent back, his squirrel's economies, his mediaeval piety and his pathetic wonderment at the deviltries of the world? Well, Butler is a vastly different man, if only because he is richer, more intelligent, and more powerful, but still, in the end, he takes on much of that reality and all of that pathos, raging homerically but impotently against an enemy who eludes him and defies him and has broken his heart.

And so, too, with the background of the story. I can imagine nothing more complex than the interplay of finance and politics in war time and during the days following, when the money kings were just finding themselves and graft was just rising to the splendor of an exact science. And yet Dreiser works his way through that maze with sure steps, and leaves order and understanding where confusion reigned. Of tales of municipal corruption we have had aplenty; scarcely a serious American novelist of today, indeed, has failed to experiment with that endless and recondite drama. But what other has brought its prodigal details into better sequence and adjustment, or made them enter more vitally and convincingly into the characters and adventures of his people? Those people of Dreiser's, indeed, are never the beings in vacuo who populate our common romances. We never see them save in contact with a vivid and fluent environment, reacting to its constant stimuli, taking color from it, wholly a part of it.

So much for "The Financier." It is the prologue rather than the play. The real tragi-comedy of Cowperwood's struggle for power and beauty will be played out in Chicago, and of its brilliancy and mordacity we have abundant earnest. Dreiser knows Chicago as few other men know it; he has pierced to the very heart of that most bewildering of cities. And, what is more, he has got his secure grip upon Cowperwood.

H. L. MENCKEN
"ADVENTURES AMONG THE NEW NOVELS"
Smart Set *43(August 1914), 153–57.*

After all, Dr. Munyon is quite right: there is yet hope. Sometimes, of course, it is hard to discern, almost impossible to embrace. Sweating through the best-sellers of the moment, shot from the presses in a gaudy cataract, one can scarcely escape a mood of intense depression, a bleak esthetic melancholia. What is to become of a nation which buys such imbecile books by the hundred thousand, and not only buys them, but reads them, and not only reads them, but enjoys them, gabbles about them, takes them seriously, even pays reverence to them as literature?

Publishers get rich printing that sort of "literature," and then use their money to bludgeon and browbeat all authors who try to do anything better. Imagine a young American bobbing up with a new "Germinal," or a new "Lord Jim" or a new "Brothers Karamazov": what a job he would have getting it between covers! But let him rise shamelessly out of the old bog of mush, dripping honey and buttermilk, and at once there is silver in his palm and praise in his ear. The Barabbases fight for him, playing one another all kinds of sharp tricks; the newspapers record his amours, his motor accidents and his table talk; the literary monthlies print his portrait (in golf togs) opposite that of Gerhart Hauptmann; the women's clubs forget Bergson and the white slave trade to study his style. In the end, he retires to Palm Beach or Tuscany with a fortune, and so becomes a romantic legend, half genius and half god.

But, as I started out to say, there is yet a glimmer of hope. A small class of more civilized readers begins to show itself here and there; a few daring publishers risk a dollar or two on fiction of an appreciably better sort; the literary monthlies forget their muttons long enough to say a kind word for Joseph Conrad; now and then a genuine artist is seen in the offing. Fate, alas, conspires with stupidity to keep the number down. Frank Norris died just as he was getting into his stride; David Graham Philips was murdered by a lunatic at the very moment of his deliverance; a dozen others, after diffident bows, have disappeared in ways just as mysterious. But there remains Theodore Dreiser, patient, forthright, earnest, plodding, unswerving, uncompromising—and so long as Dreiser keeps out of jail there will be hope.

Four long novels are now behind him, and in every one of them one sees the same grim fidelity to an austere artistic theory, the same laborious service to a stern and rigorous faith. That faith may be put briefly into two articles: *(a)* that it is the business of a novelist to describe human beings as they actually are, unemotionally, objectively and relentlessly, and not as they might be, or would like to be, or ought to be; and *(b)* that his business is completed when he has so described them, and he is under no obligation to read copybook morals into their lives, or to estimate their virtue (or their lack of it) in terms of an ideal goodness. In brief, the art of Dreiser is almost wholly representative, detached, aloof, unethical: he makes no attempt whatever to provide that pious glow, that mellow sentimentality, that soothing escape from reality, which Americans are accustomed to seek and find in prose fiction. And despite all the enormous advantages of giving them what they are used to and cry for, he has stuck resolutely to his program. In the fourteen years since "Sister Carrie" he has not deviated once, nor compromised once. There are his books: you may take them or leave them. If you have any respect for an artist who has respect for himself, you may care to look into them; if not, you may go to the devil.

In all this, Dreiser runs on a track parallel to Conrad's; the two men suggest each other in a score of ways. Superficially, of course, they may seem to be far apart: the gorgeous colors of Conrad are never encountered in Dreiser. But that difference lies almost wholly in materials; in ideas and methods they are curiously alike. To each the salient fact of life is its utter meaninglessness, its sordid cruelty, its mystery. Each stands in amazement before the human tendency to weigh it, to motivate it, to see esoteric significances in it. Nothing could be more profoundly agnostic and unmoral than Conrad's "Lord Jim" or Dreiser's "Jennie Gerhardt." In neither book is there the slightest suggestion of a moral order of the world; neither novelist has any blame to hand out, nor any opinion to offer as to the justice or injustice of the destiny he describes. It is precisely here, indeed, that both take their departure from the art of fiction as we of English speech commonly know it. They are wholly emancipated from the moral obsession that afflicts our race; they see the human comedy as a series of inexplicable and unrepresentative phenomena, and not at all as a mere allegory and Sunday school lesson. If art be imagined as a sort of halfway station between science and morals, their faces are plainly turned toward the hard rocks of science, just as the faces of the more orthodox novelists are turned toward pansy beds of morals.

Conrad tells us somewhere that it was Flaubert who helped him to formulate his theory of the novel, with Turgenieff and the other Russians assisting. The influences that moulded Dreiser are not to be stated with such certainty. Here and there one happens upon what seem to be obvious tracks of Zola, but Dreiser, if I remember rightly, has said that he knows the Frenchman only at second hand. Did the inspiration come through Frank Norris, Zola's one avowed disciple in America? Against the supposition stands the fact that "Sister Carrie" followed too soon after "McTeague" to be an imitation of it—and besides, "Sister Carrie" is a far greater novel, in more than one way, than "McTeague" itself. Perhaps some earlier and lesser work of Norris's was the model that the younger man followed, consciously or unconsciously. Norris was his discoverer, and in a sense, his patron saint, battling for him valiantly when the firm of Doubleday, Page & Co. achieved immortality by suppressing "Sister Carrie." (Some day the whole of this tale must be told. The part that Norris played proved that he was not only a sound critic, but also an extraordinarily courageous and unselfish friend.) But whatever the fact and the process, Dreiser has kept the faith far better than Norris, whose later work, particularly "The Octopus," shows a disconcerting mingling of honest realism and vaporous mysticism. In Dreiser there has been no such yielding. His last book, "The Titan," is cut from exactly the same cloth that made "Sister Carrie." Despite years of critical hammering and misunderstanding, and a number of attacks of a sort even harder to bear, he has made no sacrifice of his convictions and done no treason to his artistic conscience. He may be right or he may be wrong, but at all events he has gone straight ahead.

"The Titan," like "Sister Carrie," enjoys the honor of having been suppressed after getting into type. This time the virtuous act was performed by Harper & Brothers, a firm which provided mirth for the mocking back in the nineties by refusing the early work of Rudyard Kipling. The passing years work strange farces. Today the American publisher of Kipling is the firm of Doubleday, Page & Co., which suppressed "Sister Carrie"—and "Sister Carrie," after years upon the town, is now on the vestal list of the Harpers, who bucked at "The Titan"! The grotesque comedy should have been completed by the publication of the latter work by Doubleday, Page & Co., but of this delectable fourth act we were unluckily deprived. Life, alas, is seldom quite artistic. Its phenomena do not fit snugly together, like squares in a checkerboard. But nevertheless the whole story of the adventures of his books would make a novel in Dreiser's best manner—a novel without the slightest hint of a moral. His own career as an artist has been full of the blind and unmeaning fortuitousness that he expounds.

But what of "THE TITAN" as a work of art? To me, at least, it comes closer to what I conceive to be Dreiser's ideal than any other story he has done. Here, at last, he has thrown overboard all the usual baggage of the novelist, making short and merciless shrift of "heart interest," "sympathy" and even romance. In "Sister Carrie" there was still a sop, however little intended, for the sentimentalists: if they didn't like the history of Carrie as a study of the blind forces which determine human destiny, they could wallow in it as a sad, sad love story. Carrie was pathetic, appealing, melting; she moved, like Marguerite Gautier, in an atmosphere of agreeable melancholy. And Jennie Gerhardt, of course, was merely another Carrie—a Carrie more carefully and objectively drawn, perhaps, but still one to be easily mistaken for a "sympathetic" heroine of the best-sellers. Readers jumped from "The Prisoner of Zenda" to "Jennie Gerhardt" without knowing that they were jumping ten thousand miles. The tear jugs were there to cry into; the machinery seemed to be the same. Even in "The Financier" there was still a hint of familiar things. The first Mrs. Cowperwood was sorely put upon; Cowperwood himself suffered injustice, and pined away in a dungeon.

But no one, I venture to say, will ever make the same mistake about "THE TITAN"—no one, not even the youngest and fairest, will ever take it for a sentimental romance. Not a single appeal to the emotions is in it; it is a purely intellectual account, as devoid of heroics as a death certificate, of a strong man's savage endeavors to live out his life as it pleases him, regardless of all the subtle and enormous forces that seek to break him to a rule. There is nothing in him of the conventional outlaw; he does not wear a red sash and bellow for liberty; from end to end he issues no melodramatic defiance of the existing order. The salient thing about him is precisely his avoidance of all such fine feathers and sonorous words. He is no hero at all, but merely an extraordinary gamester—sharp, merciless, tricky, insatiable. One stands amazed before his marvelous resourcefulness and daring, his absolute lack of conscience, but there is never the slightest effort to cast a romantic glamour over him, to raise sympathy for him, to make it appear that he is misunderstood, unfortunate, persecuted. Even in love he is devoid of the old glamour of the lover. Even in disaster he asks for no quarter, no generosity, no compassion. Up or down, he is sufficient unto himself.

The man is the same Cowperwood who came a cropper in "The Financier," but he has now reached middle age, and all the faltering weakness and irresolutions of his youth are behind him. He knows exactly what he wants, and in the Chicago of the early eighties he proceeds to grab it. The town is full of other fellows with much the same aspirations, but Cowperwood has the advantage over them that he has already fallen off his wall and survived, and so he lacks that sneaking fear of consequences which holds them in check. In brief, they are brigands with one eye on the *posse comitatus*, while he is a brigand with both eyes on the swag. The result, as may be imagined, is a combat truly homeric in its proportions— a combat in which associated orthodoxy in rapine is pitted against the most fantastic and astounding heterodoxy. The street railways of Chicago are the prize, and Cowperwood fights for control of them with all the ferocity of a hungry hyena and all the guile of a middle-aged serpent. His devices are staggering and unprecedented, even in that town of surprises. He makes a trial of every crime in the calendar of roguery, from blackmail to downright pillage. And though, in the end, he is defeated in his main purpose, for the enemy takes the cars, he is yet so far successful that he goes away with a lordly share of the profits, and leaves behind him a memory like that of a man-eating tiger in an Indian village.

A mere hero of melodrama? A brother to Monte Cristo and Captain Kidd? A play-acting superman, stalking his gorgeous heights? Far from it, indeed. The very charm of the man, as I have hinted before, lies in his utter lack of obvious charm. He is not sentimental. He is incapable of attitudinizing. He makes no bid for that homage which goes to the conscious outlaw, the devil-of-a-fellow. Even in his amours, which are carried on as boldly and as copiously as his chicaneries, there is no hint of the barbered Don Juan, the professional scourge of virtue. Cowperwood pursues women unmorally, almost innocently. He seduces the wives and daughters of friends and enemies alike; there is seldom any conscious purpose to dramatize and romanticize the adventure. Women are attractive to him simply because they represent difficulties to be surmounted, problems to be solved, personalities to be brought into subjection, and he in his turn is attractive to women simply because he transcends all that they know, or think they know, of men. There must be at least a dozen different maids and wives in his story, and in one way or another they all contribute to his final defeat, but there is nothing approaching a grand affair. At no time is a woman hunt the principal business before him. At no time does one charmer blind him to all others. Even at the close, when we see him genuinely smitten, an easy fatalism still conditions his eagerness, and he waits with unflagging patience for the victory that finally rewards him.

Such a man, described romantically, would be undistinguishable from the wicked earls and seven-foot guardsmen of Ouida and the Duchess. But described realistically, with all that wealth of minute and apparently inconsequential detail which Dreiser piles up so amazingly, he becomes a figure astonishingly vivid, lifelike and engrossing. He fits into no *a priori* theory of conduct or scheme of rewards and punishments; he proves nothing and teaches nothing; the motives which move him are never obvious and frequently unintelligible. But in the end he seems genuinely a man—a man of the sort that we see about us in the real world—not a transparent and simple fellow, reacting docilely according to a formula, but a bundle of complexities and contradictions, a creature oscillating between the light and the shadow, a unique and, at bottom, inexplicable personality. It is here that Dreiser gets farthest from the wallowed rut of fiction. The Cowperwood he puts before us is not the two-dimensional cut-out, the facile jumping jack, of the ordinary novel, but a being of three dimensions and innumerable planes—in brief, the impenetrable mystery that is man. The makers of best-sellers, if they could imagine him at all, would seek to account for him, explain him, turn him into a moral (*i.e.*, romantic) equation. Dreiser is content to describe him.

Naturally enough, the lady reviewers of the newspapers have been wholly flabbergasted by the book. Unable to think of a character in a novel save in terms of the characters in other novels, they have sought to beplaster Cowperwood with the old, old labels. He is the Wealthy Seducer, the Captain of Industry, the Natural Polygamist, the Corruptionist, the Franchise Grabber, the Bribe Giver, the Plutocrat, the Villain. Some of them, intelligent enough to see that not one of these labels actually fits, have interpreted the fact as a proof of Dreiser's incapacity. He is denounced for creating a Cowperwood who is not like other capitalists, not like other lawbreakers, not like other voluptuaries—that is to say, not like the capitalists, lawbreakers and voluptuaries of Harold MacGrath, E. Phillips Oppenheim and Richard Harding Davis. And one hears, too, the piping voice of outraged virtue: a man who chases women in his leisure and captures a dozen or so in twenty years is ungentlemanly, un-American, indecent— and therefore ought not to be put into a book. But I do not think that Dreiser is going to be stopped by such piffle, nor even by the more damaging attacks of smug and preposterous publishers. He has stuck to his guns through thick and thin, and he is going to stick to them to the end of the chapter. And soon or late, unless I err very grievously, he is going to reap the just reward of a sound and courageous artist, just as George Meredith reaped it before him, and Joseph Conrad is beginning to reap it even now.

H. L. MENCKEN
"A LITERARY BEHEMOTH"
Smart Set *47(December 1915), 150–54.*

On page 703 of Theodore Dreiser's new novel, "THE 'GENIUS'," the gentleman described by the title, Eugene Tennyson Witla by name, is on his way to a Christian Scientist to apply for treatment for "his evil tendencies in regard to women." Remember the place: page 703. The reader, by this time, has hacked and gummed his way through 702 large pages of fine print: 97 long chapters: more than 300,000 words. The stage-hands stand ready to yank down the curtain; messieurs of the orchestra, their minds fixed eagerly upon malt liquor, are up to their hips in the finale; the weary nurses are swabbing up the operating room; the learned chirurgeons are wiping their knives upon their pantaloons; the rev. clergy are swinging into the benediction; the inexorable embalmer waits in the antechamber with his unescapable syringe, his Mona Lisa smile. . . . And then, at this painfully hurried and impatient point, with the *coda* already under weigh and even the most somnolent reaching nervously for his galoshes, Dreiser halts the whole show to explain the origin, nature and inner meaning of Christian Science, and to make us privy to a lot of chatty stuff about Mrs. Althea Johns, the lady-like healer, and to supply us with detailed plans and specifications of the joint, lair or apartment-house in which this fair sorceress lives, works her miracles, trims her boobs, and has her being!

Believe me, I do not spoof. Turn to page 703 and see for yourself. There, while the fate of Witla waits and the bowels of patience are turned to water, we are instructed and tortured with the following particulars about the house:

1. That it was "of conventional design."
2. That there was "a spacious areaway" between its two wings.
3. That these wings were "of cream-colored pressed brick."
4. That the entrance between them "was protected by a handsome wrought-iron door."
5. That to either side of this door was "an electric lamp support of handsome design."
6. That in each of these lamp supports there were "lovely cream-colored globes, shedding a soft lustre."
7. That "inside was the usual lobby."
8. That in the lobby was the usual elevator.
9. That in the elevator was the usual "uniformed negro elevator man."
10. That this negro elevator man (name not given) was "indifferent and impertinent."
11. That a telephone switchboard was also in the lobby.
12. That the building was seven stories in height.

Such is novel-writing as Dreiser understands it—a laborious and relentless meticulousness, an endless piling up of small details, an almost furious tracking down of ions, electrons and molecules. One is amazed and flabbergasted by the mole-like industry of the man, and no less by his lavish disregard for the ease and convenience of his readers. A Dreiser novel, at least of the later canon, cannot be read as other novels are read, *e.g.*, on a winter evening or a summer afternoon, between meal and meal, travelling from New York to Boston. It demands the attention for at least a week, and uses up the strength for at least a month. If, tackling "The 'Genius,'" one were to become engrossed in the fabulous manner described by the newspaper reviewers and so find oneself unable to put it down and go to bed before the end, one would get no sleep for three days and three nights. A man who can prove that he has read such a novel without medical assistance should be admitted to the *Landwehr* at once, without thesis or examination, and perhaps even given the order *pour la mérite*. A woman of equal attainments is tough enough to take in washing or to sing Brünnhilde. . . .

And yet, and yet—well, here comes the inevitable "and yet." For all his long-windedness, for all his persistent refusal to get about his business, for all his mouthing of things so small that they seem to be nothings, this Dreiser is undoubtedly a literary artist of very respectable rank, and nothing proves it more certainly than this, the last, the longest and one is tempted to add the damnedest of his novels. The thing is staggering, alarming, maddening—and yet one sticks to it. It is rambling, formless, chaotic—and yet there emerges out of it, in the end, a picture of almost blinding brilliancy, a panorama that will remain in the mind so long as memory lasts. Is it necessary to proceed against the reader in so barbarous a manner? Is there no way of impressing him short of wearing him out? Is there no route to his consciousness save laparotomy? God knows. But this, at all events, is plain: that no other route is open to Dreiser. He must do his work in his own manner, and his oafish clumsiness and crudeness are just as much a part of it as his amazing steadiness of vision, his easy management of gigantic operations, his superb sense of character. One is familiar with stylist-novelists, fellows who tickle with apt phrases, workers in pyschological miniature, carvers of cameos. Here is one who works with a steam-shovel, his material being a county. Here is a wholesaler in general merchandise. Here, if such a fellow as Henry James be likened to a duellist, is the Hindenburg of the novel.

And what have we, precisely, in the story of Eugene Tennyson Witla? A tale enormous and indescribable—the chronicle, not only of Witla's own life, but also of the lives of a dozen other persons, some of them of only the slightest influence upon him. And what sort of man is this Witla. In brief, an artist, but though he actually paints pictures and even makes a success of it, not the artist of conventional legend, not a moony fellow in a velvet coat. What the story of Witla shows us, in truth, is very much the same thing that the story of Frank Cowperwood, in "The Financier" and "The Titan," showed us, to wit, the reaction of the artistic temperament against the unfavorable environment of this grand and glorious republic. If a Wagner or a Beethoven were born in the United States to-morrow it is highly improbable that he would express himself in the way that those men did; if a Raphael or a Cézanne, it is even more unlikely. The cause thereof is not that we disesteem music and painting, but that we esteem certain other arts infinitely more, particularly the art of creating vast industrial organisms, of bringing the scattered efforts of thousands of workers into order and coherence, of conjuring up huge forces out of spent and puny attractions and repulsions. Witla, as I have said, tries conventional art; he even goes to Paris and sets up as a genius of Montmartre. But his creative instinct and intelligence are soon challenged by larger opportunities; he is too thoroughly an American to waste himself upon pictures to hang upon walls. Instead he tackles jobs that better fit his race and time, and so, after a while, we see him at the head of a mammoth publishing house, with irons in half a dozen other fires—a boss American with all the capacity for splendor that goes with the species.

The chief apparent business of the story, indeed, is to show Witla's rise to this state of splendor, and its corrupting effect upon his soul. To this extent Dreiser plays the moralist: he, too, is an American, and cannot escape it altogether. Witla mounts the ladder of riches rung by rung, and at each rise he yields more and more to the lavishness surrounding him. He acquires fast horses, objects of art, the physical comforts of a sultan. His wife, out of Wisconsin, is hung with fragile and costly draperies; his home is a thing for the decorator to boast about; his very office has something of the luxurious gaudiness of a bordello. Bit by bit he is conquered by his pervasive richness, this atmosphere of gorgeous ease. His appetite increases as dish follows dish upon the groaning table that fate has set for him; he acquires, by subtle stages, the tastes, the prejudices, the point of view of a man of wealth; his creative faculty, disdaining its old objects, concentrates itself upon the moulding and forcing of opportunities for greater and greater acquisitions. And so his highest success becomes his deepest degradation, and we see the marks of his disintegration multiply as he approaches it. He falls, indeed, almost as fast as he rises. It is a collapse worthy of melodrama. (Again the moral note!)

I say that this rise and fall make the chief business of the story, but that, of course, is only externally. Its inner drama presents a conflict between the two Witlas—the artist who is trying to create something, however meretricious, however undeserving his effort, and the sentimentalist whose longing is to be loved, coddled, kept at ease. This conflict, of course, is at the bottom of the misery of all men who may be truly said to be conscious creatures—that is, of all men above the grade of car conductor, barber, waiter or Sunday-school superintendent. On the one hand there is the desire to exert power, to do something that has not been done before, to bend reluctant material to one's will, and on the other hand there is the desire for comfort, for well-being, for an easy life. This latter desire, nine times out of ten, perhaps actually always, is visualized by women. Women are the conservatives and conservators, the enemies of hazard and innovation, the compromisers and temporizers. That very capacity for mothering which is their supreme gift is the greatest of all foes to masculine enterprise. Most men, alas, yield to it. In the common phrase, they marry and settle down—*i.e.*, they give up all notion of making the world over. This resignationism usually passes for happiness, but to the genuine artist it is quite impossible. He must go on sacrificing ease to aspiration and aspiration to ease, thus vacillating abominably and forever between his two irreconcilable desires. No such man is ever happy, not even in the moment of his highest achievement. Life, to him, must always be a muddled and a tragic business. The best he can hope for is a makeshift and false sort of contentment.

This is what Eugene Tennyson Witla comes to in the end. Women have been the curse of his life, from the days of his nonage onward. Forced into their arms constantly by an irresistible impulse, an unquenchable yearning for their facile caresses, he has been turned aside as constantly from his higher goals and led into smoother and broader paths. Good, bad and indifferent, they have all done him harm. His own wife, clinging to him pathetically through good and evil report, always ready to take him back after one of his innumerable runnings amuck, is perhaps his greatest enemy among them. She is always ten yards behind him, hanging on to his coat-tails, trying to drag him back. She is fearful when he needs daring, stupid when he needs stimulation, virtuously wifely when the thing he craves is wild adventure. But the rest all fail him, too. Seeking for joy he finds only bitterness. It is the gradual slowing down of the machine, mental and physical, that finally brings him release. Slipping into the middle forties he begins to turn, almost imperceptibly at first, from the follies of his early manhood. When we part from him at last he seems to have found what he has been so long seeking in his little daughter. The lover has merged into the father.

It is upon this tale, so simple in its main outlines, that Dreiser spills more than 300,000 long and short words, most of them commonplace, many of them improperly used. His writing, which in "The Titan" gave promise of rising to distinction and even to something resembling beauty, is here a mere dogged piling up of nouns, adjectives, verbs, adverbs, pronouns, and particles, and as devoid of æsthetic quality as an article in the *Nation*. I often wonder if he gets anything properly describable as pleasure out of his writing—that is, out of the actual act of composition. To the man who deals in phrases, who gropes for the perfect word, who puts the way of saying it above the thing actually said, there is in writing the constant joy of sudden discovery, of happy accident. But what joy can there be in rolling up sentences that have no more life or beauty in them, intrinsically, than so many election bulletins? Where is the thrill in the manufacture of such a paragraph as that I have referred to above, in which the apartment-house infested by Mrs. Althea Johns is described as particularly as if it were being offered for sale? Or in the laborious breeding of such guff as this, from Book I, Chapter IV:

The city of Chicago—who shall portray it! This vast ruck of life that had sprung suddenly into existence upon the dank marshes of a lake shore.

But who protest and repine? Dreiser writes in this banal fashion, I dessay, because God hath made him so, and a man is too old, at my time of life, to begin criticizing the Creator. But all the same it may do no harm to point out, quite academically, that a greater regard for fairness of phrase and epithet would be as a flow of Pilsner to the weary reader in his journey across the vast deserts, steppes and pampas of the Dreiserian fable. Myself no voluptuary of letters, searching fantodishly for the rare titbit, the succulent morsel, I have yet enough sensitiveness to style to suffer damnably when all style is absent. And so with form. The well-made novel is as irritating as the well-made play—but let it at least have a beginning, a middle and an end! Such a confection as "The 'Genius'" is as shapeless as a Philadelphia pie-woman. It billows and rolls and bulges out like a cloud of smoke, and its internal organization is as vague. There are episodes that, with a few chapters added, would make very respectable novels. There are chapters that need but a touch or two to be excellent short stories. The thing rambles, staggers, fumbles, trips, wobbles, straggles, strays, heaves, pitches, reels, totters, wavers. More than once it seems to be foundering, in both the equine and the maritime senses. The author forgets it, goes out to get a drink, comes back to find it smothering. One has heard of the tree so tall that it took two men to see to the top of it. Here is a novel so huge that a whole shift of critics is needed to read it. Did I myself do it all alone? By no means. I read only the first and last paragraphs of each chapter. The rest I farmed out to my wife and children, to my cousin Ferd, and to my pastor and my beer man.

Nathless, as I have before remarked, the composition hath merit. The people in it have the fogginess and impenetrability of reality; they stand before us in three dimensions; their sufferings at the hands of fate are genuinely poignant. Of the situations it is sufficient to say that they do not seem like "situations" at all: they unroll aimlessly, artlessly, inevitably, like actual happenings. A weakness lies in the background: New York is vastly less interesting than Chicago. At all events, it is vastly less interesting to Dreiser, and so he cannot make it as interesting to the reader. And no wonder. Chicago is the epitome of the United States, of the New World, of youth. It shows all the passion for beauty, the high striving, the infinite curiosity, the unashamed hoggishness, the purple romance, the gorgeous lack of humor of twenty-one. Save for San Francisco, it is the only American city that has inspired a first-rate novel in twenty-five years. Dreiser's best books, "Sister Carrie," "Jennie Gerhardt" and "The Titan," deal with it. His worst, "The Financier," is a gallant but hopeless effort to dramatize Philadelphia—a superb subject for a satirist, but not for a novelist. In "The 'Genius'" he makes the costly blunder of bringing Witla from Chicago to New York. It would have been a better story, I venture, if that emigration had been left out of it. . . .

H. L. MENCKEN
"A SOUL'S ADVENTURES"
Smart Set *49(June 1916), 154.*

Of the current play books, the only one that interests me is "Plays of the Natural and the Supernatural," by Theodore Dreiser, a volume containing seven pieces, four of which have been printed in THE SMART SET. Of the seven, that which shows the best promise of popular success is "The Girl in the Coffin," a somewhat obvious piece of realism but with saving overtones. The four plays of the supernatural are: "The Blue Sphere," "Laughing Gas," "In the Dark," and "The Spring Recital." In each of them Dreiser tries to depict dramatically the blind, unintelligent, unintelligible forces which lie behind all human motives and acts. Superficially, they may seem to reveal an abandonment of his "chemic" theory for mysticism, but that seeming is only seeming. The two are really no more than diverse aspects of a single philosophy. That philosophy, like Joseph Conrad's, has for its central idea the fortuitousness and inexplicability of human life, and you will find it running unbrokenly through all of Dreiser's books, from "Sister Carrie" down to this last one. The criticism which deals only with externals often praises him for making Carrie Meeber so clear, for understanding her so well, but the truth is that his achievement in his study of her consists rather in making visible the impenetrable mystery of her, and of the vast complex of muddled striving and aspiration of which she is so helplessly a part. It is in this sense and not in the current critical sense that "Sister Carrie" is a profound work. It is not a book of glib explanations, of quasi-scientific cocksureness; it is, beyond all else, a book of wonder.

Dreiser's characteristic lack of technical cunning is plainly seen in some of these plays. "The Girl in the Coffin," for example, is too long. Its content and doctrine would be better discerned if it were not so heavily blanketed with words. Again, "The Spring Recital" seems but half worked out, and "The Light in the Window," in more than one place, comes perilously close to banality. But these defects are more than made up for by the photographic observation shown in "Old Rag Picker" and by the disarming plausibility and impressiveness of "The Blue Sphere" and "In the Dark." If these pieces had been done by Maeterlinck or by some fantastic Russian, the noise of their celebrity would be filling the ears, but with Dreiser's name upon them, I doubt that they will arouse much enthusiasm among the lady critics, male and female, of our fair republic. These pious numskulls, in truth, seldom consider him as an artist; they almost always content themselves with belaboring him as an immoralist. The reviews of "The 'Genius'" themselves reviewed, would make a curious contribution to Puritan psychology, and if my health holds out, I may attempt its confection later on. The book was read with a salacious eye, as Sunday School boys read the Old Testament, and then denounced pontifically as naughty. I wonder what the smut hounds will find to shock them in his plays!

H. L. MENCKEN
"THE CREED OF A NOVELIST"
Smart Set *50(October 1916), 138–43.*

The similarity between the fundamental ideas of Joseph Conrad and those of Theodore Dreiser, so often exhibited to the public gape in this place, is made plain beyond all shadow of cavil by the appearance of Dreiser's "A Hoosier Holiday," a volume of mingled reminiscence, observation, speculation and confession of faith. Put the book beside Conrad's "A Personal Record" (*Harper, 1912*), and you will find parallels from end to end. Or better still, put it beside Hugh Walpole's little volume, "Joseph Conrad," in which the Conradean metaphysic is condensed from the novels even better than Conrad has done it himself: at once you will see how the two novelists, each a worker in the elemental emotions, each a rebel against the prevailing cocksureness and superficiality, each an alien to his place and time, touch each other in a hundred ways.

"Conrad," says Walpole (himself a very penetrating and competent novelist), "is of the firm and resolute conviction that life is too strong, too clever and too remorseless for the sons of men." And then, in amplification: "It is as though, from some high window, looking down, he were able to watch some shore, from whose security men were forever launching little cockleshell boats upon a limitless and angry sea. . . . From his height he can follow their fortunes, their brave struggles, their fortitude to the very end. He admires that courage, the simplicity of that faith, but his irony springs from his knowledge of the inevitable end. . . ." Substitute the name of Dreiser for that of Conrad, with "a Hoosier Holiday" as text, and you will have to change scarcely a word. Perhaps one, to wit, "clever." I suspect that Dreiser, writing so of his own creed, would be tempted to make it "stupid," or, at all events, "unintelligible." The struggle of man, as he sees it, is more than impotent; it is meaningless. There is, to his eye, no grand ingenuity, no skillful adaptation of means to end, no moral (or even dramatic) plan in the order of the universe. He can get out of it only a sense of profound and inexplicable disorder, of a seeking without a finding. There is not only no neat programme of rewards and punishments; there is not even an understandable balance of causes and effects. The waves which batter the cockleshells change their direction at every instant. Their navigation is a vast adventure, but intolerably fortuitous and inept—a voyage without chart, compass, sun or stars. . . .

So at bottom. But to look into the blackness steadily, of course, is almost beyond the endurance of man. In the very moment that its impenetrability is grasped the imagination begins attacking it with pale beams of false light. All religions, I dare say, are thus projected from the soul of man, and not only all religions, but also all great agnosticisms. Nietzsche, shrinking from the horror of the abyss of negation, revived the Pythagorean concept of *der ewigen Wiederkunft*—a vain and blood-curdling sort of comfort. To it, after a while, he added explanation, almost Christian—a whole repertoire of whys and wherefores, aims and goals, aspirations and significances. Other seers have gone back even further: the Transcendentalists stemmed from Zeno of Elea. The late Mark Twain, in an unpublished work, toyed with a characteristically daring idea: that men are to some unimaginably vast and incomprehensible Being what the unicellular organisms of his body are to man, and so on *ad infinitum*. Dreiser occasionally dallies with much the same notion; he likens the endless reactions going on in the world we know, the myriadal creation, collision and destruction of entities, to the slow accumulation and organization of cells *in utero*. He would make us specks in the insentient embryo of some gigantic Presence whose form is still unimaginable and whose birth must wait for eons and eons. Again, he turns to something not easily distinguishable from philosophical idealism, whether out of Berkeley or Fichte it is hard to make out—that is, he would interpret the whole phenomenon of life as no more than an appearance, a nightmare of some unseen sleeper or of men themselves, an "uncanny blur of nothingness"—in Euripides' phrase, "a tale told by an idiot, dancing down the wind." Yet again, he talks vaguely of the intricate polyphony of a cosmic orchestra, cacophonous to our dull ears. Finally, he puts the observed into the ordered, reading a purpose in the displayed event: "life was intended as a spectacle, it was intended to sting and hurt. . . ." But these are only gropings, and not to be read too critically. From speculations and explanations he always returns, Conrad-like, to the bald fact: to "the spectacle and stress of life." The bolder flights go with the puerile solutions of current religion and morals. Even more than Conrad, he sees life as a struggle in which man is not only doomed to defeat, but denied any glimpse or understanding of his antagonist. His philosophy is an agnosticism that has almost got beyond curiosity. What good would it do us, he asks, to know? In our ignorance and helplessness, we may at least get a slave's comfort out of cursing the gods. Suppose we saw them striving blindly too, and pitied them?

The function of poetry, says F. C. Prescott, in "Poetry and Dreams" (a book so modest and yet so searching that it will be years before the solemn donkeys of the seminaries ever hear of it), is to conjure up for us a vivid picture of what we want, but cannot get. The desire is half of the story, but the inhibition is as plainly the other half, and of no less importance. It is this element that gives its glamour to tragedy; the mind seizes upon the image as a substitute for the reality, and the result is the psychical *katharsis* described by Aristotle. It is precisely by the same process that Dreiser and Conrad get a profound and melancholy poetry into their books. Floating above the bitter picture of what actually is, there is always the misty but inordinately charming picture of what might be or ought to be. Here we get a clue to the method of both men, and to the secret of their capacity for reaching the emotions. All of Conrad's brilliant and poignant creatures are dreamers who go to smash upon the rocks of human weakness and stupidity—Kurtz, Nostromo, Lord Jim, Almayer, Razumov, Heyst, even Whalley and M'Whirr. And so with Carrie Meeber, Jennie Gerhardt, Frank Cowperwood and Eugene Witla. They are not merely vivid and interesting figures; they are essentially tragic figures, and in their tragedy, despite its superficial sordidness, there is a deep and ghostly poetry. "My task," said Conrad once, "is, by the power of the printed word, to make you hear, to make you feel—it is, above all, to make you *see*." Comprehension, sympathy, pity—these are the things he seeks to evoke. And these, too, are the things that Dreiser seeks to evoke. The reader does not arise from such a book as "Sister Carrie" with a smirk of satisfaction, as he might from a novel by Howells or James; he leaves it infinitely touched. . . .

Mr. Walpole, in his little book, is at pains to prove that Conrad is neither realist nor romanticist, but an intricate combination of both. The thesis scarcely needs support, or even statement: *all* imaginative writers of the higher ranks are both. Plain realism, as in the early Zola, simply wearies us by its futility; plain romance, if we ever get beyond youth, makes us laugh. It is their artistic combination, as in life itself, that fetches us—the subtle projection of the muddle that is living against the orderliness that we reach out for—the eternal war of aspiration and experience—the combat of man and his destiny. As I say, this contrast lies at the bottom of all that is vital and significant in imaginative writing; to argue for it is to wade in platitudes. I speak of it here simply because the more stupid of Dreiser's critics—and what author has ever been hoofed by worse asses!—insist upon seeing him and denouncing him as a realist, and as a realist only. One of them, for example, has lately printed a long article maintaining that he is blind to the spiritual side of man altogether, and that he accounts for his characters solely by some incomprehensible "theory of animal behaviour." Could one imagine a more absurd mouthing of a phrase? One is almost staggered, indeed, by such critical imbecility, even in a college professor. The truth is, of course, that all of Dreiser's novels deal fundamentally with the endless conflict between this "animal behaviour" and the soarings of the spirit—between the destiny forced upon his characters by their environment, their groping instincts, their lack of courage and resourcefulness, and the destiny they picture for themselves in their dreams. This is the tragedy of Carrie Meeber and Jennie Gerhardt. The physical fact of their "seduction" (they are willing enough) blasts them doubly, for on the one hand it brings down upon them the conventional burden of the pariah, and on the other hand the worldly advancement which follows widens their aspiration beyond their inherent capacities, and so augments their unhappiness. It is the tragedy, too, of Cowperwood and Witla. To see these men as mere melodramatic Don Juans is to fall into an error almost unimaginably ridiculous. The salient fact about them, indeed, is that they are *not* mere Don Juans—that they are men in whom the highest idealism strives against the bonds of the flesh. Witla, passion-torn, goes down to disaster and despair. It is what remains of the wreck of his old ideals that floats him into peace at last. As for Cowperwood, we have yet to see his actual end—but how plainly its shadows are cast before! Life is beating him, and through his own weakness. There remains for him, as for Lord Jim, only the remnant of a dream.

With so much ignorant and misleading criticism of him going about, the appearance of "A Hoosier Holiday" should be of service to Dreiser's reputation, for it shows the man as he actually is, stripped of all the scarlet trappings hung upon him by horrified lady reviewers, male and female. The book, indeed, is amazingly naif. Slow in tempo, discursive, meditative, it covers a vast territory, and lingers in far fields. One finds in it an almost complete confession of faith, artistic, religious, even political. And not infrequently that confession comes in the form of somewhat disconcerting confidences—about the fortunes of the house of Dreiser, the dispersed Dreiser family, the old neighbors in Indiana, new friends made along the way. As readers of "A Traveller at Forty" are well aware, Dreiser knows little of reticence, and is no slave to prudery. In that earlier book he described the people he encountered exactly as he saw them, without forgetting a vanity or a wart. In "A Hoosier Holiday" he goes even further: he speculates about them, prodding into the motives behind their acts, wondering what they would do in this or that situation, forcing them painfully into laboratory jars. They become, in the end, not unlike characters in a novel; one misses only the neatness of a plot. Strangely enough, the one personage of the chronicle who remains dim throughout is the artist, Franklin Booth, Dreiser's host and companion on the long motor ride from New York to Indiana, and the maker of the book's excellent pictures. One gets a brilliant etching of Booth's father, and scarcely less vivid portraits of Speed, the chauffeur; of various persons encountered on the way, and of friends and relatives dredged up out of the abyss of the past. But of Booth one learns little save that he is a Christian Scientist and a fine figure of a man. There must have been much talk during those two weeks of careening along the high-road, and Booth must have borne some part in it, but what he said is very meagrely reported, and so he is still somewhat vague at the end—a personality sensed, but scarcely apprehended.

However, it is Dreiser himself who is the chief character of the story, and who stands out from it most brilliantly. One sees in the man all the special marks of the novelist: his capacity for photographic and relentless observation, his insatiable curiosity, his keen zest in life as a spectacle, his comprehension of and sympathy for the poor striving of humble folks, his endless mulling of insoluble problems, his recurrent Philistinism, his impatience of restraints, his suspicion of messiahs, his passion for physical beauty, his relish for the gaudy drama of big cities, his incurable Americanism. The panorama that he enrolls runs the whole scale of the colors; it is a series of extraordinarily vivid pictures. The sombre gloom of the

Pennsylvania hills, with Wilkes-Barré lying among them like a gem; the procession of little country towns, sleepy and a bit hoggish; the flash of Buffalo, Cleveland, Indianapolis; the gargantuan coal-pockets and ore-docks along the Erie shore; the tinsel summer resorts; the lush Indiana farm-lands, with their stodgy, bovine people—all of these things are sketched in simply, and yet almost magnificently. I know, indeed, of no book which better describes the American hinterland. Here we have no idle spying by a stranger, but a full-length representation by one who knows the thing he describes intimately, and is himself a part of it. Almost every mile of the road travelled has been Dreiser's own road in life. He knew those unkempt Indiana towns in boyhood; he wandered in the Indiana woods; he came to Toledo, Cleveland, Buffalo as a young man; all the roots of his existence are out there. And so he does his chronicle *con amore*, with many a sentimental dredging up of old memories, old hopes and old dreams.

Strangely enough, for all the literary efflorescence of the Middle West, such pictures of it are very rare. I know, in fact, of no other on the same scale. It is, in more than one way, the heart of America, and yet it has gone undescribed. Dreiser remedies that lack with all his characteristic laboriousness and painstaking. When he has done with them, those drowsy villages and oafish country towns have grown as real as the Chicago of "Sister Carrie" and "The Titan." One sees a land that blinks and naps in the sunshine like some great cow, udders full, the cud going—a land of Dutch fatness and contentment—a land, despite its riches, of almost unbelievable stupidity and immobility. We get a picture of a typical summer afternoon; mile after mile of farms, villages, little towns, the people sleepy and empty in mind, lolling on their verandas, killing time between trivial events, shut off from all the turmoil of the world. What, in the end, will come out of this over-fed, too-happy region? Ideas? Rebellions? The spark to set off great wars? Or only the silence of decay? In Ohio industry has already invaded the farms; chimneys arise among the haystacks. And so further west. But in Indiana there is a back-water, a sort of American Midi, a neutral ground in the battles of the nation. It has no art, no great industry, no dominating men. Its literature, in the main, is a feeble romanticism for flappers and fat women. Its politics is a skeptical opportunism. It is not stirred by great passions. It knows no heroes. . . . What will be the end of it? Which way is it heading?

Save for passages in "The Titan," "A Hoosier Holiday" marks the high tide of Dreiser's writing—that is, as sheer writing. There are empty, brackish phrases enough, God knows—"high noon" among them. But for all that, there is an indeniable glow in it; it shows, in more than one place, an approach to style; the mere wholesaler of words has become, in some sense, a connoisseur, even a voluptuary. The picture of Wilkes-Barré girt in by her hills is simply done, and yet there is imagination in it, and touches of brilliance. The sombre beauty of the Pennsylvania mountains is vividly transferred to the page. The towns by the wayside are differentiated, swifty drawn, made to live. There are excellent sketches of people—a courtly hotel-keeper in some God-forsaken hamlet, his self-respect triumphing over his wallow; a group of babbling Civil War veterans, endlessly mouthing incomprehensible jests; the half-grown beaux and belles of the summer resorts, enchanted and yet a bit staggered by the awakening of sex; Booth *père* and his sinister politics; broken and forgotten men in the Indiana towns; policemen, waitresses, farmers, country characters; Dreiser's own people—the boys and girls of his youth; his brother Paul, the Indiana Schneckenburger and Francis Scott Key, author of "On the Banks of the Wabash"; his sisters and brothers; his beaten, hopeless, pious father; his brave and noble mother. The book is dedicated to this mother, now long dead, and in a way it is a memorial to her, a monument to affection. Life bore upon her cruelly; she knew poverty at its lowest ebb and despair at its bitterest; and yet there was in her a touch of fineness that never yielded, a gallant spirit that faced and fought things through. *Une ame grande dans un petit destin*: a great soul in a small destiny! One thinks, somehow, of the mother of Gounod. . . . Her son has not forgotten her. His book is her epitaph. He enters into her presence with love and with reverence and with something not far from awe. . . .

In sum, this record of a chance holiday is much more than a mere travel book, for it offers, and for the first time, a clear understanding of the fundamental faiths and ideas, and of the intellectual and spiritual background no less, of a man with whom the future historian of American literature will have to deal at no little length. Dreiser, as yet, has not come into his own. In England his true stature has begun to be recognized, and once the war is over I believe that he will be "discovered," as the phrase is, in Germany and Russia, and perhaps in France. But in his own country he is still denied and belabored in a manner that would be comic were it not so pathetically stupid. The college professors rail and snarl at him in the *Nation* and the *Dial*; the elderly virgins of the newspapers represent him as an iconoclast, an immoralist, an Anti-Christ, even a German spy; the professional moralists fatuously proceed to jail him because his Witlas and his Cowperwoods are not eunuchs—more absurdly still, because a few "God damns" are scattered through the 736 crowded pages of "The 'Genius.'" The Puritan fog still hangs over American letters; it is formally demanded that all literature be made with the girl of sixteen in mind, and that she be assumed to be quite ignorant of sex. And the orthodox teachers sing the hymn that is lined out. In Prof. Fred Lewis Pattee's "History of American Literature Since 1870" (*Century*), just published, there is no mention of Dreiser whatever! Such novelists as Owen Wister, Robert W. Chambers and Holman F. Day are mentioned as "leaders"; substantial notices are given to Capt. Charles King, Blanche Willis Howard and Julian Hawthorne; five whole pages are dedicated to F. Marion Crawford; even Richard Harding Davis, E. P. Roe and "Octave Thanet" are soberly estimated. But not a line about Dreiser! Not an incidental mention of him! One recalls Richardson's "American Literature," with its contemptuous dismissal of Mark Twain. A sapient band, these college professors!

But the joke, of course, is not on Dreiser, but on the professors themselves, and on the host of old maids, best-seller fanatics and ecstatic Puritans who support them. Time will bring the Indianan his revenge, and perhaps he will yield to humor and help time along. A Dreiser novel with a Puritan for its protagonist would be something to caress the soul—a full-length portrait of the Eternal Pharisee, a limning of the Chemically Pure, done scientifically, relentlessly, affectionately. Dreiser knows the animal from snout to tail. He could do a picture that would live. . . .

H. L. MENCKEN
"DITHYRAMBS AGAINST LEARNING"
Smart Set *57(November 1918), 143–44.*

The eleven pieces in "Free and Other Stories," by Theodore Dreiser, are the by-products of a dozen years of industrious novel-writing, and are thus somewhat miscellaneous in character and quality. They range from experiments in the fantastic to ventures into realism, and, in tone, from the satirical to the rather laboriously moral. The best of them are "The Lost Phoebe," The Cruise of the *Idlewild*," "The Second Choice" and "Free." The last-named is a detailed and searching analysis of a disparate marriage that has yet survived for forty years—an elaborate study of a life-long conflict between impulse and aspiration on the one hand and fear and conformity on the other. Here Dreiser is on his own ground, for the thing is not really a short story, in any ordinary sense, but a chapter from a novel, and he manœuvres in it in his customary deliberate and spacious manner. "The Second Choice" is of much the same character—a presentation of the processes of mind whereby a girl deserted by the man she loves brings herself to marriage with one she doesn't love at all. Those of the stories that are more properly short stories in form are less successful; for example, "A Story of Stories," "Old Rogaum and His Theresa" and

"Will You Walk Into My Parlor?" The true short story, in fact, lies as far outside Dreiser's natural field as the triolet or the mazurka. He needs space and time to get his effects; he must wash in his gigantic backgrounds, and build up his characters slowly. The mountebankish smartness and neatness of the Maupassant-O. Henry tradition are quite beyond him. He is essentially a serious man, and a melancholy. The thing that interests him most is not a deftly articulated series of events but a gradual transformation of personality, and particularly a transformation that involves the decay of integrity. The characters that live most brilliantly in his books, like those that live most brilliantly in the books of Conrad, are characters in disintegration—corroded, beaten, destroyed by the inexplicable mystery of existence.

In the midst of many reminders of his high talents, Dreiser's worst failing as a practical writer appears with painful vividness in this book. I allude to his astonishing carelessness, his irritating slovenliness. He seems to have absolutely no respect for words as words—no sense of their inner music, no hand whatever for their adept combination. One phrase, it would seem, pleases him quite as much as another phrase. If it is flat, familiar, threadbare, so much the better. It is not, indeed, that he hasn't an ear. As a matter of fact, his hearing is very sharp, and in his dialogue, particularly when dealing with ignorant characters, he comes very close to the actual vulgate of his place and time. But the difficulty is that this vulgate bulges beyond the bounds of dialogue: it gets into what he has to say himself, unpurged by anything even remotely resembling taste. The result is often a series of locutions that affects so pedantic a man as I am like music on a fiddle out of tune, or a pretty girl with beer-keg ankles, or mayonnaise on ice-cream. . . .

H. L. MENCKEN
"THE DREISER BUGABOO"
The Seven Arts *(August 1917)*.

Dr. William Lyon Phelps, the Lampson professor of English at Yale, opens his chapter on Mark Twain in his "Essays on Modern Novelists" with a humorous account of the critical imbecility which pursued Mark in his own country down to his last years. The favorite national critics of that era (and it extended to 1895, at the least) were wholly anaesthetic to the fact that he was a great artist. They admitted him, somewhat grudgingly, a certain low dexterity as a clown, but that he was an imaginative writer of the first rank, or even of the fifth rank, was something that, in their insanest moments, never so much as occurred to them. Phelps cites, in particular, an ass named Professor Richardson, whose "American Literature," it appears, "is still a standard work" and "a deservedly high authority"—apparently in colleges. In the 1892 edition of this *magnum opus*, Mark is dismissed with less than four lines, and ranked below Irving, Holmes and Lowell—nay, actually below Artemus Ward, Josh Billings and Petroleum V. Nasby! The thing is fabulous, fantastic—but nevertheless true. Lacking the "higher artistic or moral purpose of the greater humorists" (*exempli gratia*, Rabelais, Molière, Aristophanes!), Mark is put off by this Prof. Balderdash as a laborious buffoon. . . . But stay! Do not laugh yet! Phelps himself, indignant at the stupidity, now proceeds to prove that Mark was really a great moralist, and more, a great optimist. . . . Turn to "The Mysterious Stranger" and "What is Man?"! . . .

College professors, alas, never learn anything. The identical pedagogue who achieved this nonsense about old Mark in 1910 now seeks to dispose of Theodore Dreiser in the precise manner of Richardson. That is to say, he essays to finish him by putting him into Coventry, by loftily passing him over. "Do not speak of him," said Kingsley of Heine; "he was a wicked man." Search the latest volume of the Phelps revelation, "The Advance of the English Novel," and you will find that Dreiser is not once mentioned in it. The late O. Henry is hailed as a genius who will have "abiding fame"; Henry Sydnor Harrison is hymned as "more than a clever novelist," nay, "a valuable ally of the angels" (the right-thinker complex! art as a form of snuffling!), and an obscure Pagliaccio named Charles D. Stewart is brought forward as "the American novelist most worthy to fill the particular vacancy caused by the death of Mark Twain"—but Dreiser is not even listed in the index. And where Phelps leads with his baton of birch most of the other drovers of rah-rah boys follow. I turn, for example, to "An Introduction to American Literature," by Henry S. Pancoast, A.M., L.H.D., dated 1912. There are kind words for Richard Harding Davis, for Amelie Rives, and even for Will N. Harben, but not a syllable for Dreiser. Again, there is "A History of American Literature," by Reuben Post Halleck, A.M., LL.D., dated 1911. Lew Wallace, Marietta Holley, Owen Wister and Augusta Evans Wilson have their hearings, but not Dreiser. Yet again, there is "A History of American Literature Since 1870," by Prof. Fred. Lewis Pattee, instructor in "the English language and literature" somewhere in Pennsylvania. Fred has praises for Marion Crawford, Margaret Deland and F. Hopkinson Smith, and polite bows for Richard Harding Davis and Robert W. Chambers, but from end to end of his fat tome I am unable to find the slightest mention of Dreiser.

So much for one group of heroes of the new Dunciad. That it includes most of the acknowledged heavyweights of the craft—the Babbitts, Mores,

Brownells and so on—goes without saying; as Van Wyck Brooks has pointed out in *The Seven Arts*, these magnificoes are austerely above any consideration of the literature that is in being. The other group, more courageous and more honest, proceeds by direct attack; Dreiser is to be disposed of by a moral *attentat*. Its leaders are two more professors, Stuart P. Sherman and H. W. Boynton, and in its ranks march the lady critics of the newspapers with much shrill, falsetto clamor. Sherman is the only one of them who shows any intelligible reasoning. Boynton, as always, is a mere parroter of conventional phrases, and the objections of the ladies fade imperceptibly into a pious indignation which is indistinguishable from that of the professional suppressors of vice.

What, then, is Sherman's complaint? In brief, that Dreiser is a liar when he calls himself a realist; that he is actually a naturalist, and hence accursed. That "he has evaded the enterprise of representing human conduct, and confined himself to a representation of animal behavior." That he "imposes his own naturalistic philosophy" upon his characters, making them do what they ought not to do, and think what they ought not to think. That he "has just two things to tell us about Frank Cowperwood: that he has a rapacious appetite for money, and a rapacious appetite for women." That this alleged "theory of animal behavior" is not only incorrect, but immoral, and that "when one half the world attempts to assert it, the other half rises in battle." [*The Nation*, 2 Dec. 1915.]

Only a glance is needed to show the vacuity of all this irate flubdub. Dreiser, in point of fact, is scarcely more the realist or the naturalist, in any true sense, then H. G. Wells or the later George Moore, nor has he ever announced himself in either the one character or the other—if there be, in fact, any difference between them that anyone save a pigeon-holing pedagogue can discern. He is really something quite different, and, in his moments, something far more stately. His aim is not merely to record, but to translate and understand; the thing he exposes is not the empty event and act, but the endless mystery out of which it springs; his pictures have a passionate compassion in them that it is hard to separate from poetry. If this sense of the universal and inexplicable tragedy, if this vision of life as a seeking without a finding, if this adept summoning up of moving images, is mistaken by college professors for the empty, meticulous nastiness of Zola in "Pot-Bouille"—in Nietzsche's phrase, for "the delight to stink"—then surely the folly of college professors, as vast as it seems, has been underestimated. What is the fact? The fact is that Dreiser's attitude of mind, his manner of reaction to the phenomena he represents, the whole of his alleged "naturalistic philosophy," stem directly, not from Zola, Flaubert, Augier and the younger Dumas, but from the Greeks. In the midst of democratic cocksureness and Christian sentimentalism, of doctrinaire shallowness and professorial smugness, he stands for a point of view which at least has something honest and courageous about it; here, at all events, he is a realist. Let him put a motto to his books, and it might be:

> *O ye deathward-going tribes of men!*
> *What do your lives mean except that they go to nothingness?*

If you protest against that as too harsh for Christians and college professors, right-thinkers and forward-lookers, then you protest against "Oedipus Rex."

As for the animal behavior prattle of the learned headmaster, it reveals on the one hand only the academic fondness for seizing upon high sounding but empty phrases and using them to alarm the populace, and on the other hand, only the academic incapacity for observing facts correctly and reporting them honestly. The truth is, of course, that the behavior of such men as Cowperwood and Eugene Witla and of such women as Carrie Meeber and Jennie Gerhardt, as Dreiser describes it, is no more merely animal than the behavior of such acknowledged and undoubted human beings as Dr. Woodrow Wilson and Dr. Jane Addams. The whole point of the story of Witla, to take the example which seems to concern the horrified watchmen most, is this: that his life is a bitter conflict between the animal in him and the aspiring soul, between the flesh and the spirit, between what is weak in him and what is strong, between what is base and what is noble. Moreover, the good, in the end, gets its hooks into the bad: as we part from Witla he is actually bathed in the tears of remorse, and resolved to be a correct and godfearing man. And what have we in "The Financier" and "The Titan"? A conflict, in the ego of Cowperwood, between aspiration and ambition, between the passion for beauty and the passion for power. Is either passion animal? To ask the question is to answer it.

I single out Dr. Sherman, not because his pompous syllogisms have any plausibility in fact or in logic, but simply because he may well stand as archetype of the booming, indignant corrupter of criteria, the moralist turned critic. A glance at his paean to Arnold Bennett [New York *Evening Post*, 31 Dec. 1915] at once reveals the true gravamen of his objection to Dreiser. What offends him is not actually Dreiser's shortcomings as an artist, but Dreiser's shortcomings as a Christian and an American. In Bennett's volumes of pseudo-philosophy—e.g., "The Plain Man and His Wife" and "The Feast of St. Friend"—he finds the intellectual victuals that are to his taste. Here we have a sweet commingling of virtuous conformity and complacent optimism, of sonorous platitude and easy certainty—here, in brief, we have the philosophy of the English middle classes—and here, by the same token we have the sort of guff that the half-educated of our own country can understand. It is the calm, superior numskullery that was Victorian; it is by Samuel Smiles out of Hannah More. The offense of Dreiser is that he has disdained this revelation and gone back to the Greeks. Lo, he reads poetry into "the appetite for women"—he rejects the Pauline doctrine that all love is below the diaphragm! He thinks of Ulysses, not as a mere heretic and criminal, but as a great artist. He sees the life of man, not as a simple theorem in Calvinism, but as a vast adventure, an enchantment, a mystery. It is no wonder that respectable schoolteachers are against him. . . .

The Comstockian attack upon "The 'Genius'" seems to have sprung out of the same muddled sense of Dreiser's essential hostility to all that is safe and regular—of the danger in him to that mellowed Methodism which has become the national ethic. The book, in a way, was a direct challenge, for though it came to an end upon a note which even a Methodist might hear as sweet, there were provocations in detail. Dreiser, in fact, allowed his scorn to make off with his taste—and *es ist nichts fürchtlicher als Einbildungskraft ohne Geschmack*. The Comstocks arose to the bait a bit slowly, but none the less surely. Going through the volume with the terrible industry of a Sunday-school boy dredging up pearls of smut from the Old Testament, they achieved a list of no less than 89 alleged floutings of the code—75 described as lewd and 14 as profane. An inspection of these specifications affords mirth of a rare and lofty variety; nothing could more cruelly expose the inner chambers of the moral mind. When young Witla, fastening his best girl's skate, is so overcome by the carnality of youth that he hugs her, it is set down as lewd. On page 51, having become an art student, he is fired by "a great warm-tinted nude of Bouguereau"— lewd again. On page 70 he begins to draw from the figure, and his instructor cautions him that the female breast is round, not square—more lewdness. On page 151 he kisses his girl on mouth and neck and she cautions him: "Be careful! Momma may come in"—still more. On page 161, having got rid of mamma, she yields "herself to him gladly, joyously" and he is greatly shocked when she argues that an artist (she is by way of being a singer) had better not marry—lewdness double damned. On page 245 he and his bride, being ignorant, neglect the principles laid down by Dr. Sylvanus Stall in his great works on sex hygiene—lewdness most horrible! But there is no need to proceed further. Every kiss, hug and tickle of the chin in the chronicle is laboriously snouted out, empanelled, exhibited. Every hint that Witla is no vestal, that he indulges his unchristian fleshliness, that he burns in the manner of I Corinthians, VII, 9, is uncovered to the moral inquisition.

On the side of profanity there is a less ardent pursuit of evidence, chiefly, I daresay, because their unearthing is less stimulating. (Besides, there is no law prohibiting profanity in books: the whole inquiry here is but so much *lagniappe*.) On page 408, describing a character called Daniel C. Summerfield, Dreiser says that the fellow is "very much given to swearing, more as a matter of habit than of foul intention," and then goes on to explain somewhat lamely that "no picture of him would be complete without the interpolation of his various expressions." They turn out to be *God Damn* and *Jesus Christ*—three of the latter and five or six of the former. All go down; the pure in heart must be shielded from the knowledge of them. (But what of the immoral French? They call the English *Goddams*.) Also, three plain *damns*, eight *hells*, one *my God*, five *by Gods*, one *go to the devil*, one *God Almighty* and one plain *God*. Altogether, 31 specimens are listed. "The 'Genius'" runs to 350,000 words. The profanity thus works out to somewhat less than one word in 10,000. . . . Alas, the Comstockian proboscis, feeling for such offendings, is not as alert as when uncovering more savoury delicacies. On page 191 I find an overlooked *by God*. On page 372 there are *Oh, God, God curses her*, and *God strike her dead*. On page 373 there are *Ah, God, Oh, God*, and three other invocations of God. On page 617 there is *God help me*. On page 720 there is *as God is my judge*. On page 723 there is *I'm no damned good*. . . . But I begin to blush.

When the Comstock Society began proceedings against "The 'Genius,'" a group of English novelists, including Arnold Bennett, H. G. Wells, W. L. George and Hugh Walpole, cabled an indignant caveat. This bestirred the Authors' League of America to activity, and its executive committee issued a minute denouncing the business. Later a protest of American *literati* was circulated, and more than 400 signed, including such highly respectable authors as Winston Churchill, Percy Mackaye, Booth Tarkington and James Lane Allen, and such critics as Lawrence Gilman, Clayton Hamilton and James Huneker, and the editors of such journals as the *Century*, the *Atlantic Monthly* and the *New Republic*. Among my literary lumber is all the correspondence relating to this protest, not forgetting the letters of those who refused to sign, and some day I hope to publish it, that posterity may not lose the joy of an extremely diverting episode. Meanwhile, the case moves with stately dignity through the interminable corridors of jurisprudence, and the bulk of the briefs and exhibits that it throws off begins to rival the staggering bulk of "The 'Genius'" itself.

In all this, of course, there is a certain savoury grotesquerie; the exposure of the Puritan mind makes life, for the moment, more agreeable. The danger of the combined comstockian professorial attack, to Dreiser as artist, is not that it will make a *muss*-Presbyterian of him, but that it will convert him into a professional revolutionary, spouting stale perunas for all the sorrows of the world. Here Greenwich Village pulls as Chautauqua pushes; already, indeed, the passionate skepticism that was his original philosophy begins to show signs of being contaminated by various so-called "radical" purposes. The danger is not one to be sniffed in. Dreiser, after all, is an American like the rest of us, and to be an American is to be burdened by an ethical prepossession, to lean toward causes and remedies. Go through "The 'Genius'" or "A Hoosier Holiday" carefully, and you will find disquieting indications of what might be called a democratic trend in thinking—that is, a trend toward short cuts, easy answers, glittering theories. He is bemused, off and on, by all the various poppycock of the age, from Christian Science to spiritism, and from the latest guesses in eschatology and epistemology to *art pour l'art*. A true American, he lacks a solid culture, and so he yields a bit to every wind that blows, to the inevitable damage of his representation of the eternal mystery that is man.

Joseph Conrad, starting out from the same wondering agnosticism, holds to it far more resolutely, and it is easy to see why. Conrad is, by birth and training, an aristocrat. He has the gift of emotional detachment. The lures of facile doctrine do not move him. In his irony there is a disdain which plays about even the ironist himself. Dreiser is a product of far different forces and traditions, and is capable of no such escapement. Struggle as he may to rid himself of the current superstitions, he can never quite achieve deliverance from the believing attitude of mind—the heritage of the Indiana hinterland. One half of the man's brain, so to speak, wars with the other half. He is intelligent, he is thoughtful, he is a sound artist—but always there come moments when a dead hand falls upon him, and he is once more the Indiana peasant, snuffing absurdly over imbecile sentimentalities; giving a grave ear to quackeries, snorting and eye-rolling with the best of them. One generation spans too short a time to free the soul of man. Nietzsche, to the end of his days, remained a Prussian pastor's son, and hence two-thirds a Puritan; he erected his war upon holiness, toward the end, into a sort of holy war. Kipling, the grandson of a Methodist preacher, reveals the tin-pot evangelist with increasing clarity as youth and its ribaldries pass away and he falls back upon his fundamentals. And that other English novelist who springs from the servants' hall—let us not be surprised or blame him if he sometimes writes like a bounder.

As for Dreiser, as I hint politely, he is still, for all his achievement, in the transition stage between Christian Endeavor and civilization; between Warsaw, Indiana, and the Socratic grove; between being a good American and being a free man; and so he sometimes vacillates perilously between a moral sentimentalism and a somewhat extravagant revolt. "The 'Genius,'" on the one hand, is almost a tract for rectitude, a Warning to the Young; its motto might be *Scheut die Dirnen*! And on the other hand, it is full of a laborious truculence that can be explained only by imagining the author as heroically determined to prove that he is a plain-spoken fellow and his own man, let the chips fall where they may. So, in spots, in "The Financier" and "The Titan," both of them far better books. There is an almost moral frenzy to expose and riddle what passes for morality among the stupid. The isolation of irony is never reached; the man is still a bit evangelical; his ideas are still novelties to him; he is as solemnly absurd in some of his floutings of the code American as he is in his respect for Bouguereau, or in his flirtings with New Thought, or in his naive belief in the importance of novel-writing. . . .

But his books remain, particularly his earlier books—and not all the ranting of the outraged orthodox will ever wipe them out. They were done in the stage of wonder, before self-consciousness began to creep in and corrupt it. The view of life that got into "Sister Carrie," the first of them, was not the product of a deliberate thinking out of Carrie's problem. It simply got itself there by the force of the artistic passion behind it; its coherent statement had to wait for other and more reflective days. This complete rejection of ethical plan and purpose, this manifestation of what Nietzsche used to call moral innocence, is what brought up the guardians of the national tradition at the gallop, and created the Dreiser bugaboo of today. All the rubber-stamp formulae of American fiction were thrown overboard in these earlier books; instead of reducing the inexplicable to the obvious, they lifted the obvious to the inexplicable; one could find in them no orderly chain of causes and effects, of rewards and punishments; they represented life as a phenomenon at once terrible and unintelligible, like a stroke of lightning. The prevailing criticism applied the moral litmus. They were not "good"; *ergo* they were "evil."

The peril that Dreiser stands in is here. He may begin to act, if he is not careful, according to the costume forced on him. Unable to combat the orthodox valuation of his place and aim, he may seek a spiritual refuge in embracing it, and so arrange himself with the tripe-sellers of heterodoxy, and cry wares that differ from the other stock only in the bald fact that they are different. . . . Such a fall would grieve the judicious, of whom I have the honor to be one.

H. L. MENCKEN
"THEODORE DREISER"
(in A Book of Prefaces, *1917).*

Out of the desert of American fictioneering, so populous and yet so dreary, Dreiser stands up—a phenomenon unescapably visible, but disconcertingly hard to explain. What forces combined to produce him in the first place, and how has he managed to hold out so long against the prevailing blasts—of disheartening misunderstanding and misrepresentation, of Puritan suspicion and opposition, of artistic isolation, of commercial seduction? There is something downright heroic in the way the man has held his narrow and perilous ground, disdaining all compromise, unmoved by the cheap success that lies so inviting around the corner. He has faced, in his day, almost every form of attack that a serious artist can conceivably encounter, and yet all of them together have scarcely budged him an inch. He still plods along in the laborious, cheerless way he first marked out for himself; he is quite as undaunted by baited praise as by bludgeoning, malignant abuse; his later novels are, if anything, more unyieldingly dreiserian than his earliest. As one who has long sought to entice him in this direction or that, fatuously presuming to instruct him in what would improve and profit him, I may well bear a reluctant and resigned sort of testimony to his gigantic steadfastness. It is almost as if any change in his manner, any concession to what is usual and esteemed, any amelioration of his blind, relentless exercises of *force majeure*, were a physical impossibility. One feels him at last to be authentically no more than a helpless instrument (or victim) of that inchoate flow of forces which he himself is so fond of depicting as at once the answer to the riddle of life, and a riddle ten times more vexing and accursed.

And his origins, as I say, are quite as mysterious as his motive power. To fit him into the unrolling chart of American, or even of English fiction is extremely difficult. Save one thinks of H. B. Fuller (whose "With the Procession" and "The Cliff-Dwellers" are still remembered by Huneker, but by whom else?[1]), he seems to have had no fore-runner among us, and for all the discussion of him that goes on, he has few avowed disciples, and none of them gets within miles of him. One catches echoes of him, perhaps, in Willa Sibert Cather, in Mary S. Watts, in David Graham Phillips, in Sherwood Anderson and in Joseph Medill Patterson, but, after all, they are no more than echoes. In Robert Herrick the thing descends to a feeble parody; in imitators further removed to sheer burlesque. All the latter-day American novelists of consideration are vastly more facile than Dreiser in their philosophy, as they are in their style. In the fact, perhaps, lies the measure of their difference. What they lack, great and small, is the gesture of pity, the note of awe, the profound sense of wonder—in a phrase, that "soberness of mind" which William Lyon Phelps sees as the hallmark of Conrad and Hardy, and which even the most stupid cannot escape in Dreiser. The normal American novel, even in its most serious forms, takes colour from the national cocksureness and superficiality. It runs monotonously to ready explanations, a somewhat infantile smugness and hopefulness, a habit of reducing the unknowable to terms of the not worth knowing. What it cannot explain away with ready formulae, as in the later Winston Churchill, it snickers over as scarcely worth explaining at all, as in the later Howells. Such a brave and tragic book as "Ethan Frome" is so rare as to be almost singular, even with Mrs. Wharton. There is, I daresay, not much market for that sort of thing. In the arts, as in the concerns of everyday, the American seeks escape from the insoluble by pretending that it is solved. A comfortable phrase is what he craves beyond all things—and comfortable phrases are surely not to be sought in Dreiser's stock.

I have heard argument that he is a follower of Frank Norris, and two or three facts lend it a specious probability. "McTeague" was printed in 1899; "Sister Carrie" a year later. Moreover, Norris was the first to see the merit of the latter book, and he fought a gallant fight, as literary advisor to Doubleday, Page & Co., against its suppression after it was in type. But this theory runs aground upon two circumstances, the first being that Dreiser did not actually read "McTeague," nor, indeed, grow aware of Norris, until after "Sister Carrie" was completed, and the other being that his development, once he began to write other books, was along paths far distant from those pursued by Norris himself. Dreiser, in truth, was a bigger man than Norris from the start; it is to the latter's unending honour that he recognized the fact instanter, and yet did all he could to help his rival. It is imaginable, of course, that Norris, living fifteen years longer, might have overtaken Dreiser, and even surpassed him; one finds an arrow pointing that way in "Vandover and the Brute" (not printed until 1914). But it swings sharply around in "The Epic of the Wheat." In the second volume of that incomplete trilogy, "The Pit," there is an obvious concession to the popular taste in romance; the thing is so frankly written down, indeed, that a play has been made of it, and Broadway has applauded it. And in "The Octopus," despite some excellent writing, there is a descent to a mysticism so fantastic and preposterous that it quickly passes beyond serious consideration. Norris, in his day, swung even lower—for example, in "A Man's Woman" and in some of his short stories. He was a pioneer, perhaps only half sure of the way he wanted to go, and the evil lures of popular success lay all about him. It is no wonder that he sometimes seemed to lose his direction.

Emile Zola is another literary father whose paternity grows dubious on examination. I once printed an article exposing what seemed to me to be a Zolaesque attitude of mind, and even some trace of the actual Zola manner, in "Jennie Gerhardt"; there came from Dreiser the news that he had never read a line of Zola, and knew nothing about his novels. Not a complete answer, of course; the influence might have been exerted at second hand. But through whom? I confess that I am unable to name a likely medium. The effects of Zola upon Anglo-Saxon fiction have been almost *nil*;

his only avowed disciple, George Moore, has long since recanted and re-
formed; he has scarcely rippled the prevailing romanticism. . . . Thomas
Hardy? Here, I daresay, we strike a better scent. There are many obvious
likenesses between "Tess of the D'Ubervilles" and "Jennie Gerhardt" and
again between "Jude the Obscure" and "Sister Carrie." All four stories
deal penetratingly and poignantly with the essential tragedy of women; all
disdain the petty, specious explanations of popular fiction; in each one
finds a poetical and melancholy beauty. Moreover, Dreiser himself con-
fesses to an enchanted discovery of Hardy in 1896, three years before
"Sister Carrie" was begun. But it is easy to push such a fact too hard, and
to search for likenesses and parallels that are really not there. The truth is
that Dreiser's points of contact with Hardy might be easily matched by
many striking points of difference, and that the fundamental ideas in their
novels, despite a common sympathy, are anything but identical. Nor does
one apprehend any ponderable result of Dreiser's youthful enthusiasm for
Balzac, which antedated his discovery of Hardy by two years. He got from
both men a sense of the scope and dignity of the novel; they taught him
that a story might be a good one, and yet considerably more than a story;
they showed him the essential drama of the commonplace. But that they
had more influence in forming his point of view, or even in shaping his
technique, than any one of half a dozen other gods of those young days—
this I scarcely find. In the structure of his novels, and in their manner of
approach to life no less, they call up the work of Dostoyevsky and Turgenev
far more than the work of either of these men—but of all the Russians
save Tolstoi (as of Flaubert) Dreiser himself tells us that he was ignorant
until ten years after "Sister Carrie." In his days of preparation, indeed, his
reading was so copious and disorderly that antagonistic influences must
have well-nigh neutralized one another, and so left the curious youngster
to work out his own method and his own philosophy. Stevenson went
down with Balzac, Poe with Hardy, Dumas *fils* with Tolstoi. There were
even months of delight in Sienkiewicz, Lew Wallace and E. P. Roe! The
whole repertory of the pedagogues had been fought through in school and
college: Dickens, Thackeray, Hawthorne, Washington Irving, Kingsley,
Scott. Only Irving and Hawthorne seem to have made deep impressions.
"I used to lie under a tree," says Dreiser, "and read 'Twice Told Tales'
by the hour. I thought 'The Alhambra' was a perfect creation, and I still
have a lingering affection for it." Add Bret Harte, George Ebers, William
Dean Howells, Oliver Wendell Holmes, and you have a literary stew indeed! . . . But for all its bubbling I see a far more potent influence in the
chance discovery of Spencer and Huxley at twenty-three—the year of
choosing! Who, indeed, will ever measure the effect of those two giants
upon the young men of that era—Spencer with his inordinate meticu-

lousness, his relentless pursuit of facts, his overpowering syllogisms, and Huxley with his devastating agnosticism, his insatiable questionings of the old axioms, above all, his brilliant style? Huxley, it would appear, has been condemned to the scientific hulks, along with bores innumerable and unspeakable; one looks in vain for any appreciation of him in treatises on beautiful letters.[2] And yet the man was a superb artist in works, a master-writer even more than a master-biologist, one of the few truly great stylists that England has produced since the time of Anne. One can easily imagine the effect of two such vigorous and intriguing minds upon a youth groping about for self-understanding and self-expression. They swept him clean, he tells us, of the lingering faith of his boyhood—a mediaeval, Rhenish Catholicism;—more, they filled him with a new and eager curiosity, an intense interest in the life that lay about him, a desire to seek out its hidden workings and underlying causes. A young man set afire by Huxley might perhaps make a very bad novelist, but it is a certainty that he could never make a sentimental and superficial one. There is no need to go further than this single moving adventure to find the genesis of Dreiser's disdain of the current platitudes, his sense of life as a complex biological phenomenon, only dimly comprehended, and his tenacious way of thinking things out, and of holding to what he finds good. Ah, that he had learned from Huxley, not only how to inquire, but also how to report! That he had picked up a talent for that dazzling style, so sweet to the ear, so damnably persuasive, so crystal-clear!

But the more one examines Dreiser, either as a writer or as theorist of man, the more his essential isolation becomes apparent. He got a habit of mind from Huxley, but he completely missed Huxley's habit of writing. He got a view of woman from Hardy, but he soon changed it out of all resemblance. He got a certain fine ambition and gusto out of Balzac, but all that was French and characteristic he left behind. So with Zola, Howells, Tolstoi and the rest. The tracing of likenesses quickly becomes rabbinism, almost cabalism. The differences are huge and sprout up in all directions. Nor do I see anything save a flaming up of colonial passion in the current efforts to fit him into a German frame, and make him an agent of Prussian frightfulness in letters. Such bosh one looks for in the *Nation* and the Boston *Transcript*, and there is where one actually finds it. Even the *New Republic* has stood clear of it; it is important only as material for that treatise upon the patrioteer and his bawling which remains to be written. The name of the man, true enough, is obviously Germanic, and he has told us himself, in "A Traveler at Forty," how he sought out and found the tombs of his ancestors in some little town of the Rhine country. There are more of these genealogical revelations in "A Hoosier Holiday," but they show a Rhenish strain that was already running thin in boyhood. No one, indeed, who reads a Dreiser novel can fail to see the gap separating the author from these half-forgotten forebears. He shows even less of Germanic influence than of English influence.

There is, as a matter of fact, little in modern German fiction that is intelligibly comparable to "Jennie Gerhardt" and "The Titan," either as a study of man or as a work of art. The naturalistic movement of the eighties was launched by men whose eyes were upon the theatre, and it is in that field that nine-tenths of its force has been spent.

In his manner, as opposed to his matter, he is more the Teuton, for he shows all of the racial patience and pertinacity and all of the racial lack of humour. Writing a novel is as solemn a business to him as trimming a beard is to a German barber. He blasts his way through his interminable stories by something not unlike main strength; his writing, one feels, often takes on the character of an actual siege operation, with tunnellings, drum fire, assaults in close order and hand-to-hand fighting. Once, seeking an analogy, I called him the Hindenburg of the novel. If it holds, then "The 'Genius'" is his Poland. The field of action bears the aspect, at the end, of a hostile province meticulously brought under the yoke, with every road and lane explored to its beginning, and every crossroads village laboriously taken, inventoried and policed. Here is the very negation of Gallic lightness and intuition, and of all forms of impressionism as well. Here is no series of illuminating flashes, but a gradual bathing of the whole scene with white light, so that every detail stands out.

And many of those details, of course, are trivial; even irritating. They do not help the picture; they muddle and obscure it; one wonders impatiently what their meaning is, and what the purpose may be of revealing them with such precise, portentous air. . . . Turn to page 703 of "The 'Genius.'" By the time one gets there, one has hewn and hacked one's way through 702 large pages of fine print—97 long chapters, more than 250,000 words. And yet, at this hurried and impatient point, with the *coda* already begun, Dreiser halts the whole narrative to explain the origin, nature and inner meaning of Christian Science, and to make us privy to a lot of chatty stuff about Mrs. Althea Jones, a professional healer, and to supply us with detailed plans and specifications of the apartment house in which she lives, works her tawdry miracles, and has her being. Here, in sober summary, are the particulars:

1. That the house is "of conventional design."
2. That there is "a spacious areaway" between its two wings.
3. That these wings are "of cream-coloured pressed brick."
4. That the entrance between them is "protected by a handsome wrought-iron door."

5. That to either side of this door is "an electric lamp support of handsome design."

6. That in each of these lamp supports there are "lovely cream-coloured globes, shedding a soft lustre."

7. That inside is "the usual lobby."

8. That in the lobby is "the usual elevator."

9. That in the elevator is the usual "uniformed negro elevator man."

10. That this negro elevator man (name not given) is "indifferent and impertinent."

11. That a telephone switchboard is also in the lobby.

12. That the building is seven stories in height.

In "The Financier" there is the same exasperating rolling up of irrelevant facts. The court proceedings in the trial of Cowperwood are given with all the exactness of a parliamentary report in the London *Times*. The speeches of the opposing counsel are set down nearly in full, and with them the remarks of the judge, and after that the opinion of the Appellate Court on appeal, with the dissenting opinions as a sort of appendix. In "Sister Carrie" the thing is less savagely carried out, but that is not Dreiser's fault, for the manuscript was revised by some anonymous hand, and the printed version is but little more than half the length of the original. In "The Titan" and "Jennie Gerhardt" no such brake upon exuberance is visible; both books are crammed with details that serve no purpose, and are as flat as ditch-water. Even in the two volumes of personal record, "A Traveler at Forty" and "A Hoosier Holiday," there is the same furious accumulation of trivialities. Consider the former. It is without structure, without selection, without reticence. One arises from it as from a great babbling, half drunken. On the one hand the author fills a long and gloomy chapter with the story of the Borgias, apparently under the impression that it is news, and on the other hand he enters into intimate and inconsequential confidences about all the persons he meets en route, sparing neither the innocent nor the obscure. The children of his English host at Bridgely Level strike him as fantastic little creatures, even as a bit uncanny—and he duly sets it down. He meets an Englishman on a French train who pleases him much, and the two become good friends and see Rome together, but the fellow's wife is "obstreperous" and "haughty in her manner" and so "loud-spoken in her opinions" that she is "really offensive"—and down it goes. He makes an impression on a Mlle. Marcelle in Paris, and she accompanies him from Monte Carlo to Ventimiglia, and there gives him a parting kiss and whispers, "*Avril-Fontainebleau*"—and lo, this sweet one is duly spread upon the minutes. He permits himself to be arrested by a fair privateer in Piccadilly, and goes with her to one of the dens of sin that suffragettes see in their nightmares, and cross-examines her at length regarding her ancestry, her professional ethics and ideals, and her earnings at her dismal craft—and into the book goes a full report of the proceedings. He is entertained by an eminent Dutch jurist in Amsterdam—and upon the pages of the chronicle it appears that the gentleman is "waxy" and "a little pedantic," and that he is probably the sort of "thin, delicate, well barbered" professor that Ibsen had in mind when he cast about for a husband for the daughter of General Gabler.

Such is the art of writing as Dreiser understands it and practises it—an endless piling up of minutiae, an almost ferocious tracking down of ions, electrons and molecules, an unshakable determination to tell it all. One is amazed by the mole-like diligence of the man, and no less by his exasperating disregard for the ease of his readers. A Dreiser novel, at least of the later canon, cannot be read as other novels are read—on a winter evening or summer afternoon, between meal and meal, travelling from New York to Boston. It demands the attention for almost a week, and uses up the faculties for a month. If, reading "The 'Genius,'" one were to become engrossed in the fabulous manner described in the publishers' advertisement, and so find oneself unable to put it down and go to bed before the end, one would get no sleep for three days and three nights.

Worse, there are no charms of style to mitigate the rigours of these vast steppes and pampas of narration. Joseph Joubert's saying that "words should stand out well from the paper" is quite incomprehensible to Dreiser; he never imitates Flaubert by writing for "*la respiration et l'oreille.*" There is no painful groping for the inevitable word, or for what Walter Pater called "the gipsy phrase"; the common, even the commonplace, coin of speech is good enough. On the first page of "Jennie Gerhardt" one encounters "frank, open countenance," "diffident manner," "helpless poor," "untutored mind," "honest necessity," and half a dozen other standbys of the second-rate newspaper reporter. In "Sister Carrie" one finds "high noon," "hurrying throng," "unassuming restaurant," "dainty slippers," "high-strung nature," and "cool, calculating world"—all on a few pages. Carrie's sister, Minnie Hanson, "gets" the supper. Hanson himself is "wrapped up" in his child. Carrie decides to enter Storm and King's office, "no matter what." In "The Titan" the word "trig" is worked to death; it takes on, toward the end, the character of a banal and preposterous refrain. In the other books one encounters mates for it—words made to do duty in as many senses as the American verb "to fix" or the journalistic "to secure."

I often wonder if Dreiser gets anything properly describable as pleasure out of this dogged accumulation of threadbare, undistinguished, uninspiring nouns, adjectives, verbs, adverbs, pronouns, participles and conjunctions. To the man with an ear for verbal delicacies—the man who searches painfully for the perfect word, and puts the way of saying a thing above the thing said—there is in writing the constant joy of sudden discovery, of happy accident. A phrase springs up full blown, sweet and caressing. But what joy can there be in rolling up sentences that have no more life and beauty in them, intrinsically, than so many election bulletins? Where is the thrill in the manufacture of such a paragraph as that in which Mrs. Althea Jones' sordid habitat is described with such inexorable particularity? Or in the laborious confection of such stuff as this, from Book I, Chapter IV, of "The 'Genius'"?:

> The city of Chicago—who shall portray it! This vast ruck of life that had sprung suddenly into existence upon the dank marshes of a lake shore!

Or this from the epilogue to "The Financier":

> There is a certain fish whose scientific name is *Mycteroperca Bonaci*, and whose common name is Black Grouper, which is of considerable value as an afterthought in this connection, and which deserves much to be better known. It is a healthy creature, growing quite regularly to a weight of two hundred and fifty pounds, and living a comfortable, lengthy existence because of its very remarkable ability to adapt itself to conditions. . . .

Or this from his pamphlet, "Life, Art and America";[3]

> Alas, Alas! for art in America. It has a hard stubby row to hoe.

But I offer no more examples. Every reader of the Dreiser novels must cherish astounding specimens—of awkward, platitudinous marginalia, of whole scenes spoiled by bad writing, of phrases as brackish as so many lumps of sodium hyposulphite. Here and there, as in parts of "The Titan" and again in parts of "A Hoosier Holiday," an evil conscience seems to haunt him and he gives hard striving to his manner, and more than once there emerges something that is almost graceful. But a backsliding always follows this phosphorescence of reform. "The 'Genius,'" coming after "The Titan," marks the high tide of his bad writing. There are passages in it so clumsy, so inept, so irritating that they seem almost unbelievable; nothing worse is to be found in the newspapers. Nor is there any compensatory deftness in structure, or solidity of design, to make up for this carelessness in detail. The well-made novel, of course, can be as hollow as the well-made play of Scribe—but let us at least have a beginning, a middle and an end! Such a story as "The 'Genius'" is as gross and shapeless as Brünnhilde. It billows and bulges out like a cloud of smoke, and its internal organization is almost as vague. There are episodes that, with a few chapters added, would make very respectable novels. There are chapters that need but a touch or two to be excellent short stories. The thing rambles, staggers, trips, heaves, pitches, struggles, totters, wavers, halts, turns aside, trembles on the edge of collapse. More than once it seems to be foundering, both in the equine and in the maritime senses. The tale has been heard of a tree so tall that it took two men to see to the top of it. Here is a novel so brobdingnagian that a single reader can scarcely read his way through it. . . .

Of the general ideas which lie at the bottom of all of Dreiser's work it is impossible to be in ignorance, for he has exposed them at length in "A Hoosier Holiday" and summarized them in "Life, Art and America." In their main outlines they are not unlike the fundamental assumptions of Joseph Conrad. Both novelists see human existence as a seeking without a finding; both reject the prevailing interpretations of its meaning and mechanism; both take refuge in "I do not know." Put "A Hoosier Holiday" beside Conrad's "A Personal Record," and you will come upon parallels from end to end. Or better still, put it beside Hugh Walpole's "Joseph Conrad," in which the Conradean metaphysic is condensed from the novels even better than Conrad has done it himself: at once you will see how the two novelists, each a worker in the elemental emotions, each a rebel against the current assurance and superficiality, each an alien to his place and time, touch each other in a hundred ways.

"Conrad," says Walpole, "is of the firm and resolute conviction that life is too strong, too clever and too remorseless for the sons of men." And then, in amplification: "It is as though, from some high window, looking down, he were able to watch some shore, from whose security men were forever launching little cockleshell boats upon a limitless and angry sea. . . . From his height he can follow their fortunes, their brave struggles, their fortitude to the very end. He admires their courage, the simplicity of their faith, but his irony springs from his knowledge of the inevitable end. . . ."

Substitute the name of Dreiser for that of Conrad, and you will have to change scarcely a word. Perhaps one, to wit, "clever." I suspect that Dreiser, writing so of his own creed, would be tempted to make it "stupid," or, at all events, "unintelligible." The struggle of man, as he sees it, is more than impotent; it is gratuitous and purposeless. There is, to his eye, no grand ingenuity, no skillful adaptation of means to end, no moral (or even dramatic) plan in the order of the universe. He can get out of it only a sense of profound and inexplicable *dis*order. The waves which batter the cockleshells change their direction at every instant. Their navigation is a vast adventure, but intolerably fortuitous and inept—a voyage without chart, compass, sun or stars. . . .

So at bottom. But to look into the blackness steadily, of course, is almost beyond the endurance of man. In the very moment that its impenetrability is grasped the imagination begins attacking it with pale beams of false light. All religions, I daresay, are thus projected from the questioning soul of man, and not only all religions, but also all great agnosticisms. Nietzsche, shrinking from the horror of that abyss of negation, revived the Pythagorean concept of *der ewigen Wiederkunft*—a vain and blood-curdling sort of comfort. To it, after a while, he added explanations almost Christian—a whole repertoire of whys and wherefores, aims and goals, aspirations and significances. The late Mark Twain, in an unpublished work, toyed with an equally daring idea; that men are to some unimaginably vast and incomprehensible Being what the unicellular organisms of his body are to man, and so on *ad infinitum*. Dreiser occasionally inclines to much the same hypothesis; he likens the endless reactions going on in the world we know, the myriadal creation, collision and destruction of entities, to the slow accumulation and organization of cells *in utero*. He would make us specks in the insentient embryo of some gigantic Presence whose form is still unimaginable and whose birth must wait for Eons and Eons. Again, he turns to something not easily distinguishable from philosophical idealism, whether out of Berkeley or Fichte it is hard to make out—that is, he would interpret the whole phenomenon of life as no more than an appearance, a nightmare of some unseen sleeper or of men themselves, an "uncanny blur of nothingness"—in Euripides' phrase, "a song sung by an idiot, dancing down the wind." Yet again, he talks vaguely of the intricate polyphony of a cosmic orchestra, cacophonous to our dull ears. Finally, he puts the observed into the ordered, reading a purpose in the displayed event: "life was intended to sting and hurt. . . ." But these are only gropings, and not to be read too critically. From speculations and explanations he always returns, Conrad-like, to the bald fact: to "the spectacle and stress of life." All he can make out clearly is "a vast compulsion which has nothing to do with the individual desires or tastes or impulses of individuals." That compulsion springs "from the settling processes of forces which we do not in the least understand, over which we have no control, and in whose grip we are as grains of dust or sand, blown hither and thither, for what purpose we cannot even suspect."[4] Man is not only doomed to defeat, but denied any glimpse or understanding of his antagonist. Here we come upon an agnosticism that has almost got beyond curiosity. What good would it do us, asks Dreiser, to know? In our ignorance and helplessness, we may at least get a slave's consolation out of cursing the unknown gods. Suppose we saw them striving blindly, too, and pitied them? . . .

But, as I say, this scepticism is often tempered by guesses at a possibly hidden truth, and the confession that this truth may exist reveals the practical unworkableness of the unconditioned system, at least for Dreiser. Conrad is far more resolute, and it is easy to see why. He is, by birth and training, an aristocrat. He has the gift of emotional detachment. The lures of facile doctrine do not move him. In his irony there is a disdain which plays about even the ironist himself. Dreiser is a product of far different forces and traditions, and is capable of no such escapement. Struggle as he may, and fume and protest as he may, he can no more shake off the chains of his intellectual and cultural heritage than he can change the shape of his nose. What that heritage is you may find out in detail by reading "A Hoosier Holiday," or in summary by glancing at the first few pages of "Life, Art and America." Briefly described, it is the burden of a believing mind, a moral attitude, a lingering superstition. One-half of the man's brain, so to speak, wars with the other half. He is intelligent, he is thoughtful, he is a sound artist—but there come moments when a dead hand falls upon him, and he is once more the Indiana peasant, snuffing absurdly over imbecile sentimentalities, giving a grave ear to quackeries, snorting and eye-rolling with the best of them. One generation spans too short a time to free the soul of man. Nietzsche, to the end of his days, remained a Prussian pastor's son, and hence two-thirds a Puritan; he erected his war upon holiness, toward the end, into a sort of holy war. Kipling, the grandson of a Methodist preacher, reveals the tin-pot evangelist with increasing clarity as youth and its ribaldries pass away and he falls back upon his fundamentals. And that other English novelist who springs from the servants' hall—let us not be surprised or blame him if he sometimes writes like a bounder.

The truth about Dreiser is that he is still in the transition stage between Christian Endeavour and civilization, between Warsaw, Indiana and the Socratic grove, between being a good American and being a free man, and so he sometimes vacillates perilously between a moral sentimentalism and a somewhat extravagant revolt. "The 'Genius,'" on the one hand, is almost a tract for rectitude, a Warning to the Young; its motto might be *Scheut die Dirnen!* And on the other hand, it is full of a laborious truculence that can only be explained by imagining the author as heroically determined to prove that he is a plain-spoken fellow and his own man, let the chips fall where they may. So, in spots, in "The Financier" and "The Titan," both of them far better books. There is an almost moral frenzy to expose and riddle what passes for morality among the stupid. The isolation of irony is never reached; the man is still evangelical; his ideas are still novelties to him; he is as solemnly absurd in some of his floutings of the Code Américain as he is in his respect for Bouguereau, or in his flirtings with the New Thought, or in his naif belief in the importance of novel-writing. Somewhere or other I have called all this the Greenwich

Village complex. It is not genuine artists, serving beauty reverently and proudly, who herd in those cockroached cellars and bawl for art; it is a mob of half-educated yokels and cockneys to whom the very idea of art is still novel, and intoxicating—and more than a little bawdy.

Not that Dreiser actually belongs to this ragamuffin company. Far from it, indeed. There is in him, hidden deep-down, a great instinctive artist, and hence the makings of an aristocrat. In his muddled way, held back by the manacles of his race and time, and his steps made uncertain by a guiding theory which too often eludes his own comprehension, he yet manages to produce works of art of unquestionable beauty and authority, and to interpret life in a manner that is poignant and illuminating. There is vastly more intuition in him than intellectualism; his talent is essentially feminine, as Conrad's is masculine; his ideas always seem to be deduced from his feelings. The view of life that got into "Sister Carrie," his first book, was not the product of a conscious thinking out of Carrie's problems. It simply got itself there by the force of the artistic passion behind it; its coherent statement had to wait for other and more reflective days. The thing began as a vision, not as a syllogism. Here the name of Franz Schubert inevitably comes up. Schubert was an ignoramus, even in music; he knew less about polyphony, which is the mother of harmony, which is the mother of music, than the average conservatory professor. But nevertheless he had such a vast instinctive sensitiveness to musical values, such a profound and accurate feeling for beauty in tone, that he not only arrived at the truth in tonal relations, but even went beyond what, in his day, was known to be the truth, and so led an advance. Likewise, Giorgione de Castelfranco and Masaccio come to mind: painters of the first rank, but untutored, unsophisticated, uncouth. Dreiser, within his limits, belongs to this sabot-shod company of the elect. One thinks of Conrad, not as artist first, but as savant. There is something of the icy aloofness of the laboratory in him, even when the images he conjures up pulsate with the very glow of life. He is almost as self-conscious as the Beethoven of the last quartets. In Dreiser the thing is more intimate, more disorderly, more a matter of pure feeling. He gets his effects, one might almost say, not by designing them, but by living them.

But whatever the process, the power of the image evoked is not to be gainsaid. It is not only brilliant on the surface, but mysterious and appealing in its depths. One swiftly forgets his intolerable writing, his mirthless, sedulous, repellent manner, in the face of the Athenian tragedy he instils into his seduced and soulsick servant girls, his barbaric pirates of finances, his conquered and hamstrung supermen, his wives who sit and wait. He has, like Conrad, a sure talent for depicting the spirit in disintegration. Old Gerhardt, in "Jennie Gerhardt," is alone worth all the *dramatis per-*

sonae of popular American fiction since the days of "Rob o' the Bowl"; Howells could no more have created him, in his Rodinesque impudence of outline, that he could have created Tartuffe or Gargantua. Such a novel as "Sister Carrie" stands quite outside the brief traffic of the customary stage. It leaves behind it an unescapable impression of bigness, of epic sweep and dignity. It is not a mere story, not a novel in the customary American meaning of the word; it is at once a psalm of life and a criticism of life—and that criticism loses nothing by the fact that its burden is despair. Here, precisely, is the point of Dreiser's departure from his fellows. He puts into his novels a touch of the eternal *Weltschmerz*. They get below the drama that is of the moment and reveal the greater drama that is without end. They arouse those deep and lasting emotions which grow out of the recognition of elemental and universal tragedy. His aim is not merely to tell a tale; his aim is to show the vast ebb and flow of forces which sway and condition human destiny. One cannot imagine him consenting to Conan Doyle's statement of the purpose of fiction, quoted with characteristic approval by the New York *Times*: "to amuse mankind, to help the sick and the dull and the weary." Nor is his purpose to instruct; if he is a pedagogue it is only incidentally and as a weakness. The thing he seeks to do is to stir, to awaken, to move. One does not arise from such a book as "Sister Carrie" with a smirk of satisfaction; one leaves it infinitely touched.

Dreiser, like Mark Twain and Emerson before him, has been far more hospitably greeted in his first stage, now drawing to a close, in England than in his own country. The cause of this, I daresay, lies partly in the fact that "Sister Carrie" was in general circulation over there during the seven years that it remained suppressed on this side. It was during these years that such men as Arnold Bennett, Theodore Watts-Dunton, Frank Harris and H. G. Wells, and such critical journals as the *Spectator*, the *Saturday Review* and the *Athenaeum* became aware of him, and so laid the foundations of a sound appreciation of his subsequent work. Since the beginning of the war, certain English newspapers have echoed the alarmed American discovery that he is a literary agent of the Wilhelmstrasse, but it is to the honour of the English that this imbecility has got no countenance from reputable authority and has not injured his position.

At home, as I have shown, he is less fortunate. When criticism is not merely an absurd effort to chase him out of the court because his ideas are not orthodox, as the Victorians tried to chase out Darwin and Swinburne, and their predecessors pursued Shelley and Byron, it is too often designed to identify him with some branch or other of "radical" poppycock, and so credit him with purposes he has never imagined. Thus Chautauqua pulls and Greenwich Village pushes. In the middle ground there proceeds the pedantic effort to dispose of him by labelling him. One faction maintains that he is a realist; another calls him a naturalist; a third argues that he is really a disguised romanticist. This debate is all sound and fury, signifying nothing, but out of it has come a valuation by Lawrence Gilman[5] which perhaps strikes very close to the truth. He is, says Mr. Gilman, "a sentimental mystic who employs the mimetic gestures of the realist." This judgment is apt in particular and sound in general. No such thing as a pure method is possible in the novel. Plain realism, as in Gorky's "Nachtasyl" and the war stories of Ambrose Bierce, simply wearies us by its vacuity; plain romance, if we ever get beyond our nonage, makes us laugh. It is their artistic combination, as in life itself, that fetches us—the subtle projection of the concrete muddle that is living against the ideal orderliness that we reach out for—the eternal war of experience and aspiration—the contrast between the world as it is and the world as it might be or ought to be. Dreiser describes the thing that he sees, laboriously and relentlessly, but he never forgets the dream that is behind it. "He gives you," continues Mr. Gilman, "a sense of actuality; but he gives you more than that: out of the vast welter and surge, the plethoric irrelevancies . . . emerges a sense of the infinite sadness and mystery of human life. . . ."[6]

"To see truly," said Renan, "is to see dimly." Dimness or mystery, call it what you will: it is in all these overgrown and formless, but profoundly moving books. Just what do they mean? Just what is Dreiser driving at? That such questions should be asked is only a proof of the straits to which pedagogy has brought criticism. The answer is simple: he is driving at nothing, he is merely trying to represent what he sees and feels. His moving impulse is no flabby yearning to teach, to expound, to make simple; it is that "obscure inner necessity" of which Conrad tells us, the irresistible creative passion of a genuine artist, standing spell-bound before the impenetrable enigma that is life, enamoured by the strange beauty that plays over its sordidness, challenged to a wondering and half-terrified sort of representation of what passes understanding. And *jenseits von Gut und Böse*. "For myself," says Dreiser, "I do not know what truth is, what beauty is, what love is, what hope is. I do not believe anyone absolutely and I do not doubt anyone absolutely. I think people are both evil and well-intentioned." The hatching of the Dreiser bugaboo is here; it is the flat rejection of the rubber-stamp formulae that outrages petty minds; not being "good," he must be "evil"—as William Blake said of Milton, a true poet is always "of the devil's party." But in that very groping toward a light but dimly seen there is a measure, it seems to me, of Dreiser's rank and consideration as an artist. "Now comes the public," says Hermann Bahr, "and demands that we explain what the poet is trying to say. The answer is this: If we knew exactly he would not be a poet. . . ."

Notes

1. Fuller's disappearance is one of the strangest phenomena of American letters. I was astonished some time ago to discover that he was still alive. Back in 1899 he was already so far forgotten that William Archer mistook his name, calling him Henry Y. Puller. *Vide* Archer's pamphlet, The American Language; New York, 1899.
2. For example, in The Cambridge History of English Literature which runs to fourteen large volumes and a total of nearly 10,000 pages, Huxley receives but a page and a quarter of notice, and his remarkable mastery of English is barely mentioned in passing. His two debates with Gladstone, in which he did some of the best writing of the century, are not noticed at all.
3. New York, 1917; repr. in *The Seven Arts*, February 1917.
4. Life, Art and America, 5.
5. The *North American Review*, February 1916.
6. Another competent valuation, by Randolph Bourne, is in *The Dial*, 14 June 1917.

H. L. MENCKEN

"H. L. MENCKEN TELLS OF DREISER'S NEW BOOK"

New York Sun, *13 April 1919, 4.*

From the highest swing of Theodore Dreiser to his lowest stoop there is a distance so great that it seems almost fabulous—the distance, to wit, which separates all that is rarest and soundest in our literature from all that is shoddiest and most trivial. Such a book as *Jennie Gerhardt* is so brilliantly vivid, so profoundly moving, so spacious and dignified, that one turns from it with a sort of dismay to such a book as *The Genius*, with its tedious pedantry, its interminable inconsequence, its childish and irritating flatulence. It is as if Joseph Conrad, quitting a *Youth* or a *Heart of Darkness*, should proceed to a sentimental serial for shopgirls and fat women; it is almost as if Brahms should rise up out of hell to write patriotic ballads for vaudeville.

The phenomenon, unluckily, is not unmatched in our beautiful letters. The late Mark Twain, in the intervals of challenging Swift and Rabelais (and, somewhat behind the door, Nietzsche), often leaned down to challenge Artemus Ward, Charles H. Hoyt and M. Quad; it was his own incurable weakness, indeed, and not the mere imbecility of press agents, that bred the astounding doctrine that Irvin Cobb is his heir and assign. The causes of this disconcerting wabbling, though they are instructive, I need not go into here. I have touched upon them elsewhere, and shall expose them in detail in a forthcoming work. More important to the present purpose is one of the effects. It is this: That one approaches a new book by Dreiser as one always approached a new book by Mark, with a certain uncomfortable uncertainty—with one's aesthetic heart in one's mouth. It may be a new *Sister Carrie* or *Jennie Gerhardt* or *Titan* or *Hoosier Holiday*, and so praise God!—but on the other hand, it may be a new *Traveler at Forty* or *Hand of the Potter* or *Genius*, and so a thousand damns! Well, here is *Twelve Men*, just off the press. To which of these categories does it belong? Let all cognoscenti be of cheer! Not to the second, surely! But to the first? Almost I am tempted to say clearly to the first. The high swing is undoubtedly there, and though there are also occasional dips to much lower levels the general effect is that of Dreiser at his most penetrating and persuasive. In more than one way he has done nothing better since *The Titan*. It shows, with a few unimportant breaks, a deliberate return to his first manner—the manner of pure representation, of searching understanding, of unfailing gusto and contagious wonderment. There is no banal philosophizing. There is no torturing of flabby theory. There is, above all, no burden of ethical purpose, no laboring of a duty to be performed. Instead there are simply a dozen sketches of character—rotund, brilliantly colored, absolutely alive. The thing is done capitally, and, at its top points, superbly.

Most of these dozen men are real—perhaps all. The author's brother Paul—the famous Paul Dresser, author of *On the Banks of the Wabash* and *Just Tell Them That You Saw Me*—appears in his proper person. Others—for example, Muldoon, the trainer; Harris Merton Lyon and Dreiser's father-in-law—are easily recognized. But this actual reality has little if anything to do with the reality they show upon the printed page. That reality is due altogether to the extraordinary skill of the man presenting them. What he produces is not merely an objective likeness; it is a searching and at times almost shameless inner genuineness. He gets into them; he understands and interprets them; he turns them inside out. And always in a way that somehow seems casual—always with a guileless and offhand air. Not once is there any creaking of literary blocks and tackles. Not once is there a formal vivisection. It is ever a picture he presents, not a diagram.

And what a gaudy and diverting picture it often is! Consider, for instance, the chapter devoted to Dresser-Dreiser, the song writing, tear squeezing brother—the Indiana Rouget de Lisle and Francis Scott Key. Intrinsically, he was an intensely interesting man, huge in body and yet ready to weep like a flapper, a fellow of remarkable talents and yet as devoid of elementary taste as a green grocer or a Congressman, a great success and yet a pathetic failure. But even more interesting than the man himself was the world he moved in and the culture he represented—the world and culture of the old Broadway, of vaudeville theatres, of the spangled demi-monde, of facile friendships, maudlin sentiments, gross revels, shady enterprises, stupid and hoggish folk. In such scenes he was a man of mark. He was the peer and intimate of other men of mark. He drank, drabbed and whooped 'er up with the best of them. But all the while he was something far finer than the others—a man of feeling, a dreamer of grotesque dreams, almost a poet. It was the contrast that made him salient and memorable, and it is the deft and poignant evocation of that contrast that makes his brother's portrait of him so brilliant and so excellent.

Muldoon is done almost as well. He remains at the end a sort of mystery, a man essentially inexplicable, but it is a mystery mellowed and humanized—one recognizes him and takes joy in him without precisely understanding him. So, again, with the forlorn, preposterous evangelist of *A Doer of the Word*—an astonishing creature indeed, a Christian actually devoted to the practice of Christianity, but somehow made credible. So, finally, with Lyon, with the queer Admirable Crichton of the sketch called *Peter* and with the venerable White, the author's father-in-law. In each of these men there was something fantastic. Each was a neglected alien in a nation of the undistinguished. It is Dreiser's feat that he has displayed that oddity vividly without the slightest touch of caricature—that he somehow convinces us of their general humanness, and gets into his portrait of each something of the universal human tragedy.

In brief, this is a book of extraordinary qualities—novel in plan, sound in structure, and, barring a few smears of feebleness, highly adroit in execution. As I have said, it goes back to the manner of *Sister Carrie* and *Jennie Gerhardt*—a variety of representation that has room for the profoundest feeling, but is yet rather aloof and unimpassioned. It projects human existence as the greatest of spectacles, thrilling, harrowing, sometimes downright appalling, but never hortatory, never a moral tale. The trouble with Dreiser in, say, *The Genius*, was that this manner had slipped away from him—that moral pressure had forced him, on the defensive, into a posture not unlike that of the pulpit. *The Genius* presented life less as an engrossing and inexplicable spectacle than as a somewhat mawkish document against comstockery and the Methodist revelation of God. To that extent it wabbled and was flabby. To that extent Dreiser made a mess of it.

But in *Twelve Men* he has his old tools in hand and is back at the trade he knows so well. His hacking is still often crude. He has his old weakness for phrases that outrage the sensitive ear like successive fifths. He must wallow, anon, in his banalities. He must give the English language a clout or two over the head. But the work that finally emerges from his inept striving is work that bears every mark of a first rate artist, save only that of style. It is solid and soundly organized. It has a sort of rough grace. It conveys its idea massively and certainly. It is a good job.

One wonders what the campus pump critics will make of it. One wonders still more how long they will cling to the delusion that the way to get rid of an artist beyond their comprehension is to invent the hypothesis that he doesn't exist. The saddest business of our literary artists is to prove, over and over again, that the academic Schlegels and Brandes of the land are idiots. Poe did it. Whitman did it. Mark Twain did it. And now Dreiser is doing it again.

H. L. MENCKEN
"MORE NOTES FROM A DIARY"
Smart Set, *62(May 1920), 138–40.*

It is easy enough to understand the impulse which prompted Dreiser to write "*Hey Rub-a-Dub-Dub*," his new book, of essays and fulminations all compact. There come times in every sentient man's life when he must simply unload his ideas, or bust like a star-shell in the highroad. If he is at the end of the scale which touches the rising ladder of the *Simiidae* he becomes a Socialist on a soap-box or joins the Salvation Army; if he is literate and has a soul he writes a book. Hence the great, whirring, infernal machines which chew up the forests of Canada, now and then salting the dose with the leg or arm of a Canuck. Hence the huge ink industry, consuming five million tons of bone-black a year. Hence democracy, Bolshevism, the moral order of the world. Hence sorrow. Hence literature.

In every line of "Hey Rub-a-Dub-Dub" there is evidence of the author's antecedent agony. One pictures him sitting up all night in his sinister studio down in Tenth street, wrestling horribly with the insoluble, trying his darndest to penetrate the unknowable. One o'clock strikes, and the fire sputters. Ghosts stalk in the room, fanning the yellow candle-light with their abominable breath—the spooks of all the men who have died for ideas since the world began—Socrates, Savonarola, Bruno (not Guido, but Giordano), Ravaillac, Sir Roger Casement, John Alexander Dowie, Dr. Crippen. Two o'clock. What, then, is the truth about marriage? Is it, as Grover Cleveland said, a grand sweet song, or is it, as the gals in the Village say, a hideous mockery and masquerade, invented by Capitalism to enslave the soul of woman—a legalized *Schweinerei*, worse than politics, almost as bad as the moving-pictures? Three o'clock. Was Marx right or wrong, a seer or a mere nose-puller? Was his name, in fact, actually Marx, or was it Marcus? From what ghetto did he escape, and cherishing what grudge against mankind? Aha, the Huneker complex: *cherchez le Juif!* (I confess at once: my great-grandpa, Moritz, was rector of the Oheb Shalon *Schul* in Grodno). Three o'clock. . . .

Back to Pontius Pilate! *Quod est veritas?* Try to define it. Look into it. Break it into its component parts. What remains is a pale gray vapor, an impalpable emanation, the shadow of a shadow. Think of the brains that have gone to wreck struggling with the problem—cerebrums as large as cauliflowers, cerebellums as perfect as pomegranates. Think of the men jailed, clubbed, hanged, burned at the stake—not for embracing error, but for embracing the *wrong* error. Think of the innumerable caravan of Burlesons, Mitchell Palmers, Torquemadas, Cotton Mathers. . . . Four o'clock. The fire burns low in the grate. A gray fog without. Across the street two detectives rob a drunken man. Up at Tarrytown John D. Rockefeller snores in his damp Baptist bed, dreaming gaudily that he is young again and mashed on a girl named Marie. At Sing Sing forty head of Italians are waiting to be electrocuted. There is a memorial service for Charles Garvice in Westminster Abbey. The Comstocks raid the Elsie books. Ludendorff is elected Archbishop of Canterbury. A poor workinggirl, betrayed by Moe, the boss's son, drowns herself in the Aquarium. It is late, ah me: nearly four thirty. . . . Who the deuce, then, is God? What is in all this talk of a future life, infant damnation, the Ouija board, Mortal Mind? Dr. Jacques Loeb is the father of a dozen bull-frogs. Is the news biological or theological? What became of the Albigenses? Are they in heaven, in purgatory or in hell?. . . . Five o'clock. Boys cry the *Evening Journal*. Is it today's or tomorrow's? The question of transubstantiation remains. There is, too, neotranscendentalism. . . . In Munich they talk of *Expressionismus* . . . Poof! . . .

It is easy, as I say, to imagine a man beset by such reflections, and urged irresistibly to work them out on paper. Unluckily, the working out is not always as simple a business as it looks. Dreiser's first impulse as novelist, I daresay, was to do it in novels—to compose fictions full of ideas, saying something, teaching something, exposing something, destroying something. But the novelist also happened to be an artist, and at once the artist entered an effective caveat against that pollution. A work of art with ideas in it is as sorry a monster as a pretty girl full of Latin. The aim of a work of art is not to make one think painfully, but to make one feel beautifully. What is the idea in "Jennie Gerhardt?" Who knows but God? But in "Jennie Gerhardt" there is feeling—profound, tragic, exquisite. It is a thing of poignant and yet delicate emotions, like Brahms' Fourth symphony. It lies in a sort of intellectual fourth dimension. It leaves a memory that is vivid and somehow caressing, and wholly free from doubts, questionings, head-scratchings. . . . So Dreiser decided to make a serious book of it, a book of unalloyed ratiocination, a book in the manner of Herbert Spencer. The result is "Hey Rub-a-Dub-Dub"—solemn stuff, with never a leer of beauty in it—in fact, almost furious. Once or twice it grows a bit lyrical; once or twice it rises to the imaginatively grotesque. But in the main it is plain exposition—a book of speculation and protest. He calls it himself "a book of the mystery and terror and wonder of life." I suspect that he lifted this subtitle from an old review of H. L. M. If so, then welcome! From him I have got more than is to be described in words and more than I can ever pay.

But what of the thing itself? Is it good stuff? My feeling is that it isn't. More, my feeling is that Dreiser is no more fitted to do a book of speculation than Joseph Conrad, say, is fitted to do a college yell. His talents simply do not lie in that direction. He lacks the mental agility, the insinuating suavity, the necessary capacity for romanticising a syllogism. Ideas themselves are such sober things that a sober man had better let them alone. What they need, to become bearable to a human race that hates them and is afraid of them, is the artful juggling of a William James, the insurance-agent persuasiveness of an Henri Bergson, the boob-bumping talents of a Martin Luther—best of all, the brilliant, almost Rabelaisian humor of a Nietzsche. Nietzsche went out into the swamp further than any other explorer; he left such pallbearers of the spirit as Spencer, Comte, Descartes and even Kant all shivering on the shore. And yet he never got bogged, and he never lost the attention of his audience. What saved him was the plain fact that he always gave a superb show—as good, almost, as a hanging. He converted the problem of evil into a melodrama with nine villains; he made of epistemology a sort of intellectual bed-room farce; he amalgamated Christianity and the music of Offenbach. . . . Well, Dreiser is quite devoid of that gift. Skepticism, in his hands, is never charming; it is simply despairing. His criticism of God lacks ingenuity and audacity. Earnestly pursuing the true, he too often unearths the merely obvious, which is sometimes not true at all. One misses the jauntiness of the accomplished duellist; his manner is rather that of the honest householder repelling burglars with a table-leg. In brief, it is enormously serious and painstaking stuff, but seldom very interesting stuff, and never delightful stuff. The sorrows of the world become the sorrows of Dreiser himself, and then the sorrows of his reader. He remains, in the last analysis, the novelist rather than the philosopher. He is vastly less a Schopenhauer than a Werther.

But a book by Dreiser is a book by Dreiser, and so one reads it with curiosity if not with delectation.

H. L. MENCKEN
"ADVENTURES AMONG BOOKS"
Smart Set *70(March 1923), 143–44.*

The Dreiser book, a tome of more than 500 large pages, is the second volume of what is projected as a three-volume autobiography. It deals with the author's years as a newspaper reporter, and, despite his usual discursiveness and undistinguished English, it is a work full of fascination. Here we see the beginnings of the Dreiser novels and of the Dreiserian philosophy of resigned pessimism. That philosophy is not the fruit of a native sinfulness, as Prof. Dr. Sherman would have us believe; it is the fruit of an extensive and laborious observation of the human farce from a singularly favorable grandstand. While Dr. Sherman was an innocent child in Iowa, and familiar with blood only as it issued from the cut necks of domestic fowl, Dreiser was serving as a reporter at Bellevue Hospital and along the waterfront of New York. That service knocked all the ethical cocksureness of the prairie out of it, and put pity into him. He is today perhaps the only American novelist who shows any sign of being able to feel profoundly, and he is surely the only one who can arouse genuine feeling in his readers. There are plenty of others who far surpass him in technical facility, in humor and in ingenuity, but there is none who comes near him in the primary business of a novelist, which is to make the transaction depicted seem real, and important, and poignant. His poor drab, Jennie Gerhardt, is perhaps the most unattractive woman ever put into a novel as heroine. She is dull, helpless, and without imagination, and it is hard to think of her save as a frump. But Dreiser somehow makes a tragic figure of her before he finishes. In the sordid, commonplace story of her life there is a presentation of the universal misery of man. To do that is to accomplish a very rare and difficult business. The only other American novelist who seems likely ever to achieve it is Miss Cather.

Dreiser's career as a reporter was not distinguished, and the tale he has to tell is thus not very startling. He covered the usual assignments, met the usual public frauds, saw the usual horrors, diverted himself in his scant leisure with the usual carnalities of young reporters. I doubt that his newspaper writings, though they were regarded as masterpieces by the staff of the Pittsburgh *Dispatch*, had any actual merit as journalism. He is quite without the journalistic talent for superficial vividness; he must have room to manoeuvre. In "A Book About Myself" he gives himself this room, and the result, despite some windy excursions, is a volume that probably gives a better picture of the life of a young reporter than any that could be written by a better journalist.

H. L. MENCKEN
"DREISER IN 840 PAGES"
American Mercury 7*(March 1926)*, 379–81.

Whatever else this vasty double-header may reveal about its author, it at least shows brilliantly that he is wholly devoid of what may be called literary tact. A more artful and ingratiating fellow, facing the situation that confronted him, would have met it with a far less difficult book. It was ten years since he had published his last novel, and so all his old customers, it is reasonable to assume, were hungry for another—all his old customers and all his new customers. His publisher, after a long and gallant battle, had at last chased off the comstocks. Rivals, springing up at intervals, had all succumbed—or, what is the same thing, withdrawn from the Dreiser reservation. The Dreiser cult, once grown somewhat wobbly, was full of new strength and enthusiasm. The time was thus plainly at hand to make a ten strike. What was needed was a book full of all the sound and solid Dreiser merits, and agreeably free from the familiar Dreiser defects—a book carefully designed and smoothly written, with no puerile clichés in it and no maudlin moralizing—in brief, a book aimed deliberately at readers of a certain taste, and competent to estimate good workmanship. Well, how did Dreiser meet the challenge? He met it, characteristically, by throwing out the present shapeless and forbidding monster—a heaping cartload of raw materials for a novel, with rubbish of all sorts intermixed— a vast, sloppy, chaotic thing of 385,000 words—at least 250,000 of them unnecessary! Such is scientific salesmanship as Dreiser understands it! Such is his reply to a pleasant invitation to a party!

By this time, I suppose, you have heard what it is all about. The plot, in fact, is extremely simple. Clyde Griffiths, the son of a street preacher in Kansas City, revolts against the piety of his squalid home, and gets himself a job as bellboy in a gaudy hotel. There he acquires a taste for the luxuries affected by travelling Elks, and is presently a leader in shop-girl society. An automobile accident, for which he is not to blame, forces him to withdraw discreetly, and he proceeds to Chicago, where he goes to work in a club. One day his father's rich brother, a collar magnate from Lycurgus, N.Y., is put up there by a member, and Clyde resolves to cultivate him. The old boy, taking a shine to the youngster, invites him to Lycurgus, and gives him a job in the factory. There ensues the conflict that makes the story. Clyde has hopes, but very little ready cash; he is thus forced to seek most of his recreation in low life. But as a nephew to old Samuel Griffiths he is also taken up by the Lycurgus *haut ton*. The conflict naturally assumes the form of girls. Roberta Alden, a beautiful female operative in the factory, falls in love with him and yields herself to him. Almost simultaneously Sondra Finchley, an even more beautiful society girl, falls in love with him and promises to marry him. Clyde is ambitious and decides for Sondra. But at that precise moment Roberta tells him that their sin has found her out. His reply is to take her to a lonely lake and drown her. The crime being detected, he is arrested, put on trial, convicted, and electrocuted.

A simple tale. Hardly more, in fact, than a plot of a three page story in

True Confessions. But Dreiser rolls it out to such lengths that it becomes, in the end, a sort of sequence of serials. The whole first volume, of 431 pages of small type, brings us only to the lamentable event of Roberta's pregnancy. The home life of the Griffithses in Kansas City is described in detail. We make intimate acquaintance with the street preacher himself, a poor fanatic, always trusting in the God who has fooled him incessantly, and with his pathetic, drab wife, and with his daughter Esta, who runs away with a vaudeville actor and comes home with a baby. There ensues a leisurely and meticulous treatise upon the life of the bellboys in the rococo Green-Davidson Hotel—how they do their work, what they collect in tips, how they spend their evenings, what sort of girls they fancy. The automobile accident is done in the same spacious manner. Finally, we get to Lycurgus, and page after page is devoted to the operations of the Griffiths factory, and to the gay doings in Lycurgus society, and to the first faint stirrings, the passionate high tide, and the disagreeable ebb of Clyde's affair with Roberta. So much for Volume I: 200,000 words. In Volume II we have the murder, the arrest, the trial and the execution: 185,000 more.

Obviously, there is something wrong here. Somewhere or other, there must be whole chapters that could be spared. I find, in fact, many such chapters—literally dozens of them. They incommode the action, they swamp and conceal the principal personages, and they lead the author steadily into his weakness for banal moralizing and trite, meaningless words. In "The 'Genius'" it was *trig* that rode him; in "An American Tragedy" it is *chic*. Did *chic* go out in 1896? Then so much the better! It is the mark of an unterrified craftsman to use it now—more, to rub it in mercilessly. Is Freudism stale, even in Greenwich Village? Ahoy, then, let us heave in a couple of bargeloads of complexes—let us explain even judges and district attorneys in terms of suppressions! Is the "chemic" theory of sex somewhat flyblown? Then let us trot it out, and give it a polishing with the dish-rag! Is there such a thing as sound English, graceful English, charming and beautiful English? Then let us defy a world of scoundrels, half Methodist and half aesthete, with such sentences as this one:

The "death house" in this particular prison was one of those crass erections and maintenances of human insensibility and stupidity principally for which no one primarily was really responsible.

And such as this:

Quite everything of all this was being published in the papers each day.

What is one to say of such dreadful bilge? What is one to say of a novelist who, after a quarter of a century at his trade, still writes it? What one is to say, I feel and fear, had better be engraved on the head of a pin and thrown into the ocean: there is such a thing as critical *politesse*. Here I can only remark that sentences of the kind I have quoted please me very little. One of them to a page is enough to make me very unhappy. In "An American Tragedy"—or, at all events, in parts of it—they run to much more than that. Is Dreiser actually deaf to their dreadful cacophony? I can't believe it. He can write, on occasion, with great clarity, and even with a certain grace. I point, for example, to Chapter XII of Book III, and to the chapter following. There is here no idiotic "quite everything of all," and no piling up of infirm adverbs. There is, instead, straightforward and lucid writing, which is caressing in itself and gets the story along. But elsewhere! . . .

Thus the defects of this gargantuan book. They are the old defects of Dreiser, and he seems to be quite unable to get rid of them. They grow more marked, indeed, as he passes into middle life. His writing in "Jennie Gerhardt" was better than his writing in "The Genius" and so was his sense of form, his feeling for structure. But what of the more profound elements? What of his feeling for character, his capacity to imagine situations, his skill at reaching the emotions of the reader? I can only say that I see no falling off in this direction. "An American Tragedy," as a work of art, is a colossal botch, but as a human document it is searching and full of a solemn dignity, and at times it rises to the level of genuine tragedy. Especially the second volume. Once Roberta is killed and Clyde faces his fate, the thing begins to move, and thereafter it roars on, with ever increasing impetus, to the final terrific smash. What other American novelist could have done the trial as well as Dreiser has done it? His method, true enough, is the simple, bald one of the reporter—but of *what* a reporter! And who could have handled so magnificently the last scenes in the death-house? Here his very defects come to his aid. What we behold is the gradual, terrible, irresistible approach of doom—the slow slipping away of hopes. The thing somehow has the effort of a tolling of bells. It is clumsy. It lacks all grace. But it is tremendously moving.

In brief, the book improves as it nears its shocking climax—a humane fact, indeed, for the reader. The first volume heaves and pitches, and the second, until the actual murder, is full of psychologizing that usually fails to come off. But once the poor girl is in the water, there is a change, and thereafter "An American Tragedy" is Dreiser at his plodding, booming best. The means are often bad, but the effects are superb. One gets the same feeling of complete reality that came from "Sister Carrie," and especially from the last days of Hurstwood. The thing ceases to be a story, and becomes a harrowing reality. Dreiser, I suppose, regards himself as an adept at the Freudian psychology. He frequently uses its terms, and seems to take its fundamental doctrines very seriously. But he is actually a behaviorist of the most advanced wing. What interests him primarily is not what people think, but what they do. He is full of a sense of their helplessness. They are, to him, automata thrown hither and thither by fate—but suffering tragically under every buffet. Their thoughts are muddled and trivial—but they can feel. And Dreiser feels with them, and can make the reader feel with them. It takes skill of a kind that is surely not common. Good writing is far easier.

The Dreiserian ideology does not change. Such notions as he carried out of the experiences of his youth still abide with him at fifty-four. They take somewhat curious forms. The revolt of youth, as he sees it, is primarily a revolt against religious dogmas and forms. He is still engaged in delivering Young America from the imbecilities of a frozen Christianity. And the economic struggle, in his eye, has a bizarre symbol: the modern American hotel. Do you remember Carrie Meeber's first encounter with a hotel beefsteak in "Sister Carrie"? And Jennie Gerhardt's dumb wonder before the splendors of that hotel in which her mother scrubbed the grand staircase? There are hotels, too, and aplenty, in "The Titan" and "The 'Genius'"; toward the end of the latter there is a famous description, pages long, of the lobby of a New York apartment house, by the Waldorf-Astoria out of the Third avenue car-barn. It was a hotel that lured Jennie (like Carrie before her) to ruin, and it is a hotel that starts Clyde Griffiths on his swift journey to the chair. I suggest a more extensive examination of the matter, in the best Dreiser-Freud style. Let some ambitious young *Privat Dozent* tackle it.

So much for "An American Tragedy." Hire your pastor to read the first volume for you. But don't miss the second!

H. L. MENCKEN
"LADIES, MAINLY SAD"
American Mercury *19(February 1930), 254–55.*

"A Gallery of Women" is a companion to "Twelve Men," published in 1919. There are fifteen sketches, each dealing with some woman who impinged upon the author at some time in the past; if the collection is not quite as interesting as its forerunner, then that is probably because women themselves are considerably less interesting than men. Not one of them here is to be mentioned in the same breath with Dreiser's brother Paul, the shining hero of "Twelve Men," or with Muldoon the Iron Man, who plainly posed for the stupendous Culhane. Perhaps those who come closest to that high level are Regina C——, who succumbs to cynicism and morphine, and Bridget Mullanphy, almost a female Culhane. The rest are occasionally charming, but only too often their chief mark is a pathetic silliness. What ails most of them is love. They throw away everything for it, and when they can't get the genuine article they seem to be content with imitations. And if it is not love, real or bogus, that undoes them, then it is some vague dream that never takes rational form—puerile self-expression, of gratuitous self-sacrifice, of something else as shadowy and vain.

Dreiser draws them with a surety of hand that seldom falters. He is at his best in just such character sketches, and he has a special skill at getting under the skins of women. In all of his books, indeed the matter chiefly dealt with is female vagary, and to its elucidation he has brought an immense curiosity and no little shrewdness. As I have said, men are naturally more interesting, if only because they show a higher variability, but women remain more mysterious, and hence more romantic. Why should Regina C—— throw herself away as she does? Why should Esther Norn waste her devotion upon men who have no need of her, and set no value upon her? Why, indeed, should old Bridget Mullanphy stagger through life in shackles to her loafer of a husband and her abominable daughter? The common answer is that there is something noble about that sort of immolation, but Dreiser is too wise to make it. He simply sets forth the facts as he has seen them, and leaves the philosophizing to less conscientious sages. He sees into all these women, but he would probably be the last to claim that he really sees through them. They remain figures in the eternal charade, touching always but inscrutable to the last.

Dreiser's writing continues to be painful to those who seek a voluptuous delight in words. It is not that he writes mere bald journalese, as certain professors have alleged, but that he wallows naïvely in a curiously banal kind of preciosity. He is, indeed, full of pretty phrases and arch turns of thought, but they seldom come off. The effect, at its worst, is that of a hangman's wink. He has been more or less impressed, apparently, by the familiar charge that his books are too long—that his chief sin is garrulousness. At all events, he shows a plain awareness of it: at one place he pauses in his narrative to say, "But hold! Do not despair. I am getting on." The point here, however, is not well taken. He is not actually garrulous; he always says something apposite, even though it may be obvious. What ails him is simply an incapacity to let anything go. Every detail of the human comedy interests him so immensely that he is bound to get it down. This makes, at times, for hard reading, but it has probably also made Dreiser. The thing that distinguishes him from other novelists is simply his astounding fidelity of observation. He sees every flicker of the eye, every tremor of the mouth, every change of color, every trivial gesture, every awkwardness, every wart. It is the warts, remember, that make the difference between a photograph and a human being.

Most other American novelists of his generation have been going downhill of late, but Dreiser seems to be holding on pretty well. The youngsters coming up offer him nothing properly describable as serious competition. They all write better than he does, but they surely do not surpass him in the really essential business of their craft. As year chases year, such books as "Jennie Gerhardt" and "The Titan" take on the proportions of public monuments; they become parts of the permanent record of their time; there is a sombre dignity in them that will not down. The defects that are in them are defects that are common to all latter-day American fiction. They may be imperfect, but they remain the best we have.

H. L. MENCKEN
"FOOTPRINTS ON THE SANDS OF TIME"
American Mercury *23(July 1931), 383.*

. . . The writing in ["Dawn"] . . . is often dreadful, and various banal clichés (for example, "no less," "of sorts" and "if you please") are worked to death. Nevertheless, it would be idle to deny the fascination of the story. Dreiser commits every variety of literary atrocity, but all the while his narratives move and breathe. Here he shows that he can make of himself as vital and memorable a character as he made of Frank Cowperwood and Carrie Meeber. The period he covers runs from his earliest recollection as a child in Terre Haute, Ind., to his futile year at college. He is brutally frank; he rejects all the ordinary reticences; he is often lost in the dark mazes of his own garrulity. But in the end the record that he produces is seen to have the quality of a really impressive human document. The man himself is extraordinary, and his account of his youthful hopes and agonies is a piece of literature—as bespattered with defects as a farmboy with freckles, but still a piece of literature. One rejoices that it offers new glimpses of his heroic and tragic mother, already seen in "A Hoosier Holiday," and of his incomparable Brother Paul.

A PROTEST AGAINST THE SUPPRESSION OF THEODORE DREISER'S
"THE 'GENIUS'"

We, the undersigned, American writers observe with deep regret the efforts now being made to destroy the work of Theodore Dreiser. Some of us may differ from Mr. Dreiser in our aims and methods, and some of us may be out of sympathy with his point of view, but we believe that an attack by irresponsible and arbitrary persons upon the writings of an author of such manifest sincerity and such high accomplishments must inevitably do great damage to the freedom of letters in the United States, and bring down upon the American people the ridicule and contempt of other nations. The method of the attack, with its attempt to ferret out blasphemy and indecency where they are not, and to condemn a serious artist under a law aimed at common rogues, is unjust and absurd. We join in this public protest against the proceeding in the belief that the art of letters, as carried on by men of serious purpose and with the co-operation of reputable publishers, should be free from interference by persons who, by their own statement, judge all books by narrow and impossible standards; and we advocate such amendments of the existing laws as will prevent such persecutions in future:—

Preliminary List of Signers

Leonard D. Abbott
Franklin P. Adams
Samuel Hopkins Adams
George Ade
Zoë Aikins
Sherwood Anderson
Gertrude Atherton
Ralph Henry Barbour
David Belasco
Samuel G. Blythe
Van Wyck Brooks
Thompson Buchanan
Abraham Cahan
Bliss Carman
Willa Sibert Cather
Robert W. Chambers
Winston Churchill
Irvin S. Cobb
Sherwin Cody
George M. Cohan
Will Levington Comfort
Grace MacGowan Cooke
John O'Hara Cosgrave
Frances Gregg
Herbert Croly
Mabel Potter Daggett
Floyd Dell
Rheta Childe Dorr
Douglas Z. Doty

William Griffith
Francis Hackett
Philip Hale
Frank Harris
Alexander Harvey
James Hopper
Avery Hopwood
Carl Hovey
Louis How
Rupert Hughes
Herbert Hungerford
Fannie Hurst
Wallace Irwin
Thomas S. Jones, Jr.
Reginald Wright Kaufman
Charles Keeler
Edwin Lefevre
Richard Le Gallienne
Prof. William E. Leonard
Sinclair Lewis
Ludwig Lewisohn
Walter Lippman
Jack London
Amy Lowell
Alice MacGowan
Harold MacGrath
Charles Agnew MacLean
Jeannette Marks
Don Marquis

Harvey O'Higgins
James Oppenheim
Will Payne
R. W. Pence
Hugh Pendexter
Ernest Poole
Ezra Pound
John Cowper Powys
Nina Wilcox Putnam
William MacLeod Raine
Myra G. Reed
William Marion Reedy
Arthur B. Reeve
Eugene Manlove Rhodes
Mary Roberts Rinehart
Edgar Selwyn
Ida Vera Simonton
Upton Sinclair
Winchell Smith
John Spargo
George Sterling
Grant Stewart
Rose Pastor Stokes
Ida M. Tarbell
Booth Tarkington
Freeman Tilden
Charles Hanson Towne
Horace Traubel
Sara Teasdale

H. G. Dwight
Max Eastman
Arthur Davison Ficke
James Montgomery Flagg
Hortense Flexner
James Forbes
Henry B. Fuller
Garet Garrett
Susan Glaspell
Montagu Glass
Abbie Carter Goodloe
Ferris Greenslet

Edgar Lee Masters
Roi Cooper Megrue
Henry Louis Mencken
Samuel Merwin
George Middleton
Harriet Monroe
Gouverneur Morris
Montrose J. Moses
Ethel Watts Mumford
Gustavus Myers
George Jean Nathan
Meredith Nicholson

Andre Tridon
Henry Tyrrell
Alice Woods Ulman
Henry Kitchell Webster
Edward J. Wheeler
Marguerite O. B. Wilkinson
Jesse Lynch Williams
Harry Leon Wilson
Richardson Wright
Willard Huntington Wright

The following English writers have also protested against the suppression of "The 'Genius'":

Arnold Bennett
W. L. George

William J. Locke
E. Temple Thurston
Hugh Walpole

H. G. Wells
Louis Wilkinson

N.B.—The above preliminary list will be followed by other lists. Additional copies can be secured from the Secretary of the Theodore Dreiser Committee, care of John Lane Company, 120 West 32nd Street, New York City.

THE ORF'CER BOY

"He was a gran' bhoy!"—Mulvancy

Now 'e aren't got no whiskers
    An' 'e's only five foot 'igh
(All the same 'e is 'a orf'cer hof the Queen!)
    Oh, 'is voice is like a loidy's
    An' 'e's so polite an' shy!
(All the same 'e serves 'Er Majesty the Queen!)
    It is only 'bout a year ago 'e left 'is mother's knee,
    It is only 'bout a month ago 'e come acrost the sea,
    It is only 'bout a week that 'e 'as been a-leadin' me.
(That's the way 'e serves 'Er Majesty the Queen!)

'E is such a little chappie,
    Bein' only five foot 'igh,
That you'd wonder how 'is likes could serve the Queen;
You would think that when 'e 'eard the guns
    'E'd just set down an' cry—
A-forgettin' ev'rything about the Queen;
    But by all that's good an' holy, you'd be extraord'ny wrong.

'Cos 'e doesn't like no singin' 'arf as good 's the Gatlin's song.
An' 'e fights as though 'e'd been a-fightin' twenty times as long
As any other man that serves the Queen!
If you'd seen 'im when we got to where
    The Modder's deep an' wet,
You'd a-knowed 'e was a orf'cer hof the Queen!
There's a dozen of the enemy
    That ain't forgot 'im yet—
For 'e run 'is sword clean through 'em for the Queen!
    Oh, 'e aren't much on whiskers an' 'e aren't much on 'eight,
    An' a year or two ago 'e was a-learnin' for to write,
    But you bet your soldier's shillin' 'e's the devil in a fight—
An' 'e'd die to serve 'Er Majesty the Queen!

HENRY LOUIS MENCKEN
(in Ventures in Verse *[1903])*

A EULOGY FOR DREISER (1947)

At the request of Helen Dreiser, Mencken sent the following state-ment in February 1947. It was read, along with contributions by James T. Farrell and Edgar Lee Masters, at a commemorative ceremony for Dreiser at the Los Angeles Public Library on 7 March 1947.

While Dreiser lived all the literary snobs and popinjays of the country, including your present abject servant, devoted themselves to reminding him of his defects. He had, to be sure, a number of them. For one thing, he came into the world with an incurable antipathy to the *mot juste*; for another thing, he had an insatiable appetite for the obviously not true. But the fact remains that he was a great artist, and that no other American of his generation left so wide and handsome a mark upon the national letters. American writing, before and after his time, differed almost as much as biology before and after Darwin. He was a man of large origi-nality, of profound feeling, and of unshakable courage. All of us who write are better off because he lived, worked and hoped.

Dreiser, like Goethe, was more interesting than any of his books. He was typical, in more ways than one, of a whole generation of Americans— a generation writhing in an era of advancing chaos. There must have been some good blood hidden in him, but on the surface he was simply an im-migrant peasant bewildered by the lack of neat moral syllogisms in civi-lized existence. He renounced his ancestral religion at the end of his teens, but never managed to get rid of it. Throughout his life it welled up in him in the form of various fantastic superstitions—spiritualism, Fortism, medical quackery and so on—and in his last days it engulfed him in the form of Communism, a sort of reductio ad absurdum of the will to believe. If he had lived another ten years, maybe even another five years, he would have gone back to Holy Church—the path followed before him by many other such poor fish, for example, Heywood Broun. His last book was a full-length portrait of a true believer, and extremely sympathetic. Solon Barnes, like Dreiser himself, was flabbergasted by the apparent lack of common sense and common decency in the cosmos, but in the end he yielded himself gratefully to the God who had so sorely afflicted him.

H. L. MENCKEN

"THE LIFE OF AN ARTIST"

New Yorker, *17 April 1948*

Down to World War I, the late Theodore Dreiser, the novelist, lived a strictly bourgeois life in the horse latitudes of upper Broadway, a region then chiefly inhabited by white-collar workers who were slightly but not much above the rank of slaves. His modest quarters were in an apartment house with bumpy ornaments of terra cotta outside and a friendly smell of home cooking within. The somewhat grand entrance was flanked by a delicatessen to one side and an up-and-coming drugstore to the other. It was a place almost as remote to me, a chronic stranger in New York, as the Jersey Meadows, but I made the trip to it often, for Dreiser, in those days, was being strafed unmercifully by the Comstocks, and I was eager to give him some aid. Besides, I liked him very much and greatly enjoyed hearing him discourse in his ponderous, indignant way, suggesting both the sermons of a Lutheran pastor and the complaints of a stegosaurus with a broken leg.

His remarks, to be sure, sometimes set my teeth on edge, for I was a born earthworm and he had an itch for such transcendental arcana as spiritualism, crystal gazing, numerology, and the Freudian rumble-bumble, then a scandalous novelty in the world. Once, landing in his den on a rainy night, I found him nose to nose with an elderly female who undertook to penetrate the future by scanning the leaves in a teacup. She predicted in my presence that he was about to be railroaded to jail by the Comstocks, and added that he'd be lucky if he got off with less than five years in Sing Sing. Inasmuch as he was then sweating away at two books and eager to finish the manuscripts and collect advances, this threw him into a considerable dither, and it took me an hour to restore him to normalcy after I had shooed the sorceress out.

But in realms less unearthly we got on quite well. He believed, and argued with some heat, that the human race was the damndest collection of vermin in the sidereal universe, and against this I could think of nothing to say. If we differed on the point, it was only because he excepted all ruined farm girls and the majority of murderers, whereas my own bill of exceptions was confined to the classical composers, Joseph Conrad, and a bartender in Baltimore named Monahan. Dreiser believed that every politician alive, including especially the reformers, should be hanged forthwith, and I went along without cavil. The same for social workers, with stress on the so-called trained ones. The same for all persons having any sort of connection with Wall Street. The same for the rev. clergy of every known persuasion. The same for hundred-per-cent Americans. When it came to authors, we again differed slightly, for there were then, besides Conrad, half a dozen whom I admired more or less—as artists, if not as men. But Dreiser, in my hearing, never praised any save Frank Norris, who had whooped up Dreiser's own first novel, "Sister Carrie," and Harris Merton Lyon, a young short-story writer, now forgotten. He also had some respect for Balzac, but not much; I recall that he once declared that all Frenchmen were too ornery for so humane a mortuary tool as the guillotine. He read the Russians but denounced them unanimously as psychopaths of marked homosexual and homicidal tendencies. Dickens he consigned to the bilge deck of his private Gehenna, along with Howells, Henry James, and H. G. Wells. Even when it came to Arnold Bennett, who, on landing in New York, had told the gaping reporters that "Sister Carrie" was one of the greatest novels of all time, the most he would concede was that Bennett was probably tight or full of dope at the time, and hence not up to the customary viciousness of an Englishman.

What caused this highly orthodox citizen, almost between days, to throw off the shroud of correctness and precipitate himself into Greenwich Village is more than I can tell you, though I knew him well and pondered the question at length. The Village in that era had a very dubious reputation, and deserved it. Nine-tenths of the alleged writers and artists who infested it lived on women, chiefly from the small towns of the Middle West, and I never heard of one who produced anything worth a hoot. Whenever, in the pursuit of my duties as a literary critic, I denounced the whole population as fraudulent and nefarious, the elders of the community always threw up Eugene O'Neill and (later) Dreiser himself as shining disproofs, but O'Neill had actually made off at sight of the first refugee from Elwood, Indiana, and Dreiser was a famous man before he moved to Tenth Street. The typical Village ménage was made up of a Cubist painter who aspired to do covers for pulp magazines and a corn-fed gal who labored at an erotic novel and paid the bills. This gal, in the standard case, was the daughter of a rural usurer who had died leaving her three thousand dollars a year in seven-per-cent farm mortgages. Until her father's executors cabbaged the money, she was a rich woman, and a rich woman, in Schmidtsville, was a target of intolerable scandal and contumely. If her I.Q. was above 7 or 8, it inevitably occurred to her, soon or late, that her dreadful experiences would make a powerful novel, so she entrained for New York and sought the encouragement of aesthetic society. She got it without delay, for the resident bucks heard of her the moment she crossed Fourteenth Street, and fought for her ferociously. If she was above the average in guile, she made the winner marry her, but this was seldom necessary, and when it happened, the marriage did not outlast her money.

Dreiser, moving to Tenth Street, found himself in a dense mass of such Little Red Riding Hoods and their attendant wolves. They swarmed in all the adjacent courts and alleys, and spilled out into the main streets and even into Washington Square. He had no more than unpacked his quills and inkhorn and hung up his other suit when they began to besiege him, for the gals all believed that his word was law with magazine editors, and their parasites were well aware that he knew every art director in New York. They barged in on him at all hours, but chiefly between 10 P.M. and 3 A.M., and the gals all brought manuscripts for him to read. I once found him with his desk surrounded by a breastwork of such scripts at least three feet high, and in a corner was a stack of canvases showing women with purple hair, mouths like the jaws of Hell, gem-set umbilici, and three or four vermilion and strabismic eyes. He was then virtually a teetotaller, but soon he had to lay in booze for the entertainment of his guests. Their tastes, it appeared, ran to liqueurs of the more exotic kinds, and they were not slow to ask for them. He then made his first acquaintance with such fancy goods as mescal, arrack, Danziger Goldwasser, and slivovitz, and had to take to massive nightcaps of bicarbonate of soda. Once, a lady poet induced him to try a few whiffs of marijuana, and his sensations were so alarming that he preached a crusade against it for years afterward.

All this cost him more money that he could afford, for the Comstockian assault had cut off his book royalties, and his magazine market was much depleted. Moreover, his working hours were invaded by his visitors, many of whom stayed a long while, and there were days when he couldn't write a line. He was a very kindly man, and the memory of his own early difficulties made him push tolerance of neophytes to the edge of folly. One night, a bulky pythoness from the Western Reserve of Ohio broke into his studio, helped herself to half a bottle of *crème de violette*, and proceeded to read to him the manuscript of a historical novel running to four hundred and fifty thousand words. He got rid of her only by what the insurance policies call an act of God. That is to say, a fire broke out in one of the art-and-love warrens across the street, and when the firemen came roaring up and began fetching aesthetes down their ladders, the pythoness took fright and ran off. The next day, he had an extra lock put on his door, which opened directly into the street, but it worked so badly that it often locked him in without locking the Village literati out. After that, he shoved an armchair against the door, but they soon learned how to climb over it.

Toward the end of 1916, the Comstocks closed in on Dreiser with psalteries sounding and tom-toms rolling, and many of his fellow-authors began to take alarm, for if he could be suppressed for a few banal episodes of calf love in his latest book, "The 'Genius,'" then the whole fraternity might find itself facing an idiotic and ruinous censorship. Accordingly, a manifesto was circulated protesting against the attack on him, and a number of bigwigs signed it. William Dean Howells, Hamlin Garland, and a few lesser old fellows of the prissier sort refused to do so, but most of the other authors of any consequence stepped up eagerly, and in a little while the paper had a hundred or more important signatures. But then Dreiser himself took a hand in gathering them, and the first list he turned in threw the committee into a panic. For all the quacks of the Village, hearing what was afoot, rushed up to get some publicity out of signing, and their new neighbor was far too amiable to refuse them. This list and those that followed day by day were really quite extraordinary documents, for a good half of the signers had never had anything printed in magazines above the level of the pulps, and the rest had never seen print at all. The nascent Communists of the time—they were then thought of as harmless cranks—were all there, and so were the poetical advocates of free love, the professional atheists, and the great rabble of yearning females from the Cow States. The Harlem poets signed unanimously. Not a few of the hand-painted-oil-painter signatories were being pursued by the indignant mothers of runaway daughters, and several of the etchers were under police scrutiny for filling the Village art shoppes with aphrodisiacal steals from Anders Zorn.

When Dreiser began sending in the signatures of psychoanalysts—they were then called sexologists, and their books had a great undercover sale—the committee howled in earnest, and there ensued an unseemly wrangle between the beneficiary of the manifesto and its promoters. The latter had common sense on their side, but Dreiser was too adamantine a man to be moved by any such consideration. All his fellow-Villagers, of course, leaped up to defend him and themselves, and one night when I waited on him in Tenth Street I found him palavering with a delegation that insisted that he insist on retaining the signature of a Buddhist writer from Altoona, Pennsylvania, who had been collared that very day for contributing to the delinquency of a minor; to wit, a psychopathic free-verse poetess from the Upper Peninsula of Michigan. It made me dizzy to see how easily they fetched him. They had not got out a hundred words before he was pledging his life, his fortune, and his sacred honor to the Buddhist, who had got out on bail and was present in person, in a mail-order suit of clothes, with a towel wrapped around his head. I slunk out much depressed, determined to advise the committee to disband at once and tear up its manifesto, but that, happily, was never necessary, for soon afterward the Comstocks began to flush other game, and Dreiser was forgotten.

As I have said, his flat was on the ground floor of the old house he lived in, and its door opened directly upon the street. It was comfortable enough during the first six months of his occupancy, but then excavations began for the Seventh Avenue subway, and the eastern edge thereof ran along his wall. The tearing down of the house next door did not bother him much, for in the throes of literary endeavor he had a high power of concentration, but when the gangs of workmen got down to the rocks underlying Manhattan Island and began rending them with great blasts of explosives, he sometimes made heavy weather of it. More than once, his whole collection of avant-garde art came tumbling from his walls, and on several occasions he was bounced out of bed in the middle of the night. Such adventures gave him nightmares, and even when no dynamite was going off, he dreamed of being pursued by hyenas, lawyers, social workers, and other authropophagi. But the most curious of his experiences in those days did not have to do with detonations but with a quiet neighbor who occupied the basement under his apartment. In the New York fashion, Dreiser had had no truck with this neighbor, and, in fact, didn't know his name, but now and then the man could be seen ducking in or out of the areaway at the front of the house. He operated some sort of machine downstairs, faintly audible between blasts in the larval subway, and Dreiser assumed that he was a tailor, and so gave him no thought.

One day, there was a ring at the front door, and when Dreiser opened it, three men wearing derby hats brushed past him into his apartment. An ordinary author might have been alarmed, but Dreiser was an old newspaper reporter, and hence recognized them at sight as police detectives. Keeping their hats on, they got down to business at once. Who was the man who lived below? What was his name? What sort of trade did he carry on? Did he ever have any visitors? If so, who were they, and at what time of day did they visit him? Dreiser replied that he knew nothing about the fellow and couldn't answer. He had seen and heard no visitors, though the place might be swarming with them without his knowledge. Well, then what sound *did* he hear? Dreiser mentioned an occasional subdued thumping, as of a sewing machine. Was that in the morning, in the afternoon, or in the evening? Dreiser, urging his memory, replied that he had heard it at all hours. After midnight? Probably not after midnight. After eleven o'clock? Perhaps. After ten o'clock? Yes. Was it loud or soft? Soft. How long did it go on at a stretch? Sometimes half an hour; sometimes less; sometimes more. Did he hear any heavy weights being thrown about? No. Any clank or clink of metal? He couldn't recall any. Did the neighbor look suspicious when he used the areaway? Did he peer up and down the street? Did anyone ever meet him? What sort of clothes did he wear? Did he ever carry packages?

By this time, Dreiser was growing tired of his callers, and invited them to go to hell. They showed no resentment but did not move. Instead, they became confidential. The man below, they revealed in whispers, was a counterfeiter—one of the leaders of the profession. He made half dollars out of solder melted from old tin cans, and what seemed to be his sewing machine was a contraption for casting them. The dicks said that they were preparing even now to raid and jug him. Half a block down the street, two federal agents waited with a truck, and he would be taken with all his paraphernalia. Of the three cops now in attendance, one would guard the areaway and the two others would climb down through the subway excavation and rush him from the rear. As for Dreiser, he was instructed on pain of prosecution to keep his mouth shut and maintain complete immobility. If he so much as walked into his rear bedroom, it might scare the culprit off. Meanwhile, a few last questions. Had the counterfeiter ever tried to work off any bogus half dollars on him, or proposed that he help work them off on others? Had Dreiser ever smelled burning lead? Had he ever noticed any glare of flame at night? Had there been any excessive heat, as from a furnace? Had he heard any banging, bumping, booping, or bubbling?

Dreiser now renewed his invitation to his visitors to go to hell, and this time they departed. He waited a few minutes and then peeped out of the bedroom window that gave onto the yard in the rear. The two cops of the storming party were having a hard time crawling and stumbling through the subway crater, but eventually they made it and began thumping on the basement's rear door. When they got no answer, they borrowed a scantling from a subway foreman and proceeded to batter the door down. Once they were inside, Dreiser began to see copy for one of his novels in the affair and took to the excavation himself. By the time he got to the door, muddy and bruised, the dicks were preparing to depart. While they had been sweating him upstairs, the counterfeiter had made tracks, and not only had made tracks but had taken his machine with him, and not only his machine but also his spare clothes (if any) and all his secret documents. There was nothing left save half a dozen defective counterfeit coins on the floor and a note on the table. It was written in a good, round hand and read:

Please notify the Gas Company to shut off the gas.

Annotated List of Omitted Letters (1907–1945)

1.   3 October 1907 (NYP-T): TD to HLM. A business letter asking HLM to think about subjects for articles for the *Delineator*.

2.   8 November 1907 (NYP-T): TD to HLM. A business letter recording payments for articles received.

3.   11 November 1907 (NYP-T): TD to HLM. A business letter asking about Dr. Hirshberg's intentions for a third article.

4.   2 January 1908 (NYP-T): TD to HLM. TD asks HLM to read another draft of "What Science Has Done for the Child."

5.   28 April 1908 (NYP-T): TD to HLM. A note thanking HLM for a letter.

6.   28 July 1908 (NYP-T): TD to HLM. TD tells HLM that an article he revised is now acceptable.

7.   17 November 1908 (NYP-T): TD to HLM. TD sends a check for $60 and informs HLM that the Dodge Company is not interested in an anthology of contemporary plays.

8.   4 February 1909 (NYP-T): TD to HLM. TD asks for a copy of the Baltimore *Sun*.

9.   19 February 1909 (NYP-T): TD to HLM. TD refers to HLM's article based on a report by the Rural Life Commission.

10.   23 February 1909 (NYP-T): TD to HLM. A note urging HLM to do one page on the Rural Life item.

11.   25 March 1909 (NYP-T): TD to HLM. TD suggests HLM's article will be better after revision.

12.   30 March 1909 (NYP-T): TD to HLM. TD asks for a copy of the Baltimore *Sun* article dealing with the Child Rescue Conference in Washington.

13.   10 April 1909 (NYP-T): TD to HLM. TD suggests a series of articles under the heading of "A Woman as Seen by Others."

14.　22 April 1909 (NYP-T): TD to HLM. A note thanking HLM for editorial advice.

15.　30 April 1909 (NYP-T): TD to HLM. A note thanking HLM for criticism of an unidentified article.

16.　28 May 1909 (NYP-T): TD to HLM. TD asks HLM to identify Martin Dodge of Landover, Maryland.

17.　1 August 1909 (UPL): HLM to TD. HLM responds to an inquiry, saying he did not write an article that Dreiser took to be his work.

18.　3 August 1909 (NYP-T): TD to HLM. A note asking for suggestions for *The Bohemian*.

19.　[Undated, before 18 August 1909] (UPL): HLM to TD. HLM asks about the type of material TD wants for *The Bohemian*, including the possibility of a short story.

20.　18 August 1909 (NYP-T): TD to HLM. TD comments upon the quality of HLM's editorials and says he will look at a short story.

21.　17 December 1909 (UPL-H): HLM to TD. HLM notes that he had written 3, not 4, editorials for *The Bohemian*.

22.　[Undated, 1909] (NYP): TD to HLM. A note asking HLM if he will send 3 editorials for *The Bohemian*.

23.　11 May 1910 (NYP-T): TD to HLM. TD accepts HLM's "Legal Liabilities of the Best Man" for *The Delineator*.

24.　24 May 1910 (NYP-T): TD to HLM. TD sends a copy of "The Man's Page" material he is beginning to publish in *The Delineator*.

25.　[Undated, April 1911] (UPL-H): HLM to TD. A note expressing willingness to read the manuscript of *Jennie Gerhardt*.

26.　13 May 1911 (NYP): TD to HLM. A letter joking about beer consumption in New York, and a note of thanks for HLM's appreciation of "The Mighty Burke."

27.　18 June 1911 (NYP-Pc): TD to HLM. TD sends his new address.

28.　16 August 1911 (NYP): TD to HLM. A note suggesting HLM look at a duplicate of the *Jennie Gerhardt* manuscript if Harper's does not send him proofs of the book.

29.　7 September 1911 (NYP): TD to HLM. A note asking HLM if he has received the proofs of *Jennie Gerhardt*.

30.　14 September 1911 (NYP-Tel): TD to HLM. A telegram asking HLM to return letter from Eleanor R. O'Neill.

31.　24 October 1911 (NYP): TD to HLM. A note about an interviewer who came "to get my philosophy in some concrete form."

32.   [Undated, ca. November 1911] (NYP): TD to HLM. TD sends another review of *Jennie Gerhardt*.

33.   10 January 1912 (EPL-Pc): TD to HLM. A note on the good ale and food in London.

34.   8 February 1912 (EPL-Pc): TD to HLM. A note thanking HLM for a letter.

35.   22 February 1912 (EPL-Pc): TD to HLM. A note expressing delight with Rome.

36.   3 May 1912 (UPL-Pc): HLM to TD. A list of German beers.

37.   23 October 1912 (NYP): TD to HLM. TD invites HLM to stay at his apartment.

38.   [Undated, 1913] (UPL-H): HLM to TD. HLM asks if TD will be in New York, so they may schedule a meeting.

39.   9 July 1913 (UPL-H): HLM to TD. HLM asks for a copy of *A Traveler at Forty*.

40.   [Undated] (NYP): TD to HLM. TD makes a date to meet HLM at the Brevoort Hotel.

41.   [Undated] (NYP): TD to HLM. A note on an article by George Burman Foster, pointing to Foster as someone interested in HLM's Nietzsche book.

42.   [Undated, after 2 July 1914] (UPL-H): HLM to TD. HLM says he is sending a review that TD requested.

43.   [Undated, after 21 September 1914] (UPL-H): HLM to TD. HLM notes that "The Blue Sphere" will be published in *Smart Set* and that he is thinking of publishing Benjamin DeCasseres.

44.   [Undated, December 1914] (NYP): TD to HLM. TD asks if HLM knows a place in Baltimore where John Cowper Powys can lecture.

45.   [Undated, 1914] (UPL): TD to HLM. HLM sends a check for work published in *Smart Set*.

46.   12 October 1915 (UPL): HLM to TD. HLM calls attention to a review of *The "Genius"* in the *New York Times*.

47.   12 November 1915 (NYP): TD to HLM. TD says he cannot come to dinner on Monday.

48.   12 November 1915 (NYP): TD to HLM. TD says he can come to dinner on Tuesday or Wednesday.

49.   18 November 1915 (UPL): HLM to TD. HLM advises TD not to publish a play that he feels is weak.

50.   [Undated, December 1915] (UPL-H): HLM to TD. HLM notes that he will be in New York soon.

51.   22 December 1915 (UPL): HLM to TD. A note asking about poems TD promised to send.

52.   [Undated, 1915] (NYP): TD to HLM. A note thanking HLM for some "information" he had sent.

53.   [Undated, 1915] (UPL): HLM to TD. HLM says he will call next week.

54.   7 January 1916 (UPL): HLM to TD. HLM mocks a review sent to him by TD.

55.   15 January 1916 (UPL): HLM to TD. HLM asks if TD will accept the offer he made for a poem.

56.   [Undated, before 4 April 1916] (NYP): TD to HLM. A note from Savannah asking HLM to send some amusing "screeds."

57.   31 January 1916 (NYP-Pc): TD to HLM. TD sends his Savannah address.

58.   4 April 1916 (NYP-Pc): TD to HLM. A note from Philadelphia expressing regret at having missed HLM on his way north.

59.   5 April 1916 (UPL): HLM to TD. HLM tells of letters he received addressed to TD while TD was in Savannah.

60.   20 May 1916 (UPL): HLM to TD. HLM apologizes for a mistake in one of his recent articles.

61.   12 June 1916 (UPL): HLM to TD. HLM asks for the manuscript of *A Hoosier Holiday*, notes a Canadian review, mentions the war news, and reports on the price of the Dodge edition of *Sister Carrie*.

62.   23 June 1916 (UPL): HLM to TD. HLM says that the manuscript of *A Hoosier Holiday* has not arrived.

63.   3 July 1916 (UPL): HLM to TD. HLM says he will send an edited version of *A Hoosier Holiday*, and considers a trip west with TD.

64.   7 July 1916 (UPL): HLM to TD. HLM asks for a copy of the manuscript of *A Hoosier Holiday* to help him write a review of it.

65.   12 July 1916 (UPL): HLM to TD. HLM inquires about *The Bulwark* and calls for a meeting to discuss it.

66.   15 September 1916 (NYP): TD to HLM. TD expresses regret at not having seen HLM and once again speaks of the protest and the English telegram.

67.   [Undated, before 21 October 1916] (UPL): HLM to TD. HLM sends an unidentified item for TD to consider as a help in his case for *The "Genius."*

68.   21 October 1916 (NYP): TD to HLM. TD responds to an article sent by HLM; he identifies the lawyers for the *"Genius"* case; and he mentions a debate on censorship before the Twilight Club.

69.   [Undated, 1916] (UPL): HLM to TD. HLM says he is coming to New York "Saturday night" and hopes they can meet "next week."

70.   [Undated, after 7 December 1916] (UPL): HLM to TD. A note on Felix Shay's correspondence with John Sumner.

71.   [Undated, before 14 December 1916] (UPL): HLM to TD. HLM sends TD letters from signers of the *"Genius"* protest.

72.   [Undated, 1916] (NYP): TD to HLM. A note on a correction in chapter 57 of *A Hoosier Holiday*.

73.   [Undated, 1916] (NYP): TD to HLM. A note on J. Jefferson Jones's handling of one of TD's books.

74.   [Undated, 1916] (NYP): TD to HLM. A note inquiring about the play *Laughing Gas*.

75.   [Undated, 1916] (NYP): TD to HLM. A note asking "Would you monkey with a thing like this [unidentified item] if you were me?"

76.   [Undated, 1916] (NYP): TD to HLM. A note mentioning a form of puritan protest, presumably over *The "Genius."*

77.   [Undated, 1916] (NYP): TD to HLM. TD asks advice about sending an "open letter" to several newspapers.

78.   [Undated, 1916] (NYP): TD to HLM. TD asks HLM to send someone to pick up a manuscript, probably of *A Hoosier Holiday*.

79.   [Undated, 1916] (NYP): TD to HLM. TD makes a date to meet HLM at the Lafayette Hotel.

80.   [Undated, 1916] (NYP): TD to HLM. TD asks HLM to place a passage into his copy of a book manuscript.

81.   [Undated, 1916] (NYP): TD to HLM. TD notes that he sees no error in an unidentified item.

82.   [Undated, 1917] (UPL): HLM to TD. HLM jokes about the contents of a newspaper clipping that assails TD's "portrayal of America."

83.   [Undated, late March or early April 1917] (NYP): TD to HLM. TD asks about a portrait HLM promised him.

84.   [Undated, March 1917] (UPL): HLM to TD. HLM says he will discuss his trip to Europe and the war when they meet in New York.

85.   [Undated, ca. May 1917] (UPL): HLM to TD. HLM asks TD to bring to their meeting a copy of the brief for the case of *The "Genius"* and related material.

86.   [Undated, ca. May 1917] (UPL): HLM to TD. A note of thanks for sending the brief and other items relating to the *"Genius"* case.

87.   [Undated, ca. May 1917] (UPL): HLM to TD. HLM comments on the brief and notes that Willard Huntington Wright influenced Merton Yewdale's argument.

88.   [Undated, ca. May 1917] (UPL): HLM to TD. HLM asks for TD's autobiography and mentions that he has finished the *Prefaces* essays.

89.   [Undated, ca. June 1917] (UPL): HLM to TD. HLM asks for contributions to his "Thesaurus of Unprecedented Quotations" and says TD should look at the July issue of *Masses*.

90.   [Undated, ca. June 1917] (UPL): HLM to TD. A joking note on "the second coming of Christ."

91.   [Undated, ca. 29 June 1917] (NYP): TD to HLM. TD writes that J. Jefferson Jones will not have his choice of his work, and refers to the exposé of John Sumner in *Jim Jam Jems*.

92.   [Undated, ca. 29 June 1917] (UPL): HLM to TD. HLM refers to the brief of the *"Genius"* case.

93.   [Undated, 1917] (UPL): HLM to TD. HLM asks for reprints of "Creed of a Novelist."

94.   [Undated, 1917] (UPL): HLM to TD. A note asking for an un-identified "bibliography."

95.   [Undated, 1917] (UPL): HLM to TD. HLM asks TD to look into The Yearbook of United States Brewers' Association for 1916.

96.   [Undated, 1917] (NYP): TD to HLM. TD refers to his trip west and asks jokingly to have Chopin's 6th Prelude played at his funeral.

97.   [Undated, 1917] (NYP): TD to HLM. TD notes that someone took the letter HLM sent out of the envelope, and asks for a copy. He also says he will send copies of the *"Genius"* brief.

98.   [Undated, 1917] (NYP): TD to HLM. A joke note written on a copy of Mencken's poem "The Orf'cer Boy." TD writes as an English aristocrat who approves of Mencken's patriotism.

99.   31 January 1919 (NYP): TD to HLM. TD jokingly says he is try-ing to sell Mencken's poem "The Orf'cer Boy" to the magazines.

100.   21 February 1919 (UPL): HLM to TD. HLM sends TD a number of letters he received from Louis C. Hartmann, a Mencken fan who was led to Dreiser's work by his reading of the essay in *Prefaces*.

101.   [Undated, May 1919] (UPL): HLM to TD. HLM returns news-paper clippings Dreiser had sent.

102.   9 May 1919 (UPL): HLM to TD. HLM sends TD an unnamed review sent to him by Burton Rascoe.

103.   10 May 1919 (UPL): HLM to TD. HLM sends a copy of a letter that he had sent to George S. Viereck, and suggests TD send a letter to the publisher Fawcett.

104.   30 August 1919 (NYP): TD to HLM. TD sends an unidentified manuscript for consideration at *Smart Set*.

105.   13 September 1919 (UPL): HLM to TD. HLM says he will send ten copies of the October *Smart Set* and recalls that his birthday was the day before.

106.   [Undated, before 29 November 1919] (NYP): TD to HLM. TD asks HLM to translate a letter from the German.

107.   [Undated, 1919] (NYP): TD to HLM. TD criticizes a letter of an unidentified person who has commented on his work without reading much of it.

108.   [Undated, 1919] (NYP): TD to HLM. TD asks HLM if he should allow his play *Laughing Gas* to be included in an anthology.

109.   [Undated, 1919] (NYP): TD to HLM. TD asks if he should find someone else to do a piece he was asked to do.

110.   [Undated, 1919] (NYP): TD to HLM. TD praises HLM for his version of the "Declaration of Independence" and comments unfavorably on an unidentified piece from *The Mirror*.

111.   [Undated, 1919] (NYP): TD to HLM. TD asks what one is to do with "this sort of thing" (unidentified).

112.   21 February 1920. (UPL): HLM to TD. HLM mentions meeting a copyright lawyer named B. H. Stern and encloses a Cabell Protest for signatures.

113.   [Undated, after 21 February 1920] (NYP): TD to HLM. TD thanks HLM for the address of B. H. Stern and says he signed the Cabell Protest letter.

114.   13 June 1920 (UPL): HLM to TD. HLM sends his address in San Francisco while attending the national convention.

115.   24 September 1920 (NYP): TD to HLM. TD says he did not use HLM's name in a letter to Horace Liveright and discusses the issue of advances from publishers.

116.   [Undated, after 18 November 1920] (NYP): TD to HLM. TD asks HLM to comment on W. C. Lengel's letter of 18 November in which he argues that TD should not publish *A Novel about Myself* until after he publishes another novel.

117.   14 January 1921 (NYP-Tel): TD to HLM. "Please Forward to Liveright one copy of the Novel."

118.   3 April 1921 (UPL): HLM to TD. HLM asks if he should send the medallion of TD to Kirah Markham. He also says that the *Century Magazine* will probably want two or three articles from TD.

119.   10 May 1921 (NYP): TD to HLM. TD sends an article on *The Titan* and mentions his recent trip to Seattle and Vancouver.

120.   [Undated, 1921] (NYP): TD to HLM. An obscure note asking HLM to help with an enclosed item that has disappeared.

121. [Undated, 1921] (NYP): TD to HLM. TD asks HLM to indicate what articles he thinks can be gotten out of a book, probably *A Novel about Myself*.

122. [Undated, 1921] (NYP): TD to HLM. "Don't roast it"—but reference is not clear.

123. 18 April 1922 (NYP): TD to HLM. TD asks HLM to meet with John Sumner to discuss *The "Genius"* and asks his opinion on publishing a shorter version of the novel.

124. 2 June 1922 (UPL): HLM to TD. HLM sends a copy of the list of cuts he agreed upon with John Sumner.

125. 28 October 1922 (NYP): TD to HLM. TD repeats here his letter of 29 October 1922, which asks HLM not to seek less than $2,000 for the manuscript of *Sister Carrie*.

126. 18 December 1922 (NYP): TD to HLM. TD notes that he has written the Dodd-Mead firm to determine whether it will publish an unexpurgated version of *The "Genius"*; he adds that Boni & Liveright will publish the book if Dodd-Mead does not.

127. 24 December 1922 (UPL-Tel): HLM to TD. A Christmas greeting telegram.

128. [Undated, 1922] (NYP): TD to HLM. A brief note attached to an unidentified item: "This will interest you a little. Will you return it."

129. [Undated, 1922] (NYP): TD to HLM. A note from TD defending Dr. Albert Abram's practice.

130. 14 May 1923 (NYP): TD to HLM. TD says he will go with HLM to Union Hill, New Jersey, for beer.

131. 20 September 1923 (NYP): TD to HLM. TD sends his new address and telephone number.

132. 25 September 1923 (NYP): TD to HLM. TD asks if he should send an unidentified man eight books.

133. [Undated, 1923] (NYP): TD to HLM. A note stating that a "Lyon Phelps letter amuses me."

134. [Undated, 1923] (NYP): TD to HLM. TD asks for the address of a beerhouse at Union Hill, New Jersey.

135. [Undated, 1923] (NYP): TD to HLM. TD asks whether a journal he sent to HLM is "a good Scandinavian paper."

136. [Undated, 1923] (NYP): TD to HLM. TD asks why "all right" cannot be written "alright" if "all ready" is "already."

137. [Undated, 1923] (NYP): TD to HLM. An obscure reference to his writing of autobiography.

138. 8 January 1924 (UPL): HLM to TD. HLM asks why TD is going west and tries to set up a meeting in New York.

139.   4 March 1924 (NYP): TD to HLM. TD asks for a copy of the January issue of *American Mercury*.

140.   [Undated, 1924] (NYP): TD to HLM. "And you say I am not moral? Go to."

141.   30 March 1925 (UPL): HLM to TD. HLM asks about an "episode in autobiography" and proposes another trip to Union Hill, New Jersey.

142.   17 April 1925 (UPL): HLM to TD. HLM arranges a date to meet in New York.

143.   24 April 1925 (NYP): TD to HLM. TD tries to arrange a date for a meeting in New York.

144.   [Undated, 1925] (NYP): TD to HLM. TD says he is sending a copy of Burton Rascoe's book on him.

145.   [Undated, 1925] (NYP): TD to HLM. TD says he endorses an idea for a "monument," but the reference is unclear.

146.   8 January 1926 (NYP-Pc): TD to HLM. TD sends regards from Florida.

147.   18 December 1934 (UPL): HLM to TD. HLM repeats the information in his letter of 15 December 1934.

148.   12 January 1935 (UPL): HLM to TD. HLM arranges a meeting at the Ansonia Hotel on 24 January.

149.   1 April 1935 (UPL): HLM to TD. HLM says he has bronchitis and cannot come to New York this week.

150.   3 May 1935 (UPL): HLM to TD. HLM asks TD for his "permanent address in the West."

151.   5 June 1935 (UPL): HLM to TD. HLM thanks TD for his telegram on the death of Sara Haardt Mencken. This letter is a shorter version of Mencken's letter of 11 June 1935.

152.   [Undated] (NYP-Pc): TD to HLM. A card with a picture of Dreiser's Mt. Kisco house and on an X mark TD placed this inscription: "If you want to be rescued fall here."

153.   25 February 1937 (UPL-Tel): HLM to TD. HLM suggests a meeting at Lüchow's.

154.   25 February 1937 (NYP-Tel): TD to HLM. TD accepts invitation to meet at Lüchow's.

155.   [Undated] (NYP-Pc): TD to HLM. TD jokes about Edgar Lee Masters's teeth.

156.   April 1939 (NYP): TD to HLM. TD sends a newspaper clipping about a man who died as a result of his whiskers catching fire and he jokes about HLM's cutting his whiskers.

157.   24 October 1939 (NYP): TD to HLM. TD asks for a clipping from the Congressional Record.

158.   17 December 1939 (NYP-Pc): TD to HLM. TD sends a picture of a desert ranch house with a joke message about renting it to HLM. At the top of the card he writes "Remember the poor Finns."

159.   1 April 1940 (UPL): HLM to TD. HLM says TD's comments on the English delight him and asks about TD's health.

160.   [Undated, December 1945] (NYP): TD to HLM. Christmas card with joke message about using the same card next year.

161.   [Undated] (NYP-Pc): TD to HLM. TD jokingly asks HLM if he would want to be prosecuted under statute 27b of the postal code.

162.   [Undated] (NYP): TD to HLM. TD sends HLM an unidentified manuscript, "as yet unpublished."

163.   [Undated] (NYP): TD to HLM. TD jokes about the cruelty of Baltimore editors.

164.   [Undated] (NYP): TD to HLM. TD sends an unidentified piece of writing for HLM to read.

165.   [Undated] (NYP): TD to HLM. "Note this line [unidentified] of swill."

166.   [Undated] (NYP): TD to HLM. TD sends HLM an unidentified article to read.

167.   [Undated] (NYP): TD to HLM. TD asks for a copy of an unidentified article.

168.   [Undated] (NYP): TD to HLM. TD asks, "Couldn't you write to these people [unidentified] for me?"

Index of Names and Subjects

Index of Works by Dreiser
and Mencken